Contextual
Process
Digitalization

Matthes Elstermann • Albert Fleischmann •
Christoph Moser • Stefan Oppl •
Werner Schmidt • Christian Stary

Contextual Process Digitalization

Changing Perspectives – Design Thinking – Value-Led Design

Second Edition

 Springer

Matthes Elstermann
Department of Information Systems
University of Münster
Münster, Germany

Albert Fleischmann
Dr. Albert Fleischmann and Partner
InterAktiv Unternehmensberatung
Pfaffenhofen a.d.Ilm, Germany

Christoph Moser
Doka GmbH
Amstetten, Austria

Stefan Oppl
Department for Continuing Education
Research and Educational Technologies
Danube University Krems
Krems, Austria

Werner Schmidt
Business School
Technische Hochschule Ingolstadt
Ingolstadt, Germany

Christian Stary
Department of Business
Informatics-Communications Engineering
Johannes Kepler University Linz
Linz, Austria

ISBN 978-3-032-06900-9   ISBN 978-3-032-06901-6   (eBook)
https://doi.org/10.1007/978-3-032-06901-6

This work was supported by Johannes Kepler Universität Linz.

This Springer imprint is published by the registered company Springer Nature Switzerland AG
The registered company address is: Gewerbestrasse 11, 6330 Cham, Switzerland

If disposing of this product, please recycle the paper.

Preface

The new edition of this book not only makes us authors proud of the reception its content has received so far—in keeping with our motto of the original edition, *The most important innovations are those that change thinking*—it has also inspired us to consider how we can incorporate relevant developments of recent years into holistic process design for digitalization projects.

We have incorporated these developments into the second edition in the spirit of theory-driven practice by exploring exemplary fields of action for communication-oriented design work through case studies. Using examples of innovative industrial practices as well as integrative artificial intelligence algorithms and social behavior models, we can thus demonstrate the advantages of model-based coordination of functionality and interaction in process management.

The basis is an easily understandable, standardized vocabulary for capturing and specifying behavior, which not only contributes to reducing complexity but also to improving the comprehensibility and feasibility of social, organizational, and technically relevant issues.

This can create multiple bridges that facilitate digital transformation processes, for example, between Industry 4.0 and Industry 5.0, between physical and digital twins, the design and technical implementation of socio-technical systems, and between natural and artificial intelligence—bridges that can help avoid new forms of the digital divide in the coming age of the metaverse and transhumanism.

In all presentations, we have again been guided by the aphorisms of Hans-Jürgen Quadbeck-Seeger:

- *Understandability is the courtesy of an expert.* Our work is intended to inspire all those interested in the holistic digitalization of processes. Therefore, it must be understandable.
- *Luxury: cult of the unnecessary.* We want to address all those who want to understand the nature of processes and their usability in practical action, without intensive language and usage studies, but rather underpinned by practical concepts. Students may appreciate the textbook nature of the book, practitioners the examples, and researchers and developers the conceptual presentations and theoretical excursions.
- *The larger the project, the more quietly it is buried.* The concept and project of thinking about processes in a communication-oriented and thus systemic way

have existed for more than a decade. It celebrates simplicity and clarity without neglecting complex interrelationships. The drivers of the project are experiencing constant change and have increased, as can be seen from the number of authors. It is therefore time to enrich the digitalization of processes from the perspective of behavioral orientation and to align the primarily data-oriented practice with value-based information exchange.

- *Adventure tourists are drawn to places where they have no business.* Looking toward behavioral orientation is worthwhile, as it opens up a perspective that comes close to our perception of reality, coherently expands what already exists, and thus gives us new scope for action.

Our companions on the path to completing this work are also adventurers. Special thanks go to them, in particular Ralf Gerstner from Springer, for their support on behalf of the publisher in implementing our ideas, as well as Jerome Geyer-Klingeberg from Celonis SE for clarifying the process practice.

Innovations are not natural phenomena; we have to want them and implement them. With this in mind, we wish you edifying reading, successful practical actions, and feedback from Ingolstadt, Karlsruhe, Krems, Linz, and Pfaffenhofen an der Ilm.

Münster, Germany	Matthes Elstermann
Pfaffenhofen a.d.Ilm, Germany	Albert Fleischmann
Amstetten, Austria	Christoph Moser
Krems, Austria	Stefan Oppl
Ingolstadt, Germany	Werner Schmidt
Linz, Austria	Christian Stary
July, 2025	

Contents

Motivation

1

1.1 Business Processes and Business Process Management

There is no organization without processes. When people want to collaborate, they use the necessary tools and coordinate their activities to reach the desired result. Since such activities can not only be carried out by humans but also by machines and computers, their activities must also be included when aligning human requirements and technical capabilities. In particular, different types of actors are involved in at least partially automated processes.

A process is triggered by an event that may originate inside or outside the organization, such as a travel request or customer order. Coordinated and targeted action in response to such an event is called a process. In case the organization is a company, this is referred to as business process.

There is no company without business processes. There are only differences in their level of maturity. The reactions of an organization to certain business events can always be coordinated anew when these events occur, or a procedure is defined that is then executed in such cases. Events of the same type, such as purchase orders, are referred to as event classes. A predefined procedure for an event class is called a process model. The execution of the activity sequences defined in the model as a reaction to an identified concrete event, e.g., the book order of customer Huber from May 20, is termed a process instance.

Every company, irrespective of its type of business, has certain standardized processes that can be designed and tailored to the individual company. For instance, every company has an order-to-cash process designed to react to business events, ranging from the customer order to the receipt of payment, and to document these through booking. Conversely, a procurement process will exist with purchase orders to satisfy individual requirements, the concrete reference (e.g., receipt of goods and storage), and the payment of vendors. Other examples are processes for recruitment or logistics. A common classification categorizes processes according

© The Author(s) 2026
M. Elstermann et al., *Contextual Process Digitalization*,
https://doi.org/10.1007/978-3-032-06901-6_1

to their character into management, core, and support processes. The classification is company-specific and depends, among other things, on the industry sector.

The more clearly a company defines its business processes and the more consistently it implements them in its daily operations, the more efficient it will be. For many companies, their competitiveness is not (or no longer) based solely on the uniqueness of their products, but on the quality of their business processes. For example, while a publisher's business is primarily determined by its books, at Amazon the customer experience in searching, selecting, purchasing, paying, delivering, and returning products, i.e., the smooth, customer-centric process, is the key to success.

The models for such processes must be continuously adapted or completely redesigned because the reactions to an event class can change, or additional reactions to new event classes can become necessary. The resulting specifications must also be implemented in the organization and IT infrastructure so that employees can work through instances of the processes in day-to-day business. In doing so, underlying conditions, such as effectiveness, efficiency, and compliance, i.e., the requirements to deliver the desired result with the lowest possible expenditure of resources and in compliance with valid external and internal regulations (e.g., laws), must be taken into account. Business Process Management (BPM) has established itself to handle these tasks. It describes an integrated management approach for analysis, design, optimization, implementation, control, monitoring, and further development of the management, core, and support processes in a company. From a technical point of view, it also includes IT support for these sub-tasks through corresponding tools, e.g., for modeling or execution (such as process engines) or more comprehensive Business Process Management Systems (BPMS).

In Business Process Management, a company and its immediate environment are regarded as a selected part of reality for modeling and executing. In this dedicated part of the world, one party wants a deliverable from another party in the form of a physical product, a service, or a combination of both. The deliverable should be provided in accordance with associated requirements; the desire for it is the business event to which the company should react as perceived in the defined process model.

In Business Process Management, it is therefore necessary to define a model for the provision of services and apply it to the processing of business cases. This means adapting reality according to the model, i.e., analyzing affected sections of reality and changing this reality. Since this reality and the desired changes are very complex, several modeling concepts from the social sciences, business administration, and computer science are brought together and combined in BPM.

In the following sections, we outline an overall view of process management and then explain it in detail in the succeeding chapters. From the perspective of the participants on the world, the various facets of Business Process Management are presented, and a selection of models is introduced which has turned out useful in our practice. The design of such models supports the transition from a more or less unstructured or unsatisfactory way of working to a structured process handling that corresponds to the ideas of a company and its customers.

We develop the overall view step-by-step, starting from the individual perspectives of the participants on their work in a process, its structuring and harmonization, then moving forward with the specification in a model and its embedding in the organizational and IT environment of the company, and finally culminating in the joint processing of process instances in the resulting socio-technical systems. A corresponding illustration which grows with this overall view ultimately shows our comprehensive understanding of Business Process Management.

1.2 View of the World, Structuring, and Modeling

As already mentioned, it is important for a company to identify the business events of interest and to define the activities triggered by them. For this purpose, the corresponding extract of reality must be identified and examined more closely.

This extract is determined by the customers who demand a service. For the group of company employees involved in providing the service, it represents the reality that directly affects and surrounds them. In order to provide the desired service, the parties involved must cooperate directly or indirectly.

Everyone contributes in coordination with the others. Based on their personal background in terms of education, knowledge, motivation, experiences, and preferences, each group member has their own perception of the process and its context. They develop their idea of what their contribution should be, how it is provided, which events with which activities need to be considered and by whom, in which order partial steps take place, which preliminary services are expected by whom, and for whom preliminary services are provided.

As a result, all affected people possess their own mental "world model" of the extract of reality under consideration (cf. Fig. 1.1). For a successful reaction to business events, it is necessary to structure the different realities of the participants and to transform them into a consistent process model for joint, goal-oriented action. This means that the business process is "agreed upon" by harmonizing the individual, to a greater or lesser extent, matching the mental models of the people involved.

This joining of the individual ideas of those affected by a business process and the mutual coordination of the different aspects of a business process (cf. Sect. 1.3) is itself a complex process and the central aspect of BPM.

1.3 Components of a Process Description

We conceptually split a business process description into three parts (see Fig. 1.2). The first part, called process strategy, makes statements about the purpose, triggers, inputs, end, and outputs of the process. The trigger is the event that sets the service provision in motion on the basis of the initiator's expectations, i.e., generates a process instance. This impulse is accompanied by the initiator providing information or objects that are to be processed according to their expectations. These inputs must

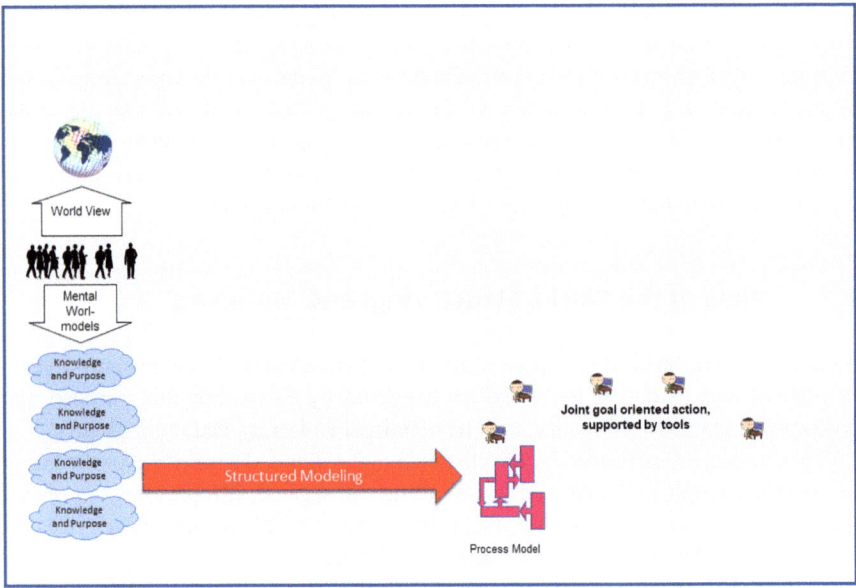

Fig. 1.1 Individual mental models of the participants

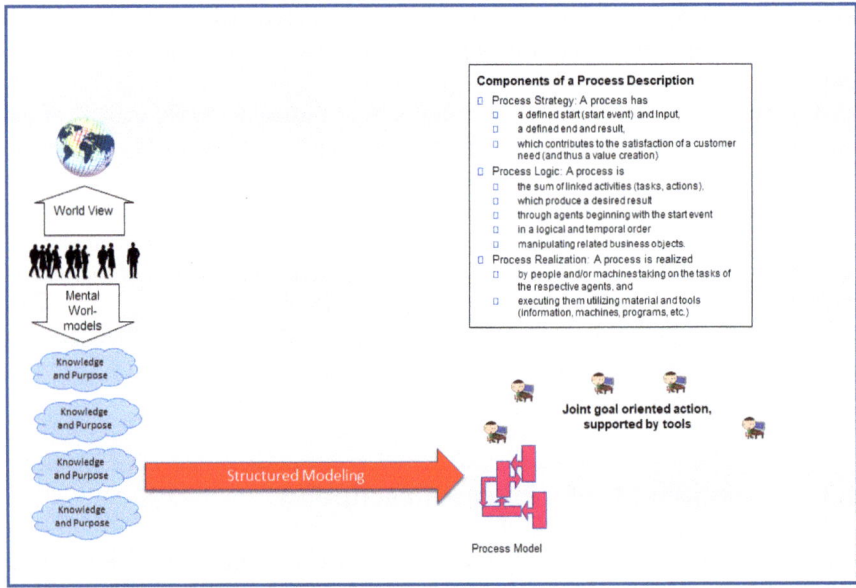

Fig. 1.2 Components of a process description

be transformed into the expected results and made available to the defined recipient. In this way, the business process creates a value for which a customer pays.

The process logic supplements this external view of a business process. This inner perspective describes the actors involved and their coordinated interaction. The actors carry out activities in a logical and timely meaningful order. They transfer the results of their actions to other actors for further processing, or to the intended recipient at the end.

Process implementation involves the provision of resources for the processing of process instances. These can be humans, machines, and software systems, which take over the activities assigned to them as concrete realizations of the involved persons. In the age of digitalization, software systems (process or workflow engines) synchronize the actors' actions by controlling the temporal and logically necessary sequence of the sub-steps according to the process model. To handle their tasks, the actors can use aids such as information, application programs, or tools where required.

Throughout process realization, it must be ensured that several process instances can be executed in parallel and independently of each other based on the defined exemplary model through appropriate resource allocation.

1.4   Determining Factors for Process Models and Process Instances

The business model essentially describes how a company affects the world and generates revenues and profits. The customer promise, as well as the resources and partners with whom this promise is fulfilled, are essential.

The enterprise architecture describes a machinery with which the business model is to be brought to life. As a typical layer concept, it defines business and IT structures and links them together. The concept of Business Engineering [1], e.g., envisages the business architecture on a strategic level with the definition of goals and services that are interwoven with the business model. At the level of the processes, as implementation tools of the strategy, the process architecture follows with its organizational and operational structure. The transition to the IT structures to support the processes leads to the level of information systems with the application architecture and the IT architecture.

As a central component of an enterprise architecture, business processes are therefore in a kind of sandwich position that illustrates how other architectural elements influence them. For example, a given organizational structure that is difficult to change can influence the procedures in processes and the way in which a company works together with external partners. The same applies to the availability of resources. But horizontal dependencies within the process organization must also be taken into account, e.g., whether a certain way of working in the ordering process has an effect on the design of payment processing.

From "below," influences affect not only the content design of the process models but also the level of detail and accuracy. For the development of IT solutions for

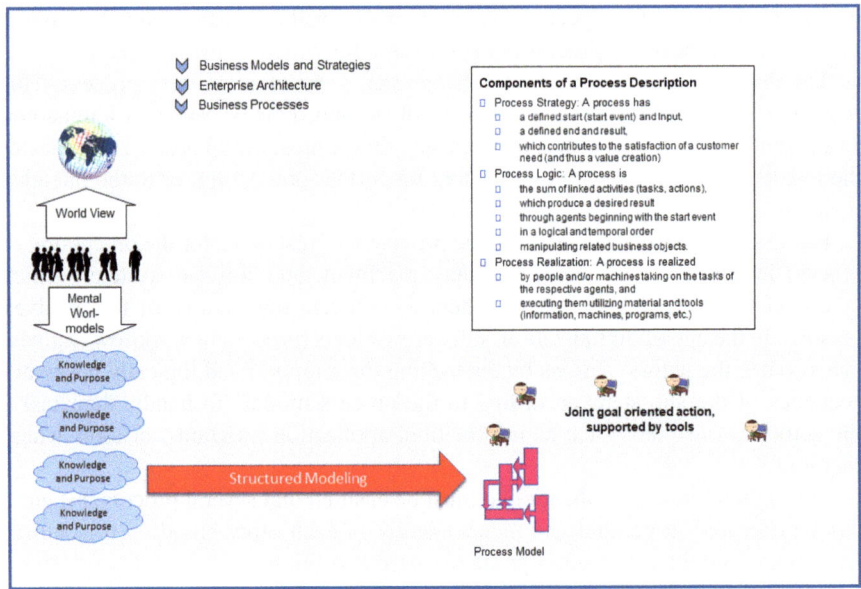

Fig. 1.3 Addition of determining factors for process definition

process digitalization, rigorous requirements apply to the model definition. Process parts that are to be executed with IT support must be specified precisely.

In addition to the internal determining factors explained above by way of example and supplemented in Fig. 1.3, external factors also have an impact on process design. Here one can see as an example test steps which have to be included in a process due to compliance regulations.

1.5   Process Metrics

The processes to be developed or changed have the general goal of supporting the implementation of the business model and the associated strategy. The relationship between the Key Performance Indicators (KPIs) from the business model and the processes is established using Process Performance Indicators (PPIs). These Process Performance Indicators are refinements of objectives from the business model (cf. Fig. 1.4).

Typical business Key Performance Indicators are derived from business models and strategies and measure business success at higher aggregation levels, e.g., revenues and costs at the overall company, division, product group level, etc. The focus here is on effectiveness ("Doing the right things"). The business processes are used to implement the strategy and bring together the elements of the enterprise architecture. The associated Process Performance Indicators aim at efficiency

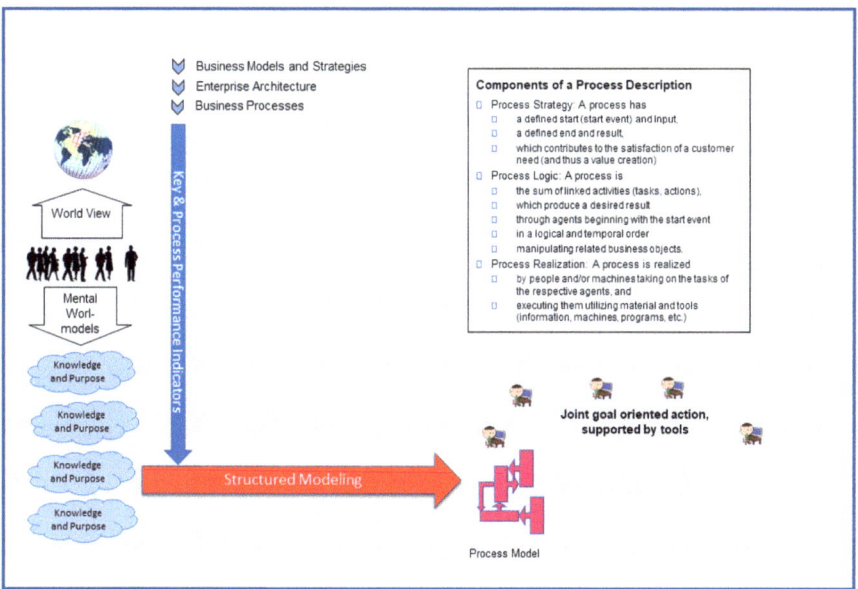

Fig. 1.4 Definition of Process Performance Indicators

("Doing things right"). They are therefore closely related to the Key Performance Indicators and are partly derived from them.

When deriving performance indicators, it must already be checked whether they can be measured with sufficient precision and justifiable effort. Under certain circumstances, this may also place demands on the process to be developed to be able to measure the performance indicators directly or indirectly. If direct measurement is not possible, targets for alternative performance indicators can also be defined, and values for the performance indicator that is actually desired can be derived from them.

Target values are defined for the Process Performance Indicators, which are to be achieved by a changed or redesigned process. Throughout the entire process, from the identification of the problem to the implementation of a modified or new process, it is important to constantly check whether the desired goals can be achieved with the resulting process.

1.6   Support Concepts

The path from individual knowledge and willingness, i.e., from the participants' mental models to a process model that can at least partially be digitalized, is complex and costly. To reduce complexity and effort, support concepts such as frameworks, process models, and description languages were developed.

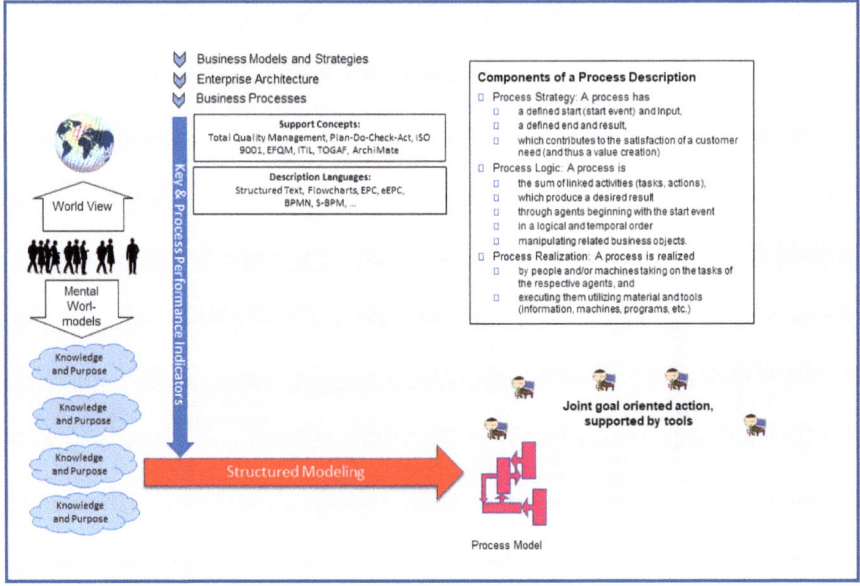

Fig. 1.5 Addition of concepts to support the process definition

The following overview comprises a thematically grouped selection of such tools which according to our experience are widely used in practice. They are inserted in Fig. 1.5 and are discussed in more detail in the chapters on models (Chap. 2) and modeling languages (Chap. 3).

Frameworks for quality management:

- Total Quality Management (TQM) TQM/PDCA
- Deming Cycle (PDCA, Plan-Do-Check-Act)
- EN ISO 9001
- European Foundation for Quality Management (EFQM)

Frameworks for Enterprise Architecture Management (EAM):

- Zachman Framework
- The Open Group Architecture Framework (TOGAF)
- Architecture-Animate (ArchiMate)

Frameworks for IT management and IT governance:

- IT Infrastructure Library (ITIL)
- Control Objectives for Information and Related Technology (COBIT)

Description languages for process logic:

- Flowcharts
- Event-controlled Process Chains and extended Event-controlled Process Chains (EPC, eEPC)
- Business Process Model and Notation (BPMN)
- Subject-oriented Business Process Management (S-BPM)

1.7   Digitalization

Today, digitalization is the keyword in the transformation of value creation. Digitalization in the economy or in organizations in general means digitalization of business models, products, and services as well as of whole processes or parts thereof. However, for processes, this does not necessarily mean full automation without any human intervention. For example, a program that controls a process may, if necessary, include actions executed by humans or by cyber-physical systems. The latter consists of communicating devices with software as well as mechanical and electronic components. In the Industry 4.0 Initiative, the aim is to achieve this comprehensive consideration of processes, i.e., the communication between people, machines, and workpieces. On the one hand, these aspects must be expressed in the process models, and on the other hand, the transfer of a business process model into digital execution must be supported as far as possible. Particularly when aspects of quality management, i.e., the continuous improvement of processes, are taken into consideration, it must be possible to implement process changes that entail a change in digitalization quickly and with as little effort as possible.

The aspects described in the previous sections must already be included in the creation of the models in order to facilitate the technical implementation of processes, but without already anticipating implementation details (cf. Fig. 1.6). The more precisely the processes are described, the easier this task becomes. Process segments whose flow logic cannot yet be precisely described at the time of modeling must be marked accordingly. However, these parts of a process can be modeled with other suitable methods according to the desired or necessary candor. Such process segments can either be described with Adaptive Case Management methods or, if a communication-oriented description language is used, as a communication loop. The latter is terminated by one of the partners involved after a corresponding result has been achieved, before continuing the process.

Important in this context is the granularity, i.e., the level of detail of the process description. Activities should be broken down in such detail that one can clearly determine whether they can be digitalized, partially digitalized (human IT, physical IT), or are performed manually by humans. The tailoring should be based on the business requirements and not on the functionality of a potentially already existing IT system. If necessary, such a system must be adapted to meet the needs of the desired business specification during process implementation.

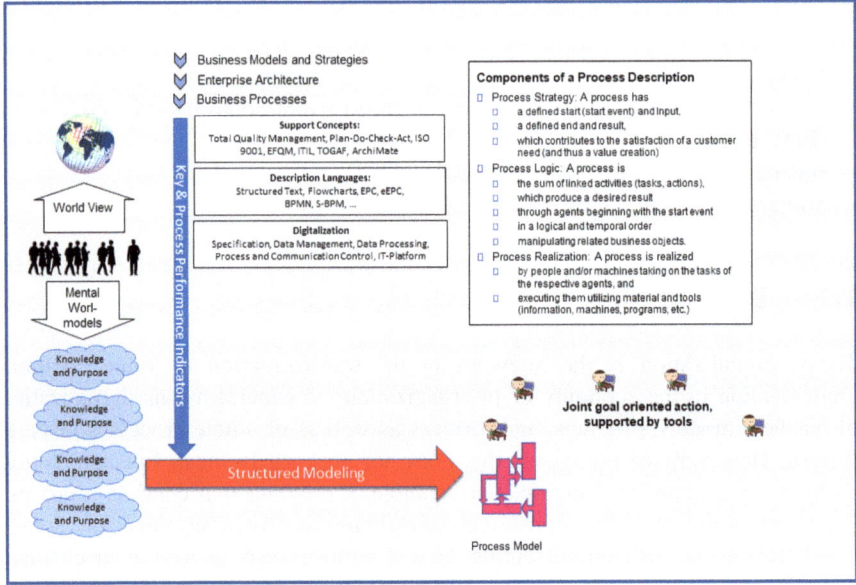

Fig. 1.6 Consideration of digitalization aspects in the model

1.8   Process for Creating Processes

The definition of the business processes cannot be done schematically or algorithmi-
cally, i.e., there is no software that when fed with the business model, the enterprise
architecture, and the Key Performance Indicators with associated target values and
support concepts, delivers a suitable process description directly.

The definition of business processes is an intuitive and creative process. Therefore, creativity techniques and knowledge management methods such as Storytelling, World Café, or Value Networks are also used, especially at the beginning
of Business Process Management activities.

For example, one can use the Design Thinking approach. This is a concept in
which interdisciplinary teams work together in an iterative process in an environment which fosters creativity to develop innovative solutions to a problem (see
Sect. 5.3). A key point thereby is to develop and consider an in-depth understanding
of the needs and motivations of people in the target group. Design Thinking offers a
comprehensive collection of methods for use in the individual steps of the approach.
With these characteristics, it can also be used for the revision or redefinition of a
business process. Under certain circumstances, extraordinary solutions can be found
that would not have been possible with the usual BPM approach.

However, a creative, innovative process concept must also be devised and
implemented in detail. Creative design is therefore embedded in a bundle of
activities that ultimately makes the process part of the real world. As such activity

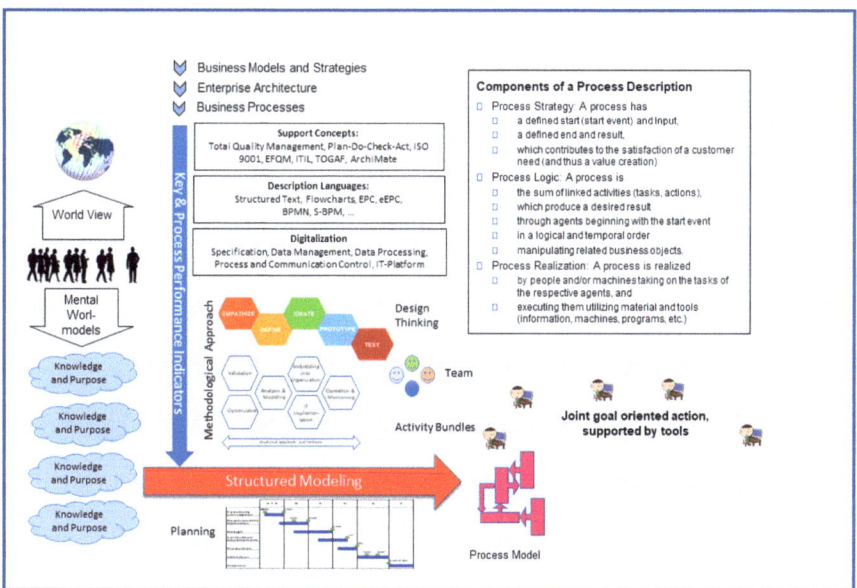

Fig. 1.7 Supplementing with process structure and planning for process changes

bundles, we identify analysis and modeling, validation, optimization, organizational implementation, IT implementation as well as operation and monitoring. These activity bundles are a further development or refinement of the Plan-Do-Check-Act cycle. They are usually arranged in a circle, which implies a corresponding flow. This does not always correspond to reality, so we present the activity bundles in Fig. 1.7 as loosely networked honeycombs. There, the phases of the Design Thinking process and the activity bundles are supplemented. Both concepts are presented in more detail in Chap. 5 and put into relation with each other.

Extensive and complex process changes usually require activities from several activity bundles and are carried out as a project. This type of project can therefore be regarded as an iteration (process instance) of the process for creating business processes. For this, a detailed project plan must be created with the activities to be carried out, responsibilities, and deadlines. The project plan should then be executed according to the methods of project management.

1.9   Organizational and Technical Implementation

Once the process model has been created, the model must be embedded in the organizational structure of a company. This determines which activity is performed by which person or organizational unit. This mapping does not have to be static but can vary from instance to instance. For example, the purchasing process can have the same flow logic for parts A and B, but a different purchasing department

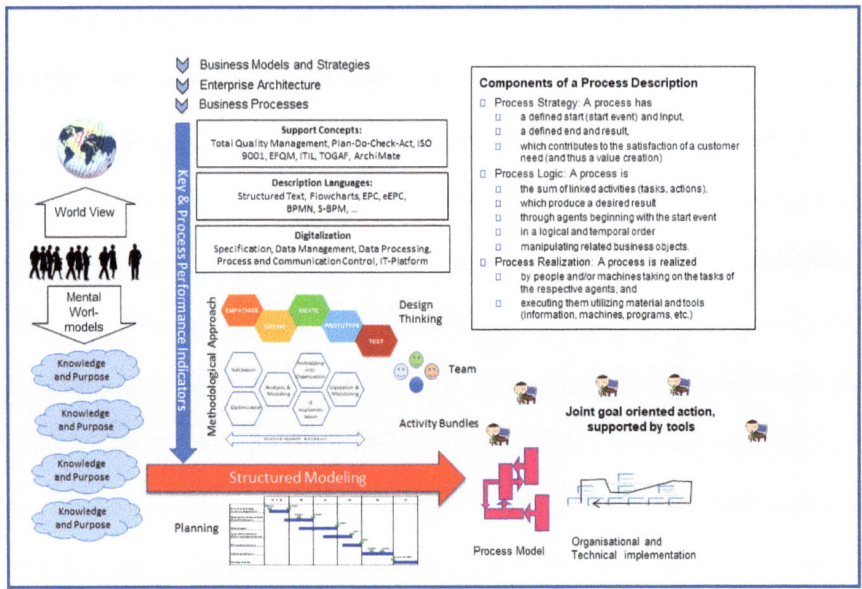

Fig. 1.8 Addition of embedding in the organization and IT environment

is responsible for purchasing parts A than for parts B. Process instances for parts A thus affect other organizational units (and persons assigned to them) than for parts B. These rules must be mapped in such a way that a process is correctly linked to the organizational structure.

In addition to activities performed by people, there may also be activities in the process that execute application programs or IT services. For this purpose, such actions must be mapped in the process model to functions of software modules, which then execute them at runtime. If during the process modeling attention was already paid to the possible digitalization, this mapping is more or less unproblematic.

Software can also control the processing of process steps and assign the tasks specified in the model to the respective persons or IT services as actors. Software systems that support this are also referred to as workflow systems (process engine, workflow engine). Ideally, process descriptions can be transferred directly into workflow systems.

After being embedded into the organization and the IT environment, a process can be used for the handling of instances, i.e., real business cases—the goal is achieved. Figure 1.8 shows the now completed path from individual mental models, including the knowledge and intentions of the participants, to the joint handling of process instances.

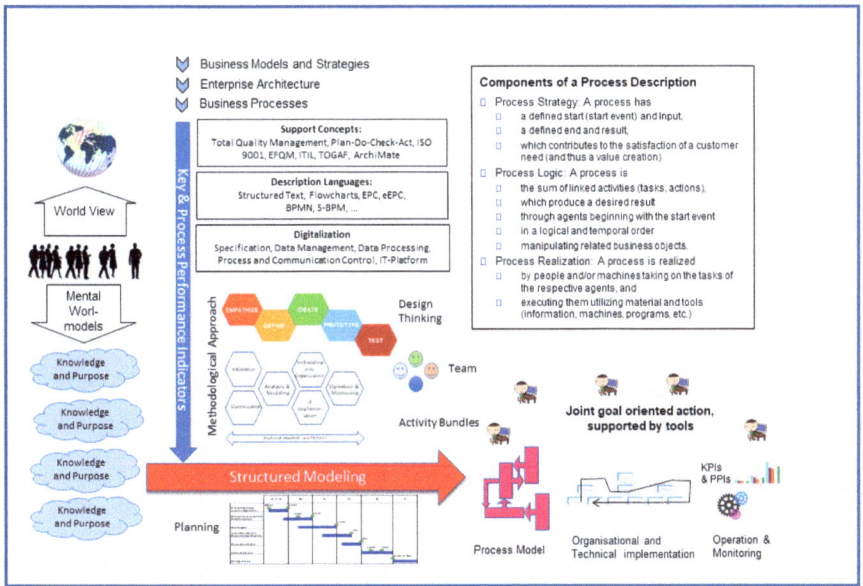

Fig. 1.9 Operation, monitoring and performance indicators

1.10   Success Measurement with Performance Indicators

When instances of a process are executed, one can check whether the target values defined for the Process Performance Indicators are reached. For this purpose, actual values for the defined Key and Process Performance Indicators (KPIs and PPIs) are measured, calculated, stored, and compared with the target values. This comparison can be made in real time or over longer time intervals. Any real-time evaluation leads to the immediate initiation of suitable countermeasures in the event of a deviation from the target. However, an evaluation of measured values over a longer period of time shows medium- to long-term trends in performance indicators and can trigger the corresponding changes. The evaluation results are visualized in the process cockpits, among other things (cf. Fig. 1.9).

1.11   Continuous Improvement

Processes are not static but are subject to changes in the internal and external determining factors described in Sect. 1.4. Developments such as business model modifications, new competitors, technical progress, or deteriorations in measured PPIs, such as lead time, may require adjustments to a process. To do this, appropriate measures should be taken within the framework of the activity and procedure bundles presented in Sect. 1.8.

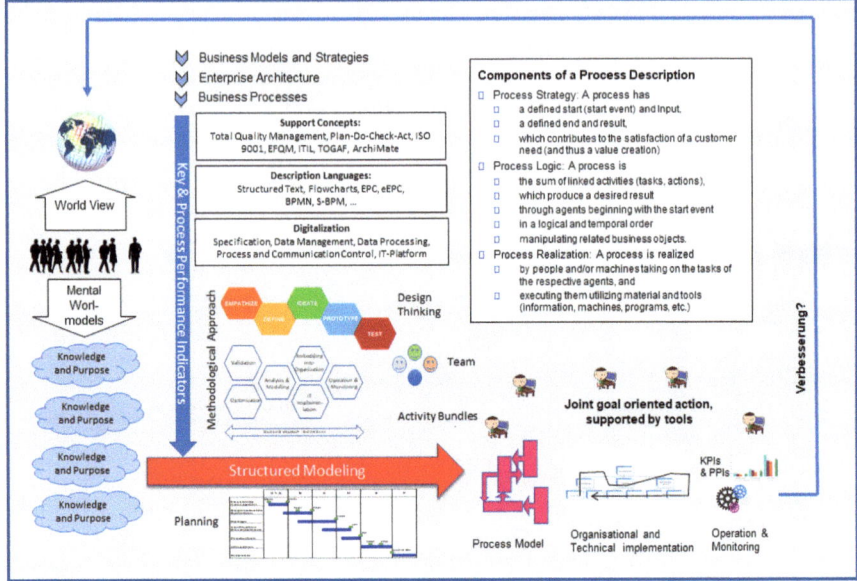

Fig. 1.10 Supplementing with continuous improvement

The feedback arrow in Fig. 1.10 indicates that the participants may again have diverging views of the selected part of reality. By harmonizing them in the way described, a new instance of the process for creating processes is started.

Continuous improvement is a very important aspect of process management. Ongoing adaptations bring one closer to the desired process. However, changes in the environment can influence this convergence. The state being pursued is therefore a "moving target."

1.12   Corporate Governance and Business Process Management

Corporate governance as an institution shapes a company. It has a decisive influence on the business model, corporate strategy, and organization. The business model and strategy are designed to open up future potential for success and thus secure the sustainable existence of the company. The enterprise architecture creates the infrastructure to exploit the potential for success. The business processes and the business objects (data) processed by them link the business and technical levels of the enterprise architecture.

The business processes are the subject of digitalization, i.e., the IT support of process execution by people and machines. In recent years, the associated requirements have increased significantly. In business processes, not only people and IT systems but also "smart" machines and devices should be able to interact. This refers to highly integrated business processes in the context of Industry 4.0 and the Internet of Things, which integrate human actors as well as individual devices and machines into a common whole. The technical players are often referred to as "smart" or "intelligent."

Corporate governance as a process describes the management activities involved in creating and exploiting the potential for success. In the context of BPM, this means the management of socio-technical systems with people is involved in processes, and machines that support people in their activities or autonomously carry out a chain of activities.

Despite the increasing importance of digitalization, the human being, as designer of socio-technical systems and user of supporting technology, is at the center of process management. Not least due to increasing agility requirements, the goal today is for employees to be able to design (model) the operative processes autonomously and independently as far as possible, and for these to then be directly supported by Information Technology without significant delays and additional effort. With a clear commitment to process orientation, management must create the conditions for this as such ("Tone from the top"). These include both the necessary infrastructure and an environment that encourages people to become actively involved in process management activities. The degree of employee involvement is determined by the image of humanity and the associated management philosophy of the company management ("Tone at the top"). In a classical, more hierarchical approach, people and their skills are seen as a resource that is the subject of managerial action, and these people ultimately execute instructions. Such a management philosophy is characterized by direct intervention of the company management and follows Theory X. According to this theory, any lack of motivation is countered by the threat of sanctioning by the company management.

In a more systemic, i.e., holistic approach, such as the one that the St. Gallen Management Model is based on, a system is to be created that works itself largely independently on the design of a Business Process Management System. All employees should be able to actively contribute. This management style follows the image of humanity according to Theory Y. According to this theory, the essential characteristics of humans are pleasure in demanding work, self-discipline, responsibility, and intellectual power.

The image of humanity is supplemented by corresponding organizational theories. The purpose of these is to explain the creation, existence, and functioning of organizations. Organizational theories implicitly assume a corresponding view of humanity. Thus, Taylorism is more based on an image of man that corresponds to Theory X. Luhmann's Systemic Organizational Theory, on the other hand, makes no ethical assumptions about the people in an organization; it only assumes that they communicate. Although the Theory of Communicative Action also focuses on communication, the world is to be changed through theory and rationality. It is assumed that man is by nature insightful and open to argumentation.

There are management philosophies and organizational theories that fit the various concepts of humanity. The nature and use of methods, techniques, and tools must be consistent with them. For example, it is not appropriate to propagate the involvement of employees if the company management then does not take their suggestions seriously or does not take notice of these suggestions at all. Before starting to design processes, a company should, therefore, be aware of the image of humanity that shapes its leadership and corporate culture.

We think that, especially for the challenges associated with digitalization, an orientation to Theory Y is necessary, which will often (and must) lead to cultural change in practice.

Reference

1. H. Österle, R. Winter, *Business Engineering: Auf dem Weg zum Unternehmen des Information-szeitalters* (Springer, Berlin, 2013)

Models

2

In the previous chapter, we outlined the various aspects of Business Process Management. Since models are often used in practice to describe these aspects, we will first take a closer look at the tasks and characteristics of models and model building in the following sections. We will then present examples of models from various fields that have proven helpful in our experience in numerous Business Process Management projects. The presentation does not claim to be exhaustive, but it can serve as a guide for readers who need to select descriptive models for their own individual projects.

2.1   Model and Reality

"You don't have to understand the world, you just have to find your way around it." This quote is attributed to Albert Einstein on the Internet. Who understands everything that happens in the world? Who knows how it works? That is why we should be concerned with our world, with the part of the world that is important to us at the moment. We should recognize that we create or construct our world every day. The section we observe is, of course, determined by our subjective interests.

Before we can observe our environment, we must decide what interests us. We decide which section of the world we want to look at and which aspects of it seem important to us. In doing so, we identify the artifacts that are essential to us and the relationships between them that are essential to us. This abstraction of a section of reality is called a model, and the aspects it contains are called attributes of the model. It may also be that the section of reality under consideration is already a model. This allows parts of an existing model to be examined more closely. This would then be a model of a model. This escalation can continue indefinitely.

© The Author(s) 2026
M. Elstermann et al., *Contextual Process Digitalization*,
https://doi.org/10.1007/978-3-032-06901-6_2

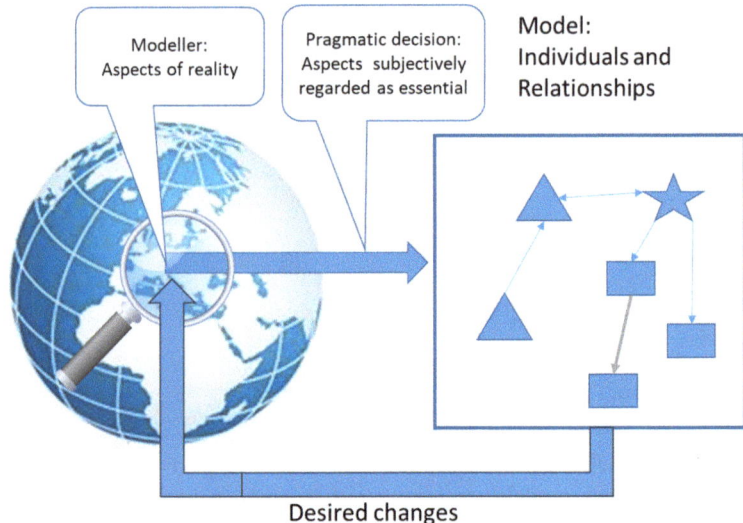

Fig. 2.1 Modeling and implementing

In his book *Allgemeine Modelltheorie* (General Model Theory), Herbert Stachowiak refers to the decision as to which aspects of the world are considered
pragmatic decisions [1]:
*"Decide what you want to understand by 'knowledge' only in relation to the
intentions (purposes, goals, goals) you have set yourself as an individual or as a
member of one or more sufficiently homogeneous groups for a certain period of
time. So, do not try to intend the absence of intention in cognition, a cognition that
is not generated by a 'knowledge of what for.'"*
The neopragmatic theory of knowledge of modelism is derived from the pragmatic decision and the concept of a model of knowledge [1]. Consequently, "all
knowledge, knowledge in models and through models, and every human encounter
with the world requires the medium of "model" [1].
Each person has their own subjective view of the world or a section of the world,
guided by their interests. Different people look at the same section of reality but
arrive at different models because they set different priorities or, in other words,
make different pragmatic decisions (see Fig. 2.1).
Each person has their own subjective view of the world or a section of the world.
Different people look at the same section of reality but arrive at different models
because they set different priorities (cf. Fig. 2.1).

2.2   Process of Systematic Knowledge Acquisition

The creation of a model and its use are subjective activities, i.e., the creator selects
the characteristics of the representation of reality according to his or her own ideas.

However, it is common for groups of actors, hereinafter referred to as subjects or agents, to agree on a model for viewing reality. Many scientific schools are based on such common models of the researchers involved.

Model building is an essential activity in all sciences, be it philosophy, sociology, physics, chemistry, engineering sciences, economics, etc. The respective models have different tasks: Either they represent the section under consideration, as is common in the natural sciences, or they serve to test certain necessary changes to the section of reality under consideration (simulation model). This is important, for example, to not endanger human lives. The safety models of cars are tested for their properties in appropriate tests before they go into series production. This is not done with humans but with models of humans, known as dummies. Two models are combined: the car model, which implements the relevant safety concepts, and the human model (dummy) to investigate the risk of injury.

The facts captured in a model can now be adjusted until the desired result is achieved for the phenomena considered with the model. For example, additional safety concepts are added to the car safety model until the desired reduction in the risk of injury is achieved. Such models are then no longer representations of reality but represent a desired reality. The desired properties are then transferred back to reality, for example, by incorporating the safety concepts tested in the model into production cars.

The goal of modeling is always to help us find our way in the world or to safely test how a corresponding change in reality would affect us. It seems that we will not succeed in understanding what holds the world together at its core in the foreseeable future. The corresponding model would then be the world that does not exist [2].

Stachowiak [1] described the process of thinking, cognition, and knowledge described above, which emphasizes the operational side of this process, in his so-called K-system (the K stands for the cybernetic orientation of this system). This K-system is to be understood as a model, i.e., it does not claim to be valid in the epistemological sense.

Figure 2.2 shows the process of knowledge acquisition according to Stachowiak's cybernetic model [1]. It shows the interaction and communication behavior between the subsystem "outside world" and individual human beings (modelers).

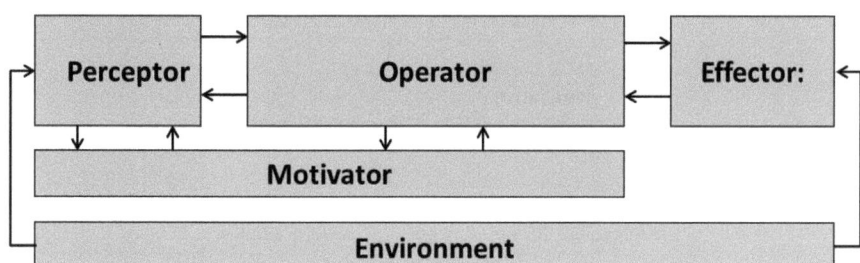

Fig. 2.2 K-system: cycle of knowledge aquisition

As an input/output system, humans receive information from the outside world. They register this information, link it to other existing information, and derive actions from it, which are fed back into the outside world via corresponding outputs, and change it. As an input/output system, humans perform various functions. The K system corresponds to a control loop in which the motivator corresponds to the reference variable. Here, the target variables are defined that relate to the purpose of gaining knowledge. The operator corresponds to the controller of the system. It ensures that the behavior of the actors in the outside world adapts to the motives, needs, desires, aspirations, etc. of the modeler.

The subsystem consisting of the perceiver, operator, and motivator is also a feedback system. The elements registered by the perceiver depend not only on the outside world but also on the motivator and ultimately on the operator. The behavior of the operator is in turn influenced by the perceptor and motivator, with the perceptor and operator influencing the motivator. This means that goals can change as a result of the perceived external world.

Based on this general model for learning, the aspects of process management outlined in Chap. 1 can now be classified. Figure 2.3 shows this classification.

In process management, the outside world corresponds to customer behavior, which in turn is embedded in the market and economic situation. The motivator function contains the corporate goal, the business model, the corporate architecture, and the description of the business processes. The perceiver perceives information from the external world, usually via process metrics or Key Performance Indicators, or suggestions for improvement from those involved in the process. This information is analyzed via the motivator-operator loop and the corresponding actions are derived. These can be changes to processes or their implementation. The effector prepares the corresponding changes, such as extensions to the process flows, and

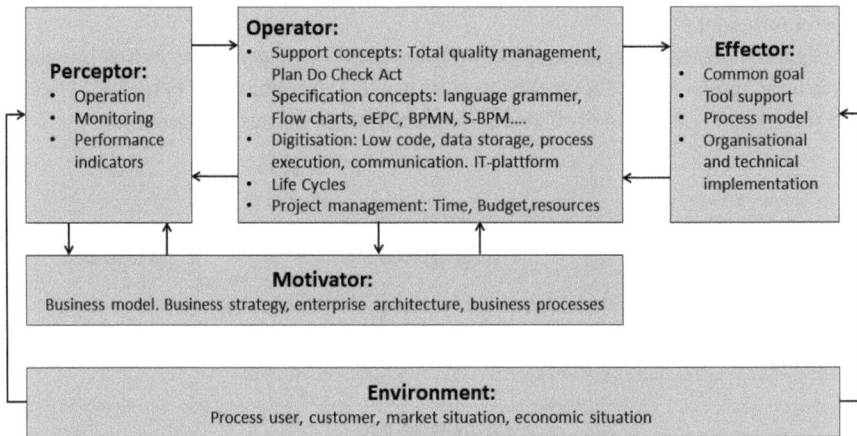

Fig. 2.3 Classification of process management aspects in the knowledge acquisition process

implements the necessary changes to the external world. This changed external world becomes a source of new information that may trigger new actions.

The knowledge gained is incorporated into models. Since all knowledge is knowledge from and in models, models are created through the K-system of knowledge acquisition. The properties of these models will be explained in more detail in the following section.

2.3   Properties of Models

Models serve both as the abstract representation of the observed reality in the sense of a cognitive function and as the design of the observed reality in the sense of a conclusion. As already mentioned, once a model is modified until it corresponds to a desired reality, it can be used as a blueprint for a corresponding transformation of reality. In natural sciences such as physics, models predominantly have a cognitive function, while in engineering sciences and business administration, they are intended to support the shaping of reality [3].

In clarifying the model concept used thus far, we follow the studies of Herbert Stachowiak. In his model theory, he examined the characteristics of models and the properties derived from these more closely [4]. Accordingly, models are identified by at least three characteristics [4, page 131]:

1: Mapping
A model is always a representation of something. It can be a depiction or representation of a natural or artificial original, whereby this original itself can again be a model. The originals can be created in a natural way, technically produced, or simply exist in some other way. Models can be described or represented in very different ways:

- Mental models: Imagination in the human mind
- Verbal models: Natural language description
- Graphical models: Technical drawings or other pictures
- Material models: Models of buildings
- Formal models: Mathematical models, computer programs, etc.

A model and the original form a class of attributes. Attributes are characteristics and properties of individuals, relations between individuals, properties of properties, properties of relations, etc. Stachowiak leaves it up to the modeling subject to determine how to conceptualize individuals. He considers individuals as attributes on level 0. Sets of attributes can be combined to form classes, which then form attributes on level 1. These classes can be combined again to form a next attribute level, and so on.

2: Reduction
In general, a model does not capture all attributes of the original but only those that appear relevant to the creator or user of the model.

Since not all attributes of the original are captured by a model, a pragmatic dimension has been introduced in the broader sense. In the "broader sense" here means that not yet specific pragmatic-operational aspects are considered, according to which the attribute classes that are to be included in a model are selected. This initial selection of attributes is intuitive and arbitrary. In the narrower sense, the reduction is pragmatic only when the intentions and operational objectives of the model creator or user influence the selection of model-relevant attributes. These adjustments to the intended practical use are made in the next step.

3: Pragmatism
After the intuitive selection of the attributes, it is checked whether the intended purpose has been achieved. Models are not clearly assigned to their originals. They serve as a replacement function:

- For certain discerning or acting model-using subjects (for whom?):
  Models are not only models of something, they are also models for someone. This someone can be a human being or an artificial model user such as a computer program. For a modeler, models can serve as a possibility to find one's way around in the world, i.e., the modeler is also a user of the model. Modelers and model users can also be two different subjects.
- Within certain time intervals (when?):
  Models also perform a function over time, i.e., their use is related to a specific point in time or to a defined time interval. During this time, the observed reality or the ideas of the modeler or model user may have changed in such a way that additional attributes should become part of the model.
- With restriction to certain mental or actual operations (why?):
  Models are created for a certain purpose, be it for better understanding a certain part of reality or for creating a blueprint for the transformation of reality.

When creating a model, modelers are always in a certain dilemma. On the one hand, the model should sufficiently reflect the desired aspects of reality, whereby it is not clearly defined what is sufficient. On the other hand, the model should not be too complex in order to remain manageable. This conflict of objectives leads to the fact that most models are developed iteratively until they reach the end of their life cycle due to increasing complexity—they are no longer manageable.

In the following sections, we present examples of models that consider aspects that are explicitly or implicitly incorporated into business process models. We have grouped the examples into models from the social sciences, business administration, business informatics, and computer science. The classification into these groups is not entirely free of overlaps, since business informatics, as a cross-sectoral discipline, considers issues from various perspectives.

2.4   Models in Social Sciences

Business Process Management has to do with people and machines. It aims at organizing their interaction while taking into account additional requirements with regard to technical, economic, and ecological feasibility. In particular, the interaction and coexistence of people has been a topic of philosophy for thousands of years. Philosophy, as the doctrine of the basic rules and structures of life, the world, and knowledge, seeks to fathom, interpret, and understand the world and human existence. The original meaning of philosophy was the teaching of good life.

In this sense, philosophy is the attempt to create a comprehensive model of our world, but this has not yet been successful. Social philosophers reduce the view and try to create a model of society as some part of reality and thus better understand its meaning and essence. In particular, social philosophies illuminate the relationship between the individual and the community as well as the structures of living together. They are therefore also regarded as variants of philosophy that touch on sociology. They should help sociologists to analyze social processes and support organizational developers in their work and help people to find their way around in the world. Numerous organizational theories focus on different aspects in their models (see [5–8]). The question of which organizational theory fits best cannot be answered. Organizational theories are models and thus, according to Stachowiak, the justified but subjective view of the modeler. Organizational theories emphasize the analysis of organizations in highly different ways and pursue different objectives. There are empirical studies on organizational theories that provide results in favor of, or against, a theory. However, the analysis methods used are controversial (see [8, page 68]).

Organizational theories are based on particular perspectives on people, and the prevailing image of people in an organization strongly influences the design of Business Process Management. Hence, in the following sections, we discuss Taylorism, Habermas's Theory of Communicative Action, and Luhmann's Social Systems as distinct organizational theories to exemplify different perspectives on human and organizational behavior.

2.4.1   Taylorism and Fordism

Taylorism introduced the "experiment" into management theory and practice and is one of the classics of organizational theory. With the so-called scientific management, organizations received an instrument to design themselves efficiently. One important characteristic is the separation between planning mental work and performing manual work. According to Taylor's view of man, workers are dumb and lazy and must, therefore, be subject to strict rules. Even today, this view often implicitly influences leadership behavior.

For Frederik Winslow Taylor, the most important goals of running a business were the perfection of the means of production and work processes, tighter organization and temporal structuring of workflows in the company, as well as a reorganization of the remuneration system. A core element of Taylorism is the design of work processes on the basis of time and movement studies. A breakdown of the production process into the smallest work steps, an exoneration of workers from mental activities, as well as a change of the wage system should lead to an optimal use of existing performance potentials. The ultimate goal is to increase the productivity of human labor. This is done by dividing the work into its smallest units, which require only little or no cognitive effort to accomplish, and which can be repeated quickly and repetitively due to their small size or the content of the work.

Taylorism is based on the following core principles:

- **Work scheduling:** The planning of the work is done by other persons than those who carry it out (separation of manual and mental work). In this way Taylor wanted to avoid the shirking that he accused the workers of. Through time and movement studies carried out by the mental workers, the least amount of movement and time required for a work step was to be determined.
- **Incentivized wages:** These time and movement studies also revealed what the workers had to achieve in a certain period of time. A bonus ensured that the workers who were classified as "dumb" and "lazy" actually tried to achieve the specified performance.
- **Selection of the most suitable workers:** One aim was to build up a first-class workforce by means of an appropriate selection mechanism. Tests were developed and used to identify particularly agile and nimble-fingered workers.
- **Reconciliation between workers and management:** Taylor believed that the system he had developed could increase productivity to such an extent that the dispute over the distribution of profits would become a minor issue. This achievement should resolve the conflict between employers and employees.

Taylorism essentially considers the structuring of work steps but does not focus on their sequence. This aspect was addressed by Henry Ford, who coordinated the individual activities by introducing the assembly line. This step created the basis for the mass production that characterized the twentieth century. The assembly line principle was also transferred to administration and strongly influenced Business Process Management. Flowcharts are the assembly line specifications for the execution of administrative tasks or the "production" of services.

2.4.2 Communicative Action According to Habermas

In contrast to Taylorism, Habermas's Theory of Communicative Action is based on insightful people who, through communication among themselves, come to a common rational action. Using his social model, Habermas explains the processes in a society, such as the search for truth, for justice, etc. Consequently, it is a model that concerns everyone, because the issues of truth and justice affect all members of societies. The central aspect in Habermas's model of society is the so-called Communicative Action.

"Finally, the concept of Communicative Action refers to the interaction of at least two subjects capable of speaking and acting that enter into an interpersonal relationship (whether by verbal or nonverbal means). The actors seek an understanding of the action situation in order to coordinate their action plans, and thus their actions, amicably" [9].

According to Habermas, communication enables an individual human being, who is not gifted with rationality on his own initiative, to overcome this deficiency. Communication between people becomes inter-subjective action and a possible source of rationality. Communicative Action means acting on the basis of mutual understanding between people.

Habermas wants to offer sociologists and politicians a model that they can use to analyze and shape society. The individual can use it to find their way around in today's societies, despite their complexity.

2.4.3 Social Systems According to Luhmann

Similar to Habermas's, Luhmann's Social Model is based on communication. The differences lie in the extent to which communication and action are combined. Luhmann only allows communication as a constituent aspect for organizations. Communication does not occur between people but between at least two information-processing processors. Luhmann thus sees communication more abstractly. According to him, society does not consist of people or parts of people. Otherwise one would cut off something from society when one cuts off something from a person. The body of a human being (i.e., as a biological system) with a conscious mind (a psychological system) is in many cases a prerequisite for the functioning of a social system, i.e., communication. However, a human being is not the social system itself. Luhmann makes no assertions about the nature of man in his organizational theory, thus leaving the perspective on humans open. People are only part of the organization insofar as they communicate with each other.

The communication between the information-processing processors consists of the so-called selections of information, message, and understanding (see Fig. 2.4).

	Two information-processing processors, usually people or social systems	
	transmitter Luhmann's "Alter"	receiver Luhmann's "Ego"
Three selections:	1. Selection of information 2. Selection of message	3. Selection of acceptance/ understanding

Fig. 2.4 Luhmann's understanding of communication

The first two selections are for the sender and the third for the recipient. Communication as a piece with at least two actors in three acts is an indivisible unit, namely, the smallest unit of a social system and the elementary operation of society [10, 11]. This view can serve as a pattern for the definition of communication in business processes, completely independent of a specific perspective on humans.

Both Luhmann and Habermas put communication at the center of their organizational theory. The fact that these two important organizational theorists so strongly emphasize the communication aspect of the organization, and that their theories are widely accepted, can be seen as an indication for considering business processes as primarily communication-oriented.

2.4.4 Organizations

Complex social systems can be divided into smaller social systems. This structure of a complex social system is called the organizational structure. The criteria according to which the division into smaller social systems takes place are subjective and depend on the respective intentions. According to Luhmann's definition of a social system, the individual social systems communicate within a more complex social system. Organizational structures are thus a model of a more complex social system.

In contrast to Luhmann's or Habermas's broad understanding of the term organization, a narrower understanding of organizations has also developed. In business administration, organization is the formal set of rules of a system based on the division of labor. In organizational sociology, it refers to a special form of social entity that can be distinguished from other social entities such as families, groups, movements, or networks. Essential characteristics of organizations are that people can join them or leave them. In addition, they have a purpose that they are geared to. Organizations have regulations on the division of labor, such as specialization according to performance, function, objects, or space, or corresponding hybrid forms. This division of labor requires the coordination of individual activities. Hierarchy is the central instrument of coordination in organizational theory. The hierarchical coordination is supplemented by cadres, commissions, task forces, etc. For one-time problems or problems to be solved for the first time, the hierarchy is supplemented by a project organization.

2.5   Models in Business Administration

Business administration is the study of economic, organizational, technical, and financial processes and structures in companies. Business Process Management is, therefore, also a part of business administration. Business processes serve to improve the economic efficiency of a company with all of the associated aspects such as customer satisfaction, employee motivation, the integration of partners, etc. For the structuring of all these aspects and for the analysis of their interaction, business administration has developed models which, when applied, have an effect on Business Process Management.

2.5.1   Business Model

The term *business model* refers to the overall concept of a company—its basic idea of how to make a profit. It represents the interrelationships as a model, how a company can generate added value for its customers and thus achieve sustainable returns. In addition to the products and services offered, the focus is on the structure of the company, the definition of the target groups (customers) and how they are addressed, as well as the design of the business processes. Beyond this understanding, there are a number of other definitions of the term business model (cf. e.g., [12]).

A business model therefore serves to understand the relationship between the company as a system of action and the creation of value. It reflects how a company works and what values it generates for specific target groups. Business models are created within the scope of a company foundation or a reorientation. They consist of several sub-models that describe which resources (materials, information, etc.) are (must be) available to a company as input variables, and how these resources are processed and transformed into marketable products or services, which are then transferred to the customer in order to generate corresponding revenues [13].

Business models can serve multiple stakeholders. The company management can thus better understand its own business and recognize existing strengths and weaknesses, as well as opportunities for further development, transformation, and improvement of its competitive position. For investors, the business model is often an important aspect of investment decisions.

A number of instruments have been developed to create business models. The best known is the Business Model Canvas by Alexander Osterwalder [14], which has found high acceptance in recent years. As the name suggests, the Business Model Canvas approach is based on a poster on which various aspects of the business model are visualized. The canvas provides a grid for nine business model aspects, which is filled with the concrete characteristics for a company at hand (see Fig. 2.5). The focus is on the value proposition (product or service).

When completing the form, a series of questions on each of the nine aspects must be answered. The following explanations briefly describe the aspects and provide a selection of associated questions.

1: Customer Segments, Target Groups
All persons or organizations for whom the company in question wants to create value.
Questions to be answered include:

- Who benefits from the product or service?
- Which customers are particularly important?

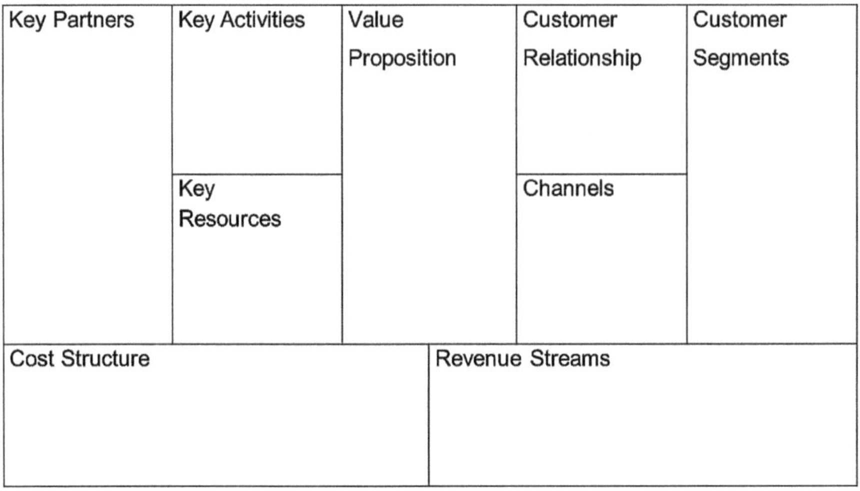

Key Partners	Key Activities	Value Proposition	Customer Relationship	Customer Segments
	Key Resources		Channels	
Cost Structure			Revenue Streams	

Fig. 2.5 Schema of the Business Model Canvas

2: Value Promise, Customer Benefit

Each customer segment has its own value proposition, the customer benefit. This is a combination of a product and service tailored to the needs of the respective segment.

Questions to be answered include:

- What benefit or value does the offer have for the customers?
- Which customer problems are solved with the offered products and/or services?

3: Channels, Sales Channels

This factor represents the specific channels through which customers are addressed and promised values are communicated to them. Sales channels determine how interaction with customers takes place. Communication, distribution, and points of sale form the interfaces between a company and its customers. The perception of the customer at these points of contact is central and determines the impression a customer has of a company.

Questions to be answered include:

- How do customers find out about the products and services offered?
- How do the products/services reach the customer?

4: Customer Relations

This section describes how dealings with customers are fostered.

Every company should think about what types of customer relationships it wants to establish with different target groups. The design of customer relationships

depends not only on the respective target group but also on the associated objectives of the company (new customer acquisition, existing customer care, etc.).
Questions to be answered include:

- What kind of relationship do the individual customer groups expect?
- How is the relationship with the customers organized?
- How much does it cost to maintain customer contact and what is the value of this particular customer?

5: Revenue Sources, Revenue Models

The company creates added value with its products and services. The central question is how much the customer is willing to pay for this. The company needs to decide on pricing models and pricing strategy (one-time payment, subscription, etc.).
Questions to be answered include:

- For what and how much are customers really willing to pay for the offer?
- How much does each of the individual revenue sources contribute to total revenue?
- How would customers like to pay?

6: Key Resources

Every company requires certain resources to prepare offers. These can be owned by the company itself, or also leased or provided by strategic partners.
Questions to be answered include:

- Which physical resources (facilities, production machines) are required to create and offer a product or service?
- Which intellectual resources (knowledge, patents, partnerships, customer base) are needed?
- Which personnel resources (teams) are required?
- What financial resources (available capital, collateral) are required?
- How can the necessary resources be procured and maintained?

7: Key Activities

Key activities are the activities necessary for the creation and utilization of services, such as production, sales, and so on.
Questions to be answered include:

- Which key activities have to be carried out in order to offer a product or a service and thus realize the customer benefit?
- Which activities are needed for which sales channels?
- Which activities are required for which customer relationships?

8: Key Partners

Key partners are business partners who provide important resources for the realization of the business model.

Companies often enter into strategic alliances with these partners. Examples are suppliers, service providers, etc.

Questions to be answered include:

- Who are key partners and what do they do for the company?
- Which key resources are provided by which partners?

9: Cost Structure

The cost structure provides information on the most important cost factors of a business model.

Questions to be answered include:

- What are the largest and most important cost factors in the business model?
- Which key resources/key activities are the most expensive?

Key Performance Indicators and associated target values for business processes can be derived from the individual parts of a business model. Conversely, the Key Performance Indicators and target values can influence the design of the processes. If the focus is on low prices, processes will look different compared to a business model focused on high quality.

2.5.2   Balanced Scorecard

The Balanced Scorecard (BSC) was introduced in the early 1990s by Kaplan and Norton [15]. It is a link between the business model, the development of a strategy, and its implementation. In the business world, strategy is classically understood as the (usually long-term) planned behavior of companies in order to achieve their goals.

A BSC starts with the vision and strategy of a company and defines the Critical Success Factors (CSF) on this basis with the help of Key Performance Indicators and associated target values. The vision of a company describes the long-term ambitious goal that an organization or company strives for. Typical visions are formulations such as "we want to become the market leader in our market segment," or "we want to become the most profitable company in our market segment."

The Key Performance Indicators promote goal setting and performance in critical areas of the strategy to achieve the vision. The BSC is therefore a management system that is derived from the vision as part of the business model and the strategy to implement said model. It reflects the key aspects of the company. The BSC concept supports strategic planning and implementation by bundling the measures taken by all entities of a company on the basis of a common understanding of its goals and by facilitating access to the evaluation and updating of the strategy.

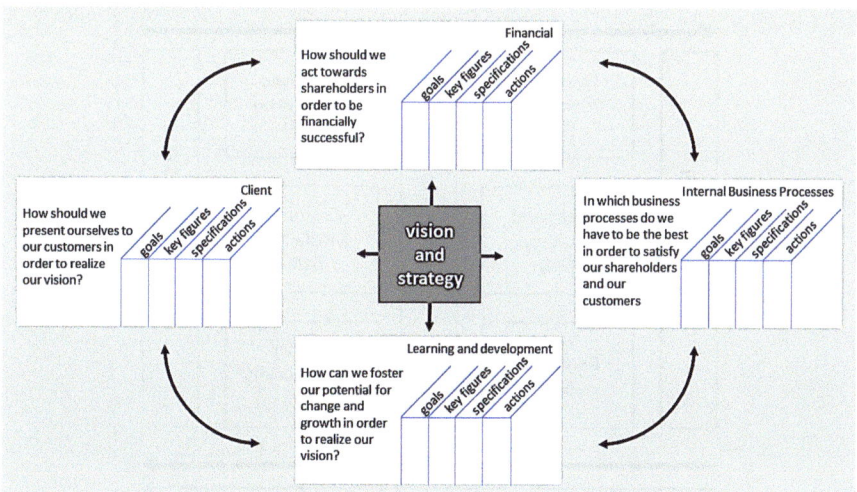

Fig. 2.6   Perspectives of the Balanced Scorecard

Since traditional management based purely on financial indicators no longer meets the requirements of companies for effective planning tools in the information age, Kaplan and Norton have introduced four perspectives for the BSC which allow the activities of a company to be assessed comprehensively. For each perspective, objectives, performance indicators, targets, and measures to be taken are defined (cf. Fig. 2.6).

2.5.3   Total Quality Management and EFQM

The term Total Quality Management (TQM) denotes the optimization of the quality of a company's products and services in all functional areas and at all levels through the participation of all employees. Optimization of quality means neither reaching the highest quality level with the given effort nor increasing the quality without consideration of costs. Rather, it is a matter of focusing on the interests of the customer and determining quality in terms of the fulfillment of customer requirements.

The management of a company decides which requirements the company places on itself and which positioning toward the customer promises the most sustainable business success. This positioning is not static. Knowledge about customer needs and about the procedures to meet these needs requires a continuous adaptation of the company.

In order to establish TQM, the European Foundation for Quality Management (EFQM) offers organizations assistance in setting up and continuously developing a comprehensive management system. Figure 2.7 shows the structure of the EFQM approach. On the one hand, this structure serves as a tool to build up a TQM and,

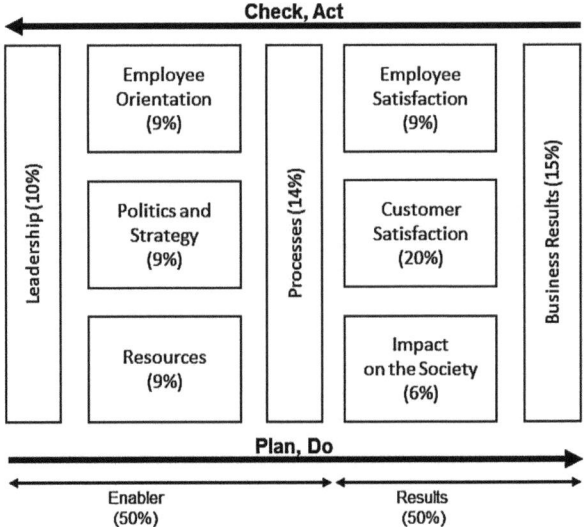

Fig. 2.7 EFQM Structure

on the other hand, to identify improvement potentials through a comprehensive evaluation system as well as to increase business success.

Enablers in the EFQM model are the methods and concepts used to achieve the results shown in the right half of the figure. The percentages in the presentation indicate the extent to which the individual aspects are included in the overall evaluation of the company.

The EFQM assumes that the enabling methods and concepts have the largest influence on the results (right side of Fig. 2.7). The model thus provides good starting points for identifying Key Performance Indicators and their target values.

In addition to the possibility of setting up a management system, EFQM also offers a very sophisticated concept for evaluating its development status. A comprehensive catalogue of questions can be used to carry out an all-round evaluation of an organization. The evaluation can be carried out by employees of the organization itself or by external consultants. The best organizations in Europe score around 750 out of a maximum of 1,000 points in such evaluations.

2.5.4   EN ISO 9001

Compared to TQM, the EN ISO 9001 standard represents a weakened form of quality management. It describes minimum requirements for a quality management system. Figure 2.8 illustrates the basic structure of the standard.

Management's responsibility means that it defines which customer requirements are met and which quality policy is pursued. The implementation of the quality policy is planned, and the corresponding responsibilities and authorities are defined

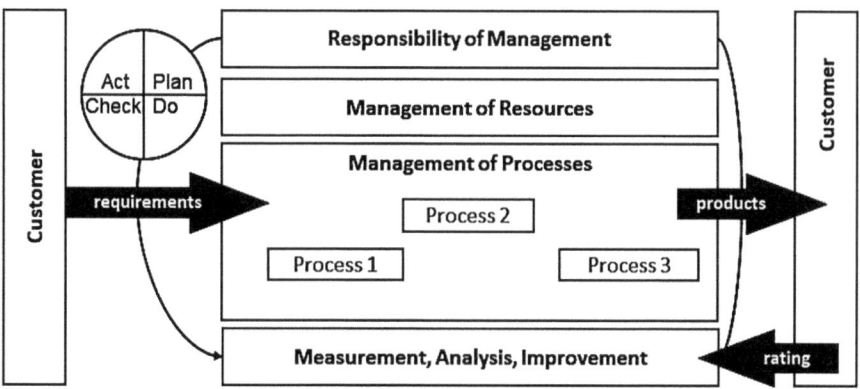

Fig. 2.8 EN ISO 9001

in the organization. Management is also responsible for evaluating the QM system at planned intervals and, in particular, taking customer feedback into account while doing so. Corporate management must also provide the necessary resources such as personnel, infrastructure, and an adequate work environment.

The core of an EN ISO 9001-compliant QM system are the processes for realizing the products and the associated customer-related services. Tasks include the planning and definition of suitable processes for the development and manufacture of products, the procurement of inputs, etc. The tools used to monitor product manufacturing and quality must be regularly checked for their suitability. The execution of the processes must be continuously monitored through measurements and analyses of Key Performance Indicators, in order to be able to initiate appropriate improvement measures in the event of deviations.

EN ISO 9001 thus provides a framework for Business Process Management. The explanations show that, strictly speaking, there is no difference between Business Process Management and quality management. Without Business Process Management, there is no quality management and vice versa.

The comparatively lower requirements of EN ISO 9001 are expressed in the fact that a company with a (merely) EN ISO 9001 compliant quality management system can only achieve about 300 points in an EFQM assessment.

2.5.5 Value Networks

The Value Networks concept was introduced by Verna Allee [16]. A Value Network is understood as roles and persons who exchange so-called tangibles and intangibles with each other. Tangible value flows are material value flows between roles and persons and correspond to the exchange of goods, services, revenues, etc. Tangible value flows represent transactions based on contracts. Intangible value flows are an additional benefit through the flow of knowledge; they are not contractually fixed or

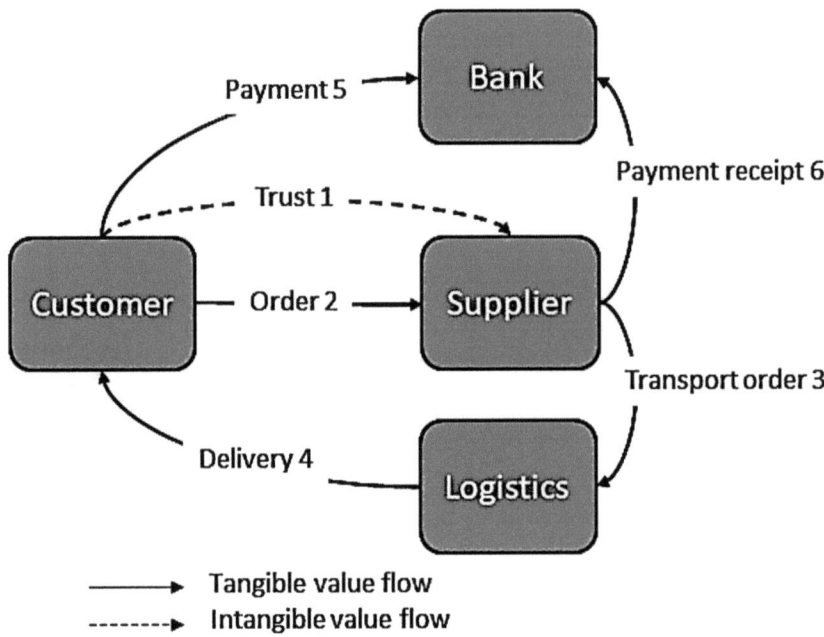

Fig. 2.9 Schema of a Value Network

subject to a charge. Intangible value flows are, e.g., strategic information, planning knowledge, as well as existing emotional components such as mutual trust, common interests, need for knowledge, security, etc.

Value Networks should enable participants and organizational developers to actively shape social and professional relationships of interaction in organizational systems by visualizing and creatively handling mutual tangible and intangible performance flows (transactions). Figure 2.9 shows a simple Value Network. The customer sends a value purchase order as a tangible value flow to the supplier. This tangible value flow is accompanied by the intangible value flow of trust. The customer and the logistics company are connected with the tangible value flow of delivery, etc. The numbers on the individual transactions express the sequence in which they are executed.

Organizations provide services as a result of their activities that ultimately contribute to the added value of a company or institution. In order to record these services and make them visible, an exchange-oriented view of organizations is recommended. This usually results in a network-like structure in which the roles within an organization and their interaction and communication channels are in the foreground. This perspective enables the transition to a communication-oriented Business Process Management.

2.6 Models in Business Informatics

Models in business informatics combine aspects from the economic and social fields with computer science to derive requirements for information systems. The models are mainly used to describe socio-technical human-machine systems. The social component covers the aspects around employees and partners. The technical dimension concerns the circumstances of Information Technology. It is important that corresponding models consider the interaction between the two domains, especially the human-machine interaction. In contrast to purely technical systems, which are regarded as deterministic, socio-technical systems can also be non-deterministic, i.e., complex, due to the involvement of social components. We limit ourselves here to the handling of frameworks for enterprise architectures and IT service management.

In order to simplify the creation of very similar process models, reference models have been defined over the years by consulting firms or standardization bodies. A well-known example of such a reference model is ITIL (IT Infrastructure Library, [17]). Due to its wide distribution, we describe it in more detail as an example of a reference model. A reference model that includes ITIL while being more focused on governance and compliance is COBIT. Due to space limitations we do not provide a representation here but refer to the extensive literature and the official Web site [18].

2.6.1 Enterprise Architectures

The understanding of architecture in the context of companies coincides with the original meaning of the term architecture. In many areas of expertise it describes the basic organization of a system with its components and their relationships to one another and to their environment.

As already mentioned in Chap. 1, an enterprise architecture specifically describes and links the business and technical elements of an enterprise. The latter include in particular the IT landscape. Both the overall architecture and its parts are described through models. The range of model types used for this purpose extends from a business model through organigrams, data models, and process models at the business level to database models, algorithms, and programs in the technical layer.

As for business models, there are also numerous frameworks for the modeling of enterprise architectures [19] has identified more than 40 frameworks with varying foci, levels of detail, and degrees of familiarity. Only four of the most relevant will be handled in the following sections.

The Zachman Framework and The Open Group Architecture Framework (TOGAF) with its extension Architecture-Animate (ArchiMate) were named as essential frameworks in surveys (see also [19]] page 5). The Architecture of Integrated Information Systems (ARIS) is widely used in practice in German-speaking countries and is of significant importance in the context of process management.

	What	How	Where	Who	When	Why
Objective/area -> Role:Planer	List of important factors in the business	List of core processes, process map	List of branch ofices	List of mportant organizations and stakeholders	List of business events	List of business goals, strategies and business models
Business model-> Role: Owner	Conceptional data model/object model	Business process model	Business logistics systems, distri- bution model	Workflow model, organizational structure	Schedule	Business plan
System model (logical) ->Role: Designer	Logical data model	Process Implementation, system archi-tecture model	Distributed systems architecture	Human interface architecture role model	Process structure	Busines rules model
Technology model (Physically) -> Role: Builder	Physical data model, class model	Technology design model, implementation model	Technology architecture	Representation architecture, system usage	Control structure, system dynamics	System requirements
Detailed presentation (from context) -> Role: Programmer	Data definitions, database structure	Program, process configuration	Network architecture	Security architecture, directory services	Schedule	System monitoring
Operations ->Role: User	Concretly available equipment	Process instances	Business locations	Execution	Current schedules	Current moods
	Inventory, material and data	Processes and functions	Spatial distribution, geometry	People and machines	Scheduling	Goals, motivation

Fig. 2.10 Zachman Framework

2.6.1.1 Zachman Framework

The framework presented by John A. Zachman in 1992 in its extended form represents a structure grid similar to the Business Model Canvas, which the user has to complete with the facts for the enterprise at hand. It consists of a matrix with different perspectives in the rows and abstractions to each perspective in the columns. Figure 2.10 shows a condensed representation; a detailed picture can be found on the Zachman International Web site (www.zachman.com).

The perspectives in the rows have the following meaning:

- Planner: Company objectives, external requirements and influences, business model
- Owner: Requirements for data, processes, structures, etc. for company management
- Designer: System design and system structure to implement the requirements
- Builder: Implementation of the system design
- Programmer: Provision of the technical infrastructure
- User: Responsible person for the operation to ensure the functionality

The columns contain the questions that the company needs to answer:

- What (inventory): What objects, equipment, data, information, etc. are required?
- How (functions and processes): How does the company work, for example, what do the business processes look like?
- Where (locations, network): Where are the company's locations?
- Who (people): Who are the people who keep the company running? Which business units are there, and what is the organizational structure like?
- When (time): When are business processes instantiated and executed? What are the time schedules for the business?

- Why (motivation): Why do we run the business the way we run it? What are the drivers of the business?.

Zachman envisages that a suitable model will be developed for each cell in the table. From this perspective, his framework is a model for a set of models that allow a closer look at different aspects of a company.

The users can deviate from the original structure in the rows and columns by changing the emphasis. This flexibility is a strength of the model frame. However, it does not contain any procedure or methodology for defining a concrete enterprise architecture. Processes for their development or transformation have to be exploited elsewhere by the users or have to be designed entirely by themselves.

2.6.1.2 The Open Group Architecture Framework (TOGAF)

TOGAF is the Open Group's framework for the development of enterprise architectures, including business processes. While the Zachman Framework emphasizes the object perspective and offers little support for the architecture development process, TOGAF focuses on the procedure for model creation. It provides methods and tools that help with the introduction, creation, use, and further development of enterprise architectures.

TOGAF distinguishes four sub-architectures:

- Business Architecture: Business aspects of enterprise architecture.
- Data Architecture: Logical and physical structures of data and resources for their management.
- Application Architecture: The application systems used and their relationships with each other as well as their relevance for the company's business.
- Technology Architecture: Software and hardware requirements for data management and application system execution. This includes, e.g., runtime environments, networks, middleware, and other operational infrastructures.

The TOGAF framework consists of the following components:

- Architecture Development Method (ADM):
  Method and procedure for the development of an enterprise architecture.
- ADM Guidelines and Techniques:
  Set of tools and guidelines that support the use of ADM (e.g., tools for iterative use of ADM).
- Architecture Content Framework:
  Structural model to define, structure, and display the results generated with ADM in a uniform and consistent way.
- Enterprise Continuum:
  Model for structuring a possible repository that can contain the respective architectures and the possible solutions such as models, patterns, architecture descriptions, etc.

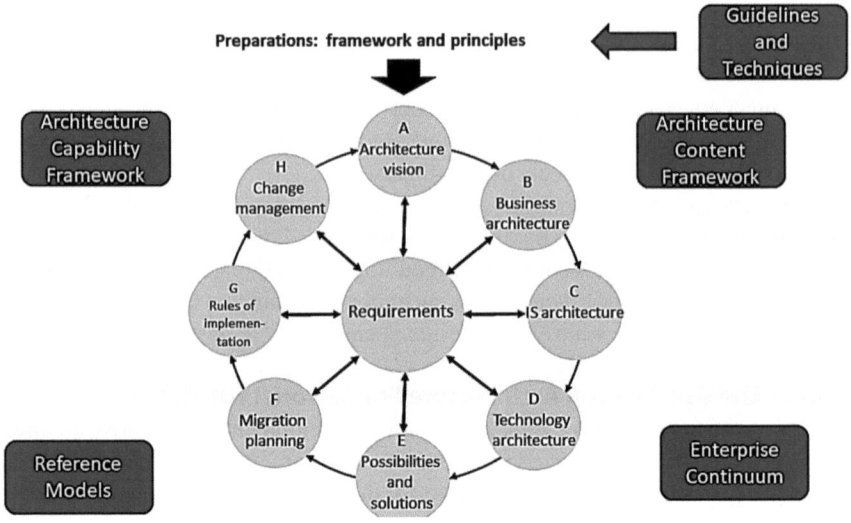

Fig. 2.11   Architecture Development Method from TOGAF

- Reference Models:
  Basic models that can be used as a basis for specific models for a company. These are the Technical Reference Model (TRM) and the Integrated Information Infrastructure Model.
- Architecture Capability Framework:
  Various reference materials for the development of specific architectural models. The Architecture Development Method (ADM) forms the core of TOGAF as an iterative process model (cf. Fig. 2.11). This creates all of the architecture artifacts. ADM can be applied at multiple levels, allowing architects to define different levels of detail of the enterprise architecture. With the help of the other components, the results are then described, structured, and stored.

The phases of the ADM are:

- Preliminary phase: Here, the organizational environment and the frameworks, methods, support tools, and important principles used are defined.
- Phase A—Architecture Vision: Here, the goals and the parties involved in updating the enterprise architecture are defined and integrated.
- Phase B—Business Architecture: The current and desired state of the business architecture is described here. The decisive differences are worked out. The desired views are defined, and the associated appropriate tools are selected.
- Phase C—Information System architecture (IS Architecture): The current and desired state of the application and information/data architecture is described here. The decisive differences are worked out. The concrete applications and data models are used for this purpose.

- Phase D—Technology Architecture: The current and desired state of the technology architecture is described here. The decisive differences are worked out. In addition, the concrete hardware systems are described.
- Phase E—Opportunities and Solutions: Here, the projects are defined which carry out the transformation from the current situation to the target state.
- Phase F—Migration Planning: The transfer from a current state to a target state is planned here.
- Phase G—Implementation Governance: The implementation into the target state is carried out and monitored here.
- Phase H—Architecture Change Management: Requirements and external influences are collected here, which then serve as the basis for the next ADM run.
- Requirements Management: The requirements management drives the ADM process continuously and is therefore at the center.

2.6.1.3 Architecture-Animates (ArchiMate)

Architecture-Animate (ArchiMate) is the name of an open and independent modeling language for enterprise architectures published by the Open Group. It provides tools that enable enterprise architects to describe, analyze, and visualize the relationships between business units and their development.

The ArchiMate language enables the description of the structure and flow of business processes, organizational structures, information flows, IT systems, and technical infrastructure. The descriptions help the participants to design changes in architectural elements and their relationships, to evaluate the consequences, and to communicate them. Figure 2.12 shows the ArchiMate framework.

The first three columns correspond to the basic concepts of ArchiMate:

- Passive structure elements:
  Passive structure elements are the objects on which the actions from the behavior (behavior elements) are executed. In general, these are information objects, but physical objects can also be modeled as passive structural elements.

	Passive structure	Behavior	Active structure	Motivation
Strategy	Resources		Resources	
Business	Business objects	Business services, functions and processes	Business actors and roles	
Application	Data objects	Application services, functions and processes	Application components and interfaces	Stakeholders, drivers, goals, principles and requirements
Technology	Artifacts	Technology services, functions and processes	Devices, system software, communication networks	
Physical	Material			
Implementation and migration	Deliverables	Work packages	Platforms	

Fig. 2.12 Elements of the ArchiMate Framework

- Active structure elements:
  Active structure elements are elements that can perform actions. Examples are people, applications, computer nodes, etc. The actions can be triggered via interfaces, which also provide the results.
- Behavior elements:
  Behavior elements represent the dynamic aspects of a company. A service is the externally visible behavior of the system that provides the service. The services are used via the corresponding interfaces. Interface events trigger the active structure elements, which then execute the corresponding service function.

These three model fragments correspond to the basic elements of natural languages: subject, predicate or verb, and object. They are considered on a total of six layers:

- Strategy layer:
  Motivation describes what a company wants to achieve. The strategy concepts describe at a high level of abstraction how a company wants to achieve its goals.
- Business layer:
  The elements of the business layer can be used to describe products and services that a company makes available externally. The business layer shows how the company realizes these products and services and is intended to help with the analysis of the corporate structure.
- Application layer:
  In the application layer, the support of the business layer is represented by applications and data.
- Technology layer:
  In the technology layer, the infrastructure needed to implement applications is described. These are essentially the required hardware and software components.
- Physical layer:
  This layer focuses on the interaction of IT and physical components such as machines, sensors, and actors.
- Implementation and migration layer:
  The implementation and migration concept describes how a defined architecture is to be implemented. In particular, it describes the work packages for implementation.

The cells of the table therefore contain the core elements for the active and passive structures as well as for the behavior in the respective layer.

The motivation column describes the reasons for designing or changing an enterprise model. These influence the modeling and give it the appropriate direction.

ArchiMate is seen as a supplement and concretization of TOGAF. TOGAF describes the process for the definition and description of an enterprise architecture (enterprise model), but it does not contain any description languages for the respective sub-models. ArchiMate aims to fill that gap. In addition to the framework shown for the architecture to be developed, it also offers languages for expressing

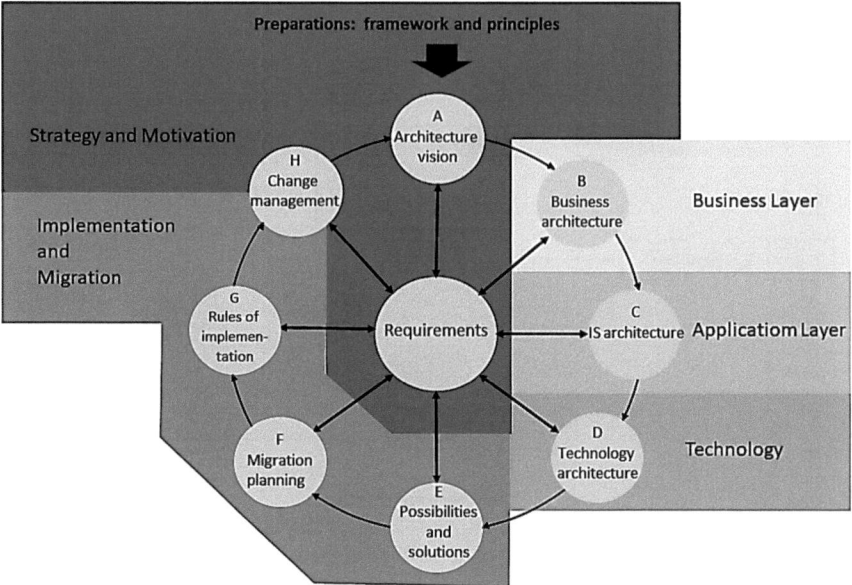

Fig. 2.13 Relationship between ArchiMate Layers and TOGAF ADM

the aspects in the individual layers. Figure 2.13 shows how the individual steps in TOGAF's architecture development method are related to the ArchiMate layers.

2.6.1.4 Architecture of Integrated Information Systems (ARIS)

The Architecture of Integrated Information Systems (ARIS) is a framework for the definition of enterprise models. It includes the data, function, organization, control, and performance views. For each view, ARIS provides a number of model types for documentation.

- Data view:
  The data view comprises the business-relevant information objects and their relationships to each other, that is, all data that is related to the activities of a company. Information objects include states such as article or customer status as well as events such as "Sales order has arrived" or "Production order has been triggered." The relevant model type is the Entity-Relationship Model (ERM).
- Function view:
  The function view describes the business-relevant activities (functions, activities) and their hierarchical relationships. Subordinate functions are sub-functions of the higher-level function. The functions perform operations on the objects described in the data view. In practice, functions are modeled with function trees.

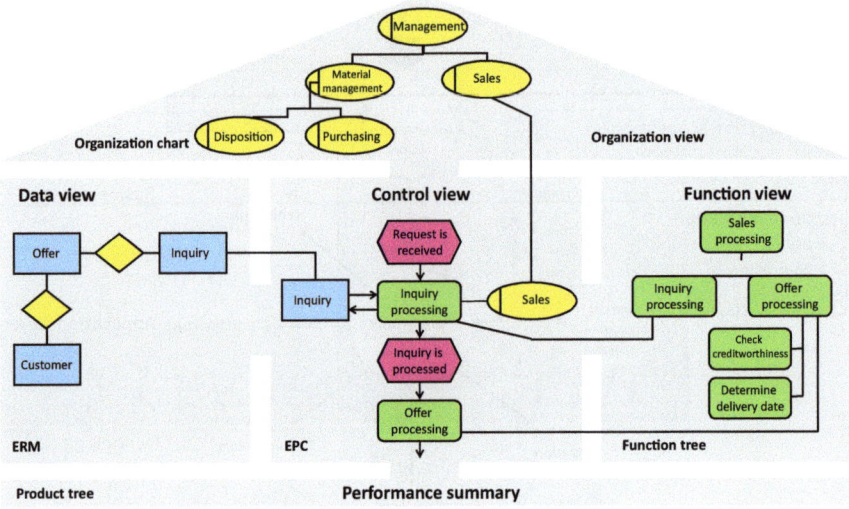

Fig. 2.14 Views and relevant model types in ARIS

- Organizational view:
  In the organizational view, the organizational structure, that is, the personnel resources of a company and their hierarchical relationships are modeled in an organizational plan. The organigram is the usual model type to represent the organizational view.
- Control view:
  The control view establishes the chronological and factual connection between the individual operational activities. It merges the data, functional, and organizational views and thus plays a central integrating role. The control layer is therefore also called the process view. The main model type is the Event-driven Process Chain (EPC).
- Performance view:
  In the performance view, the entries and results of the business process at hand are usually described using product trees.

The views, typical model types, and their context are shown in Fig. 2.14. The picture also makes clear that ARIS, with its integrated control view, places business processes, especially the sequence of activities, at the center of the consideration.

Orthogonal to the structuring carried out by the views, ARIS differentiates the abstraction levels functional concept, data processing concept and implementation on the basis of software engineering. This shows the close relationship between the models developed with ARIS and Information Technology. To solve an operational problem, a functional model is created and transferred to a corresponding data processing concept (data processing model). This ultimately serves as the basis for the concrete technical implementation.

- Functional concept:
  The functional concept describes the facts of the operational problem. At this level, data models, functional models, organizational charts, value chains or Event-driven Process Chains (EPCs), and product models are used.
- Data processing concept:
  The data processing concept specifies how the functional concept is to be implemented in IT terms. At this level, database models (data view), structure charts (functional view), network topologies (organizational view), and trigger mechanisms (control view) are considered. The purpose of the data processing concept is to adapt the functional concept to the requirements of Information Technology.
- Implementation:
  At this level, the data processing concept is converted into an executable software system. At this abstraction level, data description languages (data view), programs (function view), network protocols (organizational view), and program control (control view) are considered.

2.6.2 Framework for IT Service Management: ITIL

The IT Infrastructure Library (ITIL) is a collection of predefined processes, functions, and roles that typically occur in every IT infrastructure of medium-sized and large companies [20]. The practical assignment of activities is based on roles and functions. These are best practice proposals that have to be adapted to the needs of the company. The collection has since been supplemented by ISO 20000:2005, an ITIL-based certification model for organizations.

The IT Infrastructure Library comprises five core volumes with a current total of 37 core processes. Figure 2.15 shows the structure of ITIL. The five core volumes are based on the service life cycle. Based on the service strategy containing the process strategy development, financial management, service portfolio management, and demand management, the service is finally provided via the process groups of

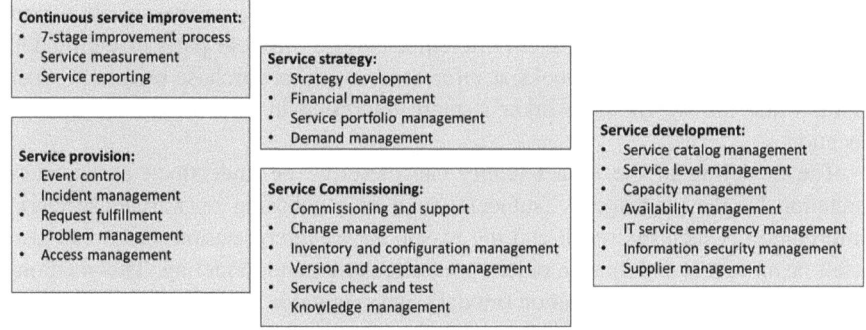

Fig. 2.15 ITIL process groups

service development and service commissioning with the processes of the service provision group. The procedures are subject to continuous improvement.

Further books such as *Software Asset Management*, *Small-Scale Implementation*, or *Building an ITIL-Based Service Management Department* supplement the core publications. ITIL thus offers comprehensive support in the development of a process system for the IT department of an organization.

2.7   Models in Computer Science

Models in computer science relate to data structure models and processes in computer systems, as well as to various essential accompanying aspects such as security, robustness, etc.

On the one hand, these models serve to illustrate a considered part of reality in order to solve a task with the help of information processing. They refer to a defined problem area or certain application areas of computer systems. This includes models that focus on data and the operations running on it, as well as models that look more at the overall structure of complex programs, i.e., their architecture. These two model categories are also called models for programming on a small scale or models for programming on a large scale, respectively.

In addition to these central model categories of computer science, there are other models that consider flanking aspects, such as access models, security models, etc. These are not the subject of further discussion here.

Instead, in the following sections, we explain several model concepts considered essential for Business Process Management.

2.7.1   Information

Information is the more central aspect of data processing, which is why it is also called Information Technology or IT. Information and information systems are models that represent an object of the real world according to the ideas of one or more subjects. The subject's ideas are oriented toward the intended purpose. For example, items in a warehouse are described by their properties such as part number, dimensions, weight, etc. Different users use different parts of the model: The purchasing department looks at information such as purchase price and order limit, while the warehouse worker is more interested in dimensions and storage location.

The modeling of the object reality can therefore be understood as an interpretation by the user agents (subjects) such as purchasing or warehouse clerk. Information is then the result and the reason for an interpretation, but it can also itself be an object and thus an object of interpretation and modeling. This relationship between subject, information (model), and original is shown in Fig. 2.16.

Information receives its value through the interpretation of the overall event by the observing subjects. This observation is partly conscious but mostly unconscious.

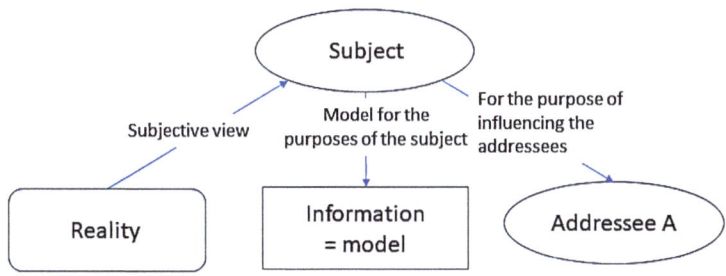

Fig. 2.16 Information is "model–from what–for what–for whom" [22]

The amount of information is reduced and filtered according to the respective need for knowledge or linked with other information.

Data is different from information. A data element is initially only a sequence of characters whose meaning is not unique. The characters can be numbers, letters, or symbols. In the marketing department of an online shop, for example, the sequence of numbers 0815 may be found. Although this sequence of characters represents a date, its meaning is not known. The string itself has no meaning except for its individual elements.

From this data, however, information can arise, if it is known in which context it is to be interpreted. By combining it with other data, a relationship is created that can be interpreted, and information can be generated. If the data 0815 is in the context "Customer Max Sample, Article 0815," the marketing department can interpret that the customer Max Sample ordered an article with the number 0815. The supplementation of data with other data depends on a subject's interest in knowledge or their intentions to use it. With the information produced in each case, a subject usually wants to influence an addressee, e.g., to perform an action. Information is thus to be understood as "statements that improve the degree of knowledge of a subject (information subject/user) about an object (information object) in a given situation and environment (information environment) in order to fulfill a task (information purpose)" [21] (cf. Fig. 2.16). Modeling is therefore a part of information management.

Information is important for politicians and business leaders, but also for every citizen of the world. It reflects a particular situation that applied at a particular point in time and usually allows an update into the future. It serves to make political, economic, or personal decisions. When using information, the question always arises of who created it and what intentions that person has. The subjectivity of models thus plays an essential role here.

2.7.2   Entity-Relationship Model

In order to turn data into information, it must be combined with other data and the relevant relationships described. This creates a data model. The best-known method

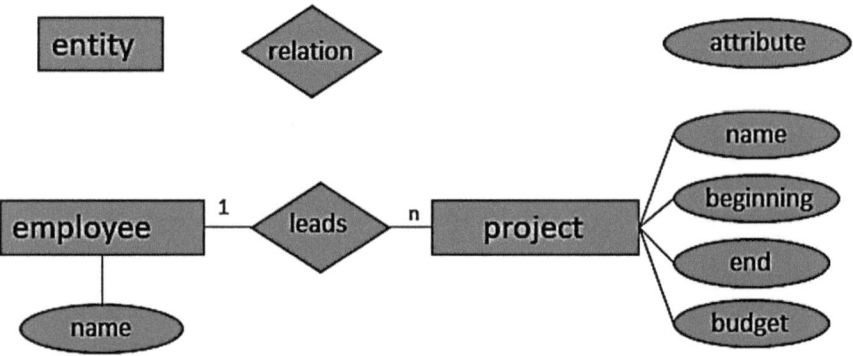

Fig. 2.17 Example of an entity-relationship diagram

for describing data models is the Entity-Relationship Model (ERM). An Entity-Relationship Model consists of three main elements:

- Entities:
  Entities are the object classes that are considered in the part of the real world that is of interest.
- Relationships or relations:
  Relations describe the relationships between entities.
- Attributes:
  Attributes are properties within the context of an entity.

Figure 2.17 shows an example of an ERM. It also indicates which symbols are generally used to express the main elements. However, one can also find ERM representations with notation elements of the Unified Modeling Language (UML).

The diagram describes the following situation:

An employee has a name. A project has a name, a start, an end, and a budget. The so-called cardinality expresses the fact that an employee can lead **several** projects, but a project **can only** be led **by exactly one** employee.

In the modeling concept of classification, objects are combined to form object types (entity sets) and relationships are combined to form relationship types (relationship sets).

These types are differentiated according to:

- Entity type: Typecasting of similar entities (e.g., employee, project)
- Relationship type: Typecasting of similar relationships (e.g., employee leads project)
- Attribute type: Typecasting of similar properties (e.g., name for the entity type employee). Attributes or combinations of attributes whose value(s) uniquely identify an entity are called identifying attribute(s) (e.g., the attribute project name identifies the entity type project).

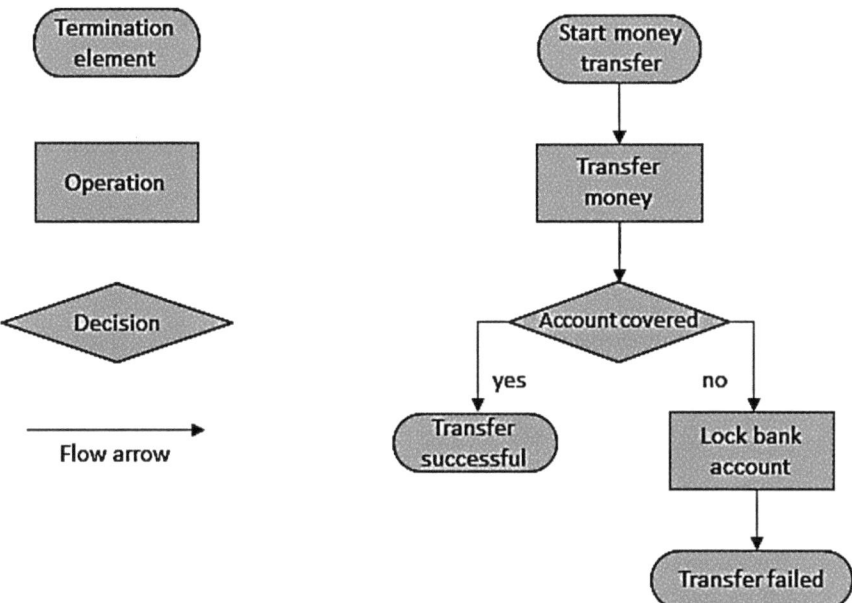

Fig. 2.18 Flowchart for account transaction

2.7.3   Flowcharts

Flowcharts illustrate an execution sequence of activities or actions and are used in numerous application areas. They can describe the order in which actions are to be performed by people or other actors. Algorithms or computer programs are often documented in the form of flowcharts (e.g., program flowcharts). Due to the broad application of flowcharts, numerous variants have developed which take into account special circumstances of the respective field of application. For data processing, the symbolism for flowcharts was defined in the standards DIN 66001:1983-12 and ISO 5807:1985. Figure 2.18 shows an example of a flowchart.

In the explanation of ARIS in Sect. 2.6.1.4, we addressed Event-driven Process Chains (EPC) as a model type for the control view. These EPCs are flowcharts of sequences of event nodes, function nodes (operations), and connectors. Arrows as edges represent control flows between the symbols. Functions and events (with the exception of start and end events) each have exactly one incoming and one outgoing edge. If functions are to create several events or if several events should trigger a function, connectors such as an exclusive or (XOR) must be used. The modeler can also express who executes a function with which IT support and what data is manipulated in doing so. For this purpose he assigns symbols for organizational units (e.g., departments, jobs, roles), information objects (data), or application systems to the function nodes. These elements must be specified in the corresponding model types. This is referred to as extended Event-driven Process Chains (eEPC).

We have already briefly indicated in Sect. 2.6.1.4 that an eEPC, as an instrument to describe the control or process view, correlates the interaction between the elements of the other views and model types. Specifically, it expresses itself in the following way:

- Control View:
  - An event is a state that occurs before or after a function. The symbol for an event is hexagonal.
  - A function (process) is an action or task that follows an event. Functions are symbolized by rectangles with rounded corners.
  - Connectors are used to split or join the control flow. The three connectors AND, OR, and XOR are available, each represented in a small circle with the corresponding symbol. The decision as to which path is followed after a connector is made by the function preceding the connector.
- Functional View:
  - The function nodes in the control view are linked with nodes from the function tree of the function view and thus specify the activity to be executed.
- Data View:
  - Information objects are entities from the data model that are bound to carriers such as documents or other data stores. They represent inputs or outputs of the function to which they are connected by a directed edge. The symbol for an information object is a rectangle, and the character as input or output is determined by the arrow direction of the connection edge.
- Organizational View:
  - Organizational units show which elements from the organizational chart, modeled according to the organizational view, execute the activities (functions) in the process. Organizational units are connected to functions by undirected edges.

Figure 2.19 shows an example for an extended Event-driven Process Chain (eEPC).

2.7.4   Petri Nets

One of the first and most widespread theoretical approaches to the description of parallelism are Petri nets.

Petri nets are used for the logical modeling of behavior. They consider the behavior of systems, usually information systems, under the following aspects:

- Activities to be carried out.
- Preconditions and postconditions of an activity.

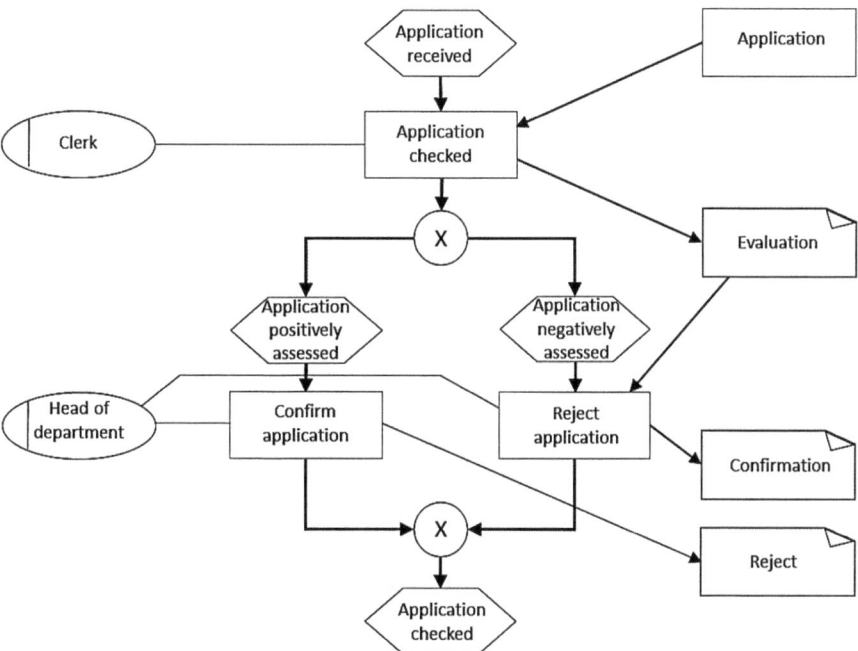

Fig. 2.19 Extended Event-driven Process Chain for an account transaction

- States of all conditions (possible values for each individual precondition or postcondition): The state of a condition is the distribution of so-called tokens as a state display to the pre- or post-range.
- Initial state (initial token).
- Procedures (possible consequences of activities).

A Petri net is a structure that is formally and mathematically precisely described as a directed graph with nodes consisting of two disjoint subsets marked with tokens. In the representation as quadruple the following applies: A Petri net is a quadruple: $PN = (S, T, K, M)$ with

- $s \, \varepsilon \, S$: Places (i.e., conditions), for the description of states and/or conditions, buffers, memories, or storage spaces. They are circular in the graph and are used to store information or tokens.
- $t \, \varepsilon \, T$: Transitions describe state transitions, events, actions, or activities and are shown in the graph as line, bar, or cuboid forms. Their purpose is the processing of information.
- $k \, \varepsilon \, K$: Arcs are possibly weighted (i.e., numbered) connections between places and transitions, shown in the graph as arrows. They indicate the course of the transitions.

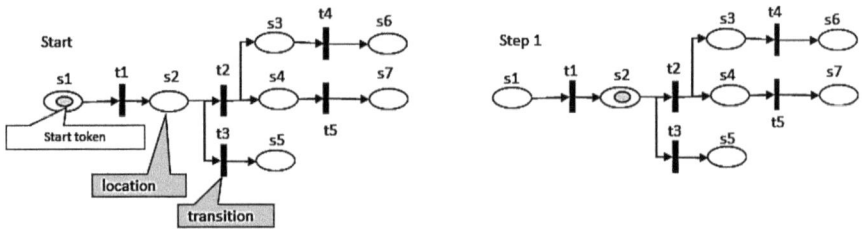

Fig. 2.20 Example of a Petri Net process model (I)

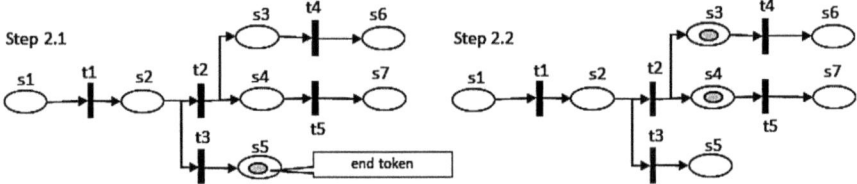

Fig. 2.21 Example of a Petri Net process model (II)

- m ε M: Tokens that represent the current state of the Petri net. Every network has an initial state, i.e., there is an initial token.

According to the above definition, arcs only go from place to transition or from transition to place. Input places of a transition t are places from which arcs run to the transition t. Output places of a transition t are places to which arcs of the transition t lead.

A transition can switch if there is at least one token in each input place. Switching means that a token is removed from each input place of the switching transition and a token is added to each output place.

The following graphics show a Petri net with its respective states after performing the switching operations. In the start state in Fig. 2.20, only the place s1 has a token, the initial token or the start token. The place s1 is the only input place of transition t1, which can therefore switch. The token is removed from s1 and a token is added to the single exit place s2. The right half of the following figure shows the state after switching t1.

The place s2 is the input place of the two transitions t2 and t3 (see left side of Fig. 2.21). So it could switch the transition t2 or t3, but not both. Which transition switches is random. This gives us a so-called non-deterministic state. If t3 switches, a token is added to the place s5 and a final state is reached, since no other arc leads out of s5. If the transition t2 switches, a token is added to the places s3 and s4, which are starting points of t2. The corresponding state is shown in the right half of Fig. 2.21.

Now either the transition t4 or t5 can switch. Here one could conclude that these two transitions switch simultaneously. But this is not allowed in Petri nets. Only one transition may switch at a time. Consequently, parallelism as observed in reality

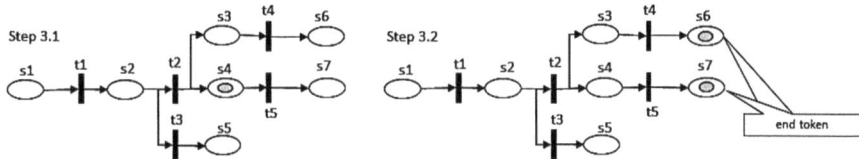

Fig. 2.22 Example of a Petri Net process model (III)

cannot be represented. However, it is arbitrary whether t4 or t5 switches first. In our example, t4 switches first and then t5. When both transitions have switched, a final state is reached again. Figure 2.22 shows the corresponding network states.

Petri net models allow the analysis and simulation of dynamic systems with concurrent and non-deterministic processes.

The type of Petri nets presented here is the basic version. It cannot be used to describe certain situations. For example, it is not possible to assign priorities for transitions which is why, for example, the right-before-left rule at traffic junctions cannot be modeled.

In order to remedy such deficits, extensions have been introduced to map further aspects of reality to the model or to describe certain situations more compactly. Examples are multivalued, colored, or prioritized Petri nets. Details of such extensions can be found in the available literature, e.g., [23].

2.7.5   Calculus of Communicating Systems

The *Calculus of Communicating Systems* (CCS) was published by Robin Milner in 1980 (see [24]). This calculus enables the formal modeling of parallel communicating systems. This permits networked systems with a static topology to be described. CCS can be used to formally investigate the properties of programs such as deadlocks, bisimilarity, etc. CCS enables the description of the following aspects:

- Communication between actors via channels
- Interaction with the environment, i.e., reactivity
- Parallel composition
- Hiding actions from the environment (information hiding)
- Nondeterministic branches

The course of a process is described as a tree, i.e., there is a root that represents the initial state and from where the individual branches originate. Each of the branches is marked. These markers represent the actions performed to move from one state to the next. A distinction is made between observable and unobservable actions. Unobservable actions can be executed at any time within a process without affecting other processes. Processes have no common variables.

Recursive expressions are used to describe the behavior of a process. Within behavior expressions, variables can be used to reference other behavior expressions.

The behavior expressions are described according to the following syntax, in which uppercase letters denote process names and lowercase letters denote actions.

- Empty Process:
  Ø
- Action:
  Process $a.P1$ executes action a and then behaves like $P1$.
- Process Name:
  With the expression $A := P1$ the process $P1$ gets the name A. Since recursive definitions are allowed, the expression $P1$ can contain the name A again.
- Choice:
  Process $P1 + P2$ can be continued with either process $P1$ or process $P2$.
- Parallel Composition:
  $P1|P2$ means that processes $P1$ and $P2$ are executed in parallel.
- Renaming:
  $P1[b/a]$ describes the process $P1$, in which all actions with the denotation a are renamed to b.
- Restriction:
  $P1 \backslash a$ denotes the process $P1$ without the action a.

Matching input and output actions in two different processes can synchronize and become an internal action τ. In general, the coaction for an action is marked with a line above the action name. These complementary actions are the send and receive actions. Figure 2.23 shows an example of the interaction between two processes.

The example in Fig. 2.24 shows how a simple holiday request process can be described with CCS.

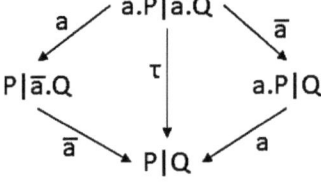

- The processes a.P and ā.Q are executed in parallel.
- Starting from a.P | ā.Q are three transitions possible.
- If a synchronization between a and ā takes place, the transition, which is invisible from the outside, originates (marked with τ) .

Fig. 2.23 Process interaction with CCS

Employee := $\overline{\text{vacation request}}$. (Rejected + Approved) . NIL

Manager := vacation request. $\overline{(\text{Rejected} + \text{Approved.approved vacation request})}$.NIL

Travel departement:= approved vacation request.NIL

Vacation application process:= Employee | Manager | Travel departement

Fig. 2.24 Example process in CCS

- P:= b̄a. b̄7.P'   Process P transmits the value a via channel b and
                      subsequently the value 7 and then behaves like P'.
- R:=b(x).b(z).x̄z.0   Process R receives any value via channel b. This
                      means in R, x and z are replaced by the received
                      values.
- Q:=a(x).Q   Process Q receives via channel a any value for x. The
                      received value is used everywhere where x is located.

- O:=P │R│Q   Entire system O

Fig. 2.25 Process description with π Calculus

In the employee process, the vacation request send action is executed (action name with overline). The system then waits for the messages "rejected" or "approved." The manager receives the vacation request message, which he replies to either with the message "approved" or "rejected." If he sends the message "approved," the message "approved vacation request" is also sent afterwards. This message is received by the travel department. Messages are exchanged asynchronously in CCS, that is, a sender waits until the receiver executes the corresponding receive action.

There are also formal rules of derivation for the informal interpretation. This makes process definitions accessible for formal evaluations.

2.7.6 π Calculus

CCS only allows static process structures. Communication relationships cannot be changed dynamically. The π Calculus (see [25]), also developed by Robin Milner, allows the representation of processes with changing structures. Any connections between components can be displayed, and these connections can also change, or new ones can be created. Thus, the π Calculus is an extension of CCS to include concurrency. The notation in the π Calculus is largely based on the CCS notation. The following example explains the modeling possibilities of the π Calculus (see Fig. 2.25).

The agent (process) P wants to send the value 7 to Q via a link a. However, the value is to be transmitted indirectly via another agent R.

In Fig. 2.26 the individual steps for the execution of system O are shown.

The processes P, R, and Q are executed in parallel. Process P sends via channel b the name a and then the name 7. Process P receives via channel b the two names. This means that each x is replaced by a and each z by 7. In Fig. 2.26 this is the result after step 2. Now the name 7 can be sent via channel a, which is then accepted by process Q. Thus, the value 7 was sent to process Q via process R. The following graphic shows how the structure of System O is changed by its process flow.

Since the channel name a is transmitted from P to R, the processes R and Q are linked via channel a after the message has been accepted. This property shows that

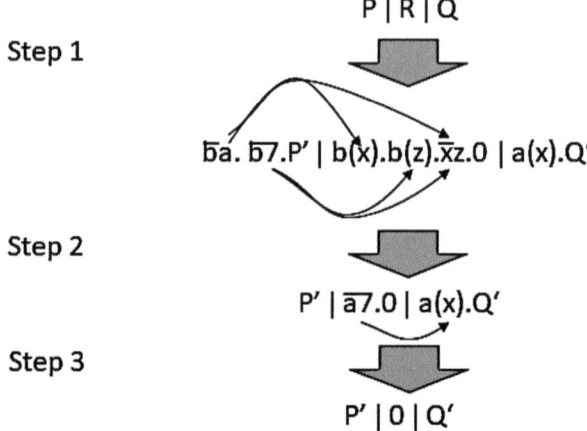

Fig. 2.26 Execution steps of system O (π Calculus)

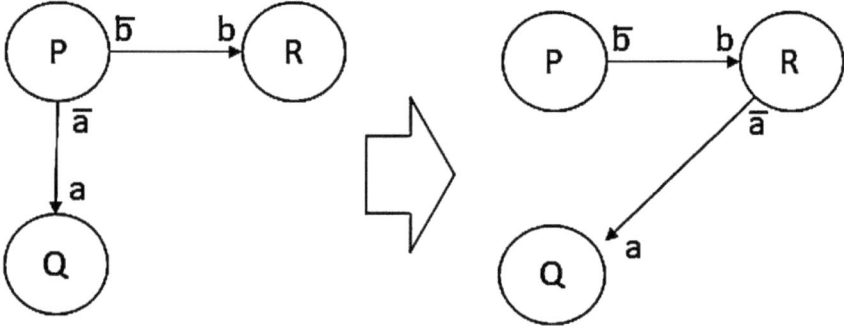

Fig. 2.27 Structural change

the π Calculus, in contrast to CCS, permits the modeling of structural changes (cf. Fig. 2.27).

2.7.7 Communicating Sequential Processes

Communicating Sequential Processes (CSP) is a methodology for describing interaction between communicating processes. The idea was first introduced by Tony Hoare in 1978 as an imperative language (see [26]). It was then developed into a formal algebra and made famous in 1985 with the publication of the book Communicating Sequential Processes (see [27]).

In CSP, as in CCS, the number of processes is static. It cannot be changed during runtime, and there are no common variables between processes. Instead, the processes "know" each other and communicate with each other by sending and receiving messages. For sending, the send process P executes the output command

$Q!(expr)$ and the receiver process Q receives the input command $P?(vars)$. Output and input commands are called corresponding if the sequence of expressions $(expr)$ and the sequence of variables $(vars)$ are of the same type in relation to their numbers and components. Analogous to CCS and the π Calculus, CSP is based on an unbuffered message exchange in which the send and receive processes must be explicitly named.

With $Q!()$ and $P?()$ a message without content is sent. Such messages are called signals and only serve to synchronize processes. If different signals are required, the distinction is made by means of type designators of the form $Q!(Signal1)$ and $P?(Signal1)$.

In addition to the unconditional message exchange described above, there is the receive instruction within a so-called guarded command. A guarded command is only executed if the preceding Boolean condition is true. The formula set

$$x > y; P?(z) \rightarrow x := x + y; y := z$$

is only executed if x is greater than y. Then the message is received by P if P is ready to send the message.

To be able to wait for messages from different senders, several guarded commands are combined to form an alternative instruction.

$$[x > y; P?(z) \rightarrow x := x + y; y := z \,\square\, x < y; Q?(z) \rightarrow y := x + y; y := z]$$

In case $x > y$ the message $P?(z)$ is expected, in case $x < y$ the message $Q?(z)$. Alternative instructions can also be executed repeatedly. Syntactically, this is expressed by a * in front of the alternative instruction.

$$* [x > y; P?(z) \rightarrow x := x + y; y := z \,\square\, x < y; Q?(z) \rightarrow y := x + y; y := z]$$

The instruction is executed until none of the conditions are true, then the repetition is terminated.

The concepts regarding the concurrency of CSP serve as a design basis for the programming language Go.

2.7.8 Abstract State Machines

In computer science, an Abstract State Machine (ASM) is a model for the formal, operational description of algorithms. The states of an Abstract State Machine are general mathematical structures. The inventor of the model is Yuri Gurevich. Egon Börger has further developed the ASM for practical application [28].

Abstract State Machines (ASM) are finite sets of transition rules of the form

If condition then action

with which the states of an ASM are changed. Condition is any logical expression and action any action. As a rule, action is a value assignment of the form $f(t1, \ldots, tn) := s$. The meaning of the rule is to execute the specified rule in the current state if the specified condition is met in that state. ASM states are generally defined as arbitrary sets of arbitrary elements with arbitrary functions (operations) and predicates defined on them. In the case of business objects, the elements are placeholders for values of any type and operations such as creating, duplicating, deleting, or algebraically manipulating objects.

A calculation step of an ASM in a certain state means that all actions for which the condition is true are executed simultaneously. Simultaneous execution can abstract from irrelevant sequences.

Several ASMs can run simultaneously and be linked via so-called controlled or monitored functions. A given ASM M can update controlled functions, but it cannot be modified by other ASMs in its environment. Monitored functions of a given ASM M can only be updated by its environment. By using controlled and monitored functions in pairs, a network of parallel coordinating ASMs can be set up.

2.7.9   Object-Oriented Models

The computer science models considered so far focus either on data or functions. The representation of data in an ERM and functions in a flowchart complement each other only in decoupled representations. The distinction between data and function views in ARIS makes this clear. Object-oriented modeling no longer reduces these individual entities into their separate parts but considers them as an integrated whole in which the individual components are interconnected and interdependent.

An object-oriented model is a view of a complex system in which the system is described by the interaction of objects. This type of modeling is intended to reduce the complexity of the description of situations to be mapped in software. The object orientation considers the entities occurring in the real world as objects. A telephone is just as much an object as a bicycle, a person, or an employee. Such objects in turn consist of other objects such as screws, rods, arms, feet, head, etc. As is usual in modeling, the objects are reduced to their properties that are significant in the respective situation. For example, an employee in a payroll accounting system is reduced to name, address, employee number, agreed income, tax class, and so on.

The objects considered in a model are not designed individually. A rough blueprint with similar properties is created for similar objects.

For example, one models the properties of books for a library application that are identical for all books. Such general descriptions of objects are called classes in object orientation. These classes are then used to create the required concrete objects (instances) within the model. The representation of reality in a model is therefore a two-stage process. First, similar objects of reality are identified and described as classes. The individual objects are then created as instances of a class. A class thus describes the structure of a set of similar objects. Figure 2.28 shows a class-object relationship according to which the book "Subject-Oriented Process

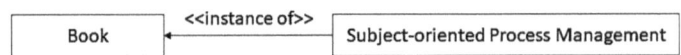

Fig. 2.28 Relationship class-object

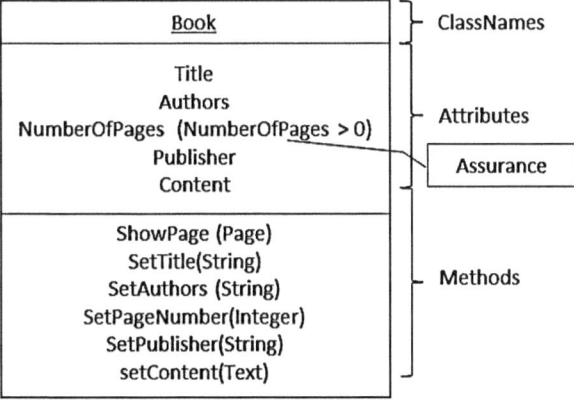

Fig. 2.29 Description of the class "Book"

Management" is an instance of the class Book. The notation used comes from the Unified Modeling Language (UML). UML is a language standardized by the Object Management Group for the description of object-oriented models.

The properties of a class are:

- Their components and the data and information they contain, also called attributes
- The operations defined on the components and their parameters (methods) with which an object can be manipulated or its status queried
- Conditions, prerequisites, and rules that the objects must fulfill (constraints)

Figure 2.29 shows an example of the description of the Book class. This class has five attributes. The Page Number attribute has a constraint that the page number must be positive. The class allows the access and manipulation of its data with six methods. Thus, the title, the authors, the page number, the publisher, and the content can be set (Set). The operation (method) DisplayPage(Page) can be used to "read" the contents of the specified page from the book.

Objects can now be instantiated from such a class definition. The operations can then be used to set the corresponding attributes for each of these instances.

An object-oriented model describes not only the definitions of the classes and the associated objects but also the relationships between the classes. The types of relationships are:

- Inheritance:
  Properties can be passed from one class to the next. This is called inheritance. The class that is used as the basis for inheritance is called the superclass, and the class that inherits is called the subclass. Thus, a class Notebook is a subclass of the class Book. The method "PageEntry(page, content)" is added to the

Fig. 2.30 Inheritance of properties from one class to another

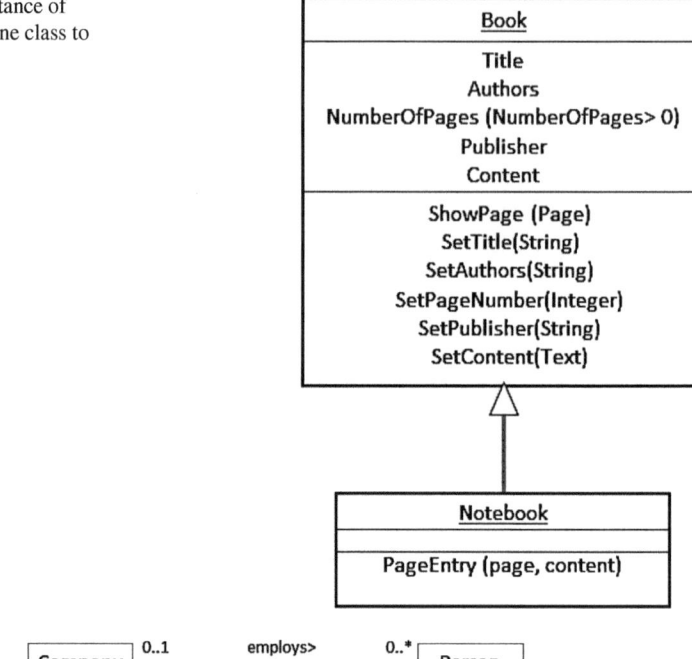

Fig. 2.31 Associations between classes

Fig. 2.32 Multilevel aggregation of classes

Notebook class. This allows a text to be entered on the specified page; otherwise, the Notebook subclass inherits all attributes and methods from the Book class. Figure 2.30 shows the inheritance relationship between Book and Notebook. The triangular arrow points from the subclass to the superclass.

- Associations:
  An association is a relationship between different objects of one or more classes. Associations are represented as a simple line between two classes. The line can be provided with a name (identifier) and number specification. The associated classes can also receive names regarding the relationship. Figure 2.31 illustrates an example of an association. A person (employee) can be employed by no company or by just one company (employer), and a company can employ one or more persons. Associations are very similar to entity-relationship diagrams.

- Aggregation:
  Aggregations are a variant of associations. This is also a relationship between two classes, but with the peculiarity that the two classes are related to each other like one part of a whole. An aggregation is made up of a quantity of individual

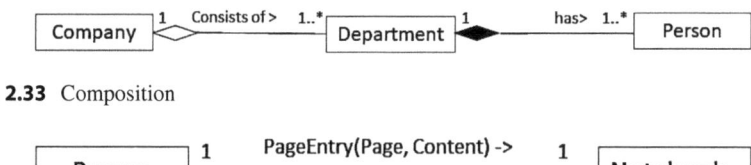

Fig. 2.33 Composition

Fig. 2.34 Message between objects

parts. Figure 2.32 shows an aggregation example in which a company consists of departments and a department of employees.

- Composition:
  A special form of aggregation is composition. Here the whole depends on the existence of its individual parts. Figure 2.31 shows a change in the above aggregation. A department does not exist anymore if no one belongs to it (Fig. 2.33).

- Objects communicate with each other, i.e., one object sends messages to another object. The messages then trigger the associated operations. An object therefore only understands the messages for which it contains the corresponding operations. Figure 2.34 shows a person's communication with the notebook to enter a new note.

The described constructs form the nucleus of the object-oriented modeling approach. In addition, there are numerous enhancements for depicting certain circumstances, such as the so-called container classes.

2.7.10 Agent/Actor-Oriented Models

So far, there is no standardized and generally accepted definition of the agent concept. The term is defined in detail somewhat differently depending on the application domain [29]. What all these definitions have in common, however, is that an agent is a scoped unit that is able to pursue the tasks assigned to it flexibly, interactively, and autonomously. The term actor is often used as a synonym for the term agent. Thus [30] define a business actor as "…an entity that is capable of performing behavior." Multi-agent systems consist of several agents that exchange messages synchronously or asynchronously. Multi-agent systems can map the structures of software systems or serve as models for social systems. Depending on the application situation, a distinction can then be made between software agents and human agents.

In a way, the processes in CCS, the π Calculus, and CSP can be seen as multi-agent systems. The term process is used there analogously to the terms agent and actor.

An agent-oriented model therefore contains the agents, the communication paths, and the messages that are exchanged. A collection of agent-oriented modeling languages and the corresponding procedures can be found in [31] and [32].

2.8   Conclusion: Models for Business Processes

Business process models depict the part of reality of business processes under consideration. The subjective understanding of the business process concept influences which process aspects are considered essential and therefore placed in the foreground in the models. The intentions and interests of the person creating the model are reflected here. Consequences are numerous interpretations of the business process concept, each of which is neither right nor wrong, but merely sets different focal points.

The following definitions of the term business process are examples of this:

1. "Sequence of value creation activities (value creation) with one or more inputs and a customer benefit generating output" [33].
2. "A process is the closed, temporal and logical sequence of activities that are necessary for the processing of a business-relevant object." [34]

Both definitions focus on the necessary activities and their consequences. The first example additionally mentions the input and the output with the customer benefit, while in the second definition the processing of the business objects is included instead.

On the other hand, neither definition includes the actors and necessary resources. They do not consider by whom and with what the activities are carried out. There is no relation to the organization in which a business process is embedded, or to which IT applications or other resources required to execute it.

We therefore follow an understanding of the term based on that of Gerhard Schewe [33] that also takes these missing aspects into account:

1. A process is the sum of linked activities (tasks)
2. carried out by actors (people, systems as task bearers)
3. in logical and chronological order
4. with aids (equipment, information)
5. for processing a business object
6. to satisfy a customer need (and thus contribute to value creation)
7. which includes a defined beginning and input
8. as well as a defined end and a result.

As already explained in Chap. 1, we will reorganize the components somewhat and group them as follows:

1. Process strategy: A process has
   a. a defined start and input (start event)
   b. and a defined end with a result
   c. that contributes to the satisfaction of a customer's needs (and thus to the creation of value)
2. Process logic: A process
   a. is the sum of linked activities (tasks)
   b. which, after the start event, are used by actors
   c. in logical and chronological order
   d. for processing a business object in order to
   e. generate the desired result.
3. Process realization: A process is realized
   a. with people and/or machines, that take over the tasks of the respective actor
   b. and carry these tasks out with tools (equipment, information, application programs, etc.).

With this understanding of business processes, the relationship between the various models from different domains described in this chapter and Business Process Management becomes clear. Figure 2.35 shows the associated integrative character of business process models.

Habermas's and Luhmann's models deal with aspects of social systems and organizations. They describe which components and relationships make up an organization and how people are positioned in it. Complex organizations can, for example, be structured into sub-organizations on the basis of operational functions,

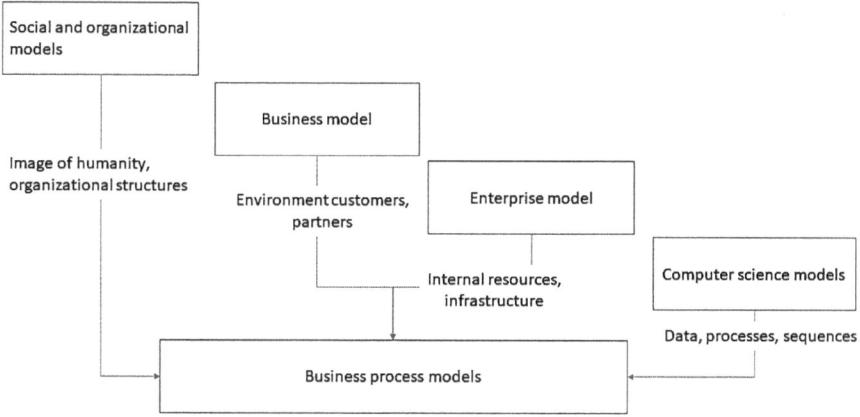

Fig. 2.35 Integration of different models through business process models

range of services, geographical aspects, or combinations of these. The result is the organization chart.

Among other things, business models consider the aspects of customers, suppliers, partners, and added value and thus look at the external service relationships on the one hand. On the other hand, they also establish the connection to the more inwardly oriented enterprise architecture, especially with value promises (products and services), activities, and resources. At the business level, the organizational structure is modeled within this enterprise architecture with the personnel resources, the processes, and the logical business objects. The linkage with the technical layer of the enterprise architecture leads to the models from computer science. These describe, for example, data structures, control flows, and algorithms for programs as well as the design and interaction of other information and communication technology components necessary for the execution of desired actions within the framework of process support and automation.

Models of business informatics generally try to unite computer science with models of social systems. These converge in business process models.

References

1. H. Stachowiak, *Allgemeine Modelltheorie* (Springer, Berlin, 1973)
2. M. Gabriel, *Warum es die Welt Nicht Gibt* (Ullstein Taschenbuch, Germany, 2015)
3. O. J. Siemoneit, *Eine Wissenschaftstheorie der Betriebswirtschaftslehre*. Dissertationsschrift (Universität Stuttgart, Germany, 2010)
4. H. Stachowiak, *General Model Theory* (Springer, Berlin, 1973)
5. A. Kieser, P. Wagenbach, *Organisation* (Schäffer-Pöschl, Germany, 2007)
6. D. Crowther, M. Green, *Organisational Theory* (Chartered Institute of Personnel Development, London, 2004)
7. G. Schreyögg (ed.), *Organisation*, 5th edn. (Gabler, Wiesbaden, 2008)
8. A. Kieser, M. Ebers (eds.), *Organisationstheorien* (Kohlhammer, Stuttgart, 2006)
9. J. Habermas, *Theory of Communicative Action Volume 1, Volume 2.* (Suhrkamp Paperback Science, Frankfurt, 1981)
10. M. Berghaus, *Luhmann Leicht Gemacht* (Böhlau, Cologne, 2011)
11. N. Luhmann, *Social Systems* (Stanford University Press, Stanford, 1995)
12. C. Scheer, T. Deelmann, P. Loos, *Geschäftsmodelle und internetbasierte Geschäftsmodelle—Begriffsbestimmung und Teilnehmermodell*. Working Papers of the Research Group Information Systems & Management (Universität Mainz, Mainz, 2003)
13. B.W. Wirtz, O. Schilke, S. Ullrich, Strategic development of business models: implications of the web 2.0 for creating value on the internet. Long Range Planning **43**(2–3), 272–290 (2010)
14. A. Osterwalder, Y. Pigneur, *Business Model Generation* (Wiley, New York, 2010)
15. R.S. Kaplan, D.P. Norton, *Balanced Scorecard* (Schäffer-Poeschel, Stuttgart, 1997)
16. V. Allee, *Value Networks and True Nature of Collaboration* (Meghan Kiffer Press, Tampa, 2015)
17. S. Franklin, A. Graesser, ITIL 4: the framework for the management of IT-enabled services. Access: 23rd October 2024
18. ISACA, *COBIT 2019 Framework: Introduction and Methodology* (ISACA, Schaumburg, 2019)
19. D. Matthes, *Enterprise Architecture Frameworks Kompendium: Über 50 Rahmenwerke für das IT-Management* (Springer, Berlin, 2011)
20. Official ITIL home page. https://www.peoplecert.org/Frameworks-Professionals/ITIL-framework last access November 2025

21. N. Szyperski, Informationsbedarf, in *Handwörterbuch der Organisation*, ed. by E. Grochla. (Verlag C.E. Poeschel, Stuttgart, 1980)
22. H. Krcmer, Information—enzyklopädie der wirtschaftinformatik, online.lexikon. Access: 23rd October 2024
23. W. Reisig, *Understanding Petri Nets* (Springer, New York, 2016)
24. R. Milner, *Communication and Concurrency* (Prentice Hall, Hoboken, 1989)
25. R. Milner, *Communicating and Mobile Systems: The Pi-Calculus* (Cambridge University, Cambridge, 1999)
26. R. Hoare, A., Comminicating sequential processes, in *Communications of the ACM*, vol. 21, Nr. 8 (1978)
27. A.R. Hoare, *Communicating Sequential Processes* (Prentice Hall, Hoboken, 1985)
28. E. Börger, R. Stärk, *Abstract State Machines: A Method for High-level System Design and Analysis* (Springer, Heidelberg, 2003)
29. S. Franklin, A. Graesser, Is it an agent, or just a program?: A taxonomy for autonomous agents. https://pdfs.semanticscholar.org/288d/7952b6648749fcbdcedabedf8f43cf7fda52.pdf. Access: 23rd October 2024
30. M. Lankhorst, et al., *Enterprise Architecture at Work* (Springer, Berlin, 2017)
31. M. Cossetino, et al., *Handbook on Agent Oriented Design Processes* (Springer, Berlin, 2014)
32. L. Sterling, K. Taveter, *The Art of Agent-Oriented Modeling* (Massachusetts Institute of Technology, Cambridge, 2009)
33. G. Schewe, Geschäftsprozess. http://wirtschaftslexikon.gabler.de/definition/geschaeftsprozess.html#definition (letzter Zugriff, Germany, 2017)
34. J. Becker, Geschäftsprozessmodellierung. http://www.enzyklopaedie-der-wirtschaftsinformatik.de/lexikon/daten-wissen/Informationsmanagement/Information-/index.html (letzter Zugriff, Germany, 2017)

Modeling Languages for Business Processes 3

Modeling languages and their underlying paradigms determine the concepts that can be used to describe an extract from perceived reality and how these concepts can be put into mutual relationship. Modeling languages thus provide a vocabulary and a grammar needed to represent real-life situations in models. They will subsequently be considered in a structured way.

The selection of a specific modeling language forms the definition basis for modeling, to which all actors involved in the modeling effort—whether they are actively involved in the creation or passively affected by the model as consumers—can refer. The term *actors* here is not restricted to humans. Humans are provided with a common, defined vocabulary by the modeling language in order to form a common understanding of the situation being modeled. But *actor* can also refer to computer systems that are given the opportunity to further process models with automation support (e.g., in order to use them as a basis for workflow support), as the semantics of model elements are exactly specified in the modeling language.

Another question is the formality of a language. Informal methods, for example, are still suitable for supporting communication between human actors, who are not bound to a strict set of rules but are usually relatively free in their choice of expression [1]. Some modeling languages are even designed to support communication among human actors and, therefore, may explicitly allow a "vague" representation of model semantics. However, if a model is intended to be used in or to discuss IT systems, modeling languages with more exact specification of syntax and especially semantics are usually required [2].

Consequently, the choice of a modeling language is highly dependent on the respective objective of the modeling process and is an important step toward successful support of the activities in which the modeling process is embedded.

In this chapter, we provide an overview and the foundations for an appropriate selection of suitable modeling languages to fulfill the requirements of both human actors as well as machines and present different languages with their respective objectives and language elements. Naturally, the focus here is on the languages to

© The Author(s) 2026   65
M. Elstermann et al., *Contextual Process Digitalization*,
https://doi.org/10.1007/978-3-032-06901-6_3

model business processes. All selected languages, therefore, allow the behavior of actors in organizations to be mapped in a broader sense. The languages, however, fundamentally differ in what is considered to be an "actor" and how the behavior of such can be described. The reasons for these differences can be found in the historical context of the languages and their respective objectives. The arrangement of the following sections, therefore, follows a historical perspective in order to clearly highlight the relationships between the languages and their origins. Finally, we discuss for each of the languages to what extent they allow the mapping of processes according to the definition used in this book and where they have their respective focal points or gaps in representation capabilities.

In principle, all languages could be used to describe processes and process systems that are supposed to be digitalized, and this chapter functions as a short reference and guide throughout the various means. If you want to consider only one for your process digitalization needs and are not bound by a specific software, the authors would advise embracing the last section, S-BPM/PASS.

3.1   Overview

Flowcharts, which are still used today, are one of the oldest modeling languages to describe processes. They were originally designed to represent the control flow in a computer program. Due to the generality of their language elements, they are also used for modeling processes in organizations and are therefore presented here as an introduction to graphical process modeling. They introduce the concept of branching in the control flow to represent alternative paths.

For a long time EPCs ("Event-driven Process Chains") were a de facto industry standard for Business Process Modeling in Europe. In addition to their capability to map process flows, they also include elements to include responsibilities, data, or services in models. This enables the modeling of business processes in their organizational context. In addition, they allow explicit modeling of parallel activities and thus go beyond the expressiveness of flowcharts in the representation of the workflow.

Historically,*UML activity diagrams can be seen* as a further development of flowcharts to model software processes. As part of the Unified Modeling Language (UML), they today represent the de facto standard for representing control flows in software. Like eEPCs, they also allow the mapping of parallel process flows. Using activity diagrams, we introduce the structuring of models through partitioning and nesting and show how models can be structured based on responsibilities and not just on the workflow itself.

BPMN (Business Process Model and Notation) is the predominant standard for representing business processes today. Originally derived from several different modeling languages, including activity diagrams, BPMN was explicitly designed for representing business processes. In this context, the idea behind BPMN was that it should enable modeling with different objectives—from communication support to execution in Workflow Management Systems. From a conceptual language point of view, BPMN is particularly interesting with regard to its possibilities for compact representation of complex process flows (such as exception handling).

S-BPM/PASS (Subject-oriented Business Process Modeling) is a modeling approach that puts the actors involved in a business process and their interactions at the center of the modeling process. The resulting modeling language, the Parallel Activity Specification Schema (PASS), is characterized by a small number of language elements and comprehensive expressiveness for mapping business processes. On the one hand, it is presented here as an example of a not primarily flow-oriented approach to Business Process Modeling, and on the other hand, it represents, in terms of language conception, an alternative to BPMN with its very extensive set of modeling elements.

3.2   Flowcharts

Flowcharts allow the depiction of simple sequences of activities, understood as a *sequential process*. A sequential process is characterized by the fact that no more than one activity is performed at any one time—thus parallel processes cannot be represented. Flowcharts were first described in the context of industrial production planning in the 1920s. At the end of the 1940s, they were adapted for the description of processes in the emerging information technology sector. Since the mid-1960s, they have been used as a standardized form of representation for computer program sequences. To this day, they are used to represent flows in computer programs or processes in organizations, as long as their complexity does not exceed the expressiveness of a flowchart [3].

The limitation of flowcharts' expressiveness is due to their historical development. In both industrial production planning and in early computer systems, it was not necessary to be able to represent parallel processes. Due to the limited computing resources available (only one CPU or only one processor core), there was no need to provide language elements to design parallel software processes.

3.2.1   Notation Elements

Flowcharts today exist in many different variants, which mainly differ in the notation used (i.e., the graphical representation). The semantics of the language elements, however, are common to all (cf. Fig. 3.1). Basically, any number of *operations* (i.e., activities, represented as rectangles) is defined. These operations are put into

Fig. 3.1 Notation elements of flowcharts

an execution sequence by means of directed connections (represented as arrows). Rounded rectangles indicate the start and end of a process.

An essential means of describing processes, both in a computer program and in organizations, is the representation of alternative operations. The selection of an alternative usually depends on a condition that can be checked—in a computer program, this could be exceeding a limit for the value of a variable; in an organization, the existence of a particular document or the decision of a person responsible for executing the process could constitute the criterion for selecting an alternative. Alternatives are represented in flowcharts by *branches* (represented as diamonds), which are connected to the previous operation via an incoming arrow and to the alternatively executed subsequent operations by two outgoing arrows. The restriction to exactly two (and not several) subsequent operations is also due to the origin of flowcharts from the representation of computer programs, since these usually are only capable of evaluating a condition in a binary way (i.e., as true or false). If a condition is to be checked for more than two values, several branches must be cascaded in flowcharts. The outgoing connections are labeled with the respective characteristic value at which the program is continued after the condition has been checked. A repeated execution of operations (e.g., as long as there are still documents that need to be processed) is represented by jumping back to an earlier operation via an outgoing connection from a branch. The other outgoing connection then progresses to the operation that is executed when the repeated execution is complete.

In addition to these basic elements, flowcharts in some variants also offer special language elements that are used mainly to represent specific operations in the area of application (such as input or output operations in computer systems). However, these are not relevant for the conceptual understanding of flowcharts and especially not for their application in Business Process Modeling.

In the following, we present the use of the notation elements using examples from Business Process Modeling. The notation used is based on the symbols defined by American National Standards Institute (ANSI) and Deutsches Institut für Normung (DIN) in the 1960s.

3.2.2 Examples

The example in Fig. 3.2 shows a process with a single operation in which an application (for which we have no detailed information here) is processed. The process ends after the processing of the application has been completed.

In the example in Fig. 3.3, the process is extended by a decision. The application is checked, and the result of this check allows a decision to be taken on its confirmation or rejection. The confirmation or rejection itself is, in turn, an operation. The outgoing connections are merged after the alternative branches are completed.

Decisions with more than two possible outputs must be represented in flowcharts using cascaded decision elements. This can be seen in the example in Fig. 3.4. Obviously, our applications are investment requests. The first decision now exam-

Fig. 3.2 Simple process flow
in flowchart

Fig. 3.3 Flowchart with
binary decision

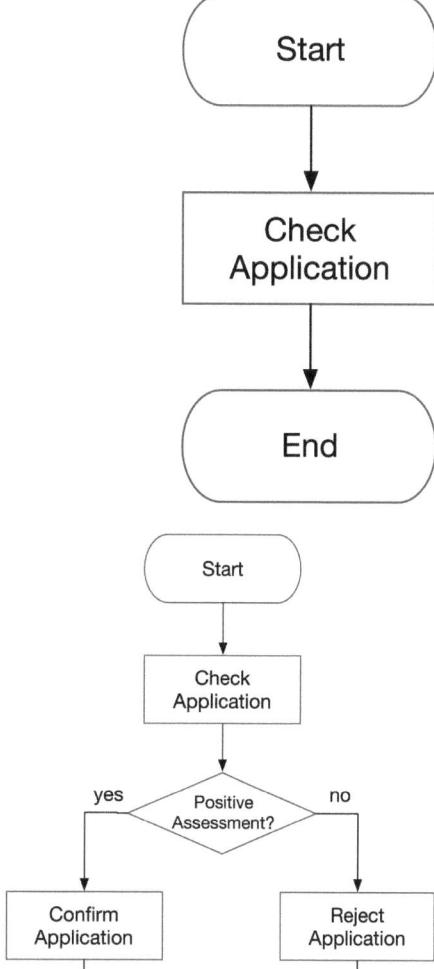

ines whether the sum of investment costs is less than EUR 1,000. If this is the
case, the request is confirmed directly. If this is not the case, a second decision
is taken. It checks whether the application sum is less than EUR 10,000. If this is
the case, the application sum is between EUR 1,000 and EUR 9,999, which leads
to an examination of the attachments to the application. If the application amount
is not less than EUR 10,000, i.e., EUR 10,000 or more, the application will be
forwarded. We don't learn anything about the destination of the forwarding here,
because flowcharts don't offer notation elements for depicting this information.

Fig. 3.4 Flowchart with
multiple-outcome decision

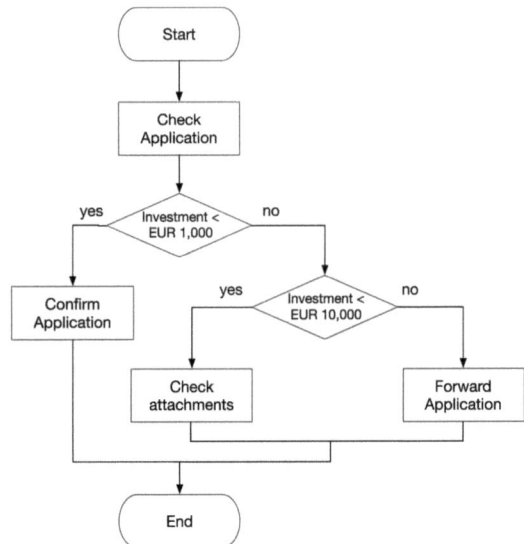

As already mentioned, branches can also be used to repeat parts of a process (loop) (cf. Fig. 3.5). To do this, the decision is inserted at the end of the part to be repeated, and an outgoing branch leads back to the point prior to the first operation to be repeated. The other outgoing branch continues the process after the repetition is completed. In the example, applications are processed as long as there are more applications available. It is important to understand that at least one application must be processed before the process can come to an end. If the process should be able to finish if there are no applications at all, an additional decision would have to be inserted at the beginning of the process ("Applications present?"), from which an outgoing connection ("no") leads directly to the end of the process. The other outgoing connection ("yes") would lead to the process flow previously described.

3.2.3   Verdict

Flowcharts are a simple way to represent business processes in terms of the logical sequence of activities they contain. Other aspects of a business process, such as data or responsibilities, are not accounted for in the language and cannot therefore be represented.

It is also not possible to represent parallel process flows. This is a major reason why flowcharts are partly being replaced by more recent languages such as UML activity diagrams or BPMN, which offer constructs for executing operations in parallel. Since flowcharts do not offer any elements to depict responsibilities, it is not possible to represent communication processes—this restriction also is addressed in more modern languages, which we introduce in the following sections.

Fig. 3.5 Flowchart with repeated execution of process parts

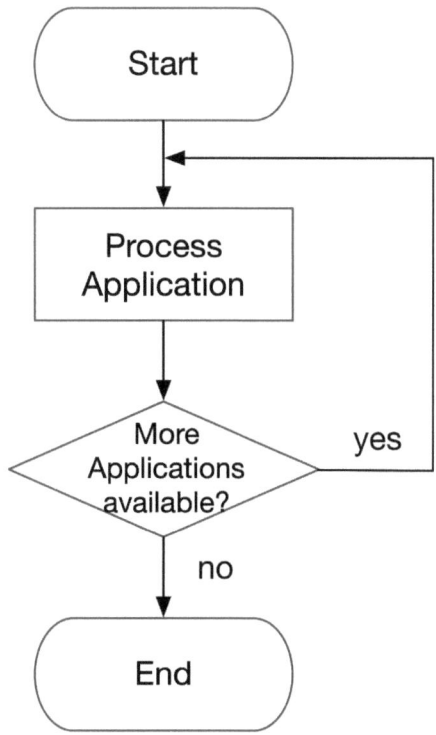

3.3 Event-driven Process Chains

For a long time, Event-driven Process Chains (EPCs) were the de facto industry standard in Europe for representing business process models. They were developed as part of the ARIS concept already presented in Sect. 2.6.1.4 and are a means to represent the control view of an organization—i.e., the view that deals with the processes in an organization and the associated links between its resources. Resources here can be both acting members and/or departments of an organization from an active perspective, as well as the required and/or manipulated data or goods from a passive perspective.

EPCs link the functions that an organization is capable of performing based on upcoming events during business operation. The basic principle of representation is that *a function* is always triggered by *an event*—that is, a function must always be preceded by an event in an EPC model in order to determine whether the execution of a function can be started. In a more comprehensive variant, "extended EPC" (eEPC), functions can be linked to the elements of the other ARIS views relevant for their execution. In particular, the responsible actors, roles, or organizational units can be assigned from the organizational view, and the relevant documents or data objects from the data view. If a function leads to a billable service, this can be represented by elements taken from the service view.

In addition to the representation of decisions, EPCs also enable the modeling of parallel process flows. For this purpose, the language provides additional notation elements: first is simply the *AND connector* that implies the split or merge of a process flow into multiple parallel flows. The *OR connector* can be used to represent processes in which one or more alternatives can be chosen, so potentially also multiple, which will run in parallel. The *XOR connector*, on the other hand, is used to represent decisions for which exactly one alternative has to be selected (this corresponds to the decision element in flowcharts).

3.3.1   Notation Elements of EPCs

The basic element for describing business processes in EPCs is the *function* (similar to the operation in flowcharts, cf. Fig. 3.6). However, the sequence of functions in a process is not determined exclusively by connection arrows. By using *events*, the sequence is specified in more detail. Every *function* is triggered by an event and subsequently creates one or more events itself. A process is thus represented by a sequence of *events* and *functions*, whereby *events* and functions always alternate. When naming them, functions should always describe a performable activity (e.g., "Check request"), while events should always describe a state (e.g., "Confirmed request" or "Rejected request").

An EPC always starts and ends with an *event. Events* that trigger a process are referred to as *start events. Events* that describe the completion of a process are referred to as *end events*. Subsequent processes can be triggered by *end events* of a previous process; that is, an end event can be a triggering *start event* in another process.

By using different connectors in combination with events, it is possible to represent different control flow variants of a process within a model. This includes the possibility of executing functions in parallel (if these are not dependent on each other). The AND, OR, and XOR logical *connectors* can be used for this purpose:

If an *AND connector* with several outgoing connections is used, all outgoing paths are traversed in parallel. These paths are then usually joined at a later point in time with another AND connector. The function after the joining AND connector is not executed until all the incoming paths have been completed.

An *OR connector* with multiple outgoing connections indicates that one or more of the following paths are traversed in parallel. These paths are usually joined again at a later point with another OR connector, whereby the subsequent function is only carried out when exactly those paths chosen at the original OR branch have been

Fig. 3.6 Notation Elements of Event-driven Process Chains (EPCs)

completed. It is important here that the paths to be activated must be selected at the time of reaching the OR connector—it cannot be used to trigger further paths at a later point in time, should this become necessary during execution. Each OR connector must be followed by an event in each of the paths that could be triggered by the function preceding the OR connector. The paths whose first events actually occur are activated during runtime.

Finally, an *XOR connector* is used for representing "exclusive OR" or "either, or" decisions. Using an XOR connector with multiple outgoing connections means that exactly one of the following paths is selected when the process is executed. It is therefore suitable for representing mutually exclusive alternatives in processes. The paths are joined again with an XOR connector, and the subsequent function is performed when the selected path has been completed. As for OR connectors, XORs must also be followed by an event on each path that could be triggered by the preceding function. These events must be mutually exclusive. The path with the first event that actually occurs is activated during runtime. In contrast to flowcharts, it is also possible to describe more than two alternatives here, as long as the events used are mutually exclusive.

3.3.2   Examples of EPCs

We here use the same examples as shown for flowcharts to visualize the differences in the notation.

The example in Fig. 3.7 shows a process with a single function in which an application (for which we have no further information here) is processed. The process ends after the application has been checked.

In the example in Fig. 3.8, the process is extended by a decision. The application is checked, and the result of this check allows making a decision on its positive or negative assessment. The confirmation or rejection itself are, in turn, functions. The outgoing connections are joined with an XOR connector after the alternate branches are completed.

Fig. 3.7 Simple EPC

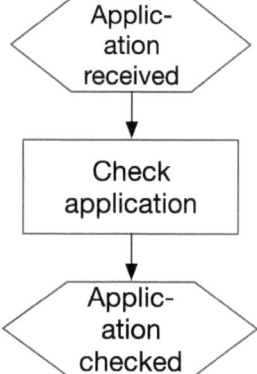

Fig. 3.8 EPC with binary
decision

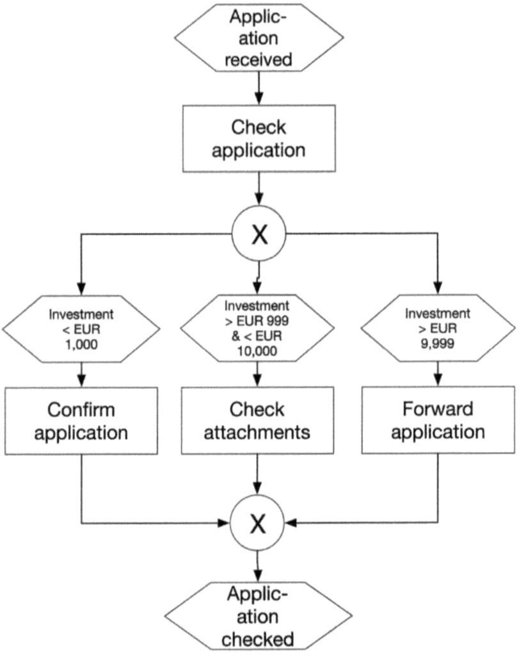

Fig. 3.9 EPC with
multi-outcome decision

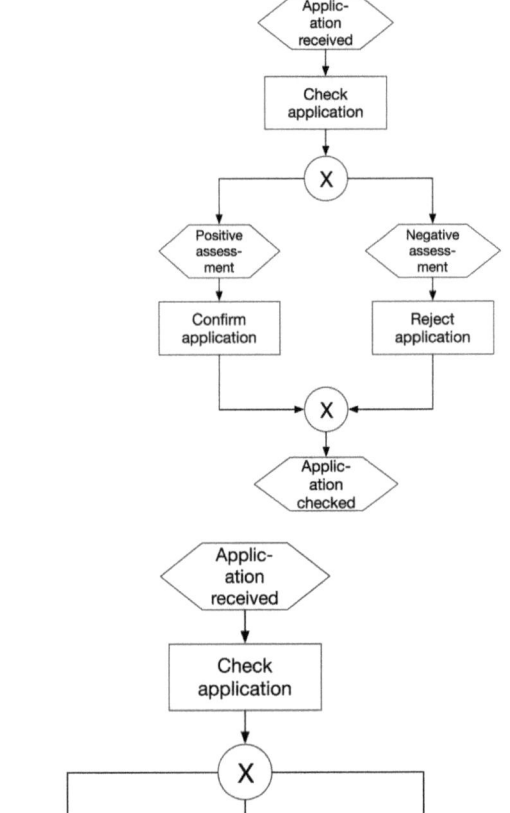

The representation of decisions that have more than two possible options is easier
here than with flowcharts. In Fig. 3.9, the XOR connector is followed by three events
that all refer to the investment amount and are mutually exclusive.

The XOR connector can also be used to repeat parts of a process (cf. Fig. 3.10).
To do this, the connector is inserted at the end of the part to be repeated and

Fig. 3.10 EPC with repeated execution of process parts

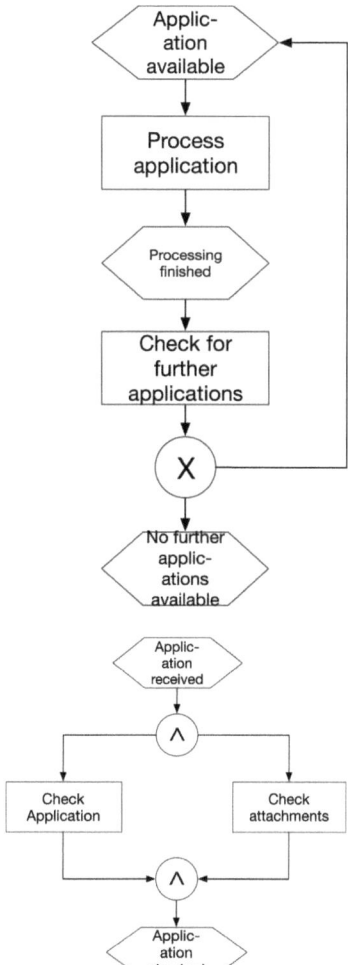

Fig. 3.11 EPC with parallel execution of process parts

an outgoing connection (line) links back to the event that triggers the part to be repeated. The other outgoing branch continues the part of the process to be executed after the repetition has been completed. It must lead to an event that triggers the termination of the repetition. In the above example, applications are processed as long as further applications are available.

The AND connector can be used if two functions can be executed independently of each other (cf. Fig. 3.11). The process modeled in the above example is therefore only correct if the attachments can actually be checked independently of the application. If this is not the case, the two functions would have to be arranged sequentially. From the point of view of modeling, the AND connector, unlike the other connectors, does not have to be immediately followed by events, since no decision is made. All outgoing branches are activated in any case.

Fig. 3.12 EPC with optional
parallel execution of process
parts

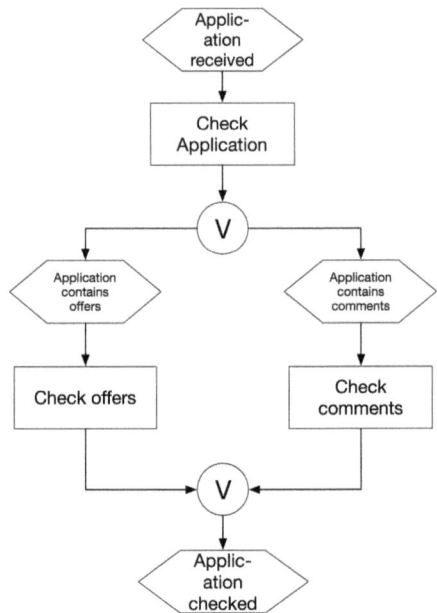

Figure 3.12 shows an example of the use of the OR connector. Here we assume that an application may contain offers or comments, or both (but must at least contain offers or comments). If offers and comments were completely optional (i.e., if both could be missing), their fundamental necessity would have to be examined with an upstream XOR connector and corresponding events. Alternatively, an additional branch could be added to the OR connector with an event "Application alone is sufficient." In both cases, the condition that events and functions must alternate on all paths through the process must not be violated. If not otherwise possible, this must be ensured by a "dummy" function that does not lead to any actual activity.

3.3.3 Supplementary Notation Elements in eEPCs

The eEPC supplements the business process depicted in an EPC with information about its execution context. In particular, responsibilities and resource requirements are assigned to the functions here. The basic rules of an EPC remain unchanged. The additional elements can only be assigned to functions—events are not affected. At this point we do not provide a complete description of the possible elements of EPCs but focus on the most common ones (cf. Fig. 3.13).

Responsibilities are represented by *organizational units*. Such units do not usually represent concrete persons but abstractly identify the name of a role (e.g., managing director) or a department (e.g., financial accounting). This ensures that the specification of a process is independent of the availability of concrete staff

Fig. 3.13 Additional notation elements for extended EPCs (eEPC)

resources. Concrete persons do not have to be assigned until the time of execution. Undirected connections (lines) are used to show the assignment to a function. In this way, an organizational unit can be assigned to several functions. It is also possible to list organizational units more than once, if the model layout can be made clearer in this way.

IT systems are modeled in a similar way. They indicate the need to use a particular IT system (e.g., an ERP system or database) when executing a function. They are also assigned to functions with undirected connections (lines).

Information objects are used to represent data processing in a business process. An information object can be arbitrarily comprehensive (i.e., a single value, as well as a complete document) and is always assigned to a function by means of a directional connection (arrow) that describes the data flow. If the arrow ends at the function, this means that the information object is required to execute the function. If the arrow ends at the information object, this means that it is created or changed by the function. An information object can have several inbound and outbound connections, which can describe both its origin and its use in a business process.

3.3.4 Example of an (e)EPC

To illustrate (e)EPCs, we use one of the examples described above and add the data flow and the human resources required (cf. Fig. 3.14). Application systems would be modeled analogously to the use in organizational units.

With regard to the data flow, we can now see that the actual application must be present in order to check the application. This check not only leads to a positive or negative assessment of the application in the process flow but also to an information object in which the assessment is stored. In the case of a negative assessment, this information-object is required to create the rejection (we can therefore assume that the rejection contains a substantive reason). If the application is confirmed, the "Assessment" data object is no longer required, so we can assume that no further justification will be given in this case.

With regard to responsibilities, we now recognize that several organizational units are involved in the process. While the application is checked by a clerk, the head of department is responsible for the final confirmation or rejection. It is important here that the events on which the decision is based are triggered by the "Check application" function, for which the clerk is responsible. In the present process model, the head of department has no possibility to revise the decision once made.

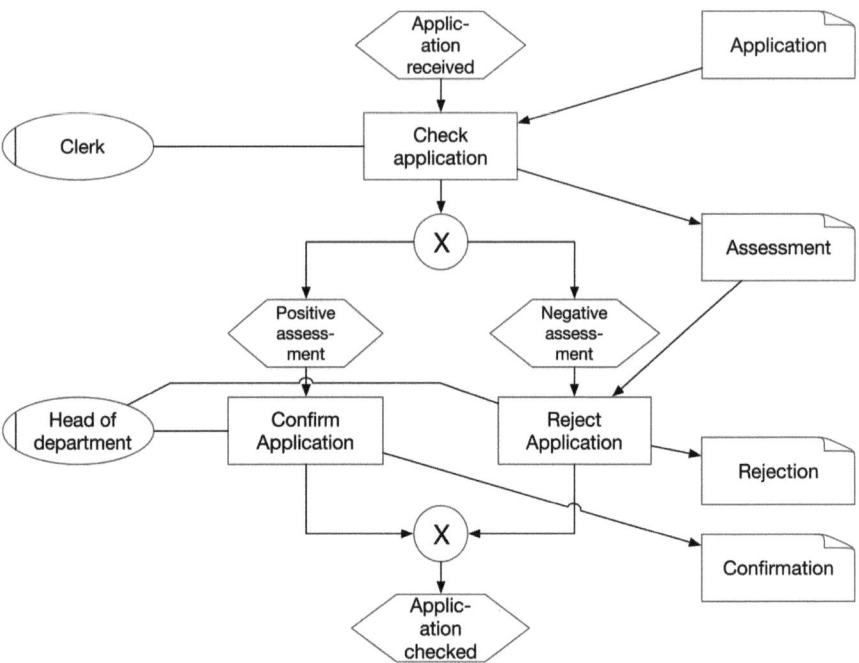

Fig. 3.14 Example of an eEPC

3.3.5 Verdict

The EPC language offers more comprehensive possibilities for representing business processes than the flowchart. What they have in common is their orientation toward using the tasks and activities within an organization as the primary structuring characteristic of the business process (i.e., all information depicted in the model is anchored in the description of the process flow). This is an obvious choice when describing organizational processes, but—as we will see later—not necessarily the only possibility. Other modeling languages use actors or data as their primary structuring elements on which all other information is anchored. This makes aspects of the process visible that can only be implicitly represented in (e)EPCs (such as the transition between responsibilities in the process and the necessary communication between the actors).

The requirement to alternate functions and events in the process flow in EPCs often leads to very extensive models that are sometimes difficult to understand. It also bears the risk of tempting modelers to formulate trivial events that do not add any information to the model (e.g., function: "Execute task," event: "Task executed"). When used correctly, however, the EPC approach offers advantages: On the one hand, processes can be described and delimited more precisely than with flowcharts; on the other hand, EPCs explicitly allow the view on the capabilities of an organization (its functions) to be linked to the view on how it uses these capabilities to react to external stimuli or events within the organization itself. Thus, organizational capabilities can be described generically and used multiple times in processes, avoiding inefficiency through replication. From a pragmatic point of view, however, practical experience has shown that the specification of generic functions, as well as process-specific events, in the necessary detail is not always feasible. More modern approaches, such as the activity diagrams discussed in the following or BPMN, therefore still use the concept of events, but only deploy these if an external stimulus (such as an incoming message, an error, or a deadline) actually needs to be addressed.

In contrast to the modeling languages with a technically oriented history (such as flowcharts or the activity diagrams described in the next section), the eEPC and the surrounding ARIS framework are concepts originally derived from business administration. They thus pursue a more comprehensive approach to the description of business processes than the technology-centric approaches. The consideration of data, responsibilities, but also goals or services (which were not discussed here), enables a comprehensive modeling of business processes, which still influences the design of contemporary modeling languages for the representation of organizational phenomena (such as business processes or enterprise architectures).

3.4   UML Activity Diagrams

The activity diagram is defined as part of UML (Unified Modeling Language), which contains a collection of modeling diagrams suitable for specifying software systems. The UML activity diagram takes a role and notation style similar to that of the original flowchart and is used to illustrate the behavior of a software system. Because of its more recent historical context, it also provides elements for the illustration of distributed and parallel process flows. Like the flowchart, the activity diagram is also suitable for representing organizational processes (i.e., business processes). While it is still used for this purpose today, the focus in the area of Business Process Modeling has shifted strongly toward BPMN (Business Process Modeling Notation). BPMN was specified by the same standardization body as UML and has adopted many elements of the activity diagram. However, BPMN focuses more explicitly on the requirements of Business Process Modeling and the organizational aspects to be represented there, which we have already discussed for EPCs.

3.4.1   Notation Elements

By definition, an activity diagram always describes an activity that consists of individual *actions* ("activity" is thus used here analogously to "process"). An action corresponds to an operation for flowcharts, or a function for EPCs, cf. Fig. 3.15).

An activity usually begins with a *start node* and finishes with an *end node* (similar to the associated elements for flowcharts). Between these nodes, the actions

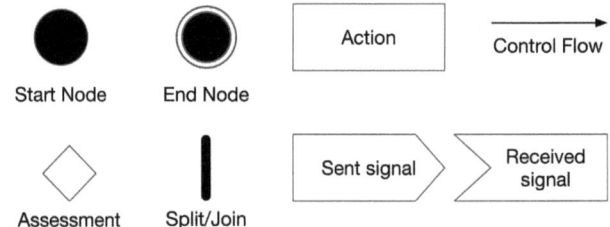

Fig. 3.15 Notation elements of UML activity diagrams

contained are specified and brought into sequence by control flow arrows. To influence the process, it is possible to insert *decision elements*. Decisions can have any number of outgoing branches, for which the activation conditions must be mutually exclusive. The conditions are listed at the outgoing connections. The semantics of the decision symbol corresponds to the XOR in the EPC—there is no equivalent for the OR connector in activity diagrams.

The activity diagram provides the *split/join element* to represent process parts that can be executed independently of each other and in parallel. When used to split the process, it can have any number of outgoing connections that are all activated at the same time. The branches created in this way should be merged again by the join element. The process is not continued until all branches have been finished.

Signals are used for communication between process parts in different activities (i.e., in different diagrams), or within an activity when information is to be provided for subsequent process parts. They are incorporated into the control flow like actions. Models do not always have to contain complete signal pairs (i.e., send and receive signals). They can also send signals for processes that are not shown in the diagram (i.e., contain only a send signal) or receive signals from a process that is not shown in the diagram (i.e., contain only a receive signal). Received signals can also trigger an activity and thus replace the start node in a diagram.

The activity diagram also provides elements to represent responsibilities and data flows (cf. Fig. 3.16). Responsibilities are represented using *partitions*. Partitions are elements that enclose parts of an activity diagram and thus determine that all elements, in particular the actions they enclose, fall under the responsibility of the

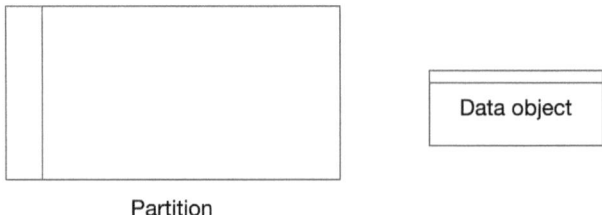

Fig. 3.16 Notation elements to represent responsibilities and data flows in UML activity diagrams

stated organizational unit (or, in the case of software systems, system component). If partitions are used (which is not mandatory), all elements of the activity diagram should be enclosed by exactly one of the partitions shown. Overlaps are not allowed. Actions outside a partition should be avoided.

Data objects in activity diagrams are directly incorporated into the control flow between actions. They can therefore (only) be used to represent the flow of information between two consecutive actions. If a data object is only needed again later in the process flow, it has to be forwarded in the control flow via all intermediate actions or passed on by means of a signal.

3.4.2 Examples

In order to work out the differences and similarities to the previously discussed modeling languages, we again make use of the examples already used above.

The example in Fig. 3.17 shows an activity with a single action in which an application (for which we have no further information here) is processed. The activity ends after the processing of the application has been completed.

In the example in Fig. 3.18, the process is extended by a decision with three possible outcomes that are mutually exclusive. The application is checked, and the result of this check allows the decision to be taken with regard to the further processing of the application.

As with the other modeling languages, we can also use branches here to repeat parts of a process (cf. Fig. 3.19). For this purpose, the decision is inserted at the end of the part to be repeated, and an outgoing branch is linked back to a closing decision before the first operation of the part to be repeated (a closing decision is used for joining alternative branches and has several incoming and only one outgoing connection). The other outgoing branch of the opening decision element continues the process after the repetition is completed.

The split/join element can be used if two action sequences can be executed independently of each other (cf. Fig. 3.20). The process modeled in the above example is therefore only correct if the attachments can actually be checked independently of the application. If this is not the case, the two actions would

Fig. 3.17 Simple UML activity diagram

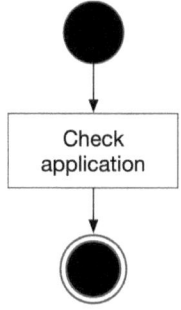

Fig. 3.18 UML activity
diagram with a
multiple-outcome decision

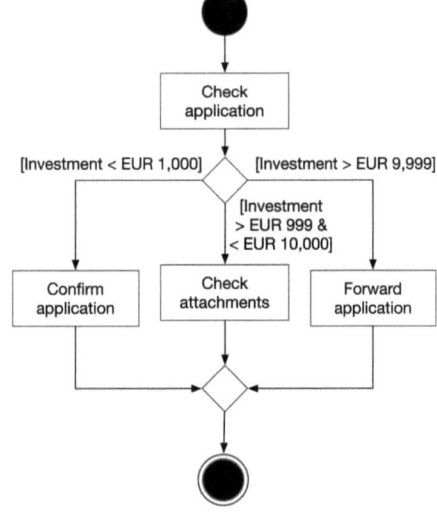

Fig. 3.19 UML activity
diagram with repeated
execution of process parts
(loop)

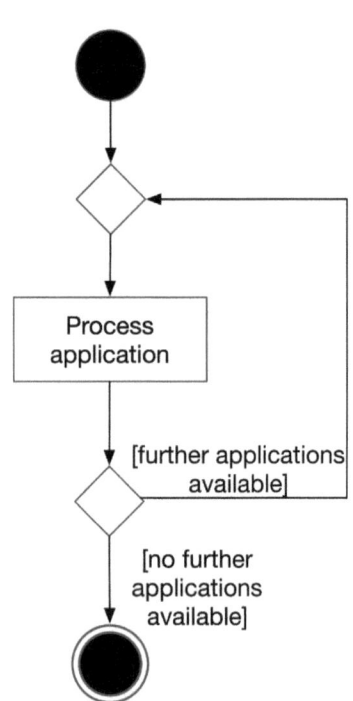

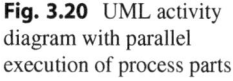

Fig. 3.20 UML activity diagram with parallel execution of process parts

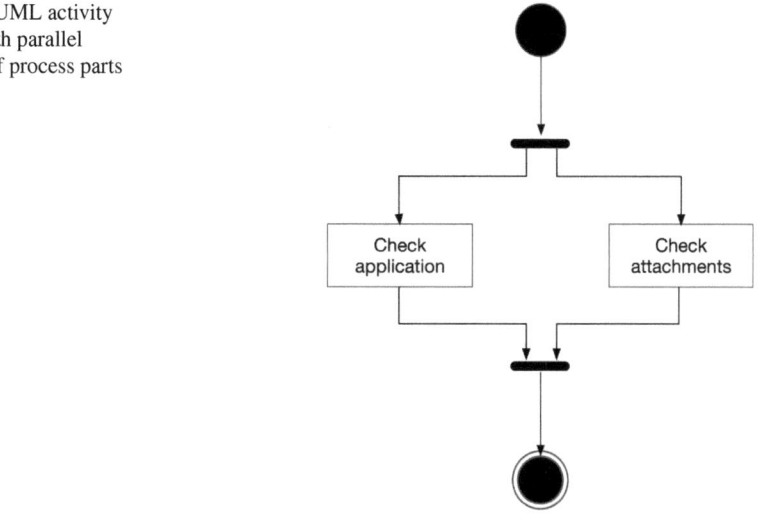

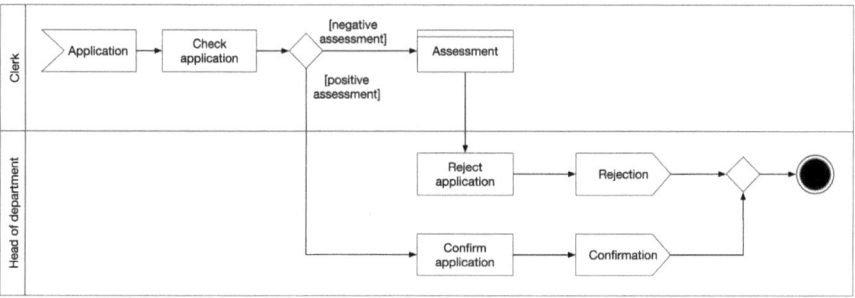

Fig. 3.21 Example of a UML activity diagram with partitions, data objects, and signals

have to be arranged sequentially. The merging join element waits for both incoming branches to be completed before continuing the process.

The example in Fig. 3.21 demonstrates the use of partitions, data objects, and signals. Partitions are used to represent the responsibilities in the process. The process is triggered by a received signal, which explicitly shows that the execution only starts when an application is received (we had previously always implicitly assumed this for the flowchart, and the other examples given for the activity diagram, but unlike EPCs, were never able to represent it in the model). Send signals are used to transmit the confirmation or rejection to the recipient (who is not shown here). The assessment of the application is only transferred in the case of a negative assessment as a data object for the action "Reject application" (we can therefore assume that the rejection contains a substantive reason). If the application is confirmed, the "Assessment" data object is not required, so we can assume that no further justification will be given in this case.

3.4.3   Verdict

Activity diagrams largely combine the simplicity of flowchart notation with the expressiveness of EPCs (with certain limitations). They allow the handling of data in the process to be represented and introduce a means of clearly representing responsibilities with the partitions. In contrast to the previously discussed languages, the availability of signals allows the depiction of communication processes between participants or with the surrounding environment of the displayed process.

The absence of an element corresponding to the OR connector in the EPC does indeed represent a limitation; however, this is rarely relevant in practice, since we are usually confronted with mutually exclusive alternatives or completely independent branches of execution in the real world. Activity diagrams are therefore a suitable tool for representing business processes on the whole, especially if the target group using the model has an Information Technology background and is already familiar with the notation. For other target groups, BPMN, which we will discuss in the next section, is preferable due to its more flexible applicability and higher expressiveness for Business Process Modeling.

3.5   BPMN

BPMN—the modeling language referred to as Business Process Model (and) Notation—was developed by IBM in 2002 and subsequently published by the BPMI (Business Process Management Initiative). The aim was to create a universally applicable standard to counter the multitude of process modeling languages used in academia and industry. This language should adopt the essential characteristics of the most common languages and make it possible, in addition to the documentation of business processes, to create models that allow for immediate IT-supported execution. BPMI, in turn, was merged with the OMG (Object Management Group) in 2005. Thus, BPMN became an OMG standard and complements the already mentioned UML (Unified Modeling Language), which is maintained by the same group.

The BPMN 2.0 standard was published in 2010. In addition to the core of BPMN, the *Business Process Diagrams*, this standard incorporates three further diagram types: the *choreography diagram*, the *collaboration diagram*, and the collaboration diagram variant of the *conversation diagram*.

In the following, we consider the basic elements of BPMN 2.0 Business Process Diagrams that enable business processes to be represented at the business level.

3.5.1   Notation Elements of BPMN Business Process Diagrams

Process diagrams created with BPMN are called *Business Process Diagrams (BPD)*. In its core, BPD follows the principles of activity diagrams, which are subsequently

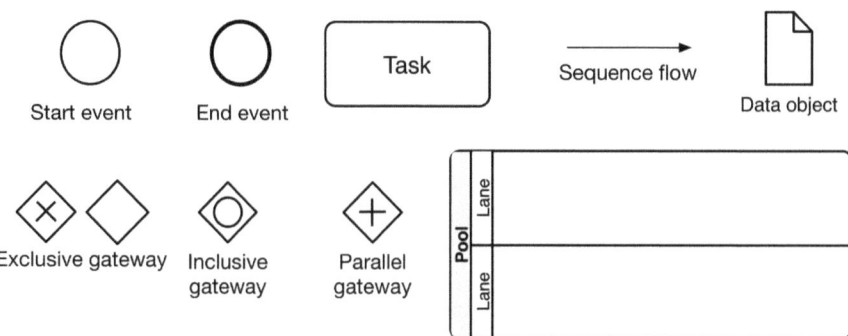

Fig. 3.22 Core notation elements of BPMN process diagrams

supplemented by elements that allow the representation of the potentially more complex control flow in business processes (cf. Fig. 3.22).

As a basic principle of representation, certain things have to be done in a process (*tasks*), but possibly only under certain conditions (*gateways*), and things can happen (*events*). These three objects are connected to each other via *sequence flows* (arrows).

Beyond that, it is often advised to make use of so-called *swimlanes* and pools and model tasks, events, and gateways only within the confinement of swimlanes, which in turn are grouped into pools. Pools and lanes are constructs used to represent responsibilities in distributed business processes. They are discussed in more detail below. If a connection is made across pool boundaries, it is modeled using *message flows*, which we will also expand on later in Sect. 3.5.7.

As stated, a process consists of *tasks*. After starting a process (by means of an event), one task follows the other until the process ends (with an event). Tasks can be atomic (i.e., not refined further) or can contain subprocesses. In such cases, tasks are refined by an additional embedded BPD, which describes the detailed sequence of sub-tasks. This detailed sequence can be "hidden" and is represented by a "+" symbol at the bottom of the task (see also Sect. 3.5.10.1).

A process begins with a *start event* and ends with an *end event*. BPMN offers a multitude of possibilities to define events that can trigger, complete, or influence the course of a process. These will be discussed later.

At this point, it is important to emphasize that a process can start with one or more start events and can end on any path through the process (see sequence flow and gateways below) with one or more end events. There must be a continuous sequence flow from each start event to at least one end event. Tasks, gateways, or intermediate events must not be endpoints in the process and therefore always require at least one outgoing sequence flow.

A gateway represents a branch in the control flow. The *exclusive (XOR) gateway* requires a condition for each outgoing control flow, which, according to the standard, must always refer to the result of an immediately preceding task.

The *parallel (AND) gateway* tracks all outgoing control flows independently and in parallel. The branched control flows can be terminated separately with end events or explicitly merged again with another parallel gateway. After this merger, the control flow only continues once all incoming control flows have been completed (as with the split/join concept for activity diagrams).

The *inclusive (OR) gateway* can follow one or more paths, whereby a condition must be specified for path selection (as with the exclusive gateway). This condition must already be testable at the time of the decision, so the necessary data must have been generated in one of the previous tasks.

Decisions, which cannot be made on the basis of previously existing data, can be represented using the event-based *gateway*. This requires an event in each outgoing branch immediately after the gateway (e.g., an incoming message event or a timer event). When one of these events occurs, its respective branch (and only this branch) is activated. We will discuss this in more detail when discussing the use of events.

3.5.2   Examples for Modeling Process Flows

In order to work out the differences and similarities to the previously discussed modeling languages, we again make use of the examples already used above.

The example in Fig. 3.23 shows a process with a single task in which an application (for which we have no detailed information here) is checked. The process ends after the "checking of the application" task has been completed.

In the example in Fig. 3.24, the process is extended by a decision with three possible results that are mutually exclusive. The application is checked, and the result of this check allows the making of a decision on how to further process the application. In BPMN, it is important that the data used as the basis for a decision is explicitly generated or received before the gateway.

Here, too, we can use branching to repeat parts of a process (cf. Fig. 3.25). For this purpose, a gateway is inserted at the end of the part to be repeated and an

Fig. 3.23 Simple BPMN
process diagram

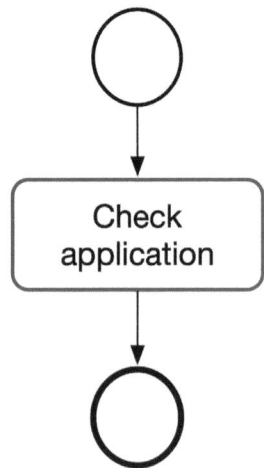

Fig. 3.24 BPMN process
diagram with
multiple-outcome decision

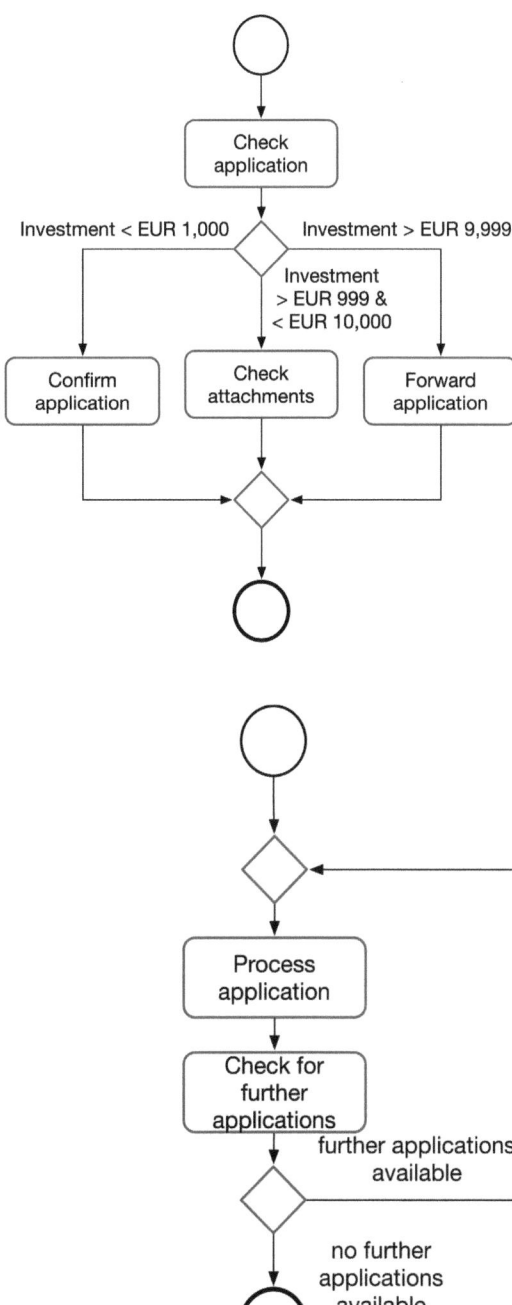

Fig. 3.25 BPMN process
diagram with repeated
execution of process parts
(loop)

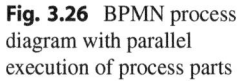

Fig. 3.26 BPMN process
diagram with parallel
execution of process parts

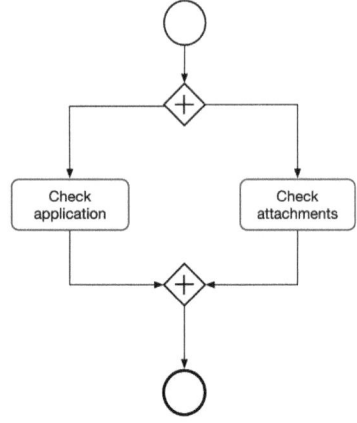

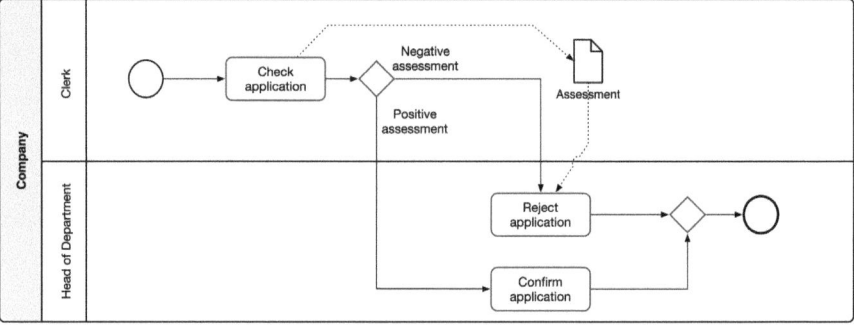

Fig. 3.27 BPMN process diagram with one pool, two lanes, an XOR Gateway, and data objects

outgoing branch is returned to a closing gateway before the first task of the part to be
repeated (a closing gateway is used for merging branches and has several incoming
sequence flows and only one outgoing). The other outgoing branch of the opening
gateway continues the process after the repetition is completed. The requirement
to explicitly create the basis for decision-making prior to the gateway is illustrated
here by the additional task of checking the existence of further applications.

The parallel gateway is used when two task sequences can be executed independently of each other (cf. Fig. 3.26). The process modeled in the example, therefore,
is only correct if the attachments can actually be checked independently of the
application. If this is not the case, the two functions would have to be arranged
sequentially. The merging gateway waits for both incoming branches to complete
before continuing the process.

The example in Fig. 3.27 shows the use of pools, lanes, and data objects. The
lanes are used to represent responsibilities in the process. With the BPMN elements
introduced so far, we cannot map communication processes. The signals available in
activity diagrams can therefore not be represented for the time being, which is why
the example here is less specific than the version represented as an activity diagram.

The use of message events, which we will introduce in a later chapter, will, however, remedy this deficiency. The assessment of the application is only transferred to the task "Reject application" in the case of a negative assessment as a data object (we can therefore assume that the rejection contains a substantive reason). In case the application is confirmed, the data object "Assessment" is no longer needed, so we can assume that in this case there will be no further justification.

3.5.3 Notation Elements for Controlling Sequence Flow with Events

A distinguishing feature of BPMN is the very detailed and comprehensive set of *event* constructs, which enables exact control of the process flow.

Events indicate that something has happened and therefore represent points in time, as opposed to tasks that take a certain amount of time and effort to be completed. So far, we have only introduced start and end events. In the following, we will describe start, intermediate, and end events in detail once again (cf. Fig. 3.28).

Events are always represented by a circle and usually an enclosed symbol. Simple circles indicate start events, double circle borders indicate intermediate events, and thick circle outlines indicate end events. If no enclosed symbol is specified, the event is of no particular type (blank) and can usually only be found at the start or end of a process or as a triggering intermediate event.

3.5.4 Start Events

Start events are used to trigger a process or subprocess. Generic (blank) events are often used if the trigger is either obvious from the context or when it is not yet known.

If a process is triggered on the basis of a particular point in time or a period of time or by a periodic event, the timer symbol (clock) is additionally used. A message symbol (letter) is used when an incoming message triggers the process (cf. Fig. 3.29).

A process can also be triggered by a *condition start event* if specific conditions need to be met in the process context in order to start it. *Signal start events* are used if some observable event from outside or inside the process should lead to the

Fig. 3.28 Fundamental event types in BPMN process diagrams

Start event   Intermediate event   End event

Fig. 3.29 Different possible start event types: basic, message, and timer start event

Application received   Application Deadline

Fig. 3.30 Combined or complex triggers for start events

Utilization > 90%   Onlinesystem down   Periodic cleaning due or Filter dirty

Fig. 3.31 Different possible end event types

Send decision

execution of a particular process. The pentagon as a symbol embedded in a start event indicates a combination of several potential start events, whereby only one of the events must occur to trigger the process (cf. Fig. 3.30).

A process does not have to be limited to a single start event; processes can also have several alternative start events.

3.5.5 End Events

Processes always finish with *end events*, whereas the same symbols are used here as for the start events, with the exception of the timer symbol, the condition, and the combination of parallel triggers. More specific end events include sending a message or issuing a signal to notify other processes about the end event at hand (for details, cf. section "Event Types").

One notable end event type is the *termination end event* (rightmost symbol in Fig. 3.31), which terminates the entire process immediately, regardless of whether other sequence flows within the process are still running or not; that is, it terminates the entire process instance. A standard end event, on the other hand, always only terminates the process branch it concludes. Any further process branches that are still running will continue to be executed.

Processes can have several end events. A process without an end event is incomplete.

3.5.6 Intermediate Events and the Event-Based Gateway

Intermediate events can be used anywhere in a process and are represented by a circle with a double border. They are used to represent intermediate results relevant for other processes, or if certain (external) events have an impact on the execution of the process at hand (e.g., an incoming message or the expiration of a certain time period).

Gateways can also be event-based if the execution of a process is dependent on the occurrence of different events, which require different reactions and therefore follow different paths. Such dependencies can be modeled with an event-based gateway.

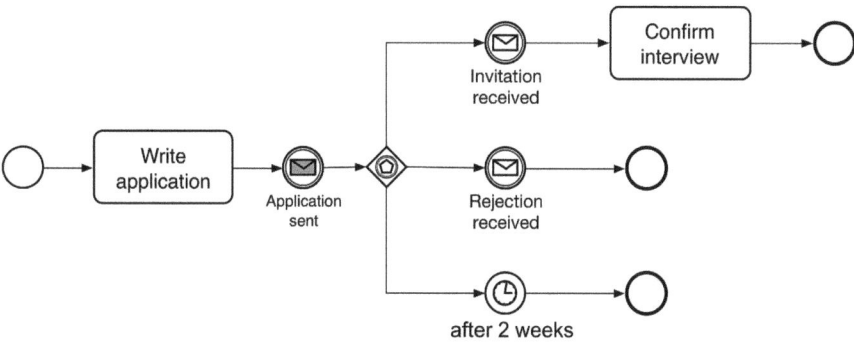

Fig. 3.32 Example BPMN process diagram showing the use of the event-based gateway

Figure 3.32 shows a process of applying for a job and waiting for different potential reactions. Depending on whether an invitation or a rejection is received, or whether a deadline of 2 weeks expires, different paths are taken in the process. The event-based gateway is the only gateway where the necessary information required to make a decision does not need to be available at the time the gateway is checked. An event-based gateway blocks the sequence flow until one of the downstream events is triggered, and then continues execution exclusively along the respective branch.

3.5.7 Notation Elements for Modeling Communication

BPMN also enables the modeling of *distributed* business processes. Although BPMN clearly focuses on the process flow during modeling (similar to flowcharts, EPCs, or activity diagrams), it also enables the structuring of the process in accordance with the participants involved and their associated responsibilities. The modeling elements available for this purpose are described in this section (cf. Fig. 3.33).

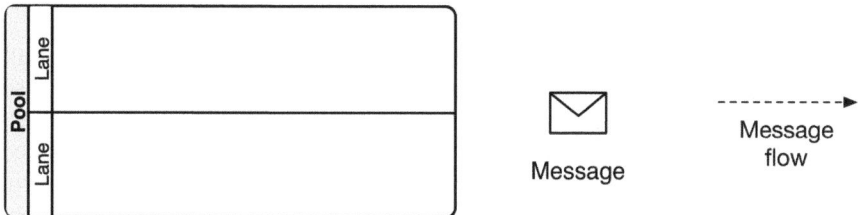

Fig. 3.33 Notation elements for modeling communication in BPMN process diagrams

A *pool* represents a company or an organizational unit in a company, such as a department. Each (swim) *lane* in a pool represents a person or role involved in the process that is assigned to this pool.

BPMN allows the representation of the interaction of two or more processes. The aforementioned pools and lanes are necessary for the representation of collaborations. Separate lanes are required for all persons or groups involved in a process, and separate pools are necessary for each process or organizational unit that is responsible for this process. Each pool thus contains its distinct processes with separate start and end events. Nevertheless, these individual processes can strongly influence each other, in which case they are coupled via message flows.

Message flows indicate that data is exchanged between different processes. Therefore, no message flow can take place within a process (pool). Consequently, there are no message flows within a lane or between different lanes of a single pool. Sequence flows show which activities are executed in which order and do not explicitly constitute an exchange of data. In contrast to message flows, they may only be used within a pool and not between different processes (pools).

Message flows can be augmented with message elements, which are used to explicitly represent the exchanged data and contain a more precise specification of the transmitted information.

Message flows can be used in different ways: they may either originate from pools and activities, and also end there, or they can be explicitly sent by send message events and received by receive message events. The first case is useful for the descriptive modeling of business processes in which a communication process is to be represented that does not necessarily have to be described exactly. A message originating from an activity or pool is sent at some point during task or process execution—the exact time remains unclear. A message ending at a pool only states that the represented organization receives this message, but not which activity it triggers or how it is handled within a process. This can be useful when modeling external organizational units, whose detailed behavior is unknown. An exact specification of communication processes, however, is only possible by using explicit send and receive events.

3.5.8 Examples for Modeling Communication-Oriented Processes

In the following, we extend the example that we used to demonstrate the use of events with the communication partner not depicted originally, i.e., we now also model the process of the company to which an application is addressed.

The example in Fig. 3.34 shows two processes (one per pool) that are linked by message flows. The company's process is triggered by an incoming application, which is represented here in the first message flow. After checking the application, the decision can be made whether to send an invitation or reject the application. In the upper pool, the applicant waits for an answer for a maximum of 2 weeks (as represented by the intermediate timer event). The event-based gateway activates the process branch whose event occurs first. The related send and receive events are

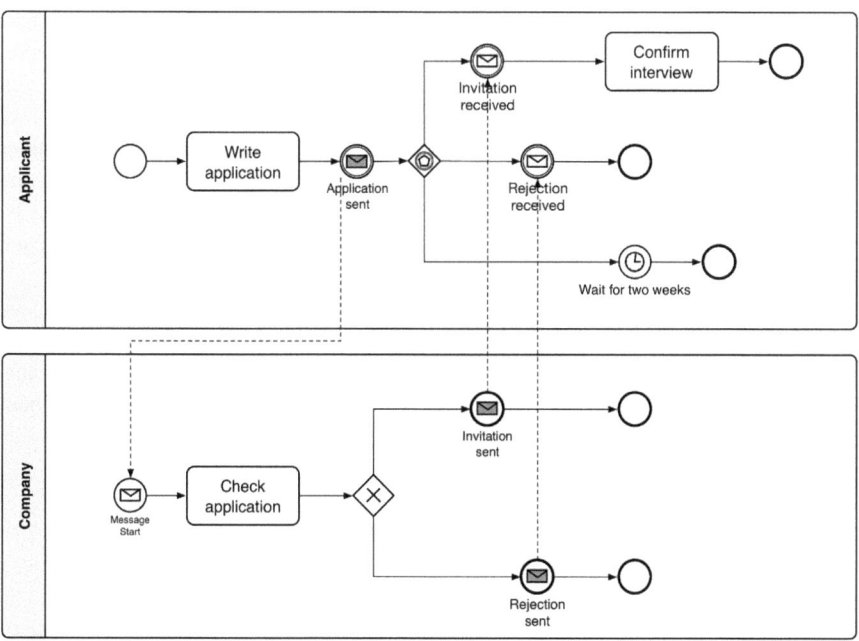

Fig. 3.34 Example BPMN process diagram showing communication-oriented processes

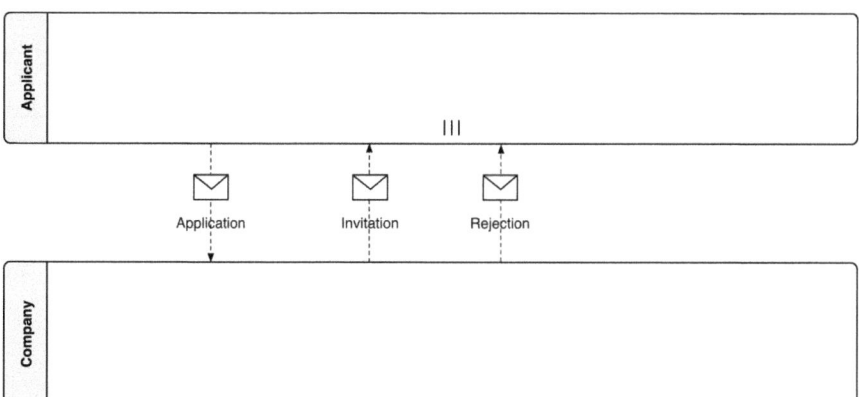

Fig. 3.35 Example BPMN process diagram showing the exclusive use of communication interactions between pools

linked via message flows. It is important to note here that message flows always represent 1:1 relationships—that is, a sent message can be received exactly once and a receive event can react to exactly one message.

The example in Fig. 3.35 shows how BPMN can be used to only represent communication acts between the actors in a distributed process. The pools are used here as black boxes, i.e., the behavior contained in them is not shown and remains unknown. All we see is that messages are exchanged, but the order of the messages is not defined. Since the specified events for sending and receiving are missing here, we augment the model with message elements attached to the message flows in order to be able to comprehensibly describe the nature of communication. Another extension of the original process model is constituted by the modifier in the upper pool, which indicates parallel multiple execution of the process contained in the upper pool. This means that the process in the lower pool could or even must be able to handle several applications arriving in parallel and independently of each other.

Empty and filled pools can also be combined as required. If, for example, we wanted to represent the process of handling an incoming application, we could leave the pool "Applicant" unspecific, since we do not know the behavior of applicants (nor is it relevant), but need to know that we can receive an application from them and that we will direct our responses to them again eventually.

3.5.9   Notation Elements for Modeling Complex Business Situations

The notation elements of BPMN introduced so far enable the representation of business processes from the point of view of the participating organizational units. BPMN allows keeping process models vague or leaving parts of them unspecified if they do not seem relevant for the objective of modeling. In some cases, however, a process needs to be defined as precisely as possible and represented in all its variants, covering all possible exceptions. This is necessary, for example, if the model is intended to serve as the basis for IT support of the work processes depicted. If aspects are omitted or abridged, the result is a discrepancy between the real work process and the support measures developed based on the model, which ultimately would lead to unsatisfactory tools and workarounds. This section describes the BPMN notation elements that enable more complex and comprehensive process descriptions. Due to the variety of scenarios that can be represented, examples are given here directly with the descriptions of the respective elements.

3.5.10   Variants of Activity Modeling

In the following section, special features for the general modeling of activities, as well as for the modeling of activities as subprocesses, are explained in more detail.

3.5.10.1 Subprocesses
As already explained, processes can include detailed specification of tasks via subprocesses. This method is mostly used to maintain a comprehensive overview of a process when creating large, extensive models, while still being able to specify detailed task descriptions. Subprocesses can be collapsed to tasks, which are then shown in the overall process with a small plus sign. If appropriate tool support is

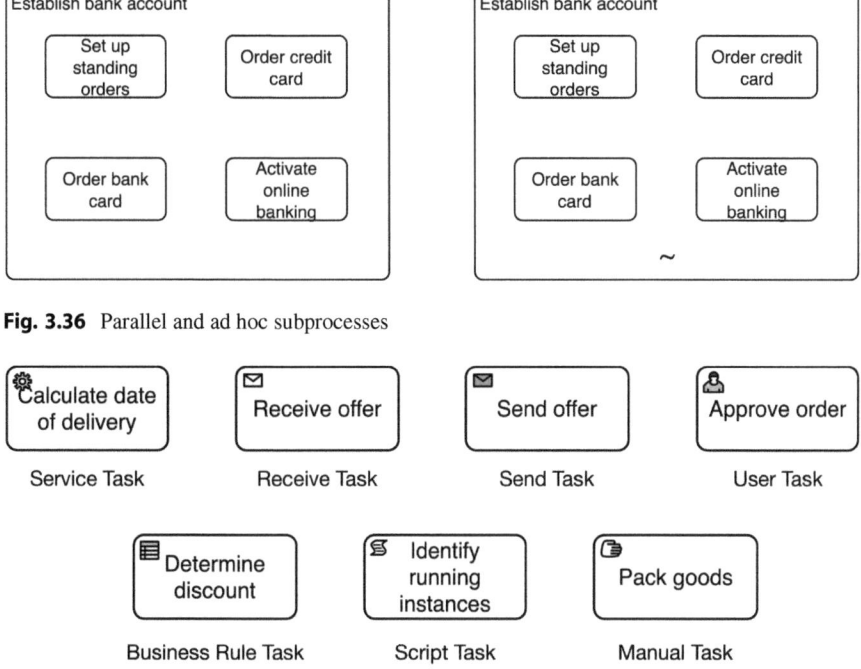

Fig. 3.36 Parallel and ad hoc subprocesses

Fig. 3.37 Different task types in BPMN process diagrams

available, collapsed tasks can be dynamically extended again to view the detailed subprocess specifying the exact execution of the task.

Subprocesses can also be used to combine several tasks in a single execution context without specifying their exact sequence. The model on the right (an ad hoc subprocess) in Fig. 3.36 only indicates that any number of the embedded activities can be performed, but makes no statement about their relationships. The left model specifies that all four embedded tasks must be executed before the subprocess is completed. It makes no assertion about their order or other relationships—the activities can be carried out in parallel or in any sequence.

3.5.10.2 Types of Tasks

Task types describe the character of a task in more detail, indicating, for example, whether it requires human involvement or can be executed automatically in an IT system. Modifiers as shown in Fig. 3.37 are used to distinguish between service tasks, receive tasks, send tasks, user tasks, business rule tasks, script tasks, and manual tasks (illustration from top left to bottom right). These modifiers do not necessarily have to be used, but they do specify the semantics of a process model in more detail.

Fig. 3.38 Task modifiers for
diverse behavior specification

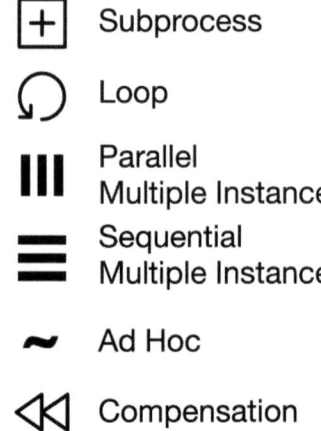

3.5.10.3 Execution Behavior of Tasks

Tasks can have different markers that describe their execution behavior. Single tasks, entire processes, or subprocesses can be executed several times in loops, in parallel, sequentially, or can be marked as ad hoc tasks or as compensation tasks (cf. Fig. 3.38).

For a looped task or process, a termination condition can be specified in addition to the symbol. If the termination condition is reached, the task or process in question is no longer executed and the superordinate process is continued. If a task can be executed several times in parallel, this is indicated by three vertical lines. For example, the "check application" task could be carried out by several agents for several received application documents. If parallel execution is not possible, but the individual cases are still independent of each other, the sequential multiple instance marker is used, which is indicated by three horizontal lines.

With ad hoc tasks, the exact sequence of the sub-tasks contained in the task is unknown a priori and is selected during the execution of the process. It is also possible to omit some of the sub-tasks and only execute those that are required in the specific situation. Such processes are indicated by a tilde (as shown above).

Compensation activities are used in transaction modeling and are described below.

3.5.11 Different Event Types Semantics

BPMN offers a large number of different events targeting different areas of application for detailed process control. While we will deal with these in detail in the following, an initial overview is provided in Fig. 3.39 to show the underlying structure of event types.

In general, events can occur in three different variants, which we have already introduced above:

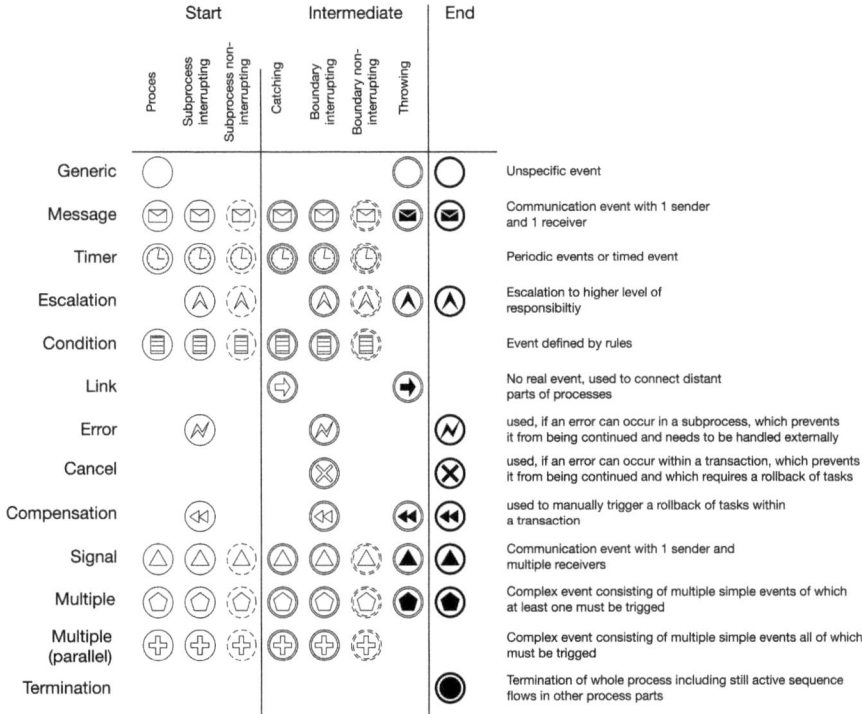

Fig. 3.39 Overview of all event types in BPMN process diagrams

- *Start events* trigger new process instances, that is, they start the execution of a process. They are always "receiving" in nature, i.e., they react to stimuli from outside (e.g., incoming messages, time sequences, etc.).
- *End events* are events that are triggered when a process instance is finished. They are always "sending" in nature, thus potentially provide stimuli for other processes or process parts.
- *Intermediate events* occur within the sequence flow, i.e., they have both an incoming and an outgoing flow (exception: link event, see below).

Start events can also be differentiated according to their surrounding modeling element. They can be used to either trigger an entire process or to trigger sub-processes. The second case is called an "event subprocess" and can be specified as an "interrupting" or a "non-interrupting" form. An "interrupting" start event indicates that the control flow is completely transferred to the subprocess, i.e., all other tasks within the respective pool are interrupted and cannot be continued. "Non-interrupting" event subprocesses are started when the respective event occurs without interrupting the execution of the task currently running within the pool in which the subprocess is placed. This can be used, for example, to react to events that should not or cannot be handled in the main process of a pool, but whose occurrence should result in a reaction without affecting the main process (such as customer inquiries about the status of an order processing while the order is being processed in the main process).

Intermediate events basically exist in "receiving" and "sending" variants. The "receiving" variants (occurring event) block the sequence flow until the specified event arrives. The process, therefore, cannot be continued until the event has occurred. The "sending" variant (triggered event) indicates the occurrence of certain events in the course of executing a process (or also an occurrence between processes from different pools). Events are often used reciprocally in comprehensively modeled processes, i.e., a receive event exists for each send event.

Receiving intermediate events also exist in a "*boundary*" form. These events are "pinned" to tasks (i.e., are graphically attached to the (lower) boundary of the task) and indicate that it is possible to react on the respective event during the execution of the task. The reaction is specified by a sequence flow originating from the attached event, which leads to the respective tasks to be performed. The boundary intermediate events in general (with some exceptions) again exist in an interrupting and a non-interrupting form. The interrupting form stops the execution of the task marked in this way and continues the sequence flow exclusively via the attached event. The non-interrupting form allows the further execution of the task marked in this way, and the sequence flow originating from the event is triggered in parallel.

The triggers that lead to the occurrence of boundary events can come from outside the tasks (e.g., incoming messages from other pools) or also from within the task, provided that these triggers are detailed by a subprocess. For example, an error in the execution of a subprocess can lead to activities in the main process via an interrupting error boundary event (such as documenting the error and escalating it to superiors).

3.5.12 The Link Event

For more complex or extensive processes, tracking sequence flows through the diagram can sometimes be difficult. Sequence flows crossing each other or sequence flows with many changes of direction are difficult to read and are detrimental to comprehensibility and clarity.

In such cases, the *link event* can be used (cf. Fig. 3.40). In contrast to the other events, it semantically does not represent a real event but merely serves as a connector between two sequence flows that are far apart. The coupling is carried out via the designation of the sending and the receiving event. There must always

Fig. 3.40 Usage of the link event in BPMN process diagrams

be a 1:1 assignment (implicit parallelization by one triggering and several receiving link events of the same name is therefore not permitted).

Link events should only be used in cases that cannot be resolved in any other way in order to increase clarity, since the effort involved in searching for related link events can even exceed the tracking of complex sequence flows (as long as there is no tool support for jumping to or visually marking related events). Choosing an alternative arrangement of activities or lanes is usually the better choice.

3.5.13 Use of Signals

In BPMN, messages can only be used for communication between pools. In addition, message-based communication always has exactly two endpoints, so it can only connect exactly one sender to exactly one receiver at a time. If information is to be made available globally within a collaborative process and this is to happen independently of pool boundaries, signals can be used. Signals can be triggered in a process (as intermediate or end events) and are then available both within the pool and in all other pools of the same collaboration.

Signals can be used, for instance, to inform all pools of a collaboration about the termination of one of the represented processes. This means that all other processes that are still running can complete their processes cleanly, and there are no dangling processes left that can no longer be completed, e.g., because an expected incoming message no longer arrives due to an aborted process of a communication partner.

3.5.14 Handling of Exceptions and Interruptions

Activities, i.e., tasks and subprocesses, can be aborted or interrupted by certain events. This is indicated by event symbols attached to the respective task. Two solid outer circular lines in the event element indicate that the task is interrupted by the event; two dashed circular lines indicate that the task is not interrupted but can be continued while simultaneously reacting on the exception that occurred. In the example in Fig. 3.41, we react on a deadline, i.e., we model that the execution of the task must not take longer than a certain time span (on the left) or requires some reaction if it lasts longer than a certain time span (on the right). In either case, the model must contain information on what has to happen when task execution takes longer than anticipated. This information is modeled as a sequence flow emanating from the attached boundary event. Reactions to unforeseen triggers, such as errors or escalations, can also be modeled and displayed in the same way using the respective event type.

3.5.14.1 Example: Non-interrupting Timer Events

Figure 3.42 shows a subprocess that includes the activities of processing an order in a fast food restaurant, which should not take longer than 5 minutes. If the processing of the order takes longer than 5 minutes, the customer should receive their money

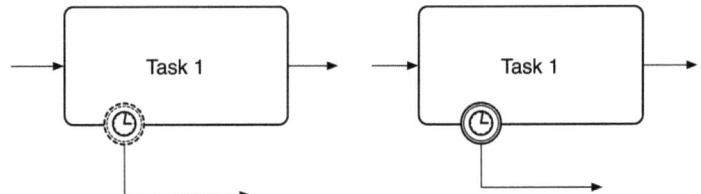

Fig. 3.41 Non-interrupting (left) and interrupting (right) boundary (timer) events

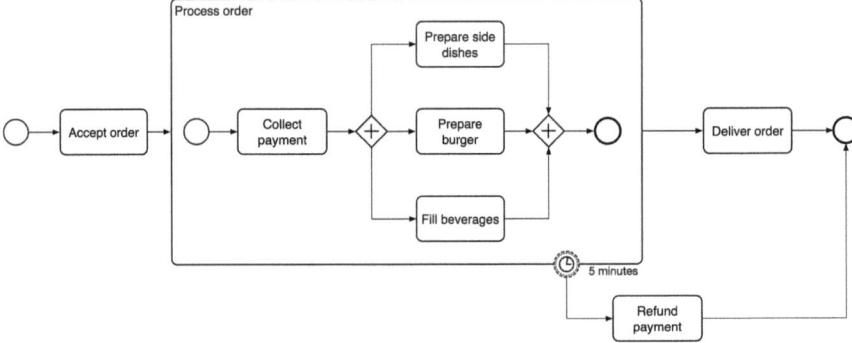

Fig. 3.42 Example for use of a non-interrupting timer event

back. The order should still be completely processed. If we had used an interrupting boundary event here, the customer would only get their money back, but not their order.

3.5.15 Different Ways of Terminating Processes

Sequence flows in a process are usually concluded with an end event. Such end events, however, only terminate the execution of the respective sequence flow. If other sequence flows are active in parallel (e.g., because they were opened by a parallel or inclusive gateway or because they were triggered by boundary events), their execution will continue to be carried out. There are several ways to terminate a (sub)process completely and immediately (i.e., terminate execution in all branches).

3.5.15.1 The Terminate Event

The terminate event aborts all active branches of a process within a pool immediately. Processes in other pools are not affected and should therefore be informed of the termination by sending a signal before the termination, if necessary (e.g., if there is a risk of waiting for further input from an already terminated process instance).

3.5.15.2 The Error Event and the Escalation Event

The error event semantically indicates the occurrence of an unforeseen error in process execution and is usually used for subprocesses. It immediately terminates the execution of the whole subprocess. The reason for the error can be given to the event as a parameter. Receiving error events can be attached to the subprocess as a boundary event for the enclosing task element to react to these errors in the superordinate process and trigger corresponding activities. Attached error events are always interrupting, i.e., they terminate the execution of the subprocess (including all active sequence flows in branches in which no error occurred). As a "weaker" variant, the "escalation event" can also be used in an identical way. The escalation event also is available in a non-interrupting form and thus allows the continuation of the execution of the subprocess in which the problem occurred.

If the effects of activities already performed have to be reversed when subprocesses are terminated, the transaction handling mechanism and constructs provided in BPMN can be used. They are described in the next section.

3.5.16 Transactions

BPMN also offers the option of representing transactions in a process. A transaction is a set of tasks that is to be executed as a whole, either completely or not at all. In particular, if a task fails, the effects of other already completed tasks need to be reversed. BPMN introduces the concept of transactional subprocesses in combination with compensation events and tasks. Compensation tasks roll back the effects of process steps that have already been executed by means of countermeasures, which are initiated in a further process step.

In a transaction subprocess (characterized in BPMN by a double border of the enclosing task element), each task is assigned a compensation task via a boundary compensation intermediate event (indicated by a "rewind" symbol). If the transaction is aborted or should explicitly be undone retroactively, the respective compensation task is executed for each task that has already been successfully completed. The abort end event (marked by an "X") can be used to abort a transaction while it is still being carried out. As an end event in a transaction subprocess, it causes its immediate termination and triggers the compensation tasks. When attached to the transaction task as a receiving intermediate boundary event, it determines the further course of the process after the transaction is terminated. As a result of the concept of compensation, transactions can also be rolled back after they have been successfully completed. Outside the transaction, a sending intermediate compensation event can be used to retrospectively trigger the compensation tasks contained in the referenced transaction.

Figure 3.43 illustrates these concepts using a travel booking process.

A travel booking consists of a flight booking and a hotel booking that can potentially be done in parallel. If one of the bookings is not possible, the other booking must be canceled if it has already been made. An error in one of

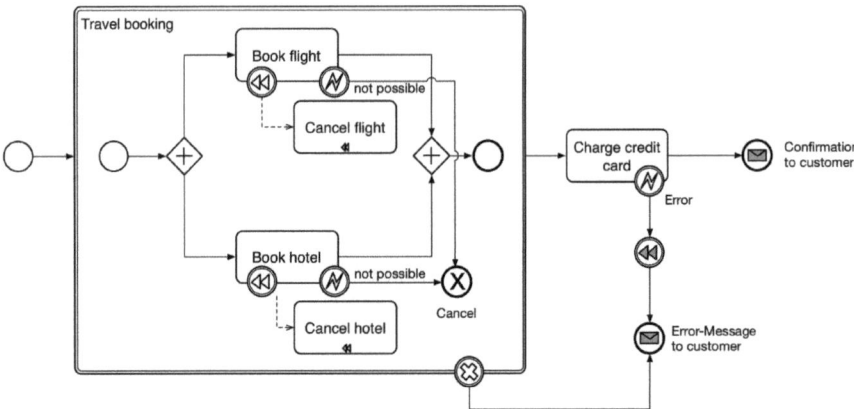

Fig. 3.43 Example for transaction subprocesses and compensation events

the bookings leads to the transaction being canceled (triggering the termination event) and leads to sending an error message to the customer. Outside the actual transaction, an error in charging the credit card leads to cancellation of the entire booking by triggering the compensation tasks retrospectively.

3.5.17 Event-Triggered Subprocesses

Event-triggered subprocesses are an alternative to boundary events when handling non-standard incidents that might occur in (sub)processes. While boundary events attached to subprocesses lead to the reaction to such incidents in the superordinate process, strictly local reactions (i.e., reactions that do not have any implications for the overall process) can be kept in the context of the subprocess by using event-driven subprocesses.

Figure 3.44 shows an example of a timer-controlled non-interrupting subprocess. It picks up on the scenario already used above to demonstrate non-interrupting boundary events and shows the process of preparing an order in a fast food restaurant.

Event-triggered subprocesses can be started with the same types of events that are available as boundary events, both in their interrupting and non-interrupting versions. Semantically, as already mentioned above, they differ only in the way the incident triggering the event is handled—locally within the subprocess or externally within the superordinate process. Depending on the process, one or the other variant can lead to a more meaningful and/or comprehensible form of representation.

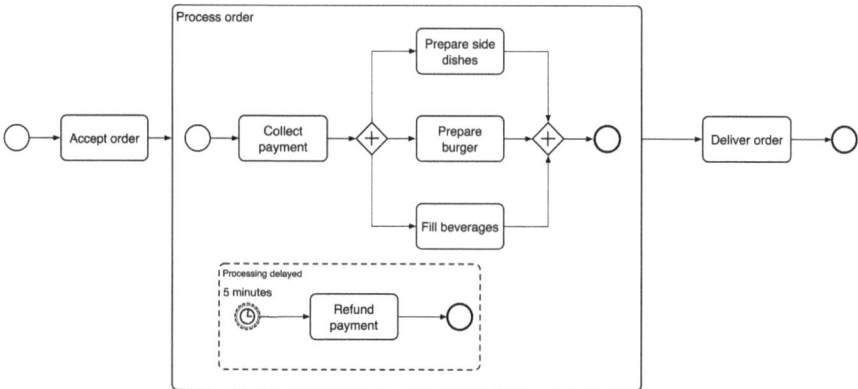

Fig. 3.44 Example for non-interrupting event-triggered subprocesses

3.5.18 Choreography Diagrams

The ability to explicitly model the interplay of actors in a collaborative process has been introduced in BPMN 2.0 in the form of choreography diagrams. A choreography depicts the process of exchanging messages between different actors. It thus provides a different view on collaboration, focusing on the sequence of the transmitted messages independently of the processes of the individual actors.

Although a representation of communication is possible in BPMN process diagrams by means of collapsed pools and the messages exchanged, the exact sequence, conditional message flows, or loops cannot be represented in this way. For instance, the example of an application process used to demonstrate the use of so-called *collapsed pools* as shown in Fig. 3.35 does not include information on whether the invitation message and the rejection message are mutually exclusive or can occur in parallel. This can be visualized with a choreography diagram.

Figure 3.45 shows the choreography representation of the application process shown above as a collaboration process. Here, the process of message exchange is the focus of representation. Choreography tasks represent the exchange of one or more messages between two or more partners. In their simplest case, they correspond to sending a single message from one partner to another.

Each choreography task is triggered by one of the partners involved by sending the first message. This triggering partner is entered in a box with a light-colored background at the upper or lower edge of the choreography activity. The names of the other party or parties involved are entered into boxes with darker backgrounds on the other side of the task. Which partner is entered at the top and at the bottom is at the discretion of the modeler. Usually, if there are several choreography tasks between the same partners, the arrangement will remain identical to allow for better comprehensibility. If corresponding collaboration diagrams are modeled, it is recommended to use the vertical arrangement of the pools as a basis for labeling the partners in the choreography tasks.

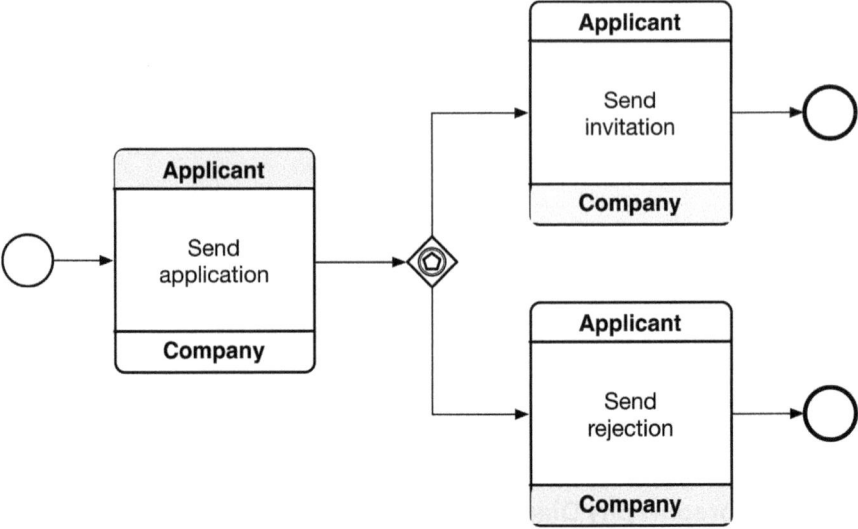

Fig. 3.45 Example of a BPMN choreography diagram

Choreography activities with more than two partners do not occur in the example shown above. In case more than two partners would be involved, several partner fields can be added at the top or bottom. However, only one field can have a light-colored background, since only one of the partners initiates message exchange with an initial message.

A sequence flow is defined in the choreography diagram between the chore-ography tasks. Modeling the sequence flow in choreography diagrams essentially corresponds to the sequence flow modeling of ordinary BPMN processes. However, certain elements of process modeling do not make sense in connection with choreography modeling and are therefore not permitted. For example, there are no message events within a sequence flow, since the message exchange is, by definition, part of the choreography tasks. Accordingly, in the diagram above, event-based gateways are not followed by events, but rather by choreography tasks. The path is selected for which the associated choreography task is first started by the respective triggering message.

If one wants to know which messages are exchanged in each choreography task, these can be added to the diagram in the form of letter symbols, which are linked to the respective partner sending the message. The letters are color-coded in the same way as partner fields. A letter symbol with a light-colored background represents the message with which a choreography task is triggered. The letter symbols of the other messages are displayed with darker backgrounds.

3.5.19 Verdict

In recent years, BPMN has advanced to be the standard choice for modeling business processes in industrial practice, and it is supported by or part of many commercially available software tools in the context of process digitalization.

Its comprehensive set of language elements makes it suitable for many application areas, from documentation to the automation-supported execution of business processes in organizations. The extensive vocabulary can at the same time be seen as a shortcoming of BPMN due to the increased complexity of the notation. In particular, the large number of event types with semantics that are sometimes hard to distinguish leads to increased effort when learning the language.

Potential issues of comprehensibility of the models when using the full set of notation elements are usually countered by using a reduced set of elements in suitable cases. For the descriptive documentation of business processes, it is usually not necessary to use the complete set of events and more complex task types. Only when a process model is to be validated or executed, for example by simulation, is it necessary to enrich the models with information on nonstandard cases or exceptions. In such cases, the simpler models can be used as a basis for supplementation.

BPMN is one of the few modeling languages that explicitly deal with modeling the communication between participating actors in a process.

However, BPMN implicitly assumes that within a pool (i.e., between lanes) it is not necessary to explicitly represent communication between actors, because they all have access to the same information infrastructure. Message flows are only modeled between different pools. They are used during execution to describe the mapping of the data structures used in the source pool to those of the target pool. A message flow, therefore, essentially corresponds to a data transfer from one information system to another and therefore always represents a communication process with exactly one sender and exactly one recipient—several recipients cannot be addressed with a single message. While this mechanism can also be used to represent nontechnical communication, its expressiveness is limited. In particular, communication between two or more actors without clearly definable messages can only be modeled in nonstandard-compliant and ambiguous ways. This limitation is owed to the claim of the executability of the created processes and also exists in other communication-oriented approaches.

Theoretically, the additional BPMN diagram types (choreography and collaboration) should supplement and alleviate the shortcomings and limitations of the BPDs, but they have the drawback of having no formal mechanism for interlinking them or making one diagram type formally dependent on the other.

In addition, BPMN focuses on processes with a fully specifiable control flow. It reaches its limits when process parts are strongly case-specific and cannot be described in detail in advance. In recent years, different approaches have emerged for such processes, which either adopt a declarative modeling approach for representing the execution conditions of process parts or focus on the communication processes between the actors involved. As an example for the latter category, we introduce Subject-oriented Business Process Modeling (S-BPM) in the next section.

3.6 PASS

3.6.1 The Paradigm of Subject Orientation

In contrast to the previously discussed modeling approaches, the following section introduces not only another workflow language. The Parallel Activity Specification Schema (PASS) has a completely different foundation. Where all(!) of the previous languages follow a procedural (or input-task-output) paradigm, PASS has the modeling *paradigm of subject-orientation* as its foundation. Subject-oriented process modeling understands and describes business processes first and foremost from the point of view of communicating actors or active system components—the subjects.

When modeling according to the subject-oriented approach, the subjects are representatives for the people or technical components involved in a process and are the focus and starting point of representation. It essentially describes who communicates with whom in which form and how the individual actors react to received messages. This simple notion implies one of two fundamental concepts of the subject-oriented paradigm: first, and in contrast to the classical approaches, that the term "process" is understood as a system of interacting active entities rather than being just a simple sequence of activities. The second fundamental concept is that during modeling in a subject-oriented way, a modeler is required to explicitly differentiate between *active elements* (subjects), passive elements (objects), and activities (verbs)—at the same time showing SOs' origin in natural human languages.

Understanding these concepts about subject-orientation is important in order to see that, as stated before, using SO/PASS is not just employing *yet another workflow language*, but adopting a different way of thinking and conceptualizing processes. Due to this fact and based on experiences made with this approach, the authors of this work would advise and encourage the use of this approach for the modeling processes with the goal of digitalizing them.

As a side note: Next to the modeling paradigm (Subject-Orientation), and the according modeling language (PASS), the term *S-BPM* is often used in the same context, standing for *Subject-Oriented Business Process Management*, a BPM methodology that naturally makes heavy use of SO/PASS but conceptually goes beyond modeling. Concepts about S-BPM can be found in [4].

3.6.2 Fundamental Notation Elements of PASS

3.6.2.1 Subject Interaction Diagrams

As explained, when modeling according to the subject-oriented approach with PASS, the subjects—abstract representations for active elements involved in a

Fig. 3.46 Notation elements of PASS Subject Interaction Diagrams (SID)

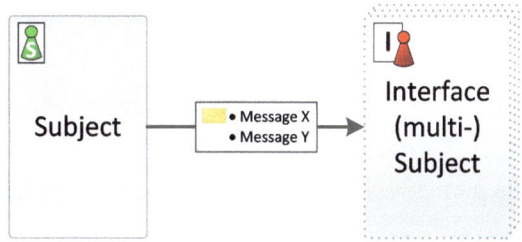

process—are at the center of attention. The modeling of a process essentially takes place in two stages with an increasing level of detail. In every PASS process model, first, a *(Subject) Interaction Diagram (SID)* is created, in which the subjects and their message exchange are described. In a following stage, the behavior of each subject is described in a separate *(Subject) Behavior Diagram (SBD)* that can be created for each subject in an SID and that is also formally dependent on its corresponding SID.

A subject is an active entity, but does not necessarily have to be a human actor. Technical systems or system components can also be subjects, as long as they play an active role in the process. Subjects must always be described abstractly, i.e., not for specific persons or machines, but on the basis of the necessary tasks to be fulfilled in the process (e.g., "application examiner" and not "Mr. Miller"). *Messages* are exchanged between the subjects. An SID only defines which messages exist and who *can* send or receive them. The order of the messages is not formally defined here.

The formal notion elements of SIDs are shown in Fig. 3.46. This includes the *Interface Subject* variant. The difference between the two subject types is that for Interface Subjects, no Subject Behavior Diagrams (see next section) are created in this model. Rather, they are left out and function as a kind of black box. A modeler can choose an interfaces subject either because they do not know the behavior of a subject in a process, or because they don't deem the behavior interesting enough (e.g., a database system that simply sends a "response" message to every "inquiry message"), or because they want to describe the behavior in a different model, in which case this subject functions as the link or interface to the other model.[1]

The Interface Subject in Fig. 3.46 is also marked to be a *Multisubject*. Both subject types can be declared to be a *Multisubject*, expressing that this subject and its behavior could exist multiple times (there could be multiple instances of it) within one single process instance (e.g., if there are multiple applicants that send their applications to the same clerk).[2]

---

[1] This mechanism allows to link subprocesses as well as process on the same conceptual level.

[2] While seemingly trivial, the multisubject mechanism is one of the most powerful modeling feature of PASS allowing for a simple, intuitive, and directly visible yet formal specification of sub (subject) instances within a process. A feature that the previous languages either do not possess or have hidden in specific runtime concerns.

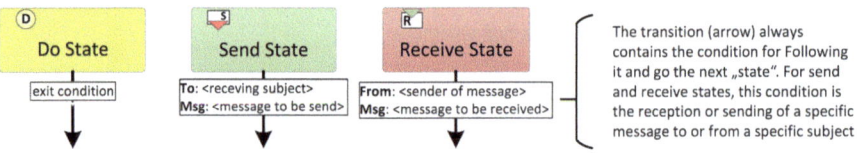

Fig. 3.47 Notation elements of PASS Subject Behavior Diagrams (SBD)

3.6.2.2 Subject Behavior Diagrams

For each standard subject, a *Subject Behavior Diagram (SBD)* describes the order in which it sends and receives messages or executes tasks. Figure 3.47 depicts the fundamental notation elements of an SBD. The individual *states* are related to each other by *transitions* (arrows) that describe the conditions of the transition from one state to the next. Each state or the idea of "being in a state," in principle, denotes that the Subject to which the SBD belongs is performing the according task. Their use depends on the type of condition used:

A *Do State* (old: Function State) simply describes what a subject is doing on its own. The possible outcomes of the activity of a Do State correspond to the outgoing connections (Do Transitions) that emanate from it. If the task can lead to different results, different subsequent states can be activated via different exit or *transition conditions* denoted on the transition arrow. This enables the representation of alternative behavior patterns.

In a *Send State*, a message is prepared and transmitted to a recipient. The subject remains in the state until the recipient is able to receive the message, and the message has actually been sent. Who the recipient of the message is and which message is transmitted is described at the outgoing connection of the send state (the transition/exit condition is that the message has actually been successfully transmitted).

The respective subject remains in a *Receive State* waiting until one of the messages that can be accepted in that state has arrived. To define which messages are to be awaited in any particular state, several outgoing *Receive Transitions* can be used to describe which message from which sender leads to which following state. In this way, it is also possible to react differently to the same message from different senders.

It is important to note that the SBDs are formally dependent and belong to an SID. An SBD can never exist alone; rather, an SID and multiple SBDs together form one process model.

3.6.2.3 Examples

In order to demonstrate the differences and similarities to the previously discussed modeling languages, we again make use of the examples already used above. In the first example, there is no communication.

The example in Fig. 3.48 shows a process with a single subject that performs a single task in which an application (about which we have no further information

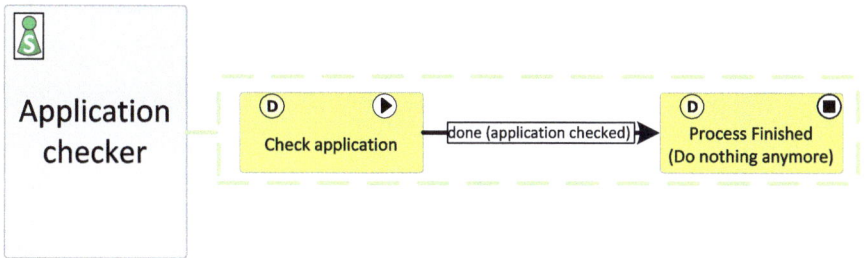

Fig. 3.48 Simple PASS process model with one subject and no interaction in the SID, and a two-state behavior diagram

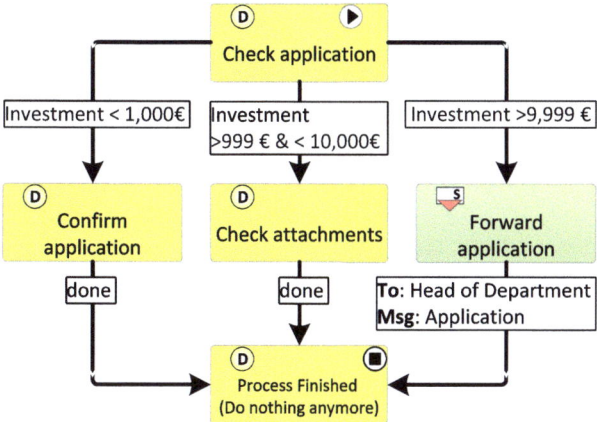

Fig. 3.49 PASS Subject Behavior Diagram with a multiple-outcome decision (SID not shown)

here) is processed. The process/behavior of the subject ends after the processing of the application has been completed. A behavior diagram must always have a *start state*, which in the example is marked by a little "Play icon" in the upper half of the shape. There must also be an *end state*, marked by a "stop icon." To fully describe the behavior of the subject, we need a transition that identifies under what conditions the state "Check application" can be left. Therefore, we insert a state "Done" here, which we mark as the final state and which does not contain any expected activities.

In Fig. 3.49, the process is extended by a decision with three possible results that are mutually exclusive, showing that all branches in SBDs follow an XOR logic. The application is checked, and the result of this examination allows a decision to be taken on further processing. In the case of an investment sum of EUR 10,000 or more, the application will be forwarded. We indicate this by a send state and specify at the outgoing connection who is to receive the request. For the process to be fully specified, a behavior diagram for the head of department would also have to be created at this point.

Fig. 3.50 PASS Subject
Behavior Diagram with
repeated execution of process
parts

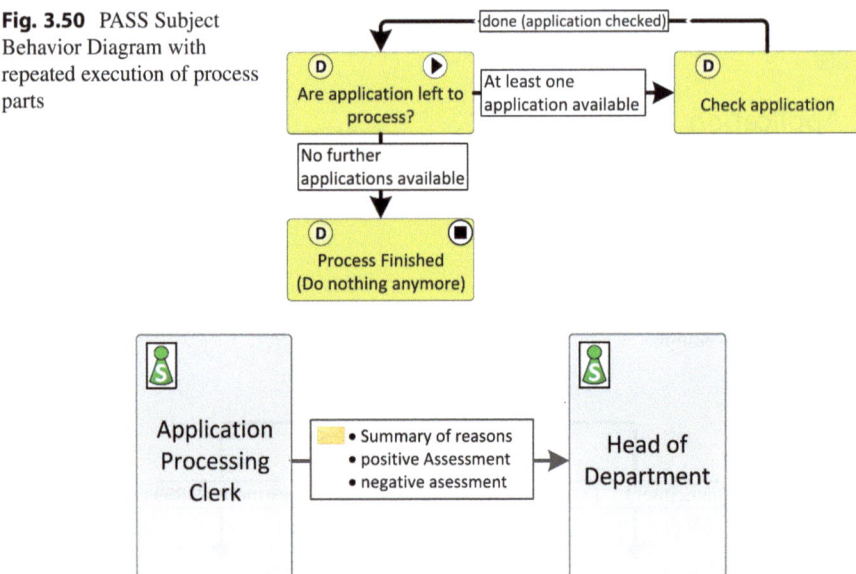

Fig. 3.51 Example of PASS Subject Interaction Diagram with multiple possible messages
exchanged between two subjects

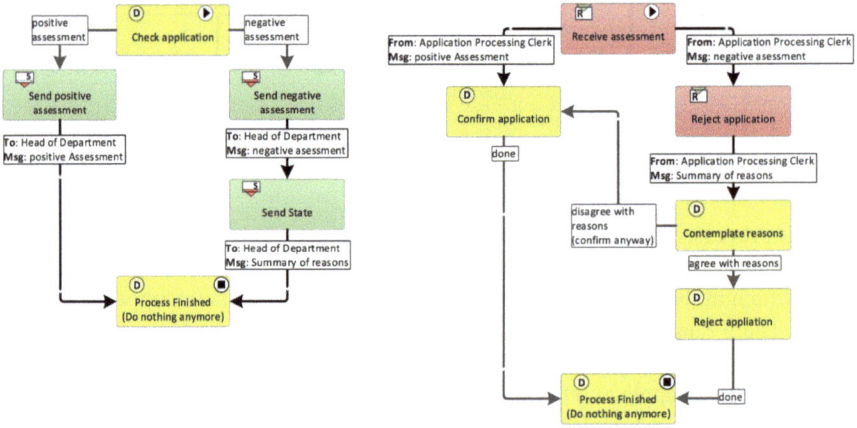

Fig. 3.52 The SBDs for the Subjects "Application Processing Clerk" (left) and "Head of
Department" (right) from Fig. 3.51

PASS also allows to define the repeated execution of parts of a process. For this
purpose, a decision to state is used that either allows going to an end state and
finishing the process or going to a state that is the part to be repeated (cf. Fig. 3.50).

The example in Fig. 3.51 shows the SID of an application process with two
subjects, a "Clerk" and a "Head of Department." Figure 3.52 shows the behavior

diagrams for both. The positive or negative assessment of an application is modeled with two different messages, leading to two different behavior branches upon their reception. The summary of reasons, giving details of the assessment, is only sent in the case of a negative assessment. If the application is confirmed, the "Summary of reasons" message is not transmitted, so we can assume that no further justification will be given in this case. Furthermore, the SBD of the Head of Department does allow them to override the original verdict and confirm the application anyway.

3.6.3   Advanced PASS Modeling

The focus of PASS on representing communication processes is reflected in a more comprehensive and flexible description of communication than in all the modeling languages considered before. In particular, PASS features several additional mechanisms that allow the representation of more complex communication scenarios: Next to the already introduced concept of multisubjects, this includes the concept of so-called *input pools* and their *restrictions*, the detailed structural description of the data structures that are being exchanged, as well as the option to include specialized behaviors, to model, e.g., reusable *Macros* or the *Guard* mechanism that allows exception handling.

3.6.3.1 Input Pools
During the hypothetical execution of a PASS process model, each subject is assumed to have an *Input Pool*. This is a kind of mailbox in which incoming messages are stored until they are required, as described in the behavior diagram.

However, in contrast to a simple mailbox, an input pool is configurable via so-called *Input Pool Restrictions*. Restrictions on the size of the input pool can be set in general for the overall number of messages, but also specific for any particular message type, sending subject, or a combination of both.

The default case is that if the input pool is not able to accept a message according to its configuration, the incoming message is *blocked* and the sender must remain in the send state until the message can be delivered. This simple approach also allows defining *synchronous* communication, simply by reducing the capacity of the input pool for a particular message to 0; in that case, the sender must always wait until the recipient is ready to receive the message directly in a corresponding receive state. In contrast, if the input pool is not restricted in that manner, which is the default case, the sender never has to wait until the receiver is in the state in which it can accept the message. This is called *asynchronous* communication (BPMN only allows the representation of this type of communication). The Input pool concept also assumes that messages can be received in any order. The messages do not have to be processed in the order they arrive but can be processed according to the recipient's requirements.

Next to a size limit and a default behavior of simply blocking an incoming message. Input Pool Restrictions allow you to configure an input pool to react differently should a size limit be reached. The alternatives are to receive the incoming message, but simply delete it directly after reception. Alternatively, to make room in the input pool for the new message, either the oldest or the newest message of the same type already in the input pool could be deleted.

3.6.3.2 Business Object Types

Business objects represent data that is required for executing the tasks in a business process. Business objects are passive, i.e., they do not initiate any interactions or trigger any actions. Business objects are processed and modified by subjects and can be assigned to messages in order to specify the transmission of data.

There is no graphical equivalent for business objects in the notation of the modeling language itself. However, some editors provide graphical means to model their structure. But in any case, saving the structural definitions can be done using existing technologies and languages that allow the definition of data types, e.g., XML-Schema or RDFS/OWL, etc. Proprietary solutions that depend on vendor definitions of the execution environments are also possible.

In general, BOs are described in a kind of tabular form. The basic structure of business objects consists of a type identifier/class name and data elements that in turn can either be primitives like strings or integer numbers, but also refer to more complex and/or nested data structure type definitions, e.g., lists. Usually, they correspond closely to the PASS process models, the accompanying. Examples are business trip requests, orders, delivery notes, invoices, etc.

Figure 3.53 shows an example of a "business trip request"-data type. This consists, among other things, of the substructure "Data on requester (employee)" with the data elements for last name, first name, and personnel number, and the structure "Data on business trip" with the data elements for start, end, and purpose of the trip.

3.6.3.3 Additional Subject Behaviors

In simple PASS, each subject can have one behavior. However, there are three types of specialized behaviors that can be added to the *base behavior* of a subject, each with its own specialized purpose: the Macro, Guard, and Extension Behaviors.

Macro Behaviors: PASS Subprocesses

One staple in the previous languages was the possibility to define so-called subprocesses, further detailed specifications that can be hidden in order to reduce the perceived complexity of a process model. This mechanism exists in PASS as well via the Macro-Mechanism. The difference is that after a *Macro Behavior* has been modeled, it can be called in any state of the base behavior. This could be done multiple times. Figure 3.55 shows on the left side a Macro Behavior that ends with a *Return-to-Origin-State*. It is indicated that this Macro is being called in the "Fill-out-bt-request" state of the base behavior and details that activity. The visualization here shows all within one Figure; however, normally Macro Behaviors are their own SBD and modeled separately.

Data structure	Meaning	Data type	Can/must	Value range/Default
Data of requester				
Name	Last name	Character	M	
First name	First name	Character	M	
Personnel number	...	Integer	M	
Organizational unit	...		C	
Pay group	...		C	
Data of trip				
Start trip	...	Date	M	Whitin 1 year from current date/ current date
End trip	...	Date	M	Start trip plus 1 year/ start trip
International trip	...	Boolean?	C	y/n; n
Travel destination (city7country)	...	Character	M	...
Reason for traveling	...	Character	M	...
Desired advance money	...	Integer	C	...
Data of approval				
Approval	Approval comment	Boolean?	M	y/n; n
Cost center	...	Integer	M	...
Desired advance money	...	Integer	C	...

Fig. 3.53 Example of business object type definition (business trip request)

Guard Behaviors: Exception Handling

Exception handling is characterized by the fact that it can occur in a process in many behavior states of subjects. The receipt of certain messages, e.g., to abort the process, always results in the same processing pattern. This pattern would have to be modeled for each state in which it is relevant. Normally, exception handling causes high modeling effort and leads to complex process models, because from each affected state, a corresponding transition has to be specified.

However, in PASS this can be modeled using the *Guard Behavior* mechanism. This allows to model a second behavior for a subject that always starts with a so-called *guard receive state*. Any message defined to be received in that state becomes a kind of interrupt message, forcing the subject to "jump" from any current activity to this specialized behavior. Normally, this Guard Behavior is active in general. However, the guard receive can also be further specified to only be active for specific states of the guarded base behavior.

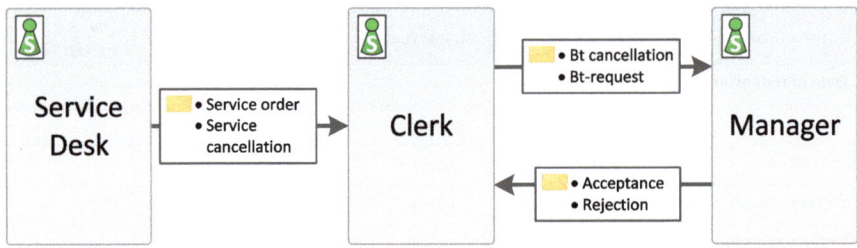

Fig. 3.54 SID of a process where an ordered service can be canceled up to the point where it could be fulfilled

To illustrate the compact description of exception handling in PASS, we use a service management process with the subject "service desk" (cf. Figs. 3.54 and 3.55). In its base behavior (grayed out in Fig. 3.55), this subject identifies a need for a business trip in the context of processing a customer order—an employee needs to visit the customer to provide a service locally. The subject "service desk" passes on a service order to an employee. Hence, the employee issues a business trip request.

In principle, the service order may be canceled at any stage during processing up to its completion whenever the customer decides to send the appropriate cancellation message. The handling of what happens if the cancellation message should arrive is described in the specialized Guard Behavior on the right side of Fig. 3.55. This Guard Behavior is limited to being triggerable only in three specific states of the base behavior.

A Guard Behavior does not necessarily have to be brought to an end; it can also return to a specified state in the base behavior or to the point where the subject was when the interrupt was triggered, with a return-to-origin, like a Macro Behavior. Exception handling behavior in a subject may vary, depending on which state or by what type of message (cancellation, temporary stopping of the process, etc.) it is triggered.

Extension Behavior: Modifying Long-Running Process Model
In an ideal world, processes are modeled once, and the model forms the base of a digitalization, possibly instantiated directly within a workflow engine. If requirements change or unforeseen circumstances occur in reality that are not captured in a process model, normally the model would be updated, and any new process instance would then be created according to the new model. However, there are certain types of processes that have long-running instances, e.g., a project management process spanning the duration of a three-year project. Simply shutting process instances down and creating a new one is rarely an option. But there might be other situations where exceptions occur in currently running operations that require updating a model to handle the unforeseen circumstances without restarting a process instance.

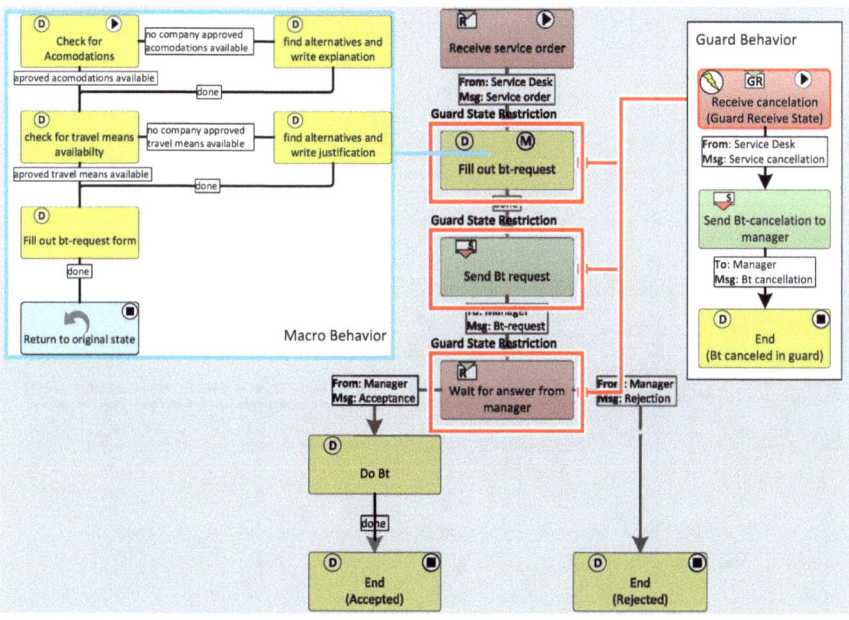

Fig. 3.55 Base behavior of subject "Clerk" in the background with Macro Behavior (left) and Guard Behavior for exception handling (right)

In that case, an extension behavior can be created that describes handling options for the new situation without modification to the original model and inserted into the running instance.

In the example case shown in Fig. 3.56, it is assumed that, due to new regulations, the employee is required, in addition to simply informing the manager, to also make sure that all cancellable reservations are reversed and expenses that will occur even if the trip is canceled will be shown explicitly. Typically, this kind of request process may be initiated months in advance, before action is taken. With a behavior extension that is being injected into all running instances of that process, the new requirements could be upheld in all cases, even if originally created under an old model.

3.6.4 Verdict

As mentioned, in contrast to the other modeling languages discussed so far, a PASS (business) process model is not a single diagram. Rather, separate behavior diagrams are created for subjects of a Subject Interaction Diagram and a formally dependent on it. The subjects are linked by describing their message exchange. PASS therefore works with a *loose (yet formal) coupling* of process parts and an easier adaptation

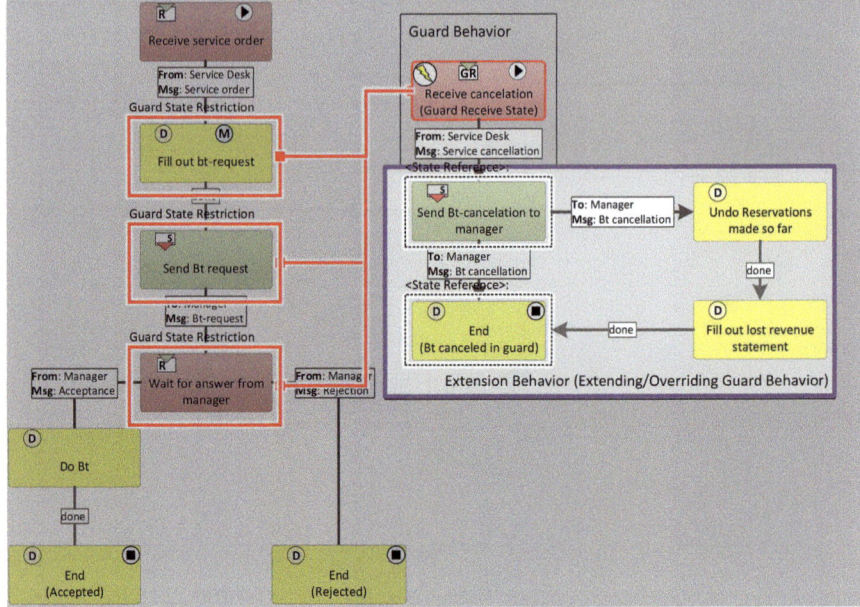

Fig. 3.56 Example for PASS Extension Behavior extending the Guard Behavior of Fig. 3.55

of the behavior of a subject, as long as its communication interface, i.e., the set of received and sent messages and their sequence, remains unchanged.

The use of state diagrams to describe the behavior of a subject also constitutes a fundamental difference from other languages. A state diagram—as already indicated by its name—describes the state of a system (here: a subject—this can be a human as well as a machine) and the events that lead to a state transition. A subject can only be in exactly one state at any one time—it is therefore by definition not able to execute process steps in parallel. Rather, the parallelity in the name of PASS is realized by the assumption that all subjects work in parallel and independently of each other. This requires a different approach to understanding and modeling processes, since constructs such as AND connectors (in EPCs), split/joins (in activity diagrams), or parallel gateways (in BPMN) are not available. At the same time, this modeling approach leads to simpler, more compact models and, in contrast to BPMN, a significantly reduced range of language constructs, which contributes to the comprehensibility of the models.

3.7   Comparison

The modeling languages considered here have different expressive power and, due to their historical development, have different focal points in their approach to representing business processes. The following section attempts to summarize these differences again systematically using the process definition presented in the former chapter and thus to compare the languages with respect to their expressiveness. We use the semantics of the presented modeling elements as a starting point.

The point of reference for the following considerations is the process definition from the last chapter, which we will reiterate here for simplicity's sake:

- Process strategy: A process has:
  - a defined start and input (start event),
  - and has a defined end with a result,
  - that contributes to the satisfaction of a customer's needs (and thus to the creation of value)
- (classical) Process logic: A process:
  - is the sum of linked activities (tasks),
  - which, after the start event, are used by actors
  - in logical and chronological order
  - for processing a business object in order to
  - generates the desired result.
- Process realization: A process is realized
  - with people and/or machines, that take over the tasks of the respective actor, and carry these tasks out
  - with tools (equipment, information, application programs, etc.).

On the basis of this definition, the concepts that should be representable in a process model in order to be able to model processes comprehensively (according to this definition) can be identified. Table 3.1 shows these concepts. Concepts that occur more than once are only mentioned when they occur for the first time, such as "result." In the case of concepts which are described in different degrees of detail, only the more concrete concepts are considered—e.g., "linked activities" as a more general formulation of "logical and chronological order."

If one now assigns the modeling elements of the languages considered to these concepts, Table 3.2 results.

The conceptual coverage obviously varies across languages. The table also shows that not all languages address all concepts to the same extent or with the same level of expressiveness. The allocation of the modeling elements to the concepts provides a first starting point for estimating the expressiveness of the respective languages.

In this overview, the different approaches and their illustration of the logical and chronological connections are only partially recognizable. However, in that aspect, the languages differ considerably: flowcharts do not offer the possibility of representing parallel processes, EPCs only allow for strong coupling of parallel activity branches by linking them within a process by means of AND or OR operators. UML activity diagrams and BPMN offer the same mechanisms (under different names) but also allow for loose coupling of processes or process parts by means of signals (for activity diagrams) or message flows (for BPMN). Especially, the latter mechanism allows a detailed description of communication processes of basically independent process parts. Flexibility, however, is restricted by the

Table 3.1 Table of concepts included in process definition

Definition model	Concept
1a	Beginning
	Input
1b	End
	Result
1c	customers necessity
2a	Acitivities / tasks
2b	start event
	Doer
2c	logical order
	chronological order
2d	Premise
3a	Human
	Machine
3b	Material resources
	Information
	Application program
	General aids

necessary unique assignment of sender and receiver for each message. PASS offers a similar communication mechanism, but is much more flexible, especially due to the subject-oriented concept of having only loosely coupled components. In PASS, a description of process parts running in parallel is only possible by distributing them to different subjects—within a subject, only one functional state can be active at a time, i.e., only alternative branches in the behavior of a subject can be represented.

In general, BPMN offers the greatest flexibility in the choice of how to represent a process. Due to the large number of modeling elements, at least theoretically, even complex real-world phenomena can be represented in a compact way. This, however, leads to higher demands on language comprehension for the model users. Activity diagrams in PASS, which are based on a compact set of modeling elements, follow a different approach here. Their approach leads to larger models in complex contexts, which in turn places higher demands on the model users with regard to their understanding of the model. However, PASS reduces the immediately visible complexity of models by distributing a process over different subjects, where not all parts have to be perceived and considered at the same time. While this leads to

Table 3.2 Concept allocation to the notation elements in different modeling languages

Definition part	Concept	Flowchart	eEPK	UML activity diagram	BPMN	S-BPM
1a	Beginning	Termination element	Event	Starting node	Start event	Starting state
	Input	-	Information object	Data object / received signal	Data object, message	Business object, message
1b	End	Termination element	Event	End node	End event	End state
	Result	-	Information object	Signal	Data object, message	Business object, message
1c	customers necessity	-	-	-	-	-
2a	Activities / tasks	Operation	Function	Action	Tasks (different types)	Functional status
2b	Start event	Only unspecific	Specifically named event	Only unspecific, perhaps by received signal	Start event (message, timer, regulate	Starting state, usually via the receipt of a message
	Actor	-	Organisational unit	Partition	Pool, Lane	Subject
2c	Logical order / Chronological order	Flow arrow & decision	Flow arrow & Connectors for alternative and parallel processes, data flow	Flow arrow, decision, Split / Join	Sequence flow, alternate and parallel gateways, message flow, exception handling, transactions, choreography	Messages between subjects, conditions for state transitions in subject behaviors
2d	Business object	-	Information object	Data object	Data object, message	Data object, message
3a	Human	-	Organisational unit	Partition	Pool, Lane, User task, manually task	Subject
	Machine	-	-	-	Service Task	Subject
3b	Material resources	-	-	-	-	-
	Information	-	Information object	Data object	Data object, message, data storage	Business object, message
	Application program	-	Application system	-	Service-Task	Subject
	Gernal aids	-	-	-	-	-

partial models that can be more easily grasped, it in turn places higher demands on modeling users and cannot be done easily without supporting modeling software that keeps the formal integrity over all parts.

When selecting a modeling language that is suitable for a given task and target group, not only should the (business) process under consideration and the intended purpose of the model be considered. The known or assumed competencies of the modelers and especially the model users and the ease of their understanding also need to be taken into consideration. A fundamental distinction can be made between languages that focus on the flow of activity (such as flowcharts and EPCs) and those that focus on the actors in a process and their communication (such as PASS). BPMN and activity diagrams are basically suitable for both types of representation, whereby BPMN offers more expressive means for representing communication processes. The final selection of a modeling language after determining the fundamentally pursued representation approach (activity flow vs. communication flow) is ultimately dependent on the preferences of the modelers or model users.

However, as mentioned, if you want to consider only one for your process digitalization needs and are not bound by a specific software, the authors would advise embracing the subject-oriented paradigm with PASS, as a personal suggestion, due to finding it the most suitable for representing complex circumstance and the modeling challenges that come when needing to describe and design the complex social-technical systems that are the overall goal in digitalizing processes.

References

1. S. Oppl, Which concepts do inexperienced modelers use to model work?—An exploratory study, in *Proceedings of MKWI 2018* (2018)
2. B. Curtis, M.I. Kellner, J. Over, Process modeling. Commun. ACM **35**(9), 75–90 (1992)
3. N. Damij, Business process modelling using diagrammatic and tabular techniques. Bus. Process. Manag. J. **13**(1), 70–90 (2007)
4. A. Fleischmann, W. Schmidt, C. Stary, S. Obermeier, E. Börger, *Subject-Oriented Business Process Management* (Springer, Berlin, 2012)

Contemporary Aspects in Business Process Modeling/Management

4

The preceding chapters discussed concrete tools and methods for describing sequences of activities within a process. However, internal organizational and especially cross-organizational processes are becoming increasingly complex with the progression of digitalization. Added to this are a growing number of possible technologies, concepts, and approaches that may play a role in modern processes within digitalization.

This chapter addresses some current challenges associated with the digitalization of processes, explains them, and places them in the context of this book.

The nature of these challenges is quite diverse, ranging from the fundamental problem of adequately representing real, complex process systems to meet requirements, to the challenge and possibility of implementing and executing process models directly in a digital format, all the way to the inclusion of current technologies such as Artificial Intelligence (AI) or the Internet of Things (IoT)).

Ultimately, all of these challenges will primarily impact the people involved. In the end, it is the social component that often constitutes the real challenge.

4.1 Describing Complex Process Systems and System Architectures

An essential challenge of digitalization lies in the fact that real business processes are often complex and involve many aspects that interact and are interwoven. If one intends to derive IT systems from process models or describe their functions accurately, the modeling methodology must allow these circumstances to be represented logically and as comprehensibly as possible.

The following sections analyze how various process modeling languages support the construction of complex model systems, how well they are suited for structuring process systems, and to what extent digital workflows can be derived from these models.

© The Author(s) 2026
M. Elstermann et al., *Contextual Process Digitalization*,
https://doi.org/10.1007/978-3-032-06901-6_4

In practically every organization with more than one business process, individual processes are formally separated but interconnected and interdependent, either directly or indirectly. For example, a sales process may be followed by an order processing process, which in turn triggers delivery processes and invoicing.

To represent such process landscapes or process architectures and their behavior meaningfully, specification languages should include mechanisms that allow complex and interrelated circumstances to be presented in a structured and comprehensible manner.

It is essential to represent the "environment" or "neighborhood" of a process and to specify what connections and relationships exist between a process and its "neighbors."

In the aforementioned case of an order handling process, its connections to the sales process and the delivery process should be representable. These are not simply sequential activities within a single process but interactions between distinct process systems. It is particularly important to name details of these interactions that concern the exchange of data and the transfer or transition of control flow.

The following sections present various options for representing and structuring such complex process systems or process architectures using the different modeling languages introduced in Chap. 3.

4.1.1   Structuring Complex Processes with Flowcharts

The only way to represent more complex structures in flowcharts is to refer to other predefined processes. These predefined processes, in turn, represent other named processes that must be described in separate models.

Figure 4.1 shows such a construction. The process model on the left refers to the delivery process shown on the right.

The control flow jumps from the original process model to the other model.

Beyond this subprocess concept, however, there is no standardized way to formally represent process architectures that provide an overview of which processes exist, how they are related, or which process uses which other (sub-)process.

In terms of data, flowcharts assume that all process-relevant data is automatically available and updated at all times within every activity. As a result, process data

Fig. 4.1 Structuring a process system model with process reference in flowcharts

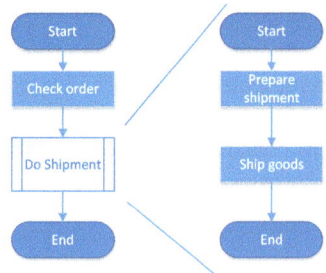

requirements or data exchange between individual processes are not considered explicitly due to conceptual limitations.

Because of these concepts, on the one hand, the process invocation mechanism and, on the other hand, implicit data sharing, flowchart process models are, when interconnected, always extremely tightly coupled (tight coupling).

This extreme tight coupling of models means that flowcharts are relatively unsuitable for representing situations in which processes are only loosely coupled or in which the flow of data plays an important role, particularly in processes that span organizational boundaries.

4.1.2   Structuring Complex Processes with Event-driven Process Chains (EPCs)

Similar to flowcharts, event-driven process chains (EPCs) use the option of referring to other processes/their models. The notation allows for ambiguity as to whether the "process reference" represents a subsequent process or a subprocess. Its symbol is described in Fig. 4.2.

The fundamental principle of this process reference is the same as in flowcharts and, for similar reasons, is insufficient to adequately represent complex process systems, especially when more than just this binary type of process relationship is to be depicted. Therefore, in the context of EPCs, there is also the value-added chain diagram (Value Chain Diagram—VCD), which theoretically allows the interaction or dependency of processes to be described.

Figure 4.3 describes the situation from Fig. 4.2, where the delivery process is triggered or invoked from the order management process. The graphical indication represents it as a triggered, subsequent process and not as a subprocess.

Fig. 4.2 Structuring a process system model with subprocess reference in EPCs

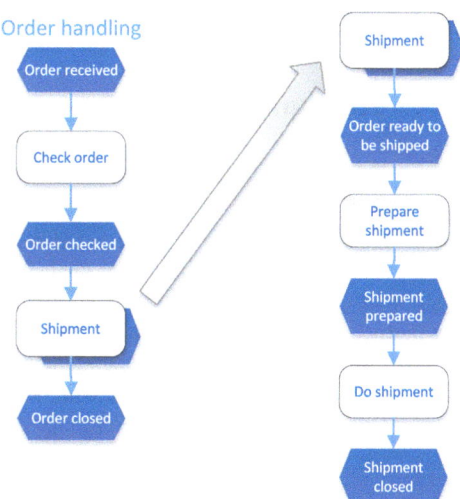

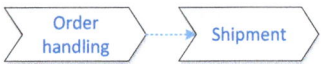

Fig. 4.3 Value chain diagram for the EPCs from Fig. 4.2–in the order management process, the delivery process is triggered

Fig. 4.4 Value chain diagram with process hierarchy

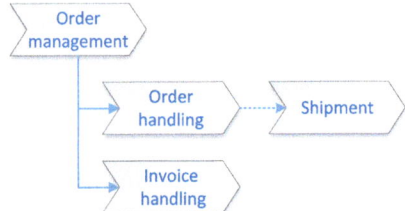

In addition to this "triggering" or following relationship, value chain diagrams also offer the possibility of denoting hierarchical relationships. This is shown in Fig. 4.4, in which the process system is described as the overarching process of order processing, which in turn consists of the subprocesses "order management," "delivery," and "invoicing."

4.1.3   Structuring Complex Processes with UML Activity Diagrams

UML activity diagrams do not offer specific notation to structurally represent the relationships of complex processes. It is not permitted to use or call an activity diagram within another activity diagram (no recursive calls). The only way to structurally link multiple processes is to connect their corresponding activity diagrams through the description of message exchanges. However, there is no dedicated symbol or higher-level diagram type to express such communication.

4.1.4   Structuring Complex Processes with BPMN

Among the various diagram types associated with BPMN, the collaboration or conversation diagram represents the highest level of abstraction. It was created to improve the comprehensibility of complex situations in which, for example, a process involves many participants, each represented by their own "pool," which may contain multiple swimlanes. Such diagrams, like the one in Fig. 4.5, show the "big picture" or an overview of the network of partners and how they communicate. However, there are no formal dependencies between such conversation diagrams and the actual process diagrams for which BPMN is primarily known, even if they belong to the same model complex and are thus conceptually related.

Fig. 4.5 Simple BPMN
collaboration or conversation
diagram

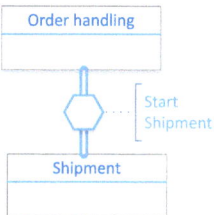

Figure 4.5 shows such a conversation diagram in which the "pools" for order management and the delivery process are represented in a compressed form and communicate with each other via the message "Execute Delivery."

Conversation diagrams represent the highest level of abstraction among all BPMN diagrams. Since it is not permitted to nest conversation diagrams, the rectangles depicted must logically be "pools," as described. Therefore, they cannot represent additional conversation diagrams on a lower abstraction level.

This leads to a rigid, two-level abstraction hierarchy consisting of the conversation diagram and the business process diagram. According to BPMN concepts, the higher-level conversation diagram formally depends on the lower-level business process diagram or merely summarizes it.

Below the business process diagram—or included within that diagram type— BPMN also includes the subprocess concept, as found in flowcharts and EPCs. However, it is subject to the same limitations described for those modeling types.

4.1.5   Structuring Complex Processes in PASS

A special role is played by the modeling methodology of the Parallel Activity Specification Schema (PASS), introduced in Chap. 3. In contrast to the other languages, PASS, based on [1], is not simply another set of symbols. Instead, it follows a fundamentally different modeling paradigm: Subject-Orientation, where the others follow a procedural or Input-task-output approach. As a result, PASS offers several additional mechanisms for representing processes in a structured and interconnected manner. This allows modelers to select and later adjust the level and granularity of abstraction according to their current requirements. The paradigm provides three separate dimensions of abstraction, each related to one of the base concepts that are distinguished in SO: subjects (active entities), objects (passive entities), and activities (verbs/tasks).

4.1.5.1 Abstraction via Activities in PASS
The dimensions of abstraction include the already known subprocess concept in the form of the Macro-Mechanism introduced in Sect. 3.6.3.3 (Fig. 4.6).

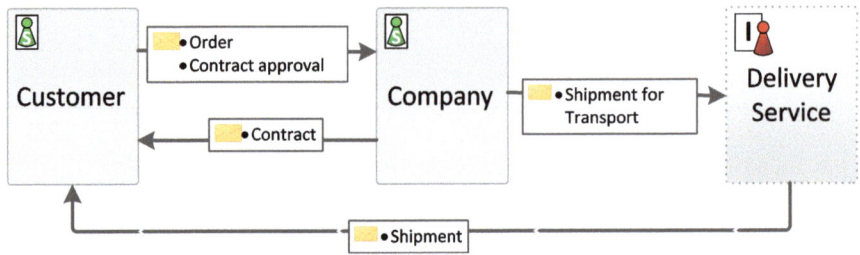

Fig. 4.6 PASS SID for the following examples

A macro is then a more detailed *"sub-behavior"*.[1] Like the other languages, this can be used to detail our activities with additional sub-activities further. This is shown in the Subject Behavior Diagram (SBD) in Fig. 4.7. The corresponding Subject Interaction Diagram (SID) is shown in Fig. 4.6.

4.1.5.2 Abstraction via Objects in PASS

The second *dimension of abstraction* in subject-orientation description is the ability to abstract over objects or messages. In subject-oriented models, messages, or rather message types, are essentially object-oriented classes that, according to the principles of object orientation, would be instantiated when the model is executed. If it is important for a modeler, subclasses can be defined for a more specific model. For example, in a business process model, a general message "contract" may exist, for which there are many more detailed variations (subclasses) such as "rental contract" or "purchase contract," which contain additional information.

One Direction of Abstraction

In object-oriented modeling/programming, the principle is that abstraction and thus dependency should occur in only one direction. This is visible in the inheritance hierarchy shown in Fig. 4.8. The subclasses all depend on and inherit from the superclass. Changes to the superclass affect all subclasses. The reverse is not true, and creating or modifying the superclass is independent of the subclasses. The formal dependency exists only in one direction. This principle is not mandatory but can be understood as a *best practice*, especially when it comes to the formal abstraction of digital systems.

This concept is also applied to subjects and entire process models in the following section. The previously discussed Macro-Mechanism in PASS also results in one-directional dependencies. However, this direction is reversed because the general

---

[1] Reminder: In a subject-oriented description, the understanding of the term *"process"* is much broader than in a classical representation where *"process"* is essentially equivalent to *"activity"*. In subject orientation, an activity may *"consist"* of "sub-activities," but an activity cannot logically consist of subjects, which in turn would constitute a subprocess.

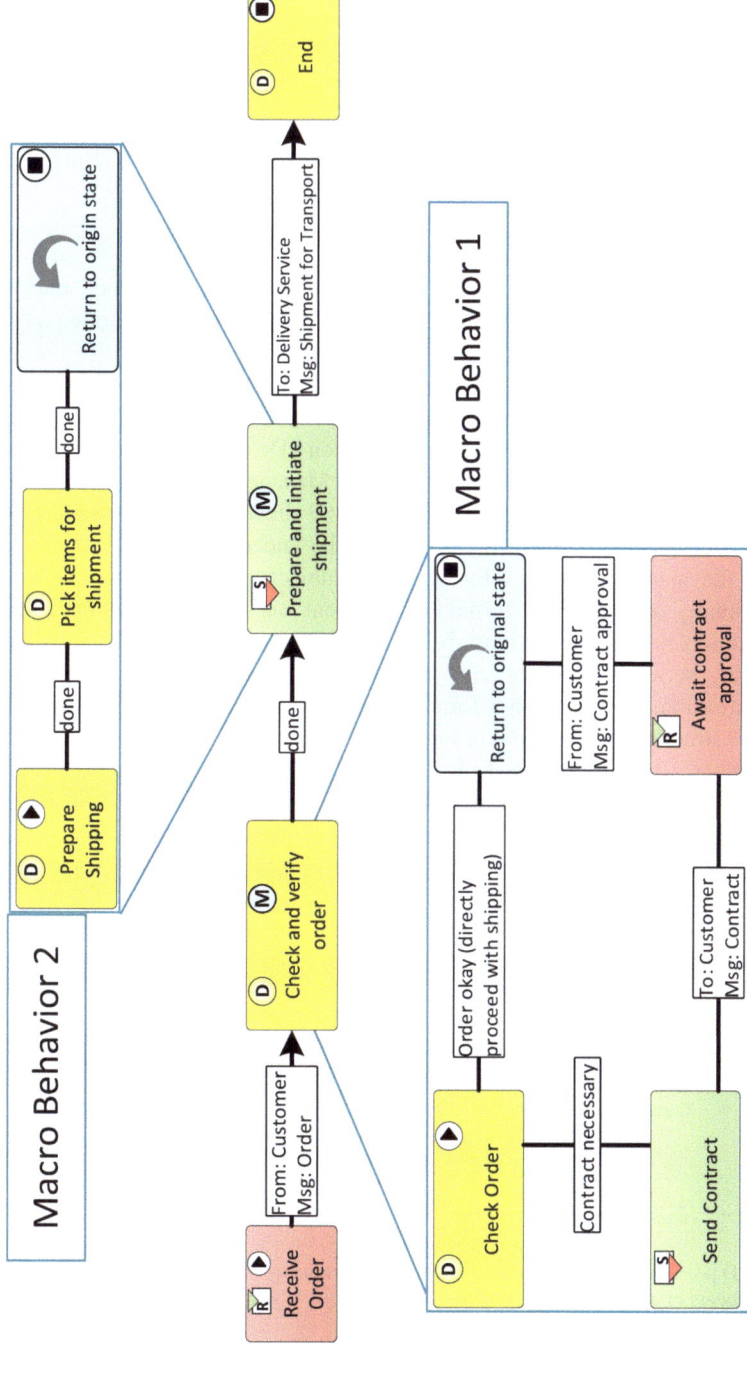

Fig. 4.7 SBD of the subject "Company" from Fig. 4.6, showing calls to Macro Behaviors (sub-activities) in PASS—symbolic representation

Fig. 4.8 Inheritance
mechanism/hierarchy (UML
notation for message (data)
objects)

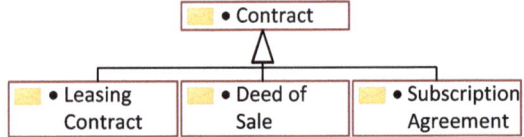

(more abstract) description must specify which Macro Behavior to call. The general description links to the more detailed one and thus depends on it.

4.1.5.3 Abstraction via Subjects in PASS

The third abstraction option in PASS is the subject dimension, which must be explicitly named in a subject-oriented description. It is the most important way to represent complex communication networks of processes.

Classically, the interface subject "Delivery Service" from Fig. 4.6 represents a single behavior not further elaborated in this model. This behavior can be described as an extended process in another model, in which "Delivery Service" appears as a standard subject alongside, for example, "Fleet Management," while "Customer" and "Company" act as interface subjects. Figure 4.9 shows such an extension.

This second process, shown in Fig. 4.9, *can* be understood as a "subprocess." However, the standard concept for interface subjects is that both models are linked mutually and are thus formally dependent on each other. A change in communication in one model must be mirrored in the other model to maintain compatibility between both. Formally, this type of model should be considered a parallel extension, where it is not formally defined whether the model in Fig. 4.6 dictates the structure of the model in Fig. 4.9, or vice versa.

If the model from Fig. 4.6 is to be a fixed specification and thus on a higher formal abstraction level, then it must not depend on Fig. 4.9. This can be expressed by modeling "Delivery Service" not as a regular interface with a fixed link to another model but as an interface to an entire process system with potentially many *"sub-subjects"*, as shown in Fig. 4.10. Such a *System Interface Subject* is an aggregation of multiple active entities (subjects). It can therefore be understood as an abstraction of a complete (subject-oriented) *subprocess system*. This subprocess

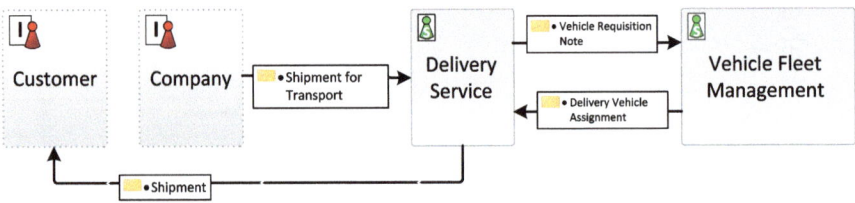

Fig. 4.9 SID process model B—extension of the model from Fig. 4.6—depending on the perspective, a subprocess or a model on the same level

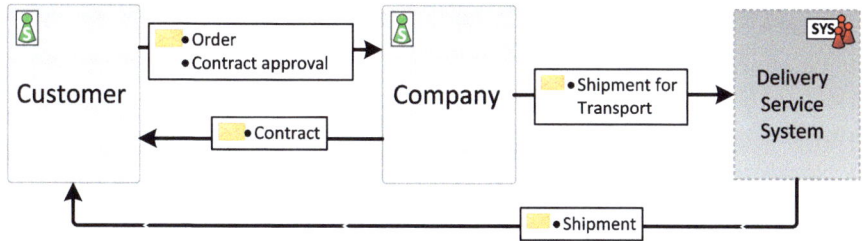

Fig. 4.10 SID showing the interface as a system without dependencies on the model from Fig. 4.9

concept differs fundamentally from that of non-subject-oriented modeling, where an (upper) activity consists of sub-activities (verbs). In contrast, here an active entity (subject) is composed of multiple sub-entities (sub-subjects).

4.1.5.4 Subject-Oriented Hierarchies and Process Architectures

The example explained in the previous section is a relatively simple abstraction. However, understanding interfaces as abstract specifications for entire subprocess systems that can be further specified in dependent models is very powerful. It allows the creation of extensive abstraction hierarchies of various models, through which different relationships and process architectures can be presented clearly and, if needed, simplified.

Figure 4.11 shows how the interaction between the ordering and delivery processes can be described in PASS at three different abstraction levels. The less abstract models depend on the more abstract one and follow its specifications (technically: they "implement" the more abstract specification).

At the highest level of abstraction, Model A (top in Fig. 4.11) only specifies that two active process systems communicate over an abstract communication channel for delivery coordination. Derived from this is the slightly more concrete Model B, which additionally specifies that within the ordering process system are the subjects "Customer" and "Company." This additional information is minimal and would typically not be described in a separate model. However, here it serves as a good example of the abstraction or refinement mechanism and how it should be used.

Model C further details Model B. The communication between Customer and Company is refined, especially the abstract communication channel is modeled. At this level, specific messages are already defined, and the Delivery Service subject functions as a so-called *border subject* for the system in which it is embedded. Finally, Model C itself can be seen and used as a specification for implementing Models (Fig. 4.12).

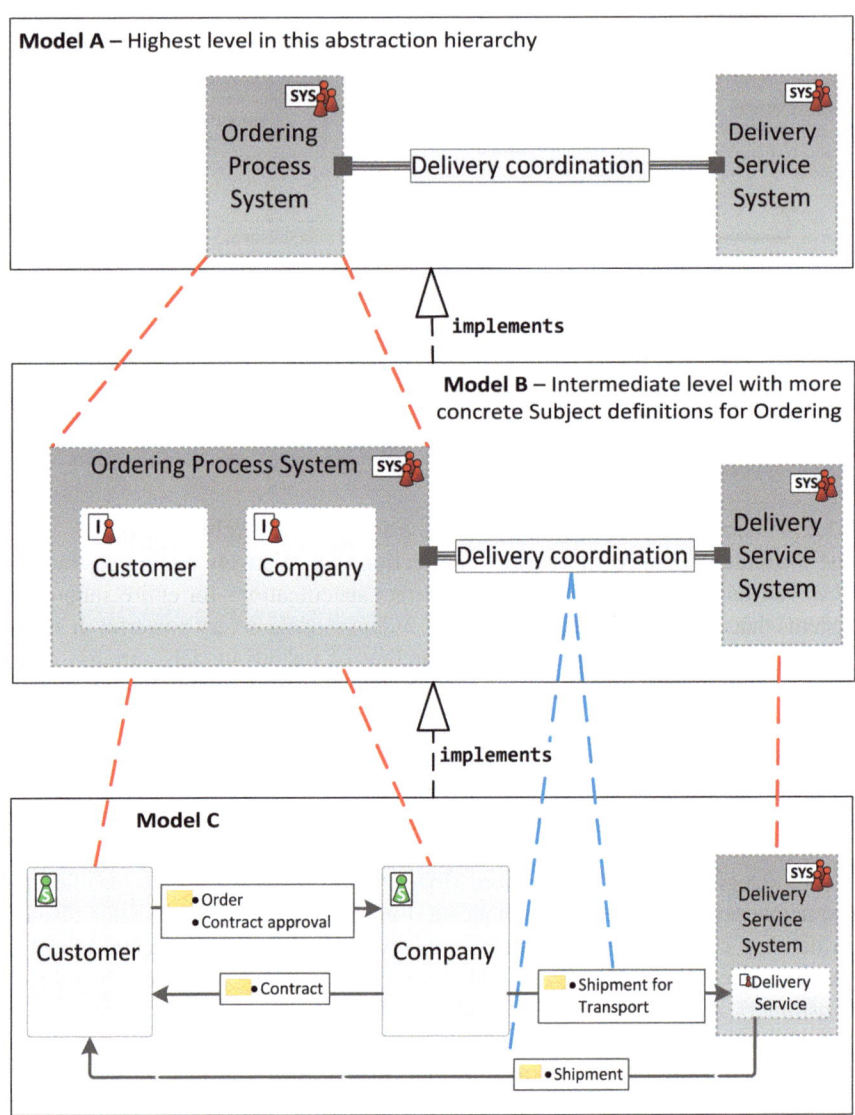

Fig. 4.11 Abstraction hierarchy with three process models

4.2   From Process Model to Digitalization: Formal Execution Capabilities

Creating complex yet semantically correct process descriptions is one of the most important prerequisites for the digitalization of processes involving more than just a few activities. As described in the previous sections, especially with the expected

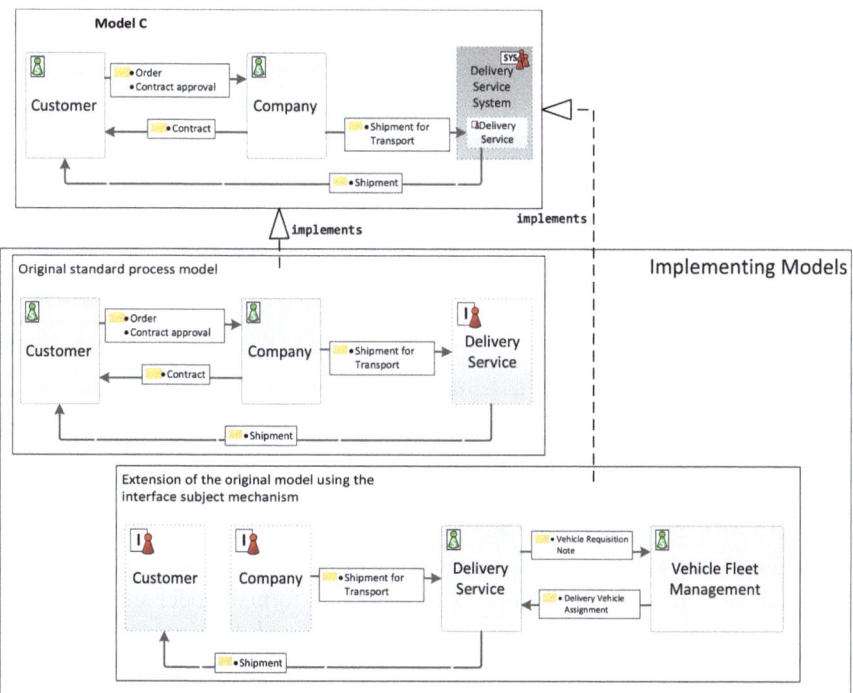

Fig. 4.12 Abstraction hierarchy with three process models—implementing models

complex processes in socio-technical systems, this depends on the expressive capabilities and formal abstraction mechanisms of the modeling language.

However, creating a process model of the process to be digitized is only the first step, followed by the activities of actual digital implementation. There are two fundamental approaches to address the principal challenges on the path to digitalization.

4.2.1   Indirect Execution

The first challenge is independent of the process modeling language used and involves giving the created model to a programmer or involving them in the creation of the process model. The stakeholders must then use the knowledge contained in the process model to configure or program the actual IT systems. The process is thus digitalized, but the model only plays an indirect role or is executed indirectly by the IT system (see Fig. 4.13).

The obvious disadvantage of this approach is that errors or misunderstandings may occur when a human translates the model into code. Unlike simply "drawing" graphics, a formal modeling language with verifiable structure and syntax rules can

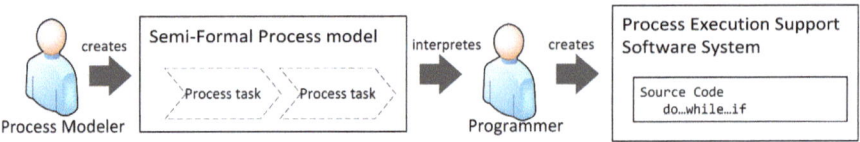

Fig. 4.13 Indirect/implicit execution of process models [2]

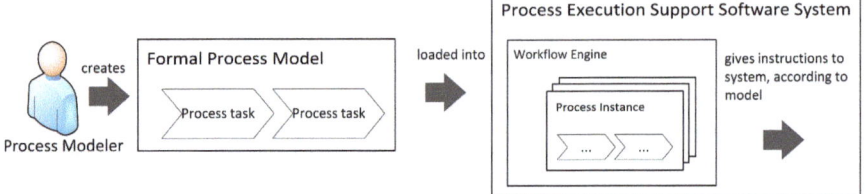

Fig. 4.14 Direct/explicit execution of process models [2]

improve the situation, as the model to be transferred can be automatically checked for correctness. If both the creators and readers of a formal model are sufficiently trained in modeling and understanding it, the likelihood of misunderstandings is also reduced.

4.2.2   Direct Execution

A formal modeling language also offers the fundamental option of directly execut-ing a model digitally. This requires that a formal execution semantics exists for the language and that it is implemented in a so-called workflow engine. If this prerequisite is met, a programmer may no longer be needed; a sufficiently trained business expert can load the process models they created into the software and then execute or instantiate them, as shown in Fig. 4.14.

However, not all modeling approaches discussed in this book provide the same prerequisites for accurate, direct, or at least indirect digital implementation. The following sections examine the capabilities of each language.

4.2.2.1 Digital Implementation Capabilities of Flowcharts

Due to their long-standing existence and wide use [3], understanding the syntax of standard flowcharts can be considered common knowledge. However, there is neither a formal, precise definition of the language's syntax nor an official execution semantics. There is also no official data format to enable the exchange between different modeling tools, databases, or project management systems. Due to their widespread use, flowchart-like description approaches serve as the foundation for visual programming languages [4], which are used in, for example, *low-code platforms*. As the name suggests, these approaches are more intended for programming specific systems and not for modeling business processes. The same applies to all flowchart-like workflow languages that were explicitly created to specify concrete systems and thus only function within the context of those systems.

4.2.2.2 Digital Implementation Capabilities of EPCs

There are many software tools for creating EPC-based process models. However, there is no standardized format for storing and exchanging these models. The most widely used tool for creating and partially executing EPCs is ARIS.[2] ARIS uses its own proprietary file format, which cannot be transferred to other tools. There have been research projects aimed at generating an open data format for EPC models [6] and making EPC models executable via the Business Process Execution Language (BPEL) [7]. However, these did not establish themselves in practice. Further approaches are not known, especially with regard to the direct execution of EPC-based process models.

4.2.2.3 Digital Implementation Capabilities of UML Activity Diagrams

There are many tools for creating digital UML activity diagrams—a list of various options can be found, for example, in [8]. An official XML exchange standard by the Object Management Group (OMG) also exists, which can theoretically be used to exchange models between different tools. In practice, however, this exchange can be tedious: many tool vendors support only their own dialect, i.e., not all notation elements are supported, or proprietary definitions and elements are added. Most tools also offer a function to generate program code for various programming languages. However, in each case, it must be determined whether this is limited to UML class diagrams or also includes UML activity diagrams—the latter is rare. Still, there are fundamental approaches and proposals for this, such as [9]. However, [9] refers only to code generation for real-time systems, and the question remains as to whether this concept or approach is generally suitable for business processes. A UML-based tool with an explicit recommendation for digitally implementing business processes is not known to the authors.

4.2.2.4 Digital Implementation Capabilities of BPMN

The official BPMN standard also includes an XML schema definition intended to enable the exchange of process models and their use in different programs. This works only moderately well in practice because many tools specialize in various aspects of BPMN usage, and manufacturers interpret the standard differently. As a result—similar to UML—the exchange of models can be quite labor-intensive [10].

The official definition of the BPMN standard's execution semantics exists in English, i.e., in a natural language with all the drawbacks of misunderstandings and misinterpretations. Additionally, a formal definition was created by the Software Competence Center in Hagenberg, Austria, for BPMN process models [11]. The

---

[2] The software tool by Software AG—not to be confused with the similarly named "Architecture of Integrated Information Systems (ARIS)" [5], on whose concepts the ARIS software is based.

execution semantics were also analyzed using the Abstract State Machine (ASM) formalism [12], identifying several ambiguities, inherent inconsistencies, and gaps [11].

This particularly affects tools for executing BPMN process models. The majority of these tools do not fully implement the BPMN standard but support only a limited subset of BPMN symbols for execution. In addition, some symbols are interpreted or executed differently, leading to varying and incompatible execution results for the same process model [13].

4.2.2.5 Digital Implementation Capabilities of PASS

For PASS, the only truly subject-oriented process modeling language originating from [1], two formal specifications exist that easily enable digital implementation.

First, there is the formal exchange standard for PASS models, based on the works of [14] and [15], which led to an official ontology-based specification maintained by the *Institute for Innovative Process Management (I2PM)* and published under [16]. This official technical standard enables the exchange of process models between various IT tools for modeling or execution.

As the specification and exchange language, the Web Ontology Language (OWL) specified by the W3C [17, 18] is used. Although more complex than, for example, an XML-based approach, OWL offers numerous advantages in terms of expressiveness, flexibility, extensibility, and the ability to natively represent complex graph structures of a process model, rather than reducing them to the tree structure of an XML format [15].

This OWL standard specifies the core elements of PASS models and the relationships between them. The actual models are also stored in OWL—but using the part of the language for describing concrete data instances rather than the structural specification.

Figure 4.15 shows a visualization of a segment of the PASS OWL standard with model elements for describing subject behavior diagrams (*Behavior Describing Components*). The structure depicted, which is included in the Standard PASS Ontology, essentially corresponds to the PASS structure introduced in Sect. 3.6.

However, specifying the static model structure is only half of what is formally necessary for simple, direct digitalization of processes. The second important aspect is a formal specification of the execution semantics of a modeling language. That is, a uniform definition of a workflow engine's behavior would have when executing a corresponding process model so that any engine conforming to the specification would execute the same model 100%

For S-BPM/PASS, such a specification exists based on the Abstract State Machine (ASM) formalism [12]. It was published in [19]. Figure 4.16 shows an excerpt of the various ASMs that together form the formal execution specification for an interpreter intended to execute subject behavior diagrams (SBDs). Additionally, a more recent specification for PASS execution is defined in PASS itself [20]. It covers aspects that the original interpreter spec did not mention, e.g., the formal handling of macro behaviors.

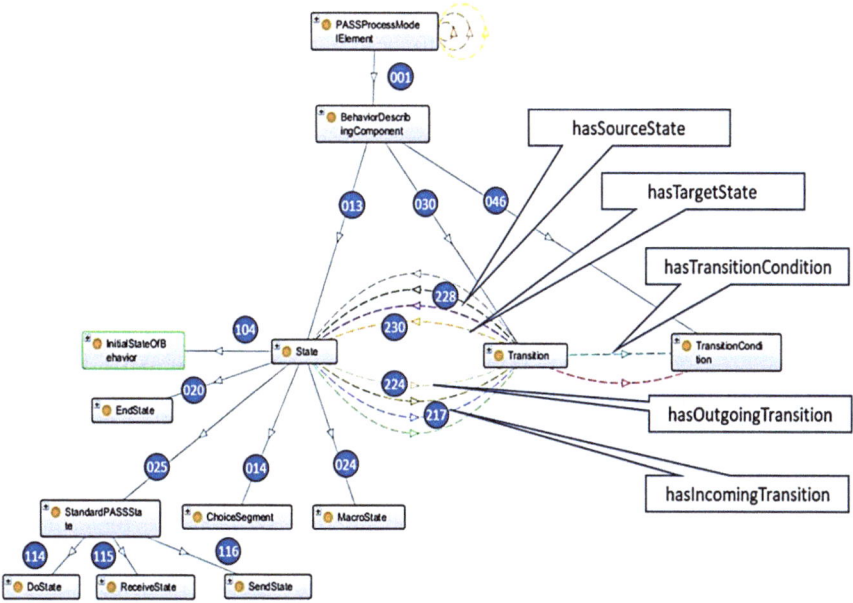

Fig. 4.15 Visualization of the OWL class structure in the Standard PASS Ontology for model components for behavior description

Behavior_{subj} (D) = {Behavior(subj, node) | node ∈ Node(D)}

Behavior(subj, state) =

   if *SID_state(subj)* = *state* **then**
      if *Completed(subj, service(state), state)* **then**
         let *edge* = *select_{Edge}({e ∈ OutEdge(state) | ExitCond(e)(subj, state)})*
            Proceed(subj, service(target(edge)), target(edge))
      else *Perform(subj, service(state), state)*
   where
      Proceed(subj, X, node) =
         SID_state(subj) := *node*
         Start(subj, X, node)

Fig. 4.16 Part of the formal Execution Semantics Specification of PASS in ASM Notation— excerpt from [19]

The significance of both standard specifications—the Standard PASS Ontology/OWL for the static model structure and interpreter specification for the dynamic execution aspects of PASS—arises from their combination, as described in [21]. Each has its purpose, and together they enable interested software developers to create workflow engines or other digital tools for process digitalization. A prototype of such a system was successfully demonstrated as a proof-of-concept by [22]. An overview of additional tools conforming to these standards can be found in [23].

Thus, from a formal perspective, Subject-Orientation with PASS offers the most extensive capabilities among all approaches mentioned here for directly and efficiently implementing or executing processes or process models digitally.

4.3   Incorporating the Internet of Things

Contrary to its name, the Internet of Things (IoT) is not a different or special type of network. It is still the conventional Internet, as an interconnected system of computers exchanging data via the Internet Protocol (IP). The term IoT, however, stands for a change primarily in the number of connected devices and their size. Unlike the classical structure, where only large, system-sustaining machines were effectively connected to the Internet, the concept of IoT aims to realize much smaller, more diverse, adaptive, and interactive systems. This is made possible by the fact that the connected active computers can be tiny and, for example, represent individual sensors or actuators. In traditional contexts, sensors would have been hard-wired electrically to corresponding control computers, something that previously would have been relatively inflexible or even impractical to implement.

Current software solutions, referred to as *IoT platforms*, are necessary to coordinate a corresponding multitude of very different devices at the technical level. However, the actual goal behind the concept of IoT is the simple and effective design of so-called cyber-physical systems (CPS). To enable these, not only are technical prerequisites required but also a shift in thinking that concerns the design of processes in such systems. This shift means changing the understanding of a process from a linear sequence of activities, which can be described hierarchically, toward a networked way of thinking about processes as networks of active entities.

This insight is not new but was already expressed, for example, in [24] in 2013. Figure 4.17 shows an excerpt based on this publication. The classical understanding

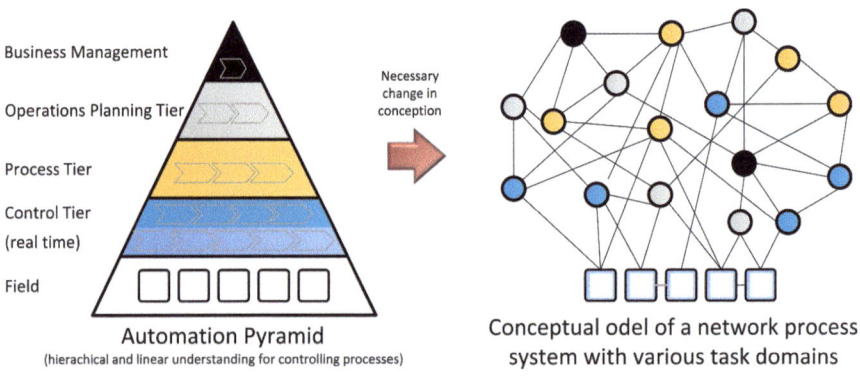

Automation Pyramid
(hierachical and linear understanding for controlling processes)

Conceptual odel of a network process system with various task domains

Fig. 4.17 Illustration of the need for a different understanding of processes—adapted from [24]

of organization within the automation pyramid is shown on the left-hand side. Here, the machines and sensors are located on the lowest level, follow a linear process and are controlled by a hierarchically organized control system. However, the statement or demand of the publication is that this concept or mental model is incorrect, especially when it comes to designing processes and technical operations in cyber-physical systems. The right-hand side of Fig. 4.17 provides the reasoning for this. The machines and sensors in the lower part of the automation pyramid on the left certainly still exist, as they perform actual work, even if they are no longer necessarily structured strictly linearly. The functional areas mentioned on the left also still exist. However, in the real world, the corresponding processes of these functional areas are not organized linearly and hierarchically but are instead highly interconnected, as depicted on the right. It is important to emphasize that the graphic on the right does not represent a special case, but rather the standard of a digitized world and the processes taking place within it.

An apparent demand from this circumstance is that a methodology used to describe processes in such a world must reflect this interconnectedness. It should enable the inclusion of various distributed entities and allow for efficient and straightforward communication about them. According to [2], among the modeling approaches presented in this book, only the subject orientation using the PASS modeling language meets the requirements to be used effectively and without excessive effort.

To demonstrate this utility, we will examine the flagship discipline of CPS development and IoT systems in the following sections: the digital twin. More precisely, we will consider model-driven development and a process-based architectural approach based on digital twins (DTs), especially since the topic of the digital twin itself already represents a challenge in the context of process digitalization.

4.3.1 Digital Twins

Many companies face a wide range of challenges in the digital transformation toward cyber-physical systems (CPS) and applications of the Internet of Things (IoT) or Internet of Behaviors (IoB) [25, 26]. These challenges range from accounting for changing component locations, to interoperability due to component heterogeneity, to management issues in the development of such systems (cf. [27–29]).

CPS are socio-technical systems that link physical devices to digital information processing in operational processes via sensors or actuators. As soon as system components are connected, IoT technologies are used. IoT or IoB usually refers to a conceptual[3] network of physical devices and other objects, in which network

---

[3] The devices are often technically connected via the Internet itself, typically using corresponding technologies/protocols such as TCP/IP or HTTP and physical technologies like 5g, Wi-Fi, etc.

technology enables the embedding of electronic elements (software running on other devices, sensors, or actuators) to collect and exchange data.

Digital twins (DTs), in turn, support the development and operation of CPS, as shown by the wide variety of application domains. These include agriculture (cf. [30]), medicine (cf. [31]), logistics [32], and digital manufacturing (cf. [33]). The rapid penetration of diverse application areas has led to a multitude of development methodologies for DTs [34]. Originally, DTs were conceptualized as virtual, *"active" models* to mirror individual physical objects or entire systems composed of such objects. However, they can be equipped with functionalities that extend beyond the original performance scope of the physical object, such as predicting setup times based on big data and machine learning applications.

Moreover, DTs enable behavioral modifications and simulations to examine various processes before the physical object is involved (cf. [35, 36], https://www.ibm.com/topics/what-is-a-digital-twin). The Digital Twin Consortium includes processes in its DT definition, which are represented in digital form in addition to the physical object. These serve in particular for the simulation of "predicted futures"—cf. https://www.digitaltwinconsortium.org/initiatives/the-definition-of-a-digital-twin/:

> "A digital twin is a virtual representation of real-world entities and processes, synchronized at a specified frequency and fidelity: Digital twin systems transform business by accelerating holistic understanding, optimal decision-making, and effective action; Digital twins use real-time and historical data to represent the past and present and simulate predicted futures; Digital twins are motivated by outcomes, tailored to use cases, powered by integration, built on data, guided by domain knowledge, and implemented in IT/OT systems."

Digital Process Twins (DPTs) aim to synchronize system components for future deployments (cf. [37]). This should be done at the highest possible level of abstraction: *"[This] macro level of magnification, shows how systems work together to create an entire production facility. Are those systems all synchronized to operate at peak efficiency, or will delays in one system affect others? Process twins can help determine the precise timing schemes that ultimately influence overall effectiveness"* (https://www.ibm.com/topics/what-is-a-digital-twin). As soon as the macro level of DPTs is addressed, however, the execution and simulation of models requires a detailing of individual component behavior in terms of behavior modeling and structuring to equally consider control, interaction, and processing within an integrative design and implementation process [38].

From the perspective of business process management, the concept of a "process twin" can be seen either as an independent idea or as redundant or overly specific, since it essentially involves the description, representation, or prediction of workflows executed by a particular component (as a subject), e.g., a production system, which is then part of the corresponding digital twin. If the attempt is made to describe a mirrored process that is meant to act on an object—e.g., a product being manufactured—possibly involving several different actors—a kind of passive process—this makes sense as soon as a subject-oriented perspective is adopted within the modeling context, in which a consistent distinction is made between active subjects and passive objects. However, even in that case, active entities will always be required for execution, which again necessitates corresponding digital twins that are at least implicitly present in the process twin.

With considerations toward synchronous interaction of physical and digital CPS components, i.e., the real-time integration of DTs, further differentiations of DTs have been proposed [39]. Such elaborations should be critically examined, as they often highlight specific use cases of digital twins without fundamentally changing or extending their structure and functionality:

- Virtual Twin: A digital representation based on a physical object (in the cloud) is created.[4]
- Predictive Twin: Data on physical conditions or from hybrid models based on a digital model are used to generate predictions about the behavior of a physical asset.[5]
- Twin Projection: The data obtained by the predictive twin is successively analyzed to gain insights into the underlying operations and processes.[6]

In all cases, networks and sensors are used in DT deployment within CPS to communicate with other systems and their environments or to retrieve data from them, thereby realizing the core functionality of DT communication[7] CPS essentially includes the physical assets, such as a plant or production facility, and the digital representation of these physical objects (cf. [40]). As a DT is confined to its digital model, it cannot exist without a connection to the physical world and without the existence of the physical asset. Suppose physical components are controlled via a DT, then the DT must be regarded as an inherent part of a CPS and its development, with IoT-technology spanning the network and facilitating the data exchange between physical components.

Challenges for DT-based CPS development arise particularly from the requirement that DTs be developed to match the physical counterpart and its operating conditions [39]: To meet requirements for privacy, security, and quality, technologies such as cryptography, blockchain, and big data are used. Real-time communication is supported by compression techniques or suitable communication technologies, including 5G and IoT protocols. Both real-time modeling and the handling of

---

[4] The attempt here seems to be to emphasize that the representation (see "Visualization" in the later reference model in Sect. 4.3.3) of the physical object is carried out using virtual reality (VR) technologies.

[5] With reference to the reference model in Sect. 4.3.3, this label emphasizes the potential technical component of "prediction" that a DT can have.

[6] This expresses that the predictive capabilities of the DT are more complex (possibly because the system mirrored by the DT is itself more complex and consists of multiple subsystems and components).

[7] Cf. e.g., "external monitoring systems" or component managers and the corresponding messages in the reference model.

previously unrecorded events or unanticipated situations require reduced-order modeling to gradually construct, continuously update, and adapt CPS models.

In the technological and organizational linking of physical components, in addition to networked sensor technologies, the simulation of physical components and human-accessible interaction mechanisms based on data-driven models is essential. CPS operation, maintenance, and further development should be based on transparent and interoperable distributed architectures that allow for hybrid analysis and modeling.

A recent study examined the cross-industry development of digital twins [34]. Although there appears to be a unified understanding of DT construction at a high level of abstraction, there exists a wide variety of refinement strategies covering different abstraction layers to develop operational DTs. For DPTs, system developers should be supported in efficiently designing and effectively implementing integrated process twins. Such support through digital twins must enable the integration and interoperability of the heterogeneous systems that comprise CPS in a modular, efficient, and robust way [38].

The behavior-centered approach for structured development of PDTs, already proposed based on subject-orientation, is founded on recent conceptual developments [41, 42] as well as extensive application experience with subject-oriented modeling and corresponding execution models [43–46].

4.3.2   An Exemplary Use Case

We use a traffic management system as a showcase for describing a CPS using subject-oriented representation (see also [41]), based on several smart city studies conducted in this field. Figure 4.18 demonstrates the approach as a demonstrator, consisting of nine participants represented by subjects that communicate with each other. The communication paths are depicted by arrows. The gathering subject counts the cars reported by the four detector subjects and forwards the numbers to the subject "Traffic Management," which exchanges data with "Environment

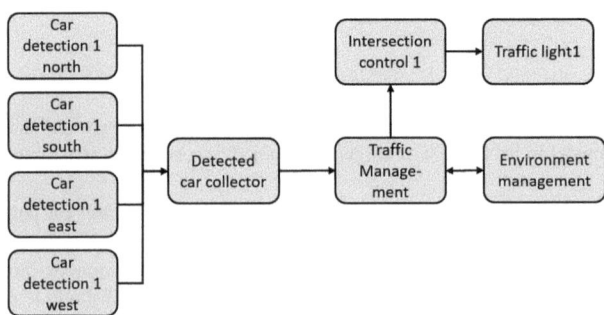

Fig. 4.18 Communication structure of a simple traffic management system

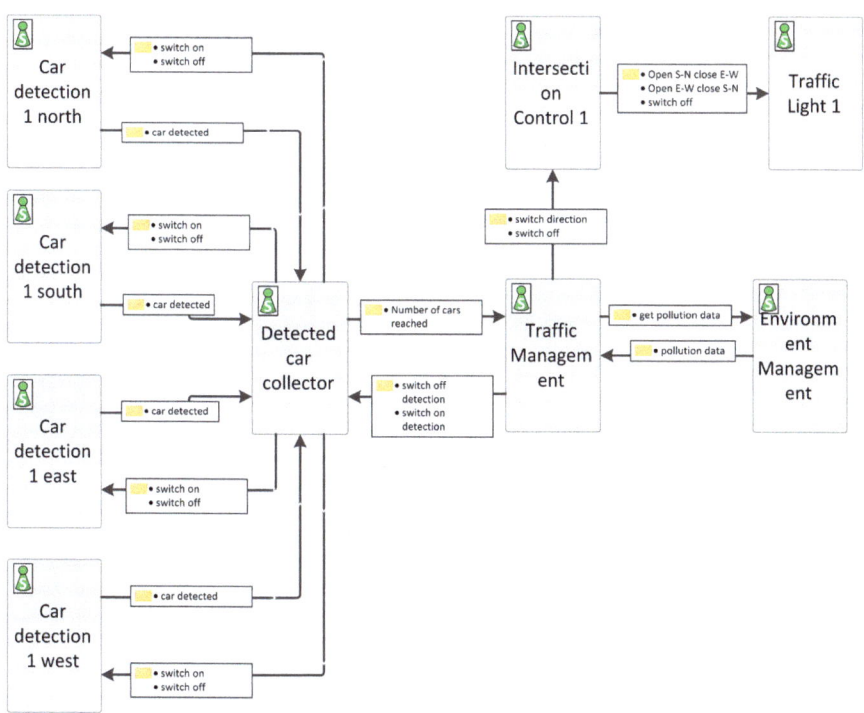

Fig. 4.19 Subject Interaction Diagram of the traffic management system

Management." It also communicates with "Intersection Control 1," which in turn controls "Traffic Light 1."

The logical behavior of a subject, as intended for behavior diagrams, contains the sequences in which messages are sent or received, and the actions that are executed on local objects/data. For this purpose, Fig. 4.18 is enriched with the messages exchanged between the involved subjects to form a Subject Interaction Diagram (cf. Fig. 4.19).

Figure 4.20 shows, as an example, the behavior of the subject "Car Detection 1 North." Upon receiving the message "Switch on," the sensor begins detecting cars. This is represented by the internal action "wait for car." As soon as a car is detected, a message "Car detected" is sent to the subject "Detected car collector."

The subject "Car Detection 1 North" can receive the message "Switch off" at any time. Therefore, it must always be ready to receive this message. This is realized by means of a so-called guard (Guard Behavior) (cf. Sect. 3.6.3). These take care of messages with high priority or act as a kind of interrupt for the standard behavior. As soon as such a guard message with high priority is placed in the input pool, the current behavior sequence is interrupted and the affected subject switches its behavior to the Guard Behavior. In our case, the message "Switch off" is accepted

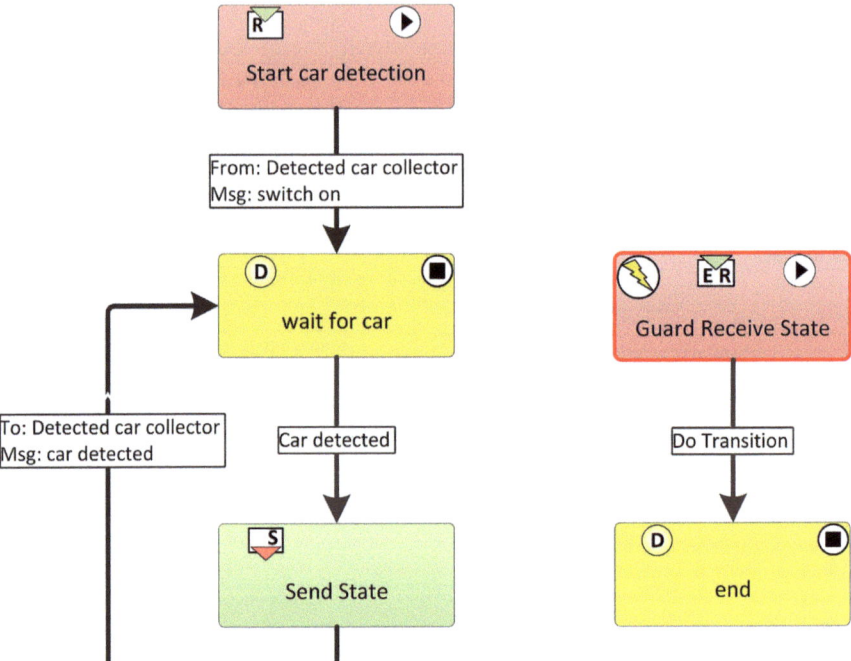

Fig. 4.20 Behavior diagram of the subject "Car detection 1 north" from Fig. 4.19

and the sensor switches to the "end" state. Guards or guard behaviors are a means of specifying responses to unforeseen and unwanted events.

On the corresponding side, the message "Car detected" is stored in the input pool of the subject "Detected car collector" after being sent. This subject can receive messages from all car detectors, count the cars in its behavior, and inform the subject "Traffic Management" when a threshold is reached. The latter then controls "Intersection Control 1," which in turn switches the subject "Traffic Light 1" by sending the appropriate messages. Figure 4.21 shows that part of the behavior in which the subject "Detected car collector" receives the messages "Car detected" from the various "Car detection" subjects.

4.3.3   A Subject-Oriented Reference Model

A different approach to addressing the topic of process digitalization and under-standing digital twins originates from [47]. The model shown in Fig. 4.22 utilizes the subject-oriented modeling paradigm to create a reference model that represents the fundamental functionality of a process system that can be referred to as a Digital Twin System (DTS).

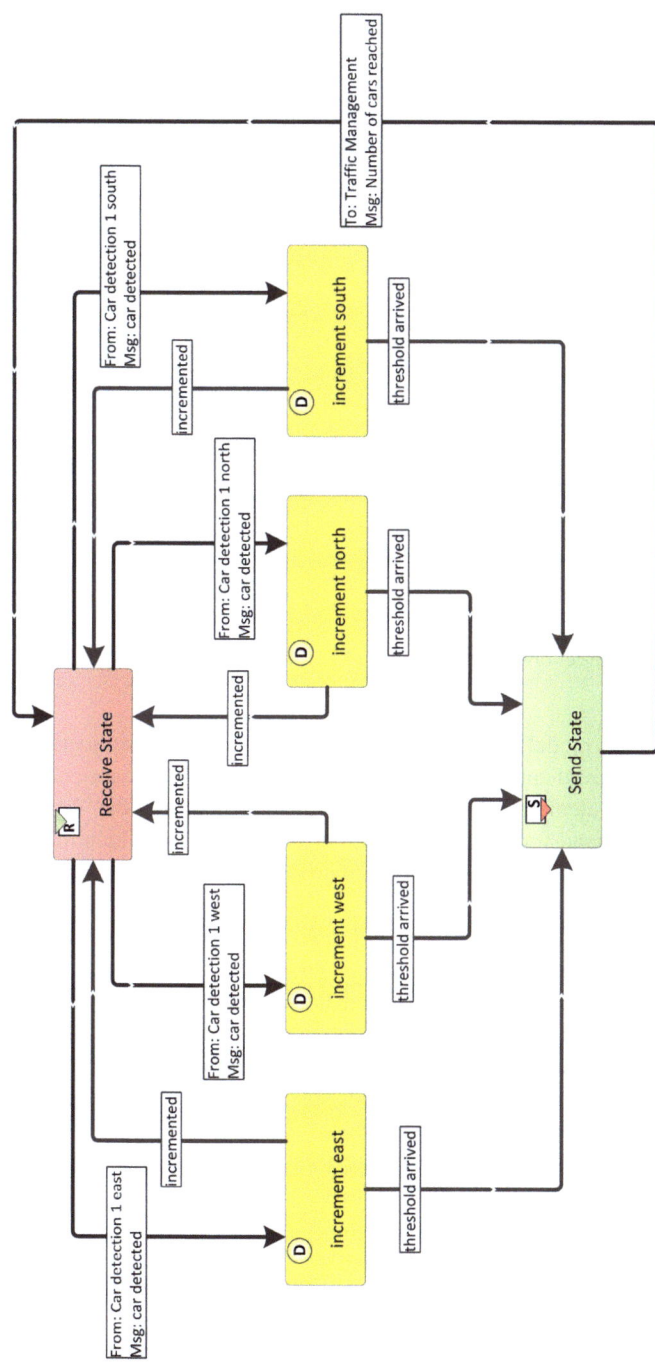

Fig. 4.21 Part of the behavior of the subject "Detected car collector"

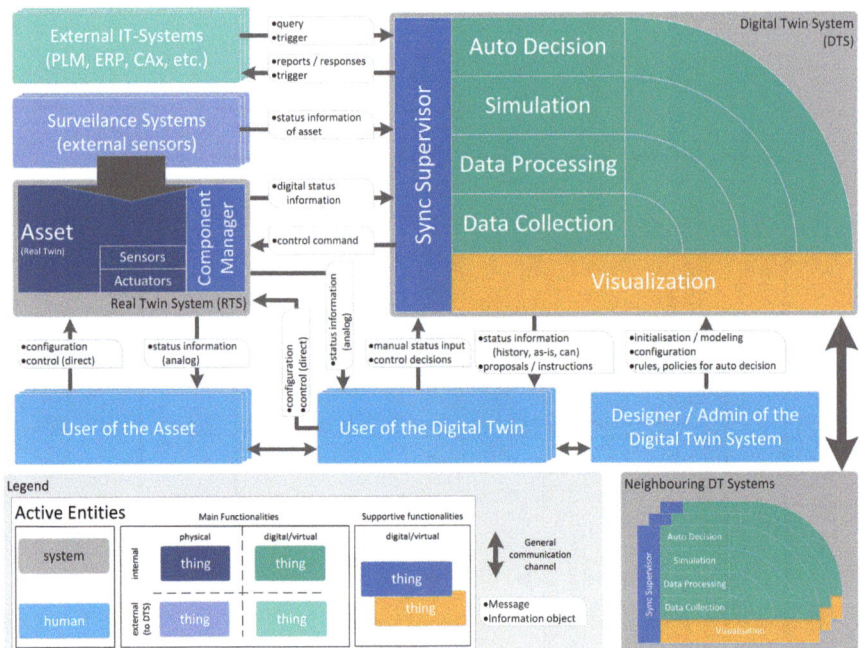

Fig. 4.22 SID of a subject-oriented reference model for digital twins from [47]

What makes this model special is its consistent application of subject orientation. The model is conceived entirely in subject-oriented terms, which particularly affects the labels of model elements. Readers can rely on the fact that all the "boxes" shown do not arbitrarily stand for concepts or methods, but for clearly identifiable, active elements of a Digital Twin System or for data objects exchanged between system components.

The model is especially intended to help people unfamiliar with the concept of a DTS to answer basic questions such as: "WHO does WHAT with WHAT?" or "WHERE does which information come from?", thereby helping them to understand what a DTS is. It is therefore primarily an explanatory process system model intended for interpersonal communication and discourse about digital processes. As such, it exemplifies a different kind of role that process models can play in addressing the challenges of digitalization.

To better understand this approach, the following sections briefly explain the structure of the model and the subjects it includes.

4.3.3.1 Structure of the Reference Model

The fundamental idea of the model is to represent all types of Digital Twin Systems (DTS), even if they exhibit different characteristics or levels of maturity. In real DTS implementations, only a few of the active components shown will actually be present. Several examples of concrete configurations are illustrated in [47].

4.3.3.2 The Real Twin System

At the core of the model is the *"Real Twin System"* (RTS), which is mirrored by the eponymous *"Digital Twin System"* (DTS). Essential within the RTS is the actual *"Asset"*. Depending on the actual nature of this asset, it may also have its own *"sensors"* or *"actuators"*, which enable the asset to monitor and control itself. For assets without their own processing. To represent a physical asset in the digital domain and to coordinate communication with its digital twin and to connect sensors/actuators, a software component is generally required, here referred to as the *"Component Manager"*.[8] This component can, for example, be part of a technical *Industry 4.0* software solution or an architecture framework. Again and depending on the nature of the asset, the Component Manager may be executed on hardware that is physically part of the RTS. However, it can also be executed on external devices if the asset itself does not have its own or sufficient computing resources.[9]

In any case, and as long as the asset has the corresponding capabilities, it will exchange information with the DTS. This fundamentally involves reports about its own state (*"digital status information"*), which are sent to the DTS. If the asset is correspondingly equipped, then control commands (*"control commands"*) can in turn be sent back from the DTS, which, when executed, can lead to a change in the state of the asset. In addition to direct control commands, this can also include, for example, software updates.

External Surveillance As mentioned, it may be the case that the asset is a primitive physical object without its own sensors, e.g., an engine block that passes through a production facility. For a digital twin in this case to receive the necessary *"status information"* about its asset, external surveillance systems (*"Surveillance Systems"*) or sensors are required, which are initially not specifically intended to monitor a single asset and are therefore also not an explicit part of the DTS. Examples of this are surveillance cameras or temperature sensors that belong to a factory building, or also systems for tracking RFID labels in logistics. It is important here that these systems must be explicitly queried by the DTS for information about the individual asset, or their data must be explicitly evaluated.

4.3.3.3 Actual Digital Twin System

As already described, the actual *"Digital Twin System (DTS)"* stands in contrast to the asset or the RTS. The actual nature and capabilities of a DTS can be very diverse and depend heavily on the technologies with which it is itself created. A DTS fundamentally has six main functions, four of which represent the actual value-creating tasks of a digital twin: *"Data Collection"*, *"Data Processing"*, *"Simulation"*, and *"Auto Decision"*. These build on each other or are partially

---

[8] The concept of the *Component Manager* is roughly based on the idea of the *Administration Shell*, created by the Platform Industrie 4.0 initiative. [48].

[9] For the concrete realization of these aspects, as explained in the previous section, IoT technologies play a major role.

dependent on each other. However, not all functions are always present in every DTS. This depends on its maturity level[10] or the requirements of a specific use case. In addition, the four core functions are supplemented by two functions that are necessary to actually be able to use a DTS. These are, on the one hand, the *"Sync Supervisor"*, a component responsible for communication between the virtual world and the physical world of the asset, as well as the *Visualization*, which is necessary for the exchange between the DTS and the people using it. In the following, the individual functions and their tasks are explained in detail again.

Data Collection The collection and storage of data (*"Data Collection"*) is the most essential function that every DTS should possess. It forms the basis for providing users with visibility (*Visibility*) over the current and past (actual) state of a mirrored asset and is also the basis for the other functions. The functioning of *"Data Collection"* is in turn particularly dependent on the functioning of the *"Sync Supervisor"*.

Data Processing The (pre-)processing and evaluation of data (*"Data Processing"*) is the next level of capabilities that a digital twin should have. In contrast to the mere collection and storage of data, this functional block includes all methods for summarizing and preparing data, and for improving the transparency (*transparency*) of information about the asset for users. This can involve simple statistical evaluation procedures. But more complex forms, for example, using methods of artificial intelligence (AI), are also in principle applicable for this type of task. Another typical task of *"Data Processing"* is, for example, the discretization of time series and the identification of events contained therein, which can in turn trigger further actions of the DTS.

Simulation The next maturity level that a DTS can reach includes the ability to make predictions about one or more possible states of the RTS in the future based on the collected and processed data. "Predictive Maintenance" is probably the best-known use case for this. The term *"Simulation"* is the most appropriate umbrella term here, encompassing a wide variety of methods and techniques, ranging from established statistical methods such as regression analysis, through classical agent-based computer simulation, to machine learning (ML) techniques. Which of these are used again depends on the nature and functioning of the RTS and which methods and techniques are available for estimating future development from a present point in time.

Auto Decision First of all, the results and possible scenarios created by simulation components can, of course, be evaluated manually by people. They can then make

---

[10] The functional areas of the model coincide relatively well with the Industry 4.0 Maturity Index (I4.0 MI) model of the German Academy of Science and Engineering—acatech. https://en.acatech. de However, these are not to be seen as abstract stages but as task areas or functions.

corresponding decisions based on the predictions and are also responsible for them. The actual vision for digital twins, especially within the concept of Industry 4.0 as described, for example, by Schuh et al. [49], however, includes the idea that decisions are made partially or even completely autonomously by systems (*Auto Decision*) and are possibly also implemented directly by the functions of the DTS. This can basically be technically solved in two ways. The simple way is a rule-based approach, in which the detection of a certain event in the collected or possibly simulated data triggers certain predefined actions. This is conceptually very similar or identical to existing methods of control engineering.

The second approach is the exploratory approach, in which it is the task of the digital twin to determine what state the RTS should ideally assume. The possible optimal state can be determined from past and present as well as future (simulated) data, with internal optimization algorithms together with rules and constraints set by humans being applied. The possibilities of technically implementing this range from direct and fixed rule sets, through dynamic "business rules" in various domain-specific forms (e.g., the Semantic Web Rule Language—SWRL), to self-learning AI systems. Furthermore, the actual degree of independence with which a DTS can make its own decisions depends on the preferences of its users, who should be able to make corresponding settings.

Synchronization The *"Sync Supervisor"* represents all technical components of a DTS that are responsible for establishing, managing, and maintaining the connection with the RTS as well as other external systems, or for restoring it in the event of a failure or restricting the DTS accordingly as long as no connection exists. This supporting function must necessarily be present in every Digital Twin System, at least rudimentarily, since a complex, possibly network-based IT system can never have one hundred percent availability. Possible reasons for at least a temporary loss of connection between DTS and RTS are, for example, changing latencies, network or power outages, lack of monitoring options, human error, or intentional sabotage.

Visualization The second supporting function of a Digital Twin System is visualization (*"Visualization"*). Its task is to make the data and information that a DTS contains about an RTS as intuitively and understandably accessible as possible to human users, and possibly also to give its users control over the RTS via the DTS. Of all the functions, visualization is probably the most important when it comes to presenting the capabilities of a digital twin externally to its users. How something can or should actually be displayed depends heavily on the respective use case and which of the core functionalities are implemented. The technical possibilities range from the complete absence of visualization (e.g., for DTSs that are technical subcomponents of more complex overarching systems and have no human users), through simple 2D representations of tables and diagrams in so-called dashboards, to fully immersive virtual or augmented reality (VR/AR) environments. In principle, however, other concepts that form an interface between the digital twin and human users are also included in this component; for example, a voice instruction generated by the DTS for factory workers.

4.3.3.4 The Human Component

Like any other IT system, digital twins should, in principle, serve the benefit of people. Therefore, these also play a correspondingly important role in the reference model. More precisely, the model distinguishes three different, fundamental roles that people can have in the context of DTS. According to the concept of subject-oriented description, a person could fulfill all these roles at different points in time.

User of the Asset In most cases, there will be people who interact directly and exclusively with the physical asset and may not even be aware of the existence of a digital twin (*"Users of [the] Asset"*). An example of this would be a factory worker who operates a production machine on site or makes changes to it, but does not know about the data that flows to a central information system. Another example would be the driver of a modern automobile, who does not have to know that the manufacturer operates a DTS for the vehicle in order to, for example, fix problems more quickly in the event of a breakdown or to prevent them from occurring in the first place through improved maintenance (predictive maintenance).

User of the Digital Twin The actual benefit of a DTS can only be realized for people who directly check the state of the RTS via the digital twin or, conversely, manually enter data about the asset into the DTS. Of course, instructions from the DTS can also go to this type of user, whose execution results in a change to the RTS. But also (simulation) data generated and prepared by the DTS can, for example, have an impact on managers who evaluate them and then have changes made to the configuration of the asset. If it is a controllable asset, these types of users can of course also control the asset via the DTS or give corresponding instructions that have an effect on the behavior of the asset.

Designer of the Digital Twin The third role that a person can have in the context of a Digital Twin System is that of the *"Designer"* or *"Admin"*. In contrast to a normal user, who simply uses a preconfigured system passively, a corresponding designer has the possibility to shape and adapt the digital twin. In addition to the original initialization, programming, and configuration, an administrator has the possibility after the start of a DTS to change rules (business rules) or guidelines that, for example, have an impact on the autonomous decisions of the system.

4.3.3.5 Other IT Systems

In addition to the various human roles, the actual RTS, and potentially monitoring sensors, a DTS also interacts with two further principal types of entities.

External IT Systems The first type of these entities represents a wide variety of external technical information systems that are neither a direct part of the DTS nor otherwise responsible for monitoring the RTS. Examples include connected Enterprise Resource Planning (ERP) systems, through which the DTS can, for instance, automatically order maintenance services or spare parts—this presupposes a correspondingly capable *Auto Decision* component. Another possible scenario is the automatic retrieval of construction drawings or other engineering information from PDM/PLM systems, which may be needed for simulations. The communication between the DTS and these systems is described very generically in the model. The possibility is shown that the DTS can make targeted queries (*queries*) to these external systems, which should then be answered (*"reports/responses"*). In addition, quite generally, the reporting of events (*"trigger"*) can mutually trigger further responses in both systems.

Other Digital Twins Technically speaking, other Digital Twin Systems with which the system under consideration interacts are initially "external IT systems." The reference model, however, considers the interaction with other DTS to be somewhat more specific and complex. In principle, the same information is exchanged there (triggers, queries, and responses). However, the actual form of communication depends on the type of relationship in which the two DTS stand to each other. There are basically three different types of relationships.

The first is one in which both digital twins are conceptually equal or equivalent and must coordinate with a *peer-to-peer* strategy. For example, two autonomous robots that have to transport something together.

The second relationship variant is that of a simple association. Here, the nature of the represented assets differs greatly, but both interact at least temporarily in a defined way, such as the digital twins of a product and the production facility in which it is currently being manufactured.

The third variant exists when the physical assets of both digital twins are in a hierarchical relationship to each other. An example of this is a single production machine (with its own dedicated DTS), which is at the same time a fixed part of a larger production facility whose DTS coordinates all the machines contained within it. At the same time, there can also be digital twins for subcomponents that are fixed parts of the individual production machine. In this case, the twins of the subcomponents transmit the state of their assets to the superior system, so that, for example, *predictive maintenance* for the machine can be realized. On the other hand, the DTS of the factory is "authoritative" toward that of the individual machine, for which, however, it needs forecasts regarding capacity utilization and availability.

All three scenarios are potentially complex, but within the possible application concepts that exist for digital twins. The consideration of a scenario with only one single, concrete digital twin is the simplest use case. However, since the main purpose of this model is comprehensible explanation, this section has been simplified and only a general communication channel with other digital twins is shown (*"Neighboring Digital Twin Systems"*).

4.3.3.6 Conclusion

As a conclusion on the reference model it should be noted here that as soon as a reader perceives a reference model as simple and easy to understand, and possibly describes obvious circumstances, then it fulfills its function to the fullest extent.

Also note that due to the subject-oriented paradigm employed, this reference model does not work with the concept of *"process twin"* as *"a process"* is neither an asset nor any active entity itself that can be communicated with. However, it is also not necessary and possibly an advantage since it avoids ambiguities that the term *process twin* might come with: e.g., what is the digital process twin of a "production process" twinning? The whole production system on a factory floor, the production process running on a single machine, the production of a product type that summarizes the handling concerns of multiple product instances, or the production process of an individual product instance? In all of those cases the physical asset that is actually being twinned can and is already identified in the example given. Instead of calling it a Process Twin, a DT can, and from a subject-oriented viewpoint *should*, be named accordingly: the digital twin of the product system, with its subcomponents of the digital twins of the production machines, that communicate with individual product digital twins, that in turn are responsible for facilitating the production process of their asset.

4.4   Artificial Intelligence

Another, and perhaps currently the most prominent, challenge for the digitalization of processes is the complex topic of Artificial Intelligence (AI).

There is little doubt that the information technologies summarized under the term AI will have and already have a significant impact on the digital working world of the coming years. A detailed analysis of the specific application possibilities, challenges, or risks lies far beyond the scope of this book, and even more so beyond the limits of a single section within a single chapter.

However, three basic impact scenarios of this technology will be outlined here to explain how AI can be understood or applied in the context of digital processes.

4.4.1   Artificial Intelligence as a Replacement for Processes?

A long-standing dream, perhaps dating back to the earliest days of digital computers, is that machines will take over tedious work entirely from humans; that a user only needs to state their problem via voice command, and the solution will be determined automatically. For business processes, this would mean that neither users nor developers would need to concern themselves with anything, because an AI system would "magically" plan, execute, and monitor all workflows necessary for the success of an organization entirely on its own—making manual design and digitalization of processes obsolete (and this book relatively useless).

To avoid repeating the predictive mistakes often made throughout the history of digitalization regarding what computers can or cannot do, it should not be denied that this scenario might become possible at some point. However, not in the near future—and initially only for relatively simple processes and workflows. That is, workflows that are fully digitally observable and for which a large amount of training data is available for AI applications, as well as workflows that occur frequently enough that automating and monitoring them via a custom-trained AI system is worthwhile and low-effort.

Setting an alarm via voice assistant already works adequately—whether using Siri, Cortana, or Google Assistant. But this is a routine process executed millions of times daily and therefore well-suited to training AI systems. A similar case is quality monitoring in production processes where many components must be inspected individually. Assuming a clear quality definition, an AI-based system that filters out faulty parts is relatively easy to implement. Whether such examples should even be considered "processes" depends on the reader's preferred definition.

The preliminary conclusion to be drawn here is that it is certainly imaginable that routine tasks and subprocesses can be easily automated using AI. However, for the foreseeable future, this will not relieve developers or users from at least thinking about the coordination and orchestration of activities—i.e., higher-level business processes.

4.4.2   Integrating Artificial Intelligence Approaches into Processes

While a fully automated design and execution of an organization's business processes through AI remains a distant dream, it is certain that individual task blocks within processes will be taken over by IT components that are not classically programmed but developed using various AI technologies.

The resulting question is: How can or should AI be integrated into processes?

There are numerous overviews of where and how different types of AI are being successfully applied (e.g., [50] or [51]), and that was even before the widespread adoption of generative AI tools based on Large Language Models and similar. The problems and tasks solved by AI are usually very specific and well solvable once a suitable dataset with measurable and classified data is available—i.e., in recurring workflows and relatively stable process contexts.

To coordinate these workflows within higher-level processes, two modeling perspectives are possible.

On the one hand, AI activities can be described in a traditional activity diagram simply as function calls. However, their significance can easily be overlooked or hidden, thereby potentially reducing or hindering communication about their use.

Figure 4.23 shows what this type of representation in a process model might look like. Without the explicitly shown comment, the AI support would be completely missed. And even with the comment, it is hardly more than a side note.

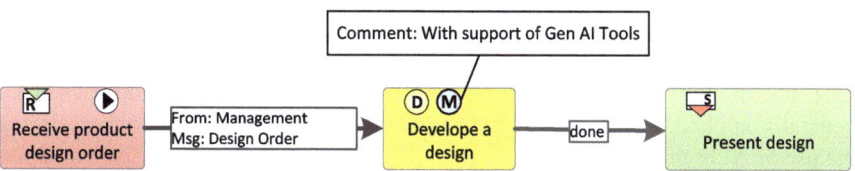

Fig. 4.23 Easily overlooked depiction of AI use in a process as a note within an activity diagram

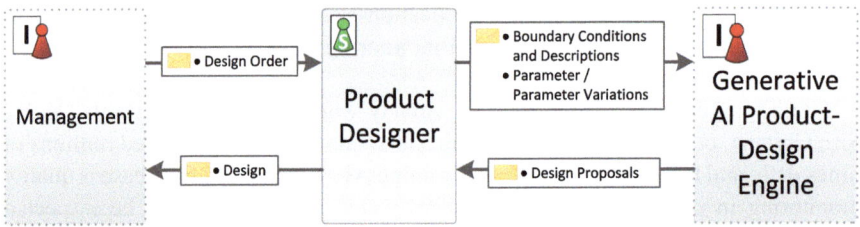

Fig. 4.24 Explicit modeling of AI usage as an explicit and active process element—in the form of a subject in a SID

However, once user acceptance and human-centered design of technical systems are prioritized, transparency becomes highly valuable. It is therefore advisable to treat corresponding AI functions as explicit active process components or modules that must be efficiently embedded within an organizational framework.

This kind of representation, as shown in Fig. 4.24, illustrates the explicit use of AI in a process, with the corresponding component appearing as a subject in an interaction diagram. The specific internal workflows of the AI can be described in detail but may also be omitted as a black box—since for the human-involved process flow, only the result is immediately relevant. Nevertheless, it is important to consider during process design how the black box will interact with its environment. *"What information is needed?"* and *"What exactly will be returned?"* are essential questions that help determine who is responsible for using the AI and interpreting its results. Simply by doing this, socio-technical system processes can and should demonstrate that while AI is used, its purpose and expected outcomes are still defined by humans. AI should thus be understood and designed as another tool in the digitalization of processes, not as something magical to which process participants are subjected.

A clear representation is a prerequisite for integration into processes. But traceability of AI decisions is also necessary to regard it as a trustworthy process participant. The relevant research keyword here is *Explainable AI*—see, e.g., [52]— a discipline that will become increasingly important in this context in the coming years but is still in its early stages.

4.4.2.1 Artificial Intelligence in Process Management

Process management (Business Process Management—BPM) is itself a process. It is therefore logical to expect that AI-based support systems will also become part of workflows in this domain.

Many automation activities in this area fall under the umbrella term *Process Mining* Typically, process modeling or discovery (Process Discovery), monitoring (Conformance Checking), and possibly improvement (Enhancement) are mentioned [53]. For digitalizing this type of process, traditional algorithmic approaches are generally applied. However, there are numerous research contributions exploring the use of AI in this field of digitalization (e.g., [54,55], or [56]).

4.4.3   Understanding AI Through Process Models

A third way to relate AI technologies to process management is to regard and describe their internal functionality and application workflows as processes themselves. The capabilities of process modeling can thus be used to foster better understanding of different AI technologies and their applications.

Figure 4.25 shows, as an example, a Subject Interaction Diagram from [57]. It is intended to explain the interaction between various entities, such as the AI trainer, the user, and different technical components, during the use of the AI technology of artificial neural networks.

Another example using process models to describe AI-related systems comes from [58], where the authors are concerned with describing support systems that try to handle a phenomenon in AI/machine learning systems called *Concept Drift(CD)*. CD occurs sometimes after an AI system, usually for classification, e.g., optical fault detection for quality control in a production process, has run for some time. It has been observed that over time the quality of classifications is reduced or drifts from an originally calibrated point. To adapt to this drift and avoid this reduction in quality, according to compensation systems, the concept drift adaptation systems are used. The referential process model SID describing such a system is shown in Fig. 4.26.

Such models can help increase understanding and convey opportunities for AI design to a broader audience, thereby fostering acceptance of the overall approach.

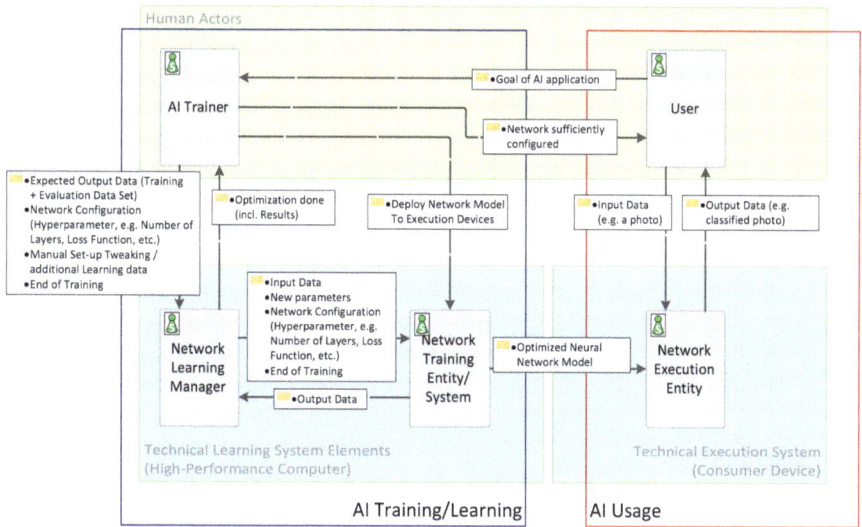

Fig. 4.25 SID of a model describing the fundamental application process of artificial neural networks (from [57])

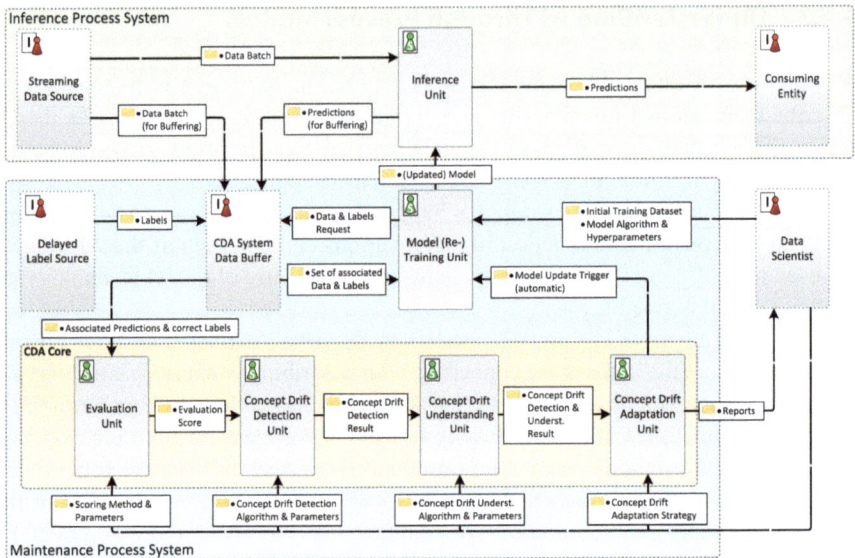

Fig. 4.26 Referential model (SID) for concept drift adaptation systems from [58]

4.5   Integration of Social Behavior Patterns into Process Modeling

The final challenge addressed in this chapter concerns the actual interplay between humans and digital processes. As long as humans are to play a role in digitized processes, they and their particularities should be explicitly taken into account when designing digital process systems. Acquiring knowledge to that respect can start with elicitation techniques like storytelling [59] to engage stakeholders in a nonintrusive way. However, such approaches require further structuring and processing by means of metadata applications, e.g., using Rhetorical Structure Theory [60].

However, subject-oriented modeling offers suitable means for expressing social behavior (patterns), as it abstracts from both, material and immaterial characteristics. This includes the ability to represent social behavior patterns as well as technical functions within the same subject-oriented process model. Therefore, we will now focus on constructing behavior models using subject-oriented modeling, incorporating socio-emotional aspects in accordance with current research on human-system integration (see [61]).

This evolution from, for example, digital twins to so-called *Digital Selves*, as presented in [62], considers not only functional or cognitive aspects of socio-technical systems but also socially relevant behavior of actors in cyber-physical environments. We will first explain the basic concept before detailing the development of subject-oriented representations of *Digital Selves*.

4.5.1   Conception

Models that expand functional aspects with elements of social behavior can be based on empirical findings and/or simulations of social systems. This behavioral extension enables the integration of socially motivated behaviors that are not necessarily grounded in functional roles, alongside task-specific behaviors of role holders. As a starting point for developing extended models, functional roles are used, such as credit processing, recruiting, learning facilitation, facility management, or product management. Less typical but still functional behavioral abstractions relate to activities that represent cross-organizational or cross-departmental tasks. Examples of this kind include people responsible for information gathering, data protection officers, quality management departments, crisis coordinators, or safety officers—all of which are roles, but at the same time the humans performing those activities, naturally, are part of a multitude of their own processes. However, these processes are usually not described or considered in the same way as the so-called main or core business processes, in which subjects of the first category appear. They are not of lesser importance, though, as they concern essential support or cross-sectional functions. Both types of roles can be combined with social behavior descriptions.

Since subjects are abstract roles within the context of a specific process, and *Digital Selves* are a kind of extended subject, every instantiation of an extended subject is linked to an implementation in a socio-technical environment, which in turn is described by the process model in which the subject appears. Typical implementations include robots that detect emergencies and initiate an appropriate procedure, components that autonomously provide information services, or customer services that configure Internet-of-Things systems in a smart home environment in coordination with their users.

Internally, each socially extended subject either performs local activities or sends messages to or expects messages from others. However, when emotional aspects are detected, each performing activity can be associated with another subject that influences behavior in subsequent steps. Such "influencer" subjects can be equipped with parameters referring to previous activities and thus provide decision support for selecting further activities of the initiating subject in the sense of socially motivated behavior.

Subjects performing internal activities can thus be combined with other subjects into a socio-emotionally relevant system behavior. In this context, the previously separated "specifications of subject behavior" need to be aligned with the corresponding desired behavior patterns. Behavior patterns that include functional tasks such as order processing can be combined with socially relevant aspects, such as constant change requests from customers and the associated time-consuming customer interaction or order handling. These aspects can subsequently influence the functional states of a subject. Typical examples include:

- A learner subject *feels* restricted in their ability to act when collaborating with other students and begins to question the contributions and behavior of other actors (represented through subject interactions) and changes their behavior to implement individual ideas.
- A facilitator subject feels the need to address an impending conflict between actors (subjects) in a project in order to avoid a possible escalation and, consequently, project failure.

Communication based on sending and receiving messages (including data) can—just like in functional models—include patterns of socio-emotional information exchange. This may result in bypassing institutional regulations that would otherwise require formal verification, as the following example illustrates: A "Facility Manager" subject wants to expedite the evacuation of a building in the event of an emergency and directly requests support from the safety officer—sending the message "Clear Building" directly to the "Safety Unit" subject.

When specific aspects or events such as emergencies are the subject of consideration, it is advisable to include the system-of-systems perspective in the modeling approach (see [63–65]). This allows the bundling of requirements for addressing a specific situation at the modeling level—for example, implementing specific regulations that affect all actors in an organization in a given context. Thus, the (partial) behavior of systems can be modeled and adapted in a situation-specific manner.

4.5.2 Development Structure

A subject-oriented model enriched with social behavior patterns (Digital Self), like the specification of digital twins, requires several steps:

- Definition of the relevant section of observable reality, such as a business case in which socio-emotional behavior must be taken into account
- Identification of actors or active components that are defined as subjects involved in this business case or process
- Determination of the interactions in which the active components or subjects are involved
- Detailing of the messages that the active components or subjects send or receive as part of functional or socio-emotional interactions
- Modeling of socio-emotionally relevant behavior of subjects that can influence the functions for handling the business case and interaction activities

Figure 4.27 shows the generic steps of how subject-oriented description concepts are applied to embed socio-emotional aspects into functional/cognitive digital representations of Digital Selves.

For example, socio-cognitive behavior in a classroom situation requiring emergency management can be considered. Involved are at least the actors (subjects)

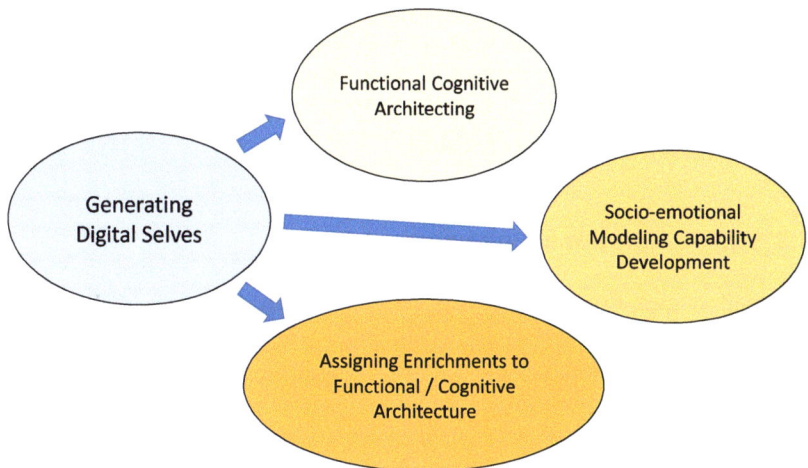

Fig. 4.27 Generating socio-cognitive representations of Digital Selves

responsible for the functional flow, i.e., teachers, students, facility management, and the safety unit. Examples of interactions in the emergency include Teacher–Facility Management and Facility Management–Safety Unit. Exchanged messages include emergency notification, emergency confirmation, evacuation request, and delivery of evacuation plan.

The control and information flow included is as follows: a teacher sends an emergency notification to the facility management of the building operator. They receive an emergency confirmation and the evacuation plan from the safety unit. This is implemented, provided that the on-site situation does not change in the meantime, e.g., due to events triggered by the social behavior of those involved or affected.

The behavior of each participating system component such as facility management and safety unit is also modeled in a subject-oriented way. Initially, the recognizing subject—e.g., the teacher in the classroom—executes an internal function to create the emergency notification. Once this function is completed, the notification is sent. In the following state, a message with the emergency notification is sent to the subject "Facility Management." After this message is sent, the subject "Teacher" transitions into a waiting state until the next incoming message.

However, depending on the students' social behavior, an action independent of the incoming confirmation may be taken. If environmental conditions change—for example, students begin moving toward the exits instead of waiting for assistance—the teacher may lead the students outside before receiving a response from facility management. This would need to be captured in the behavior diagram.

The functions in the behavior diagram relate to the processing of data or objects required to report an emergency. Data from updated sensor components is to be expected if the classroom is equipped with Internet-of-Things components and room usage is thereby monitored. Objects are data and/or applications affected by a subject's internal functions or processes and processed by services. For example, the function for generating the emergency notification uses internal data to promptly prepare the corresponding message. This notification data constitutes the payload of the emergency notification to its recipient.

4.5.3 Socio-Emotional Behavior

In addition to cognitive behavior patterns, human-to-human interaction and emotionally driven behavior are of particular importance in socio-cognitive models. When multiple individuals are involved in a situation at a single location, their (social) behavior may have a decisive impact, regardless of their primary functional role. In the classroom example, the teacher is engaged in knowledge transfer (cognitive behavior), while also representing facility management in organizational matters on-site—such as at the beginning and end of class sessions or during emergencies. Functional role-holders present in the building, including facility managers, initially play no active role in the (knowledge transfer) context—only upon corresponding activation (by the teacher).

Human-to-human interactions are important aspects that determine both role-to-role behavior among task bearers and the reaction/action behavior of individuals as well as recurring behavior patterns in organizations. The latter arises from people's tendency to observe others' responses to critical situations and to adjust their behavior accordingly. Zhu et al. [66] identified several categories of human-to-human interaction behavior in their empirical behavioral study:

- *Herding behavior* as a specific category of human-to-human interaction refers to a person following what others do, even when perceived situational information suggests otherwise. In the case of classroom evacuation, this may mean a person chooses the most congested route because it is the most popular choice rather than selecting alternative routes with fewer people. Herding can occur under high stress or rationalization of perceived situations. It is influenced by environmental factors (e.g., number of peers, exits nearby, visibility) as well as personal factors (e.g., individual attitudes).
- *Avoidance behavior* is also related to location and environmental factors. For example, in crowded places like lecture halls during class time, uncertainty—such as blocked visibility—can lead people to avoid others. In low-uncertainty situations, e.g., when nearby exits are overcrowded, most people prefer more distant exits to avoid delay.
- *Grouping behavior* is similar to herding and avoidance but considers the social connectedness of individuals. While herding and avoidance occur among strangers, grouping behavior arises from social bonds—e.g., peers from the same study group or class move as a unit and actively seek fellow group members.
- *Helping and supportive behavior* is linked to existing or emerging collective identities in critical situations. These foster interpersonal relationships and are

strengthened through shared experiences, enhancing collective identification and cooperation. However, increasing risk—e.g., an initial incident (a falling object) escalates into an earthquake—may reduce willingness to help.

- *Competitive and selfish behavior* can occur under high stress and perceived loss of personal space. A person may prioritize self-evacuation without regard for others, competing for exits or safety. Such behavior can impair group crisis management. The choice depends largely on existing or newly emerging social relationships, such as in the classroom scenario.
- *Leader-following behavior* arises when professional and/or social roles influence behavior. Individuals may assume leader or follower roles based on knowledge, experience, and personality. Many tend to adopt follower roles in critical situations; fewer choose to lead. Leadership is often assumed by authority figures, who should guide others based on their understanding of the situation and perceived surroundings.
- *Information sharing* is a key factor in critical situations and a driving force in human-to-human interaction. Once a critical event occurs, people begin "hunting for information" to better understand the severity of the situation. They consult peers or responsible actors—or even form ad hoc "crisis committees." The information they obtain helps assess options for next actions. While this can aid crisis management, it may also complicate it by causing delays or further incidents due to unproductive or time-consuming exchanges.

Each behavioral category can occur in combination with others, producing coupled effects. For instance, following and helping behaviors can intertwine when leaders exhibit supportive behavior while guiding others—interrupting leadership duties in favor of assistance. Moreover, individuals who do not panic in critical situations can process received information, whether from their group or the surrounding environment.

Managing critical situations may also involve roles not initially considered. For example, employees such as facility managers may act as first responders, guiding people to exits or instructing them on using emergency equipment. Role-specific behavior therefore influences not only individual actions but also interactions, particularly in the context of group-related behavior.

4.5.4   Relevant Interactions

Human-object-critical-situation interactions play a significant role due to the differing behavior triggers and patterns of the involved actors. For example, when facility managers are involved from the outset in the procurement, operation, and maintenance of facilities and/or inventory, the human-critical-situation interaction is influenced by their prior knowledge and informed behavioral responses. Often, trust in role-specific behavior triggers leader-following patterns.

Figure 4.28 summarizes the mapping of interaction types to modeling constructs for digital modeling. Since we pursue a communication-centered approach, the

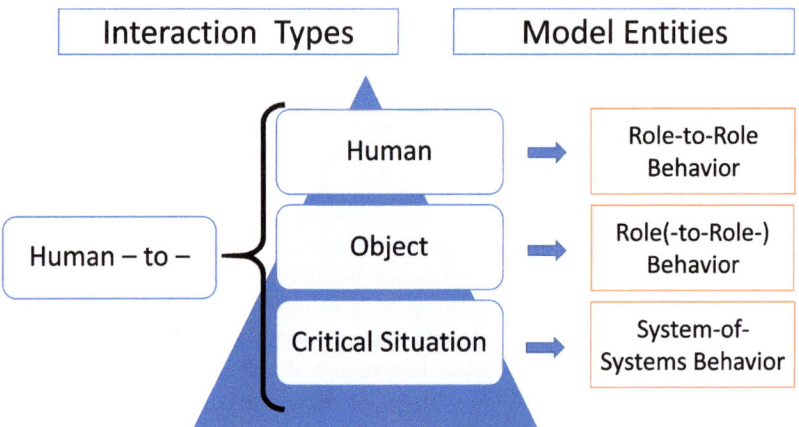

Fig. 4.28 Assignment of interaction categories to modeling functions

representation is oriented toward roles and task behavior. Accordingly, human-to-object interaction is based on behavior entities that represent individual procedures for handling or dealing with objects. In our case, since cyber-physical components fulfill dedicated tasks—such as the preprocessing of sensor data—these interactions may also occur from role to role, i.e., between designated task bearers within an organization.

Human-to-human interaction is traditionally based on role-to-role behavior. According to the subject-oriented modeling approach, subjects represent role abstractions independent of their actual implementation and can thus be implemented by physical, digital, or hybrid systems. For interaction between humans and critical situations, a controlling subject is required, as this necessitates a point of origin—both regarding what actors do and which objects in the environment are affected in a specific situation. Hence, we already consider human-critical-situation interaction as an interaction "of the second order," as it implicitly includes human-object-critical-situation interaction.

4.5.5   Modeling Integration

To capture the teaching environment in our example, the modeling must consider the organizational framework. Each involved actor and system, such as student administration or facility management, is created as a subject in an interaction diagram and modeled with a corresponding behavior diagram.

The occurrence of a critical situation is modeled using message Guard Behavior (1) where a decision is made as to whether learning in the classroom can continue as planned or (2) whether dedicated behavior sequences should be selected to address the critical situation. The latter corresponds to the treatment of a complex event and requires decision-making regarding behavior options. The sender of the guard/interrupt message is a general "observer" or a warning system or sensor, which can be represented as an interface subject without more specific behavior.

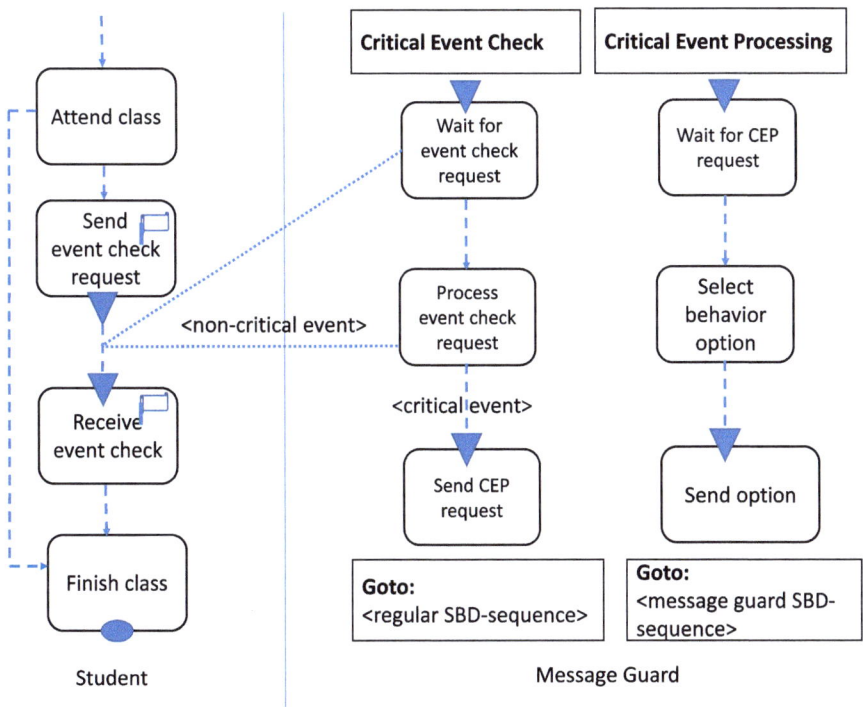

Fig. 4.29 Occurrence of a critical situation and initial assessment of criticality (base behavior diagram and Guard Behavior of a student)

Figure 4.29 shows the occurrence of an event from a student's perspective, leading to an initial check to determine whether a critical situation is present. This behavior diagram represents a human's handling of a critical situation and serves as the control mechanism for the situation. The message guard is activated as soon as a critical situation is detected and requires specific assessment. This may trigger the behavior of other actors, if they are also informed of the situation's occurrence through a guard message.

Human-to-object interactions are not represented as role-to-role interactions in behavior-oriented models. The actual interaction with an object is described as an activity within the behavior diagram. When messages refer to object manipulations or location-specific changes, then in the first case, data about digital or physical objects is transmitted via messages to other actors (subjects), which is shown in the interaction diagram. In the latter case, movements or manipulations of other subjects are reported as information. If objects themselves are transferred, this is naturally also visible in the interaction diagram.

For socio-cognitive modeling, social contextual conditions must be considered— consistent with already evaluated model simulations such as in [62]: We assume a population of unconditional cooperators. When viewing learners as a population in which actors can work alone or in groups, they can reach a certain level of

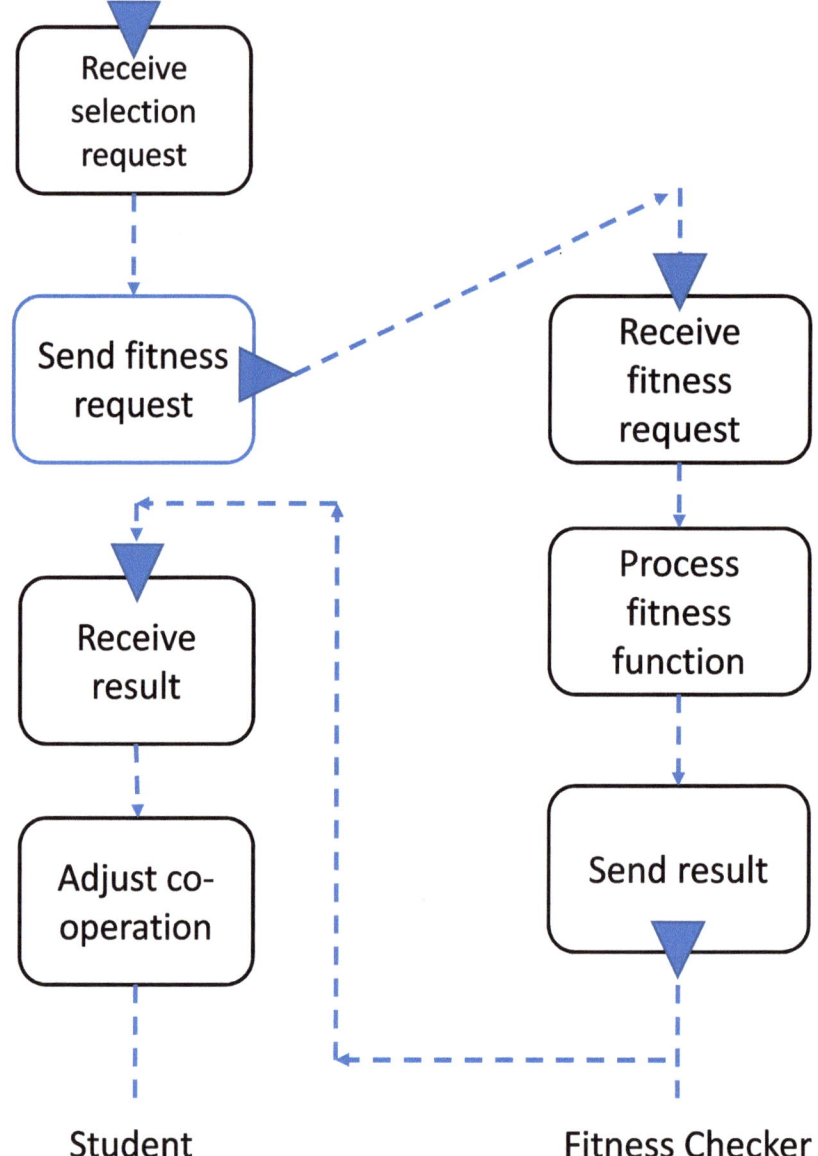

Fig. 4.30 Adjusting cooperation behavior based on the fitness of available knowledge

fitness (i.e., capability to handle a challenging situation) once they attain expected knowledge.

Figure 4.30 illustrates the activation of the function for adapting cooperation behavior. The adaptation involves collaboration from different perspectives within a group according to specific actor types:

- Emotionally stressed individuals work toward a goal under certain conditions and cooperate until the counterpart has reached a certain level of fitness (i.e., to handle the situation).
- Egoists maximize fitness by acting and cooperating only to the extent that expected fitness costs allow.
- Cooperative individuals participate unconditionally and cooperate in any case.

Based on these fitness-driven behavior types, (re-)actions in critical situations can be categorized. For instance, the desire to please others may, depending on the fitness threshold to be achieved, be attributed to either emotionally burdened cooperation partners or egoists when assigning student and teacher behaviors. Another example is the adherence to normative rules, such as waiting for instructions in the classroom—either from the safety unit outside the room or from the teacher present. Such adherence can relate not only to rules but also to cultural norms, including "unwritten laws," and may be linked to rewards like public praise.

Figure 4.31 illustrates an exemplary specification of human-to-human interaction behavior when students' cooperation behavior is based on fitness. The dotted lines indicate the relative order of activities, as additional functions may need

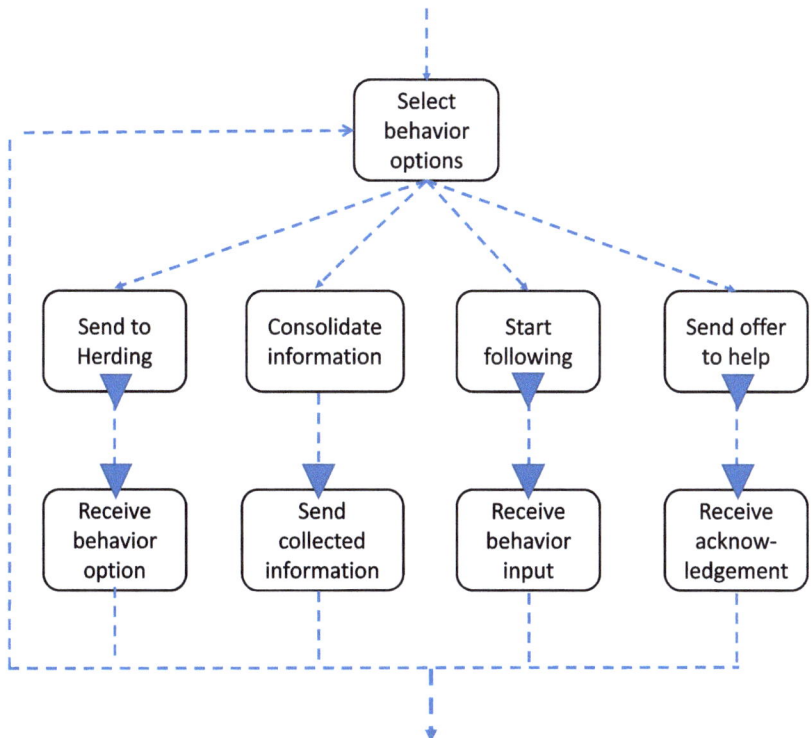

Fig. 4.31   Selection of behavioral options

to be executed. Considering only basic patterns for now, four categories can be distinguished, corresponding to the behavior types mentioned above:

- Herding corresponds to observation by a subject that, at runtime, reports on all instantiated student subjects. Once behavioral changes are observed, they are reported and received by students who select the herding behavior.
- Sharing information requires consolidating individual information, which is modeled as a functional state for this purpose. Once consolidated, it can be sent at runtime to all other instances of the student subject.
- Following is triggered by a leader subject, such as the teacher or a peer group member, i.e., a student or another role holder (e.g., facility manager), who can be addressed during the runtime of the modeled system.
- Helping involves informing others so that they can request support if needed. It is modeled as a broadcast message to instantiated subjects at runtime.
- Human-to-human interaction from the student's perspective includes herding, sharing information, following a leader, and helping.

Figure 4.32 shows the specification of human-to-human interaction behavior for teachers who are in the classroom along with students in case of an emergency. In addition to adjusting their own social behavior, a functional interaction with the facility manager is required for further instructions in critical situations. In the event of an interruption, the facility manager receives a timely report and transmits the procedure to be followed.

Figure 4.33 illustrates interpersonal interactions affecting the teacher's behavior, taking into account the various types of cooperation behavior in relation to the fitness of the available knowledge:

- Egoistic behavior becomes evident when requesting restoration of the classroom state—such as (immediately demanding) repair of a damaged item to maintain control over the learning and teaching process.
- When delegating, the teacher expects another role bearer—either facility management or even a student—to handle the entire critical situation. This can be triggered by noncooperative motives.
- Evacuating the room affects all instantiated subjects at runtime and results in leaving the room according to the facility's evacuation principles. In a way, this corresponds to assuming a leadership role and prompting others to follow.
- Helping informs students in the classroom how they can receive or provide support in handling the critical situation—for example, organizing a replacement item or removing damaged parts from the room. Like the evacuation call, this information is modeled as a broadcast message to instantiated subjects at runtime.

If the teacher is implemented by a software component or supported by digital models to handle the class socio-emotionally, a corresponding subject can provide information on how students are likely to react in emergency situations. In this

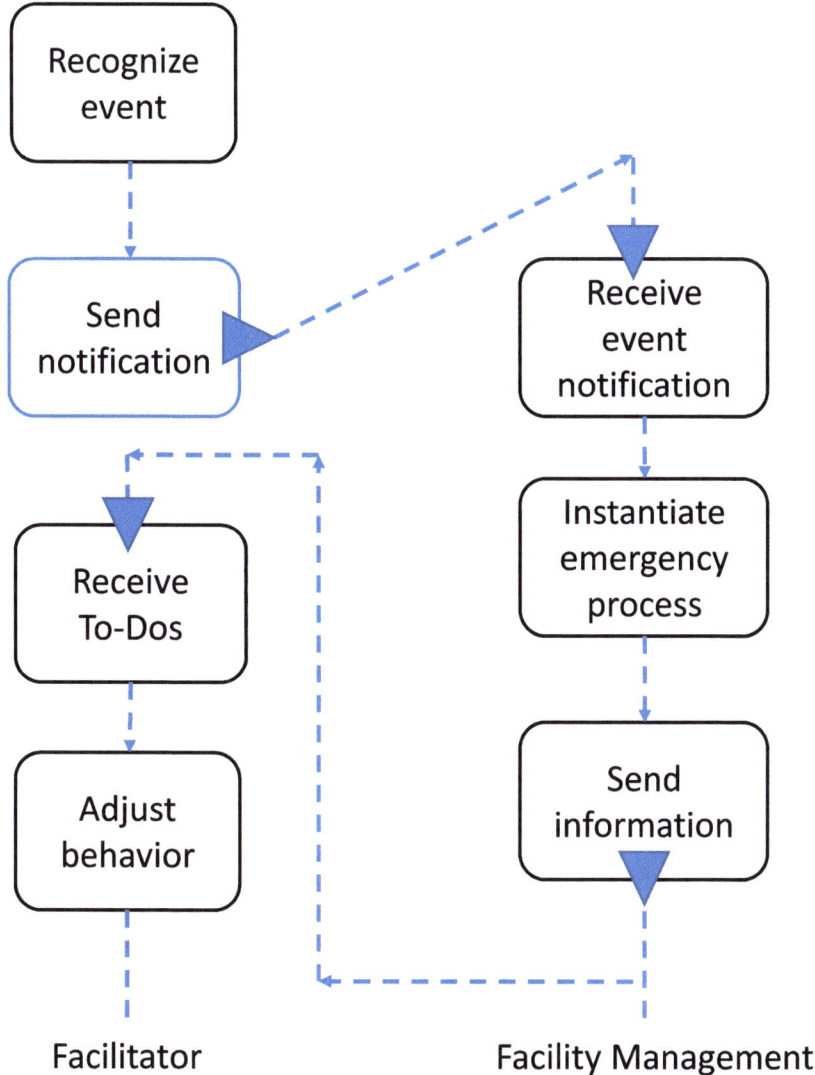

Fig. 4.32 Role-specific behavior of the teacher and facility management in critical situations

case, a digital model is available that can be provided to the teacher—e.g., as a simulation—to better predict what will happen next. Another process model can then describe how a subject "teacher" should act. He or she then sends a corresponding request message to a subject "student behavior," which provides predictions about this group's behavior. Based on known individual characteristics of the existing student population, an assessment can be generated, and the teacher can evaluate or activate appropriate behavioral options accordingly. Egoists will

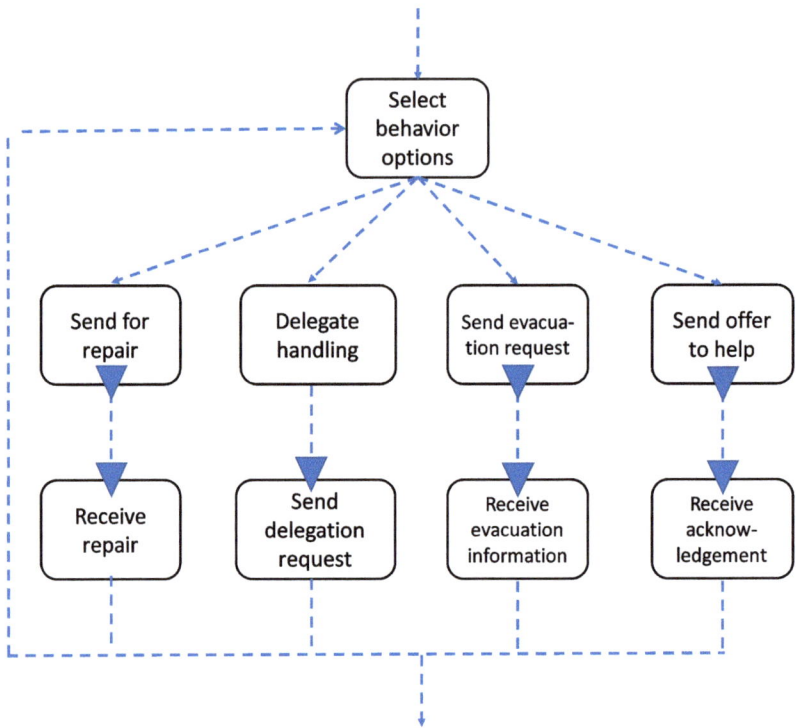

Fig. 4.33 Human-to-human interaction from the teacher's perspective: restoring the original state, delegating further steps, evacuating the room, and initiating help

instrumentalize facility management according to their preferences. Moderately socially oriented teachers will seek incentives to help, while cooperative ones will help immediately without waiting for facility management. This enables the creation of an appropriate socio-cognitive behavioral repertoire in the modeling.

References

1. A. Fleischmann, *Distributed Systems—Software Design and Implementation* (Springer, Berlin, 1994)
2. M. Elstermann, *Executing Strategic Product Planning—A Subject-Oriented Analysis and New Referential Process Model for IT-Tool Support and Agile Execution of Strategic Product Planning* (KIT Scientific Publishing, Karlsruhe, 2019)
3. R. Laue, H.C. Mayr, B. Thalheim, 100 years of graphical business process modelling: Guest editorial. Enterprise Modelling and Information Systems Architectures (EMISAJ) **17**, 3–1 (2022)
4. B.A. Myers, Visual programming, programming by example, and program visualization: a taxonomy. ACM Sigchi Bulletin **17**(4), 59–66 (1986)
5. A. Scheer, *ARIS—Modellierungsmethoden, Metamodelle, Anwendungen* (Springer, 3., völlig neubearb. und erw. aufl. ed., 1998)

6. J. Mendling, M. Nüttgens, Transformation of ARIS markup language to EPML, in *EPK* (2004), pp. 27–38
7. O. Kopp, *Abbildung von EPKs nach BPEL anhand des Prozessmodellierungswerkzeugs Nautilus*. PhD thesis (Stuttgart, Universität Stuttgart, Diplomarbeit, 2005)
8. Ihpiv, List of unified modeling language tools (2022). https://en.wikipedia.org/wiki/List_of_Unified_Modeling_Language_tools. 2022-07-24
9. S. Backhauß, *Code Generation for UML Activity Diagrams in Real-Time Systems*. PhD thesis, Master's thesis (Institute for Software Systems, Hamburg University of Technology (TU Hamburg), 2016)
10. M. Dirndorfer, H. Fischer, S. Sneed, Case study on the interoperability of business process management software, in *International Conference on Subject-Oriented Business Process Management* (Springer, Berlin, 2013), pp. 229–234
11. F. Kossak, et al. *A Rigorous Semantics for BPMN 2.0 Process Diagrams* (Springer, Berlin, 2014)
12. E. Börger, R.F. Stärk, *Abstract State Machines: A Method for High-Level System Design and Analysis* (Springer, Berlin, 2003)
13. M. Geiger, S. Harrer, J. Lenhard, G. Wirtz, BPMN 2.0: the state of support and implementation. Futur. Gener. Comput. Syst. **80**, 250–262 (2018)
14. M. Elstermann, Proposal for using semantic technologies as a means to store and exchange subject-oriented process models, in *S-BPM ONE 2017—Darmstadt, Germany—March 30–31* (2017)
15. M. Elstermann, F. Krenn, The semantic exchange standard for subject-oriented process models, in *Proceedings of the 10th International Conference on Subject-Oriented Business Process Management*, S-BPM One '18 (Association for Computing Machinery, New York, 2018)
16. I2PM, Standard-pass-ontology (2022). https://github.com/I2PM/Standard-PASS-Ontology/releases
17. D. McGuinness, F. Van Harmelen, et al., Owl web ontology language overview. W3C Recommendation **10**(10), 2004 (2004)
18. W. Org, The web ontology language (2012). https://www.w3.org/TR/owl2-overview. Accessed: 2020-01-14
19. E. Börger, A subject-oriented interpreter model for S-BPM, in *Subjektorientiertes Prozessmanagement*, ed. by A. Fleischmann, W. Schmidt, C. Stary, S. Obermeier, E. Börger (Hanser-Verlag, München, 2011)
20. M. Elstermann, Proposal for a recursive interpreter specification for pass in pass, in *International Conference on Subject-Oriented Business Process Management* (Springer, Berlin, 2023), pp. 187–201
21. M. Elstermann, A. Wolski, Matching execution and modeling semantics for subject-oriented process models, in *Subject-Oriented Business Process Management: The Digital Workplace—Nucleus for Transformation*, ed. by M. Freitag, A. Kinra, H. Kotzab, H.-J. Kreowski, K.-D. Thoben. Communications in Computer and Information Science, , vol. 1278 (Springer, Berlin, 2020)
22. A. Wolski, S. Borgert, L. Heuser, A coreASM based reference implementation for subject-oriented business process management execution semantics, in *Proceedings of S-BPM ONE 2019*, ed. by M.L.S. Betz, M. Elstermann. S-BPM ONE (ACM, New York, 2019)
23. A. Fleischmann, S. Borgert, M. Elstermann, F. Krenn, R. Singer, An overview to S-BPM oriented tool suites, in *Proceedings of the 9th International Conference on Subject-oriented Business Process Management*, ed. by M. Mühlhäuser, C. Zehbold. S-BPM ONE (ACM, New York, 2017)
24. K. Bettenhausen, S. Kowalewski, Cyber-physical systems: chancen und nutzen aus sicht der automation, in *VDI/VDE-Gesellschaft Mess-und Automatisierungstechnik* (2013), pp. 9–10
25. M. Javaid, A. Haleem, R.P. Singh, S. Rab, R. Suman, Internet of behaviours (IoB) and its role in customer services. Sens. Int. **2**, 100122 (2021)

26. C. Stary, The internet-of-behavior as organizational transformation space with choreographic intelligence, in *International Conference on Subject-Oriented Business Process Management* (Springer, Berlin, 2020), pp. 113–132
27. V.A. Wankhede, S. Vinodh, Analysis of barriers of cyber-physical system adoption in small and medium enterprises using interpretive ranking process, in *International Journal of Quality & Reliability Management*, vol. ahead-of-print (2021)
28. V.A. Wankhede, S. Vinodh, Analysis of Industry 4.0 challenges using best worst method: a case study. Comput. Ind. Eng. **159**, 107487 (2021)
29. S. Yang, N. Boev, B. Haefner, G. Lanza, Method for developing an implementation strategy of cyber-physical production systems for small and medium-sized enterprises in China. Procedia CIRP **76**, 48–52 (2018)
30. C. Pylianidis, S. Osinga, I.N. Athanasiadis, Introducing digital twins to agriculture. Comput. Electron. Agric. **184**, 105942 (2021)
31. I. Voigt, H. Inojosa, A. Dillenseger, R. Haase, K. Akgün, T. Ziemssen, Digital Twins for multiple sclerosis. Front. Immunol. **12**, 669811 (2021)
32. A. Rudskoy, I. Ilin, A. Prokhorov, Digital Twins in the intelligent transport systems. Transp. Res. Procedia **54**, 927–935 (2021)
33. D. Hartmann, H. Van der Auweraer, Digital Twins, in *Progress in Industrial Mathematics: Success Stories*, ed. by M. Cruz, C. Parés, P. Quintela, (Springer International Publishing, Cham, 2021), pp. 3–17
34. W. Heindl, C. Stary, Structured development of digital Twins—a cross-domain analysis towards a unified approach. Processes **10**, 1490 (2022)
35. M. Batty, Digital twins. Environ. Plann. B: Urban Anal. City Sci. **45**, 817–820 (2018)
36. C. Herwig, R. Pörtner, J. Möller, *Digital Twins* (Springer International Publishing, Cham, 2021)
37. R. Rosen, G. von Wichert, G. Lo, K.D. Bettenhausen, About the importance of autonomy and digital twins for the future of manufacturing. IFAC-PapersOnLine **48**(3), 567–572 (2015)
38. P. Sobhrajan, S.Y. Nikam, Comparative study of abstraction in cyber physical system. Int. J. Comput. Sci. Inform. Technol. **5**(1), 466–469 (2014)
39. A. Rasheed, O. San, T. Kvamsdal, Digital twin: values, challenges and enablers from a modeling perspective. IEEE Access **8**, 21980–22012 (2020)
40. Y. Lu, C. Liu, I. Kevin, K. Wang, H. Huang, X. Xu, Digital twin-driven smart manufacturing: connotation, reference model, applications and research issues. Robot. Comput. Integr. Manuf. **61**, 101837 (2020)
41. C. Stary, Digital twin generation: re-conceptualizing agent systems for behavior-centered cyber-physical system development. Sensors **21**, 1096 (2021)
42. F. Barachini, C. Stary, Beyond data: unifying behavior modeling, in *From Digital Twins to Digital Selves and Beyond* (Springer International Publishing, Cham, 2022), pp. 21–33
43. A. Fleischmann, W. Schmidt, C. Stary, S. Obermeier, E. Börger, *Subject-Oriented Business Process Management* (Springer Berlin Heidelberg, Berlin, 2012)
44. A. Fleischmann, W. Schmidt, C. Stary (eds.), *S-BPM in the Wild* (Springer International Publishing, Cham, 2015)
45. M. Neubauer, C. Stary (eds.), *S-BPM in the Production Industry* (Springer International Publishing, Cham, 2017)
46. C. Stary, M. Elstermann, A. Fleischmann, W. Schmidt, Behavior-centered digital-twin design for dynamic cyber-physical system development. Complex Syst. Inform. Modeling Quarterly **30**, 31–521 (2022)
47. J. Bönsch, M. Elstermann, A. Kimmig, J. Ovtcharova, A subject-oriented reference model for digital twins, in *Computers & Industrial Engineering* (2022), p. 108556
48. Verein Deutscher Ingenieure e.V. and VDI/VDE-Gesellschaft Mess- und Automatisierungstechnik, Industrie 4.0: Gegenstände, entitäten, komponenten: Statusreport (2014)
49. G. Schuh, R. Anderl, R. Dumitrescu, A. Krüger, M. ten Hompel, Industrie 4.0 maturity index: Managing the digital transformation of companies: Update 2020 (2020)
50. M. Javaid, A. Haleem, R. Singh, R. Suman, Artificial intelligence applications for industry 4.0: A literature-based study. J. Ind. Integr. Manage. **7**(01), 83–111 (2022)

51. I. Ahmed, G. Jeon, F. Piccialli, From artificial intelligence to explainable artificial intelligence in industry 4.0: a survey on what, how, and where. IEEE Trans. Industr. Inform. **18**(8), 5031–5042 (2022)
52. D. Gunning, M. Stefik, J. Choi, T. Miller, S. Stumpf, G. Yang, XAI—explainable artificial intelligence. Sci. Rob. **4**(37), eaay7120 (2019)
53. W. Van Der Aalst, *Process Mining: Data Science in Action*, vol. 2 (Springer, Berlin, 2016)
54. N. Mehdiyev, P. Fettke, Explainable artificial intelligence for process mining: a general overview and application of a novel local explanation approach for predictive process monitoring, in *Interpretable Artificial Intelligence: A Perspective of Granular Computing* (2021), pp. 1–28
55. F. Veit, J. Geyer-Klingeberg, J. Madrzak, M. Haug, J. Thomson, The proactive insights engine: process mining meets machine learning and artificial intelligence, in *BPM (Demos)* (2017)
56. A. Pery, M. Rafiei, M. Simon, W. van der Aalst, Trustworthy artificial intelligence and process mining: challenges and opportunities, in *International Conference on Process Mining* (Springer, Berlin, 2022), pp. 395–407
57. M. Elstermann, J. Bönsch, A. Kimmig, J. Ovtcharova, Human-centered referential process models for AI application, in *International Conference on Human-Centered Intelligent Systems* (Springer, Berlin, 2021)
58. M. Trat, M. Elstermann, J. Deckers, J. Ovtcharova, Modeling a reference architecture for concept drift adaptation systems (2025)
59. C. Stary, M. Maroscher, *Wissensmanagement in der Praxis:-Methoden-Werkzeuge-Beispiele* (Carl Hanser Verlag GmbH Co KG, München, 2012)
60. C. Stary, How business process modeling can benefit from rhetorical structure theory, in *International Conference on Subject-Oriented Business Process Management* (Springer, Berlin, 2024), pp. 105–124
61. G.A. Boy, Model-based human systems integration, in *Handbook of Model-Based Systems Engineering* (Springer, Berlin, 2022), pp. 1–29
62. F. Barachini, C. Stary, From digital twins to digital selves and beyond: engineering and social models for a trans-humanist world (Springer, Cham, 2022)
63. C. Stary, D. Wachholder, System-of-systems support—a bigraph approach to interoperability and emergent behavior. Data Knowl. Eng. **105**, 155–172 (2016)
64. C. Stary, System-of-systems design thinking on behavior. Systems **5**(1), 3 (2017)
65. R. Heininger, C. Stary, Capturing autonomy in its multiple facets: a digital twin approach, in *Proceedings of the 2021 ACM Workshop on Secure and Trustworthy Cyber-Physical Systems* (2021), pp. 3–12
66. R. Zhu, J. Lin, B. Becerik-Gerber, N. Li, Human-building-emergency interactions and their impact on emergency response performance: a review of the state of the art. Saf. Sci. **127**, 104691 (2020)

From Model to Digital Execution

5

5.1 Overall Context

In the previous chapters, we have shown that what happens in organizations (companies, administrations, etc.) is based on models from various disciplines. Business models, which represent enterprise architectures with models for products and services, organizational structure, processes, data, and IT infrastructure, describe in which area a company does business, how it does this, which exchange relationships it has with partners, which technical infrastructure it is supported by, etc. In the course of digitalization, the operational processes designed by domain experts using modeling languages must be turned economically into workflows supported by information and communication technology.

Both the appropriate incremental improvements of existing processes and fundamental process innovations are based on creative design accomplishments, which should lead from process models to executable systems. In this chapter, we will therefore first deal with the concept and typical activities of Business Process Management, including analysis and modeling, validation, implementation, and operation and monitoring. With the approach of Design Thinking, we then illuminate a methodical approach to creatively produce something new and solve complex problems. Subsequently, we relate both concepts to each other.

5.2 Activity Bundles in Business Process Management

5.2.1 Overview

In Chap. 1.8, we have already mentioned that the design of business processes up to their execution as instances in the processing of concrete business transactions ("operational business") itself represents a process. This is often understood as

© The Author(s) 2026
M. Elstermann et al., *Contextual Process Digitalization*,
https://doi.org/10.1007/978-3-032-06901-6_5

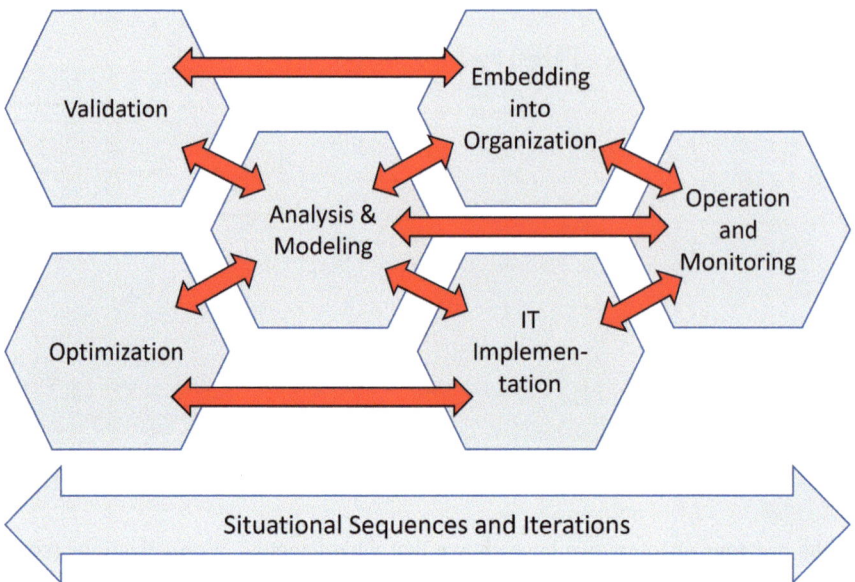

Fig. 5.1   Activity bundles in Business Process Management

a Business Process Management cycle with phases such as strategy, design, implementation, and controlling [1].

In practice, however, the sub-activities are often not clearly distinguishable from each other. We therefore see them less as a circle with a sequential sequence and consequential as *phases*, but rather as networked and interwoven, as the honeycomb structure in Fig. 5.1 suggests. The diagram also shows that we differentiate the tasks somewhat more and identify them as *bundles of activities*: analysis and modeling, validation, optimization, embedding into the organization, IT implementation, and execution and monitoring.

Although the usual representation as a cycle suggests that in process management projects all activity bundles are run through as a sequence, their selection and sequence depend on the concrete situation, e.g., the maturity level of a process. The Sects. 5.2.2–5.2.7 explain the activities using an example process. Here, the steps are first run through completely and also in the specified sequence. Such a scenario is realistic, for example, when a process is designed for the first time or completely reorganized. In Sect. 5.2.8, we discuss several scenarios for improvements that can be derived from the experience gained during operation of the originally designed process environment. They illustrate the situationally different paths through the activity bundles in the further development of the process.

5.2.2   Analysis and Modeling

The analysis serves to gather information about why a process exists or should be implemented, which goals an organization pursues with it within the framework of its strategy, and how it is currently working. The objectives are the documentation and the acquisition of indications for improvements. The modeling uses, among other things, the results of the analysis and deals with the design of future working methods, i.e., process changes and innovations. If further information is required, the participants switch back to the analysis mode to collect it and then act again creatively. Therefore, analysis and modeling cannot be clearly distinguished from each other. Validation and optimization also usually take place here, when the participants develop the model iteratively to the best of their knowledge and belief, taking into account the weak points identified in the analysis and trying out and discussing possible solutions.

In addition to considering determining factors such as strategic significance, objectives, and risks, analysis and modeling are essentially concerned with analyzing or specifying (see also Sect. 1.3)

- which actors (e.g., people, machines),
- perform which activities,
- according to which business rules,
- on which business objects (e.g., information linked to certain carriers, physical objects),
- using which tools (e.g., IT systems), and
- how they interact in order to achieve the desired process goals and results.

To develop process models based on these findings, the modeling languages presented in Chap. 3, along with their associated graphical notations are used.

During analysis and modeling, the ground is usually also laid for operational process controlling in the operating activity bundle. In addition to the process attributes already mentioned, performance parameters (indicators), in particular Process Performance Indicators (PPIs), are defined, systematized in a measurement system, and provided with target values (see [2], p. 265). Typical examples of PPIs are lead time, output per time unit, error rate, customer satisfaction, etc. The PPIs and the target values planned for them form the basis for business process monitoring, that is, operational process control during execution (see Sects. 5.2.7 and 7.3.3).

Analysis and Modeling in a Case Study
As a case study, we use the highly simplified process for handling loan applications in a bank that is similar to the examples of Chap. 3. There, applications for a real estate loan are received from interested parties for the granting of credit. Before making an offer, the clerks check the creditworthiness of the respective customer and the value of the property being mortgaged. If the result of both checks is

Process characteristic	Result of analysis
Actors / Roles:	Interested party, real estate loan administration, head of department real estate loan, executive board
Activities:	Apply for credit, check credit application (completeness), check customer creditworthiness, estimate value of object to be financed, determine financing conditions, Create offer, approve offer, send offer
Business objects:	Credit application with attachments, credit offer
Business rules:	Credit offers over 200,000 € must be approved by the department management, over 500,000 € by the board.
Interactions:	Customer - Bank (incoming mail), real estate loan administration - Head of real estate loan department, Head of real estate loan department - Executive board, real estate loan administration - customer
Aids:	Internet portal of the bank (web form), backend system of bank, workflow system of bank, SCHUFA web form, e-mail, telephone
Process metrics	Observation of the behavior of instances using: • Processing time from the receipt of a credit application to the dispatch of an offer (target: average max. 3 days), • Frequency per week including distribution • Rejection rate of applications by the bank • Rate of rejection of offers by interested parties

Fig. 5.2 Characteristics of example process and information obtained for it

positive, the clerk prepares an offer with data such as loan amount, interest and repayment rate, and term. If the loan amount is less than 200,000, the clerk signs the offer and sends it to the customer. Otherwise, the clerk must first obtain approval from the department head and, for loans exceeding 500,000, that of the board of directors. If the creditworthiness check or property inspection reveals any indications of risk, a clerk contacts the interested party to coordinate the next steps, e.g., reducing the loan amount. As part of an analysis of the process, this information was collected and structured (see Fig. 5.2). It serves as a basis for modeling the process.

In the case at hand, we use the PASS modeling language from S-BPM, described in Sect. 3.6, to represent the process, as it exists in a highly interaction-oriented description. Generally speaking, the specification would also be possible using any other modeling language that allows the mapping of responsibilities (such as eEPC or BPMN).

Figures 5.3, 5.4, and 5.5 show an excerpt of the model for the loan request process using the S-BPM modeling language. The overall model consists of the Subject Interaction Diagram (SID) and a Subject Behavior Diagram (SBD) for each subject involved. Figure 5.3 depicts the Subject Interaction Diagram, including the subjects (agents) and the messages they exchange during the process flow in the SID.

The interaction begins with the "Loan Request" message, which the "Interested Party" subject sends to the "Real Estate Credit Application Processing," from which

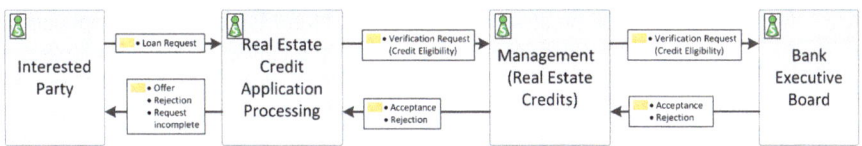

Fig. 5.3 Subject Interaction Diagram (SID) of the actors in the loan request process

Fig. 5.4 Subject Behavior Diagram (SBD) of the subject "Interested Party"

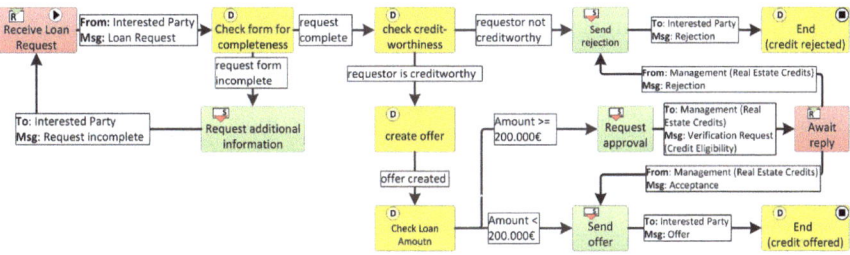

Fig. 5.5 Subject Behavior Diagram (SBD) of the subject "Real Estate Credit Application Processing"

it can receive the "Offer," the "Rejection," or the "Request incomplete" message. According to the requirements of the process, the other subjects exchange the messages visible in the SID. The communication structure in the Subject Interaction Diagram does not yet imply the order in which the messages are exchanged. This order is described in the behavior of the subjects. Figures 5.4 and 5.5 show the Subject Behavior Diagrams of the "Interested Party" subject and, in part, the behavior of the "Real Estate Credit Application Processing" subject.

The initial state in Fig. 5.4 (marked by a black triangle in a circle) stands for formulating a loan request. This is usually done by filling out a corresponding form. Its content would be part of the specification of the "loan request" business object.

After the request has been created, it is sent to the "Real Estate Credit Application Processing" subject. A response from this subject is then awaited. This response can either be the "Offer" or "Rejection" message. In both cases, the subject's behavior is terminated by reaching the respective end states, which are marked as such by small black squares. The circles of the graphical language symbols indicate the type of state ("D" (Do) for function, "S" (Send) for sending, "R" (Receive) for receiving). Diagram 5.5 shows an excerpt of the behavior description of the "Real Estate Credit Application Processing" subject. In the initial state (marked with a black triangle in a circle), the subject receives the message "Loan Request" from the subject "Interested Party." This provides the subject with the form (business object) containing the loan request data.

In the next state, a check is made to determine whether this data is complete. If not, the message "Request incomplete" is sent to the subject "Interested Party." The reception of this message is not yet included in the behavior description of the "Interested Party." If the information is complete, the interested party's creditworthiness is checked. A negative result of this check leads to sending the message "Rejection" to the "Interested Party."

In case of a positive result a credit offer is created and another condition set by business rules of the bank needs to be considered: If the requested loan amount is less than 200,000, the message "Offer" is sent to the subject "Interested Party." If the amount exceeds 200,000, the offer must be verified by the management and the message "Verification Request (Credit Eligibility) is sent to the subject "Management (Real Estate Credits)." Their decision comes back as "Acceptance" or "Rejection" and determines the subsequent steps. For credit requests of more than 500,000, the "Management (Real Estate Credits)" even involves the "Bank Executive Board" subject in the same way. The behavior of the subjects "Management (Real Estate Credits)" and "Bank Executive Board," not depicted here, need to be modeled respectively in order to meet this process logic.

5.2.3 Validation

In the BPM context, validation means checking whether the designed process generates the output expected by the (external) customer and process owner, for example, in the form of a service or product. This question with regard to effectiveness already refers to the results of partial steps, i.e., process participants of their own organization as customers. For example, it is necessary to evaluate whether an upstream process step provides all the information that a processor requires for a decision in his or her sub-task (for instance, approval). We have already mentioned that parts of a model are repeatedly subjected to validation, even during its step-by-step development. In addition, the object of validation is the completely finished process model, the effectiveness of which should be ensured before it is implemented in terms of Information Technology (cf. Sect. 5.2.6). Otherwise, errors are discovered too late and lead to correspondingly high costs for their elimination.

Validation in the Case Study
The process model for the example process was validated during its development
as well as at the end. In doing so, it was initially discovered that the original loan
application did not include a field for the applicant's employment status and thus
lacked an important risk assessment factor. This led to the extension of the business
object and to a positive validation result in the corresponding iteration.

5.2.4 Optimization

While validation aims at ensuring the effectiveness of business processes, optimization is about efficiency. Process efficiency can be expressed by process attributes
for resource consumption such as duration and costs. Optimization means finding
the optimal design of a process with regard to such process parameters. Essential
starting points are improvements in operational and structural organizational design
as well as IT support. Strictly speaking, optimization is not an independent
activity bundle but makes use of modeling, organizational implementation, and IT
implementation (see Sects. 5.2.2, 5.2.5, and 5.2.6).

Simulation is a well-known method for comparing alternatives in process execution or resource allocation. It can be used to obtain quantitative information on the
development of process parameters for a large number of process instances (orders,
production pieces, etc.). The simulation enables the evaluation of a process model
with a certain combination of parameters. These can be deterministic or stochastic
quantities described by probability distributions. Through the use of parameter
changes and alternative process designs, different design options can be analyzed
with respect to their behavior. This allows insights to be gained into bottlenecks or
inefficiencies and the sensitivity of parameters. The extension of a process model
and the gathering of necessary information for conducting simulations can cause
considerable effort. Attributes relevant for optimization are often interdependent and
contradictory, which makes optimization difficult and requires balancing efforts. A
process alternative can, for instance, have a shorter lead time relative to another but
cause higher costs. The decision for an alternative therefore also depends on the
priority of the process objectives.

Optimization in the Case Study
The model could already be optimized during its design. The steps for checking customer creditworthiness and value of the property, which were initially sequentially
planned, were redesigned to be executed in parallel.

5.2.5 Embedding into an Organizational Context

For productive operation, validated processes need to be embedded into the existing,
redesigned, or newly created organizational environment. This is also referred to as

the organizational implementation of a process. It quite often requires an adaptation of the surrounding operational and organizational structure.

A single process is usually part of an entire value creation environment (value chain, value creation network) into which it must be seamlessly assimilated. Therefore, with regard to the operational integration into the process map, particularly the interfaces with other processes must be considered. This can lead to changes to be carried out at the interfaces of an upstream or downstream process. Such circumstances usually are already taken into account in the upstream activity bundles. Therefore, the implementation should be limited to the chronological coordination of the go-live procedure. This means that processes that are connected via interfaces must go live again at the same time if a change has occurred at an interface that has also made modifications necessary in the partner process.

The organizational embedding comprises the assignment of concrete actors, i.e., people as job or role holders, to the actors abstractly specified in the model. One of the challenges is the consideration of the organizational context when using workflow engines. These must be able to dissolve, for instance, dynamic substitute regulations at runtime, as well as the fact that persons can assume different roles in the same process. For example, a superior in a vacation request process can be the approver of vacation requests for his own employees but can also be the applicant for his own vacation, which in turn must be approved by his own superior. Therefore, the software must have organizational knowledge that facilitates the correct routing of a process instance through the processing units and steps.

Further qualitative and quantitative aspects have to be taken into account during organizational embedding. Care must be taken to ensure that the employees have the necessary qualifications (skills) to carry out the modeled behavior or can gain them through training. Adequate qualification is not only a prerequisite for successful work in the currently valid version of the process; it can also foster improvement proposals by process participants.

The number of people assigned to the abstract actors in the model influences the capacity for processing process instances and thus affects parameters such as lead time.

Embedding into an Organizational Context in the Case Study
Column 2 in Fig. 5.6 shows the number of employees who in general are qualified to be assigned to the identified and modeled roles. The third column contains the actual capacity used (short-term absences, e.g., due to illness, are not taken into account). The heads of real estate and consumer credit departments stand in for each other, both in disciplinary and domain-specific matters. This also applies to the members of the executive board.

5.2.6   IT Implementation

Most processes cannot be carried out economically without IT support. Especially when a high degree of automation is strived for, the quality of the mapping of

Actor/Role	Total number	Assigned according to personnel deployment plan
Real Estate Credit Application Processing	9	5 full-time employees
Management (Real Estate Credits)	1	1 manager (Head of consumer credit department) 1 deputy
Bank Executive Board	3	1 head of private customers division 1 head of business customers division 1 head of investment management division

Fig. 5.6 Potential and concrete assignment of roles

the process in IT becomes very important. But also, and in particular, for steps where human actors are involved (e.g., entering data, making decisions), the user-centered/friendly design of the IT systems is of high importance.

IT-related implementation of a process means mapping it as an IT-supported workflow with integration of a suitable user interface, the execution logic, and the IT systems involved. For this purpose, it is necessary first of all to transfer the more or less formal model description (see Chap. 3) into a language interpretable by a workflow engine, i.e., into an executable program. This enables the engine to control the execution of a process instance at runtime according to the model. For the completion of individual subtasks during processing, a whole series of software applications and services usually have to be integrated into the process. Typical examples are ERP transactions and document and content management systems.

A relatively new approach to automation of standardized, repetitive work procedures is Robotic Process Automation (RPA). This term stands for tools that "perform [if, then, else] statements on structured data, typically using a combination of user interface interactions, or by connecting to APIs to drive client servers, mainframes or HTML code" [3]. Thus, software robots, for example, imitate the behavior of humans when using the graphical user interface of information systems [4]. This allows, for instance, the quick linking of heterogeneous IT systems and automated data transfer between, or data input in, various existing applications without the need for these to be modified. Artificial Intelligence and machine learning functionality promise to facilitate learning and automated adaptation of RPA tools to changes in the underlying IT systems [5].

Extensive testing of the implemented overall solutions must ensure the quality of the process support provided by IT.

IT Implementation in the Case Study

Figure 5.7 shows the essential elements of the IT environment, which was designed and implemented to support the process and its sub-steps, together with their most important process-relevant functions.

IT system/service	Selection of functions that are essential for the process
Portal of the bank	• Provides information material on financing and an electronic form for the customer or a real estate loan officer to enter the loan application. • ...
Workflow engine	• Instantiates the process when the customer saves the request in the portal. • Controls instances according to the model, including users and other systems or services as needed. • Records log data for the operations. • Generates messages and reports based on log data • ...
Backend system of the bank	• Manages customers • Categorizes customers (scoring) • Determines conditions • Generates offers • ...

Fig. 5.7 IT environment established for the process

5.2.7   Operation and Monitoring

Implemented processes go live after their approval by the responsible authorities. This means that those involved in a process execute it in the form of instances in the organizational and IT environment set up for day-to-day business.

In order to obtain information for the deliberate management of processes, it is necessary to observe their behavior during everyday operations. This monitoring records measurement data and calculates actual values for the Process Performance Indicators (PPIs) defined during analysis and modeling. An immediate comparison with defined target values leads to escalations along the management hierarchy and, if necessary, to short-term measures in the event of deviations. Medium- and longer-term evaluations reveal structural opportunities for improvement. The analysis of the process behavior and possible deviations allows conclusions to be drawn about causes and triggers feedback into other activity bundles.

Operation and Monitoring in the Case Study
Since the release of the process, the bank has been processing credit applications from interested parties in the described form and environment. Monitoring for the past quarter revealed the following average figures:

- Interested parties had submitted 50 applications per week.
- The bank rejected 20% of them, half of it due to lack of creditworthiness.
- For the remaining applications the interested parties received an offer within 4 days.
- In 30% of the cases the interested party accepted the offer and signed a contract.

Since competitors advertise with very short processing times, the bank assumes that the 4 days until applicants receive an offer, all other conditions being equal, is one of the reasons why customers do not sign a contract. This duration also deviates significantly from the previously formulated target of 3 days.

5.2.8   Optimization Scenarios

The following scenarios show how further analyses of the monitoring results can be used to investigate the causes of the long lead time and to branch out into suitable activity bundles for improvement measures (optimization).

In each case, the target point of the branch-out determines the further path through the activity bundles, i.e., which subsequent activities are necessary before the redesigned process can be put into day-to-day operation. In the interests of simplification, we limit our consideration to one measure per scenario. In reality, several optimization possibilities will usually be pursued in parallel.

5.2.8.1 Optimization Scenario 1

The frequency distribution for credit application occurrence has shown that on Mondays 25, Tuesdays 15, Wednesdays 6, Thursdays 2, and Fridays also 2 applications are submitted. This could be due to the fact that interested parties tour and check out real estate, take purchasing decisions, and think about financing mainly on weekends. The analysis of the idle time until the real estate credit department processes a request reveals a bottleneck at the beginning of the week, due to the high number of parallel applications. With the currently available capacity of five full-time clerks, the average idle time is 2 days. In order to reduce the latter and thus also the overall lead time, additional processing capacity, such as available part-time staff, could be employed on Mondays and Tuesdays. In this case, only organizational implementation in terms of staffing is concerned; the process does not change, and no further activities are necessary.

5.2.8.2 Optimization Scenario 2

A more detailed analysis has shown that the high average lead time is caused by the applications with amounts between 200,000 and 500,000, because the idle time until the department management ("Management (Real Estate Credits)") approves the application is very high relative to the other proportions of the total duration. This is due to the fact that the availability of department heads and substitute for approvals is limited, e.g., due to frequent business trips.

The bank's internal process analyst proposes a change of the business rule for approval. In the future, clerks should be allowed to sign and send offers for amounts up to 500,000 themselves. This reorganization affects several bundles of activities. First of all, it requires a change in the model, as the approval loop via the department management is no longer required. The model change requires subsequent validation to ensure that the changed process (still) leads to the desired result. As part of the IT implementation, the modification of the model must also be transferred to the workflow software and tested. The omission of the approvals changes the task structure of the department management. For the clerks the tasks remain the same, but competence and responsibility increase. These changes have to be taken into account in the organizational implementation, for example, through updated task descriptions and possibly through the qualification of the clerks through training, e.g., for a more comprehensive risk assessment. Compared to case 1, this scenario intervenes massively in the way the process is conducted and therefore requires much more extensive activities.

5.2.8.3 Optimization Scenario 3

The bank obtains creditworthiness data on the applicants from the associated credit bureau (e.g., SCHUFA in Germany). For this purpose, the real estate loan processing clerks transfer the necessary customer data from the loan application to the credit bureau's Web form. They then enter the results of this query into the banking system for further processing in the bank's own scoring system. The clerks report on time-consuming copying of the data using copy and paste, the errors that occur in doing so, and the resulting reworking. In order to push forward digitalization, the bank decides to use the credit bureau's Web service instead of their Web form-based Internet information service. The Web service can be integrated into the workflow in such a way that the process engine triggers it when the clerk pushes a button and transfers the customer data as parameters. The service automatically returns the result to the process engine, which then transfers it to the banking system.

In this case, the only activity bundle to be dealt with is the IT implementation, including corresponding software adaptations and subsequent tests, before going live with the modified solution. The work procedures of the participants change only slightly; qualification measures are not necessary. The elimination of manual data transfer relieves them of mindless, time-consuming, and thus cost-intensive and error-prone routine tasks. The more intensive use of IT saves processing and lead time as well as costs, while increasing customer satisfaction.

5.2.8.4 Optimization Scenario 4

In Sect. 5.2.4, we described that the customer creditworthiness check and the property value check were deliberately parallelized during modeling in order to save lead time. The analysis showed that the bank rejects five applications per week for creditworthiness reasons. In these cases, however, clerks had already spent effort doing the parallel value check of the real estate in question. Saving on this could initially speak in favor of first checking the creditworthiness and only carrying out the value check if the result is positive. A model change with validation and adaptation of the workflow application would be necessary.

However, the sequential order would again increase the lead time and lead to a conflict of objectives. Therefore, it is important to further consider whether the effort for value checking could be reduced through automation so that unnecessary value checks no longer play a role. It is conceivable, for example, that the banking system could be enhanced with valuation functions. It could then calculate a value index after automatic transfer of parameters from the loan application (type, size, year of construction, address, etc.) and being enriched with comparative information (values from the bank's own experience and reference value tables) and geo information (infrastructure with schools, shopping facilities, transportation connections, etc.). This index would accelerate the final value estimation carried out by the clerk. With this option, the parallel execution of the steps could remain. Instead of a model change, the additional functionality in the IT implementation would have to be realized and tested, and the clerks would have to be trained in how to use the software extension.

5.3 Introduction to Design Thinking

5.3.1 Essence

Design Thinking (DT) is a methodical approach to be creative and constructive in order to develop something new and to solve complex problems. It is characterized by innovative approaches to solution-oriented design. Problems can be better solved by focusing on the needs of the (potential) users during continuous iterations and "making solution ideas comprehensible and graspable" through prototypes. This basic understanding of Design Thinking is shared by practitioners and scientists alike (for an overview of examples of definitions see [6]). The spectrum covered by the approach, on the other hand, is not seen uniformly.

There are, for example, interpretations that see it as a mindset, as a process, or as a toolbox [7]. An empirical investigation proves the perception in the continuum between the two poles of toolbox and mindset (cf. Fig. 5.8) [8].

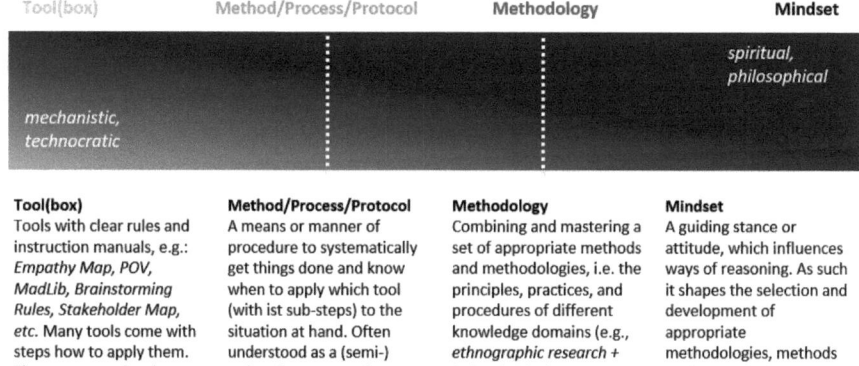

Tool(box)	Method/Process/Protocol	Methodology	Mindset
Tools with clear rules and instruction manuals, e.g.: *Empathy Map, POV, MadLib, Brainstorming Rules, Stakeholder Map, etc.* Many tools come with steps how to apply them. The more complex these steps become, the more they are perceived as self-contained methods.	A means or manner of procedure to systematically get things done and know when to apply which tool (with ist sub-steps) to the situation at hand. Often understood as a (semi-) ordered sequence of actions, for example the x steps in *'the' design thinking process, waterfall model, or other process representations.*	Combining and mastering a set of appropriate methods and methodologies, i.e. the principles, practices, and procedures of different knowledge domains (e.g., *ethnographic research + industrial design + creativity methods etc.*), which might constitute a coherent whole for an application context at hand. Examples might be *Lean Start-up, Six Sigma or Design Thinking* itself.	A guiding stance or attitude, which influences ways of reasoning. As such it shapes the selection and development of appropriate methodologies, methods and tools. The frequent application of the latter three might influence the mindset and vice versa.

Fig. 5.8 Understanding Design Thinking

On the one hand, this is due to the different roots, but on the other hand, it is also a consequence of the inherent, constant, experience-led further development and adaptation of the concept in different contexts.

Larry Leifer, one of the protagonists of the approach at the d.school in Stanford, states that its permanent enhancements are an important part of Design Thinking and that it would make itself unrecognizable if it were to publish a fixed manifesto one day [9].

The approach traces back to David Kelley from the design agency IDEO and professors Larry Leifer and Terry Winograd from Stanford University. In particular, the latter two recognized, when training engineering students, that the development of marketable products should focus much more on user-related aspects and less on purely technical aspects. This insight led to the development of the DT concept from the 1980s onwards and is still manifested today in the Stanford course on Mechanical Engineering 310—Design Innovation (me310.stanford.edu). Hasso Plattner made a significant contribution to the further dissemination of this knowledge in research, academic teaching, and business practice with his support of the institutions named after him at the d.school Institute of Design at Stanford University and the School of Design Thinking at Potsdam University (HPI D-School).

Due to its origin, DT was originally primarily concerned with the development of physical products. However, it is now used in a wide variety of areas, such as the development of services or entire business models, and is increasingly gaining importance in organizational design and Business Process Management.

5.3.2   Core Elements

Core elements are a mixture of mindset, procedures, and concrete facilities such as work areas. This is reflected in the rough division into the three "Ps," namely, into the areas people, process, and place.

Design Thinking begins with the creation of deep empathy for those affected by a (problem) situation. It identifies the optimal solution in the overlapping area of human desires (human-psychological aspect), feasibility (technological aspect), and profitability (business aspect) [10]. The innovation to be developed should be something

- That people really like (desirability)
- That is feasible from a technological and process-related point of view (feasibility)
- That is successful from an economic point of view (viability)

To achieve this, an interdisciplinary team (people) on variable, creativity-promoting premises (place) goes through a procedure (process) with many iterations, whereas a variety of methods can be used.

5.3.2.1 People

Focusing on the human being takes place in two respects:

On the one hand, representatives of the target group of the innovation, i.e., customers or users, with their needs are in the center of interest. Developing empathy for them, putting oneself in their position in the context under consideration, and thus gaining a deep understanding of the problem is the cornerstone for successful innovation and encompasses a large part of the process described in the "Process" subsection below.

On the other hand, Design Thinking strongly focuses on the people involved in the project as individuals and as a team. It aims for increasing the quality of results by using the diversity in interdisciplinary teams. Team members should be "T-Shaped", i.e., both experts and generalists. As experts, they are deeply rooted in their specialized field and bring in the appropriate expertise (vertical line of the T). This can also involve the professional representation of a stakeholder group (e.g., sales, production, IT). Looking at a problem from different perspectives and synthesizing know-how and experience from different domains often helps to develop new approaches to solutions. The quality as generalists is a prerequisite for changing from one's own perspective to that of other participants and for being open to cooperation at the (functional) interfaces (horizontal line of the T, "We" thinking) [11, p. 122]. Lewrick et al. plead for interdisciplinary versus multidisciplinary teams because the former truly and collectively generate ideas and stand behind them, whereas the members of multidisciplinary teams often overestimate their own perspective when finding solutions. The latter rather leads to compromise solutions, which are not fully supported by all. Ideally, an interdisciplinary team is made up heterogeneously of representatives not only from as many areas of expertise as possible but also from different age groups, nationalities, sexes, etc.

The success of a Design Thinking project is largely determined by the individual characteristics of the members of the associated team and the resulting collaborative working culture and way of thinking. The focus here is on showing high esteem and empathy for people as the starting point for all activities, both for colleagues in the team as well as for users or customers. In addition, the team members should have qualities such as the ability to cooperate, curiosity, joy of experimentation, integrative thinking, and optimism. A further success factor is the guidance of the team by a facilitator who is experienced in the process and the use of the method. This person provides orientation for the respective activity bundle of the process and for which instruments can best be used there, without, however, intervening in terms of content.

5.3.2.2 Process

Design Thinking follows a process model with a series of steps. Although slightly different variants of the so-called microcycle with alternative names of the phases have developed over time, their content only differs marginally. We follow the model of the d.school in Stanford, which is based on five phases of the Design Thinking process, also known as working modes (cf. Fig. 5.9).

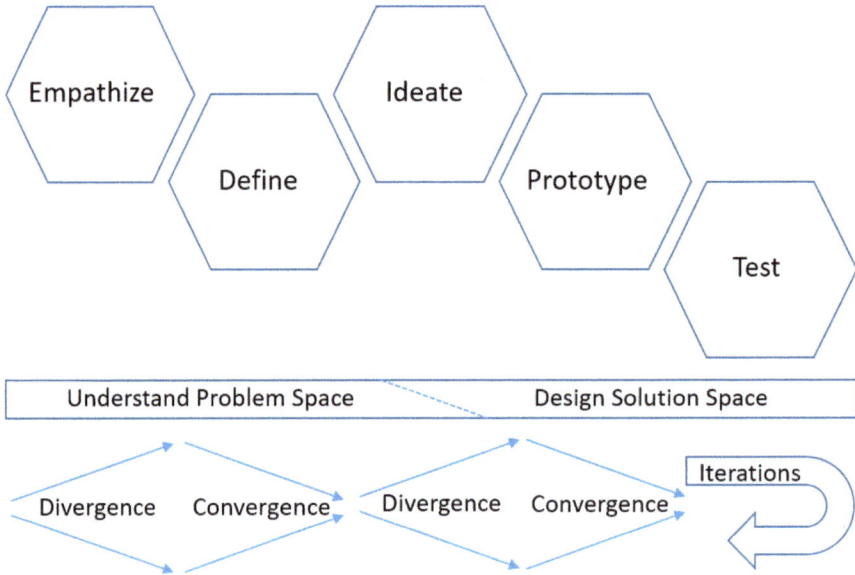

Fig. 5.9 Design Thinking process according to Stanford d.school

All models are characterized by the alternation between divergent and convergent viewing, thinking, and acting, both in understanding the problem space and shaping the solution space. The transition between the expansion of the creative space with an ever-increasing amount of information and focusing through containment is called a groan zone, i.e., a "creaking" hinge [11, p. 28f]. Deliberate iteration is also a fundamental element in the DT process, which is expressed in the motto "fail early, fail often" or "fail forward" in an open culture allowing errors. It describes the idea that ideal solutions can only be found through multiple and early experimentation, testing, and consideration of the feedback of the target group, which can lead to more or less extensive new runs of previous modes. The multiple iterations as a so-called macrocycle should lead from the understanding of the problem to the concretization of a vision for a solution and finally to an implementation plan [11, p. 37]. In all process phases the principle "Be visual & show" applies, which means that thoughts, ideas, and results are to be visually and vividly documented and presented, for example, through post-its with keywords and drawings, mind maps, process maps, tangible prototypes, etc. Because of this principle it is sometimes suggested to speak of Design Doing rather than Design Thinking.

For the successful work of a team along the process, a number of rules and tips (rules of engagement) have proven to be helpful, some of which should also be followed in group work in general. They should be communicated at the beginning of a project and called to mind later by the facilitator if necessary:

- User-oriented way of thinking and working (development of empathy)
- No specification or limitation of ways of thinking, ways of finding solutions or fixed solutions (openness, autonomy, "Go for quantity")
- Concentration on the topic (focus), therefore no distraction by smart phones, computers, smart watches, etc. unless they are to be used deliberately, e.g., for research or prototype creation
- Active participation of each team member (own articulation, disciplined listening ("One conversation at a time") and building on ideas of others
- Encourage the development of different perspectives and wild ideas
- No value judgment during idea generation ("Defer judgment," "No killer phrases")
- Time boxing to avoid falling in love with a particular idea

The following sections briefly describe each phase together with tables including a selection of methods and tools that are used in each phase, respectively. More detailed explanations can be found, for example, in the bootleg of the d.school[1] and in Lewrick et al. [11, p. 36].

Empathize (Building Empathy)
Empathy is the heart of a human-centered design process. To develop it means to build a deep understanding for the members of the target group with regard to the problem and its context. The aim is to understand why and how people do things, how they think about the world, and what is important and useful to them, as well as to learn about their physical and emotional needs. This means observing users, listening to them, interacting with them, imagining and empathizing with their situation, and thus immersing into their conscious and unconscious world of feelings, values, and needs (engage, observe, immerse). This is the basic prerequisite to steer innovations in the right direction.

So-called personas are an essential instrument for documenting the learnings about the target group. Personas represent fictional customers or users together with their objectives, behavior, needs, and attributes relevant for the solution to be developed. In the model of the Hasso Plattner Institute, the "Empathize" phase encompasses the stages "Understanding" and "Observing." Figure 5.10 shows common instruments for the activities included in this phase.

Define (Defining Problem)
This mode is about building on the findings from the "Empathize" mode, sharing and bringing them together, structuring, weighing, and interpreting them. This synthesis serves to test and further develop the personas for ideal-type users and, if necessary, to adopt the perspectives of various stakeholders. The results are a deeper understanding of the users and the problem space as well as a more concrete, meaningful problem definition (design challenge). The latter is reflected in a single

---

[1] https://dschool.stanford.edu/resources/The-Bootcamp-Bootleg.

Activity/Theme	Selected methods and tools
Open up the context of the problem and develop a common understanding of it	• Brain dump • Business Process and Value Maps, Concept Maps, Business Model Canvas
Structure the problem context	• Structuring/Clustering frameworks
Identify and understand target group (user, customer)	User Profile Canvas with • Persona • Jobs-to-be-done • Gains & Pains • Use cases
Understand the target group (user, customer)	• Needfinding discussion, interview for empathy (incl. preparation), e.g. with W questions (What? How? Why? Who?) according to the AEIOU method (Activities, Environment, Interaction, Objects, User) • Empathy map • Future user

Fig. 5.10 Methods and tools for the "Empathize" phase

Activity/Theme	Selected methods and tools
Share insights	• Story share and capture (Storytelling)
Interpret insights, draw conclusions	• Saturate and group • Empathy map • Customer/User Experience Journey (with actions, mindset, touch points, pain points, moments of truth)
Understand the target group (user, customer) even better	• Persona • Composite Character Profiles • Power of Ten • 2x2 Matrix • Why-How-Lladdering • Point of view • 360-degree view • A day in the life of …

Fig. 5.11 Methods and tools for the "Define" phase

sentence which, as a so-called Point of View (POV), forms the question for the subsequent phase of idea generation [11, p. 73]. In practice, different POV questions are used. A typical formulation is the "How might we?" question, for example, "How might we help [user, customer] to reach [a certain goal]?" [11, p. 74].

In the Hasso Plattner Institute model, "Define" corresponds to the "Define point of view" phase. Figure 5.11 lists common tools for the activities included in this phase.

Activity/Theme	Selected methods and tools
Generate ideas (iteratively)	• General brainstorming based on POV (e.g. How might we?) with stimulation through creativity techniques • Targeted brainstorming (critical functionalities, benchmark, dark horse, funky prototype) • Power of Ten, Bodystorming • Quick&Dirty Prototyping
Sort and condense ideas	• Swap Sort, 2x2 Matrix • Concept/Systems/Mind Maps, idea profiles
Evaluate and prioritize ideas	• Four-category method; Post-it voting, Spend your budget

Fig. 5.12 Methods and tools for the "Ideate" phase

Ideate (Finding Ideas)

The aim of idea generation is to develop a wide range of solutions, i.e., to develop and visualize as many ideas, and as many different ideas, as possible. The starting point is the point-of-view question; however, all the insights gained so far are incorporated into this phase, including user profile canvas, empathy map, and customer/user experience journey. The basic instrument is brainstorming, which can be further and repeatedly stimulated by creativity techniques and specific tasks (e.g., generating ideas for certain functions). The design and testing of initial "low fidelity" prototypes can also provide further food for thought for solutions and trigger iterations. The use of methods in this mode should enable going beyond obvious solutions and thus increase the innovation potential by using the collective perspectives and strengths of the team. Unexpected solution directions should be able to emerge and contribute to the quantity and diversity of ideas. This results in a multitude of ideas, which are sorted, condensed, and evaluated. The entire process should be strictly separated between the generation and evaluation of ideas, so as not to restrict the creative flow at an early phase.

In the Hasso Plattner Institute model, "Ideate" corresponds to the "Finding Idea" phase. Common instruments for the activities contained in this mode are shown in Fig. 5.12.

Prototype (Creating Prototypes)

Prototyping picks up the most highly rated ideas from idea development and continues to develop them further. In doing so, the principle of Design Thinking is implemented: to visualize issues, products, and results as early as possible and to test, discuss, and further develop them with potential users, incorporating their feedback into tangible models. Prototypes are thus created in order to learn to clarify open questions and discrepancies, to start a conversation or a discourse, and to recognize dead ends quickly and at an early stage, which in turn saves costs.

Activity/Theme	Selected methods and tools
Create prototypes	• Low-fidelity prototypes, e.g. from handicraft material (Lego, modelling clay, etc.) • Role plays, storytelling, storyboards • Wireframes, Screen design tools • Shooting and editing video

Fig. 5.13 Methods and tools for the "Prototype" phase

Prototyping transfers ideas from the mind into the physical world. A prototype can therefore be anything that takes on a physical form and follows the maxim "don't tell me, show me!": a wall with post-it notes, a role play, a room, an object, a storyboard, or any combination of different means of expression.

The granularity of the prototype should correspond to the progress of the project. In the early stages of a project, prototypes should be created that can be made quickly and cost-effectively (low fidelity, quick and dirty), but already generate useful feedback from users and colleagues. In later stages, the prototypes should be refined and allow careful investigation of specific issues. They serve to deepen empathy, to test, and to gain further ideas and inspiration.

In the Hasso Plattner Institute model, "Prototype" corresponds to the "Develop prototype" phase. Figure 5.13 shows common tools for the activities included in this phase.

Test (Testing Prototypes)
As discussed in the previous section, testing is closely linked to prototyping. The recommendation "Prototype as if you know you're right, but test as if you know you're wrong" describes the way of thinking that illustrates this relation. Testing offers the opportunity to receive qualitative feedback on the prototypical solutions, to make them better, to learn more about the users, and thus to deepen the empathy for them. The test mode is an iterative learning mode in which the prototypes are placed in the context of the potential user, then used and evaluated by them. Important principles are, like already mentioned: "Don't talk, show!", create experiences, and enable the user to make comparisons. The feedback during the tests can lead not only to changes but also to complete rejection and thus to a fundamental iteration over more distant previous phases. This procedure is also described by Lewrick et al. [11, p. 34] with the slogan "Love it, change it or leave it." In principle, each iteration loop, regardless of its scope, must reflect which previous results (e.g., personas, user/customer experience journey) have to be adapted as a result of the feedback.

In the Hasso Plattner Institute model, "Test" corresponds to the "Testing" phase. Figure 5.14 contains instruments for the activities carried out during this phase.

Activity/Theme	Selected methods and tools
Gather feedback	• Feedback grid • "I like, I wish, What if?" • A/B testing with digital tools

Fig. 5.14 Methods and tools for the "Test" phase

5.3.2.3 Place

For the work of the interdisciplinary teams in the described modes, it is necessary to create a creativity-fostering environment, so-called make or creative spaces. This applies in particular to the availability, size, and furnishing of premises as well as to visualization and prototype design tools and materials. The main aim is to provide the teams with freely and permanently available work, interaction, relaxation, and storage areas. Flexible furniture with castors, describable and erasable surfaces (walls, tables, boards), as well as good and fast access to information (Internet, libraries, etc.), tools, working materials, and catering add to a suitable environment [10, p. 216]. Lighting, ventilation, and air conditioning are also important factors to be considered.

In practice, teams are sometimes given the opportunity to design the environment themselves (e.g., build their own furniture), especially in the case of long-term projects. Doorley and Witthoft have published instructions and experiences, among other things, in the design of creative environments for the d.school [12].

5.4   Connecting the Concepts

5.4.1   Overview

As shown, Design Thinking aims at the innovation of products and services, business models, and business processes. The focus is on user centricity, creativity, and agility in an experimental, iterative process that interdisciplinary teams traverse.

Process management pursues a comparable objective with agile and creative process design of new, or redesign of existing, processes under consideration of customer needs.

In the following, we put the concepts into relation to one another and discuss the promising use of Design Thinking elements for process management.

We pay particular attention to the digitalization of processes, i.e., the reasonable use of information and communication technology for process improvement and innovation. Prototypes and final solutions are therefore always workflow applications with different degrees of automation.

5.4.2   User Centricity

During process analysis traditional BPM approaches usually involve those participating with interviews and workshops. However, the "hard" facts of the work
in the process with the characteristics listed in Sect. 5.2.2 are in the foreground
of the activity-related and process-related interview questions, card techniques, or
observations. Aspects such as understanding users' motivation, ways of thinking,
and values, which are expressly emphasized for the development of empathy in
Design Thinking, are largely ignored here. Newer concepts such as Social BPM
have changed little in this regard.

The Subject-oriented Business Process Management (S-BPM) approach, which
was already used in the case study at the beginning of this chapter, can build
an interesting bridge. It focuses on the subjects as actors in the process. With
the associated methodology and language (see Sect. 3.6) as well as suitable tool
environments, representatives of subjects involved in the process can participate in
iterative solution development not only as respondents or observers but also as active
designers. They not only explicitly specify the behavior of the subject they represent
and its interactions with other participants but can also immediately test and change
the result of their design by executing the resulting model. In doing so, they can
implicitly bring in the "soft" factors mentioned above.

5.4.3   Agile Process with Iterations

In practice, more extensive process management projects are often still carried
out using traditional project management methods in clearly defined phases with
milestones, comparable to the waterfall model in software development.

This means that the path from analysis of the design of the business model and its
organizational and IT implementation to an executable workflow application takes
an extensive amount of time. It also increases the likelihood that the resulting IT
solution will deviate from the evolving needs and desires of users.

For process digitalization in particular, it is therefore advantageous to adapt the
agile, iterative process of Design Thinking. This opens up the possibility of meeting
the increasing dynamics with regard to the emergence of new processes and changes
to existing processes, for example, due to new or changed business models such as
servitization. For further considerations, we compare the modes of Design Thinking
with the activity bundles in process management (cf. Fig. 5.15).

Together with the explanations in Sects. 5.2.2 and 5.3.2.2 the illustration shows
that DT makes a stronger distinction between problem understanding and solution
design. The latter only begins with "Ideate." Before this, the actual situation is
extensively illuminated and, for example, documented and visualized along the
way via personas in the customer/user experience journey, before the point-of-view
question is formulated as the starting point for generating ideas.

BPM Activity Bundles

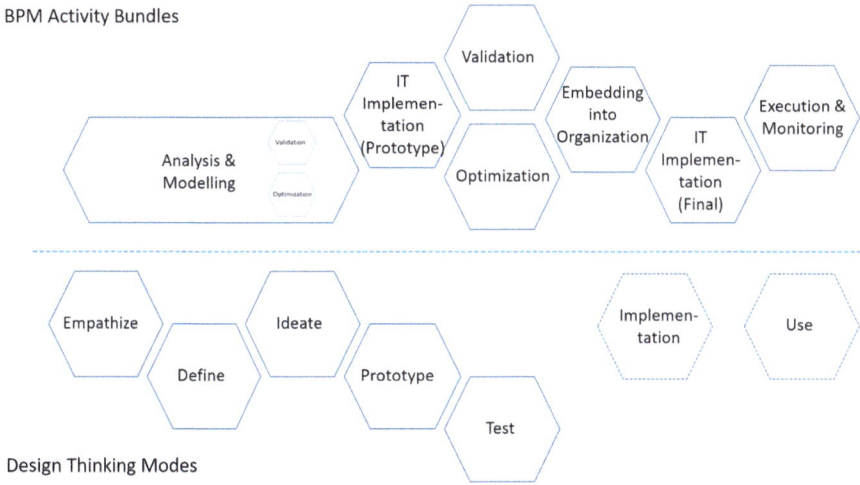

Design Thinking Modes

Fig. 5.15   Assignment of Design Thinking modes and BPM activity bundles

In process management, on the other hand, the problem is usually clearly formulated at the beginning. When renewing existing processes, it is usually derived from the desire for improved process performance (e.g., shorter lead times). In practice, therefore, only weak points in the current state are documented and analysis information is used to develop and visualize a new target model, just like in a new process. The creative, design-related part begins earlier than with Design Thinking and tends to be underpinned by less information when being started. It is driven more analytically (e.g., by performance indicators) than by the "soft" factors identified in the course of empathy development in Design Thinking. Regardless of the somewhat different concrete design, the activity bundle **Analysis and Modeling** can be assigned to the DT modes Empathize, Define, and Ideate.

The use of proven DT instruments is ideal for a more comprehensive capturing of the problem context and the resulting expansion of the spectrum of solutions for process innovation. Especially when developing a new process, the team members can broaden their horizon and develop a common understanding with a brain dump concerning the problem environment and the discussion of the results.

With the help of personas for the process participants in their respective roles as well as interviews and observations, customer/user experience journeys can be described.

If participants in the process are team members themselves, they can also visualize their own experiences as journeys. This extends the information base beyond the classic, objective process characteristics to include the user's perspective. This broader foundation for the development of solution ideas should justify the higher effort.

In Sect. 5.2.2 we had explained that effectiveness and efficiency, at least of model excerpts, are already taken into account during the analysis and modeling of processes. This is especially true if the future users do this themselves, as in subject orientation. Therefore, the activity bundles **Validation** and **Optimization** are assigned to the DT mode Test, but also cover Empathize, Define, and Ideate.

With the focus on process digitalization, the DT Prototype mode corresponds to the activity bundle **IT implementation** in process management. Prototyping in Design Thinking makes the claim to produce a prototype quickly and with simple means, i.e., cost-effectively, in order to quickly obtain feedback from the user (Test mode) and to utilize it. By applying this "fail early, fail often" principle to process management, the team must be able to create an executable model with minimal effort. The focus is therefore on creating a functional prototype in the form of software that allows users to experience what their work with the IT solution would look like. However, assigning the prototype to the IT implementation should not mean that programming is necessary. Rather, it must be possible in the interests of rapid iterations to generate a prototype automatically from the model and have it tested by the users in the activity bundle of validation. In the same way, subsequent model changes based on feedback again lead to a new prototype, until a version is found that satisfies the users. Such low-cost and early prototyping possibly prevents more complex reworking during the later realization of the real runtime environment. Using a comparable approach, the user interface can be designed according to the principles of user experience design.

Since the respective process model is not only the basis for prototypes, but in its ultimately adopted version also for the workflow application strived for, the activity bundle IT implementation includes also their realization in the way described in Sect. 5.2.6. If software which goes beyond the model-based workflow control has to be developed for this purpose, SCRUM as a user-centered, agile software development method serves as a good choice. In the context of IT implementation, it is also important to decide to what extent the strategy of minimum viable products, often used by software start-ups, should be pursued. This would mean making software with minimal functionality available to customers or users not only prototypically but also productively in order to obtain their feedback for further development. This could be risky with IT solutions for business-critical processes; on the other hand, it could possibly give an edge over competitors by familiarizing customers with features at an early stage.

As explained in Sects. 5.2.5 and 5.2.7, the model must also be embedded into the organization (**Organizational Embedding**) before the process can go live (**Operation and Monitoring**).

In Design Thinking, comparable steps follow for the implementation, for example, of a product on the basis of an accepted prototype as well as for its use. However, these steps no longer belong to the modes in the narrower sense (dotted forms in Fig. 5.15).

Conclusion

In order to meet the requirements of digitalizing processes, a process management approach should combine Design Thinking and process management concepts.

It must be suitable for quickly mapping processes and their changes both (business) domain-related and in IT, while at the same time adequately involving the users in short iteration cycles in order to approximate the resulting solution to their ideas.

In addition to the instruments that can be used for the Design Thinking modes Empathize, Define, and Ideate, easy-to-handle methods and tools are particularly necessary for this purpose, with which the team and/or the process participants themselves are able to:

1. Articulate their individually different mental models of work
2. Harmonize these different mental models
3. Develop ideas for solutions and concrete proposals for solutions in the form of models
4. Automatically convert these models into executable prototypes and test them
5. Transfer released models to live workflow applications with limited effort

An example of a concept to support (1) and (2) is Compare/WP (see Sect. 6.1.2). Requirements (3), (4), and (5) are, for example, covered by the S-BPM approach and BPM tools based on it [13, 14].

5.4.4 Interdisciplinary Team

The importance of the interdisciplinarity of the facilitator-led team in Design Thinking was explained in Sect. 5.3.2.1.

BPM projects are also usually carried out by teams. We distinguish thereby between four roles:

- **Governors** set the determining factors for the project. These essentially comprise the scope, i.e., the delimitation of the process system worked on in the project, as well as the methodology and tools, specifically related to analysis and modeling.
- **Actors** are the present or future actors who carry out the actions in the runtime instances of the process to be changed or developed. They are therefore the carriers of concrete execution-related process knowledge for their part in the creation of the process result, i.e., they know which sub-steps they carry out in which order, which information and tools they need for this, and with whom they interact.
- **Experts** support the other roles with methodical and domain-related knowledge. They are, for example, domain experts (specialists) who have expertise in the relevant field that goes beyond that of the actors, and which they can contribute as such. Method experts help the participants, especially the actors, to articulate and harmonize their mental models and to implement them with one of the modeling

languages presented in Chap. 3. Finally, IT experts are called in for the technical implementation of the business process models. If required, experts in the various fields from outside the company's own organization are also involved as external consultants.

- **Facilitators** moderate and coordinate the approach and the cooperation of the participants. For example, they ensure that actors coordinate the interfaces between their work steps and, if necessary, identify and involve suitable experts for particular problems. In the course of all this, facilitators motivate involved people to act compliantly in accordance with the determining factors set by governors and monitor their behavior respectively.

With the traditional phase-oriented approach in BPM, usually a project leader as a facilitator coordinates the collaboration of domain and method specialists as actors and experts during analysis, modeling, validation, and optimization.

The implementation of the approved business process models is then carried out by IT experts. In Sect. 5.4.3, we have already identified long duration and the resulting deviation from the stakeholders' needs as probable disadvantages of this approach.

For some time now, the **BizDevOps approach**, which is intended to take into account the increasing agility requirements in the course of digitalization, has been becoming more widespread. It strives for a comparatively closer integration of the business departments (business, biz), IT development units (development), and IT operation units (operations).[2] Right from the start, the agile team includes representatives from all areas in the roles described, who jointly design the process solution. The concept can thus both improve business and IT alignment and also foster enabling through IT. The former means that the degree of coverage of the business departments' needs increases through appropriate IT services. In enabling, IT gives impetus to the use of information and communication technology for business model and business process innovations.

Like Design Thinking, the BizDevOps approach therefore involves an inter-disciplinary team. The challenge in such teams is to establish the "We" thinking among "T-shaped" individuals. This is due to the fact that line units from which the participants originate (various business departments involved in the process, IT development, IT operations) pursue different goals and often tend to give them a higher priority than a goal to be achieved jointly (innovative or improved process solution). In addition, creativity may be hampered by the involvement of domain experts. On the one hand, process participants are often aware of weak points in existing processes and of ways for improvement. On the other hand, they may be "operationally blind" and too restricted in their consideration of the problem space and, in particular, the solution space. Recruitment should therefore not only

---

[2] When looking beyond company boundaries, one could add partners in the value creation network such as suppliers, customers, or logistics service providers (Network Partners) and speak of NetBizDevOps.

take into account diversity aspects such as gender, age, and cultural background. Rather, a meaningful balance needs to be found between domain experts and team members who have a background in other fields and have no strong self-interest in the appearance of a solution. The shift in emphasis can be made dependent on whether the goal is more a process improvement in which the experiences and inputs of those familiar with the existing process can be helpful. If, on the other hand, the focus is on a more radical process innovation, this could possibly have a limiting effect. Of course, even with the original objective of improvement, ideas for a fundamental innovation of the process under consideration should not be ignored.

References

1. T. Allweyer, *Geschäftsprozessmanagement: Strategie, Entwurf, Implementierung, Controlling* (W3l GmbH, Dortmund, 2005)
2. H.J. Schmelzer, W. Sesselmann, Geschäftsprozessmanagement in der praxis (8., überarb. u. erw. aufl.), in *München: Hanser* (2013)
3. C. Tornbohm, C. Dunie, *Market Guide for Robotic Process Automation Software, Gartner Report G00319864* (Gartner, Stamford, 2017)
4. J. Geyer-Klingeberg, N. Nakladal, F. Baldauf, F. Veit, Process mining and robotic process automation: a perfect match, in *Proceedings of the Dissertation Award, Demonstration and Industrial Track at BPM 2028* (2018). [Online; accessed 2025-05-21]
5. W. van der Aalst, M. Bichler, A. Heinzl, Robotic process automation. Bus. Inf. Syst. Eng. **60**(4), 269–272 (2018). [Online; accessed 2025-05-21]
6. D.R. Schallmo, K. Lang, et al., *Design Thinking erfolgreich anwenden* (Springer, Berlin, 2017)
7. W. Brenner, F. Uebernickel, T. Abrell, Design thinking as mindset, process, and toolbox, in *Design Thinking for Innovation* (Springer, Berlin, 2016), pp. 3–21
8. J. Schmiedgen, H. Rhinow, E. Köppen, *Parts Without a Whole?: The Current State of Design Thinking Practice in Organizations*, vol. 97 (Universitätsverlag Potsdam, Potsdam, 2016)
9. L. Leifer, F. Hoffmann, Über design thinking, bad guys, experimente, jagd und organisationalen wandel. OrganisationsEntwicklung **2**, 8–13 (2012)
10. F. Uebernickel, W. Brenner, B. Pukall, T. Naef, B. Schindlholzer, *Design Thinking: Das Handbuch* (Frankfurter Allgemeine Buch, Frankfurt , 2015)
11. M. Lewrick, P. Link, L. Leifer, N. Langensand, *Das Design Thinking Playbook: mit traditionellen, aktuellen und zukünftigen Erfolgsfaktoren* (Vahlen, Munich, 2018)
12. S. Doorley, S. Witthoft, et al., *Make Space: How to Set the Stage for Creative Collaboration* (Wiley, New York, 2012)
13. A. Fleischmann, W. Schmidt, C. Stary, Subject-oriented BPM= socially executable BPM, in *2013 IEEE 15th Conference on Business Informatics* (IEEE, New York, 2013), pp. 399–407
14. A. Fleischmann, S. Borgert, M. Elstermann, F. Krenn, R. Singer, An overview to S-BPM oriented tool suites, in *Proceedings of the 9th International Conference on Subject-oriented Business Process Management. S-BPM ONE. ACM* (2017)

Preparing an Implementation

6

The aim of the process preparation in the sense of a subsequent implementation is a precise description of the process with a description of the process strategy and process logic. The preparation includes the activity bundles on the left side of the open cycle, i.e., analysis, modeling, validation, and optimization (see figure below). The result of these activity bundles is a process description that is sufficiently precise for implementation. The preparation is split into the activities analysis combined with modeling, validation, and optimization. These activities are not carried out in a strict order, but rather the respective priorities can change frequently between activities—see Fig. 6.1.

The following sections present selected methods for these activity bundles.

6.1   Analysis and Modeling

Analysis and modeling cannot be sharply separated. The analysis focuses on the strategic aspects of processes, while modeling focuses on the process logic. In the analysis the starting point with its associated input, the end state with its generated output, and the therewith satisfied customer needs are clarified. In the analysis, the framework and the essential aspects of the process logic are also defined.

In practice, however, the process logic of the actual state is hardly explicitly described when revising processes in this phase. The analysis of the current process logic is accomplished within the framework of the definition of the desired target process. An exclusive reference to the current situation usually makes little sense and is also as a rule unpleasant for all participants to document—What has been "done wrong" lately?

As long as one is using the tool "natural language," the focus is more on the activity of analysis than on that of modeling. The transition from natural language to a more formal process modeling language corresponds to the transition to modeling activities. The modeling can be preceded by a more or less intense analysis method.

© The Author(s) 2026
M. Elstermann et al., *Contextual Process Digitalization*,
https://doi.org/10.1007/978-3-032-06901-6_6

Fig. 6.1 Integration of the preparation in the process management model

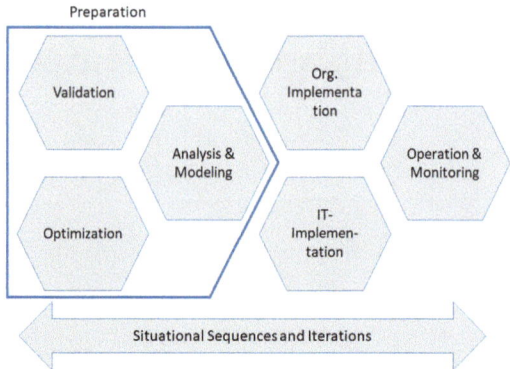

In extreme cases, a process model is immediately created without prior natural linguistic analysis. However, it is recommended that at least the strategic aspects of the process under consideration are known and defined.

In the following, guidelines for the articulation and coordination of process-relevant knowledge, which can be supported methodically and tool-wise, are presented. An essential element is the understanding of roles which the participants consider relevant for the handling of processes. In addition, it is advisable to consider the exchange relationships between actors, to evaluate their quality for the further design of processes and, if necessary, to derive potential for change from this information.

6.1.1 General Information on Articulation and Coordination

In most cases, knowledge about workflows and organizational processes rests in the minds of the actors. A context-sensitive, structured survey and analysis is therefore of crucial importance. The survey serves to articulate experiential knowledge and in most cases is carried out within the framework of modeling. However, if it is already handled in advance, the variety of approaches to solving tasks or problems in BPM projects can be dealt with in a more structured way. Nevertheless, in the context, the coordination and alignment of different approaches play an essential role. Supporting these contributes significantly to the development of solutions that are capable of integration, despite a high degree of diversity and individual approaches to the fulfillment of tasks. This section therefore deals with the survey and negotiation methods and instruments that enable individuals to articulate within the framework of collective reflection and negotiation processes.

How people carry out their work, how they react to perceived specifications or deviations, and how they cooperate with others are essentially determined by their perception of organizational reality. The interpretation of the perceived determining factors as well as the derivation of the reaction considered adequate of the acting workers can be explained by the cognitive theory of mental models. This theory can also be used as a basis for explaining learning and change processes in organizations that are initiated by operatively active persons. In this section, it therefore forms the basis for the derivation of measures which should enable workers to become aware of their work processes and the organizational interrelationships and determining factors characterizing them.

The concept of "mental models" is used to explain how people understand the world—more precisely: how they use their knowledge to make certain phenomena of the world subjectively plausible [1]. Mental models are explanatory models of the world that are formed by people on the basis of everyday experience, previous knowledge, and conclusions based on these. A mental model is used by each individual as a basis to understand the world and, if necessary, to make predictions about its behavior [1].

The knowledge that shapes mental models can be based on everyday experience or can be founded on conveyance or instruction. Seel [1] describes the modification and expansion of one's own knowledge bases and the (further) development of the cognitive abilities necessary for drawing conclusions as "learning." Learning is linked to the processing of individual experiences with, and information about, the world, its structure and evidence, and can be understood as a process of permanent conceptual change [2]. Learning thus presupposes the ability and willingness to understand and accept conveyed world views and then to base one's own mental constructions on them [2].

There are two basic difficulties in changing mental models about work processes. In the case of mental models that have already been recognized as inadequate, there is a fundamental willingness to change (in the sense of adapting the mental model to the environmental conditions perceived as changed), but the challenge is to obtain the necessary information and have it adequately presented. A further difficulty arises in situations in which not all individuals involved perceive the situation as "problematic" and therefore show no fundamental willingness to change their underlying assumptions with regard to their way of working (i.e., their mental models). This occurs especially in situations where collaborative reflection is not carried out from a generally perceived problem situation but is either initiated with a purely planning character or in situations which are perceived as "problematic" only by certain individuals involved.

These problems can be countered with explicit support for the reflection process. Such support must ensure that artifacts are created to represent the individual mental models, which can then serve as the basis for mutual understanding of the respective views on the work process. Such artifacts can serve to coordinate aspects of a work process and to ensure that the ostensive view of a work process encoded in artifacts can be implemented in work practice through performative subjective action know-how based on it. From a methodological point of view, it must be ensured that all persons involved in the real work process are organizationally and methodologically capable of participating in the collaborative learning process. This requires above all that they can understand and actively use the forms of expression utilized. This, in turn, is a learning challenge that must be explicitly addressed.

A widely accepted option for externalizing and harmonizing mental models in the educational sciences is the formation of conceptual models. At the same time, such models can form the basis for the specification of work processes and the configuration of work support systems, as long as they make use of a formally specified semantics (such as BPMN or S-BPM). In accordance with the objective of this section, conceptual models thus represent a means of enabling workers to reflect on their work, to coordinate it, to make the results of these coordination processes accessible to third parties, and to make them usable within the framework of existing system boundaries to support their own work processes.

Models are representations of reality that are provided for a particular purpose. Models never represent the real phenomenon as a whole but contain only those aspects of reality that the modeler considers relevant for the achievement of the respective goal. For modeling, this raises the question of the defining power of these models and the social reality they represent. If a model does not only fulfill an objective of the modeling individual but is used by other persons, the model influences the mental models of these persons, and thus also their behavior.

The active involvement of operative workers in the specification of work processes is therefore an opportunity for their self-empowered development of organizing their work. To this end, however, it is necessary to enable workers to understand such models, to design them by themselves, and to assess their impact on their work processes. Current approaches, on the other hand, continue to assume the need for a process analyst who translates the views of workers into a process model. This can lead to deviations between the real work process and its model representation. In addition, this approach deprives the operatively active persons of the opportunity to sharpen their mental models in the sense of model-based learning and to coordinate them with those of the other participants.

In order to enable workers to understand such models, the learning of basic approaches to the creation and interpretation of conceptual models must be the subject of education or training. Workers must be able to identify the models underlying the systems in which they are embedded. In addition, they should be able to assess the implications of external or self-implemented changes to these models and to plan interventions accordingly.

For this purpose, the following points need to be methodically supported.

1. To enable the individual articulation of one's own mental models with respect to work in order to enable individual reflection and thus to make gaps and inconsistencies individually perceptible, as well as to prevent that perspectives of individual persons are not taken into account and that these cannot subsequently establish a reference to their working reality
2. To support the agreement on a common vocabulary in order to identify different understandings of terms and subsequently to be able to communicate clearly about the work in question and to prevent the same real phenomenon from being described by different terms, or vice versa the same term from being used for different real phenomena

3. To support the development of a common understanding of collaborative work to provide a basis for reflection of individual mental models
4. In the context of the above, to enable the identification and resolution of conflicting points of view, in order to make differences in those mental models that directly affect collaboration between workers visible, and to facilitate their coordination.

The following sections show some of the methods used to implement these requirements.

6.1.2 CoMPArE/WP

The requirements described above are implemented exemplarily in the "CoMPArE/WP" method. CoMPArE/WP stands for "Collaborative Multi-perspective Articulation and Elicitation of Work Processes." In the application of CoMPArE/WP, the reflection on a real collaborative work process creates awareness of the cooperation in a concrete individual case. Due to its anchoring in concrete work processes, the method is also suitable as a means of organizational development. The form of cooperation of the method is basically determined by its implementation with a card laying technique. The participating operative workers are the essential actors and carry out the components autonomously, by which articulation and inquiry roles can change. The concrete form of the cooperation differs in the components and is, therefore, described in the procedure mentioned there. A facilitator is available to support implementation but does not intervene regarding content.

The method should support the articulation and coordination of mental models with respect to work and at the same time impart basic skills for their expression in conceptual models. The combination of these two sub-objectives has an impact on the framework of the method. From the point of view of teaching modeling competence, it makes sense to introduce the necessary skills step by step with increasing complexity. From the point of view of articulation support, an approach can be characterized by three components. Figure 6.2 gives an overview of these three components.

Component 1 is used to find a common understanding of where and how the work process to be coordinated begins and ends and to find a common vocabulary. Component 2 is used for the articulation and reflection of the respective individual contribution to the work. Each participant creates here a structured model of their point of view on their respective work contribution, individually and without interaction with others. Due to the uniformly structured presentation of the individual contributions, a collaborative alignment of these is possible in component 3. This alignment is intended to uncover conflicting points of view and to create a common view of the overall work process.

The objectives of skill development in modeling are anchored in these components. Component 1 aims to convey the verbalization of mental models and the

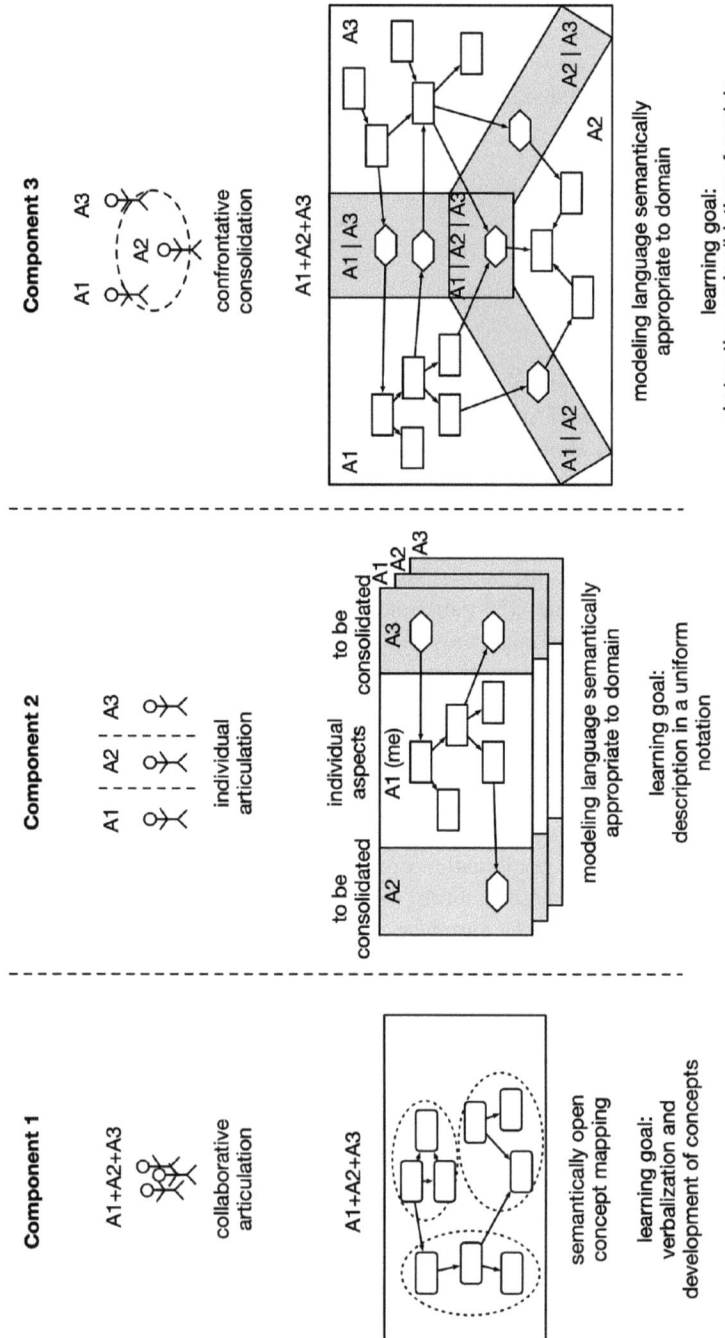

Fig. 6.2 Three components of CoMPArE/WP

concept formation based on them. In component 2, the description of the verbalized contents must be represented by means of a predefined category scheme and a notation. In doing so, it needs to be determined which elements of the category scheme remain in the responsibility of the articulating individual and which need to be validated and possibly abstracted or become the subject of negotiation during alignment in component 3.

Concrete implementation of component 1. It cannot be assumed that all participants have a common understanding of the concepts they use when describing their work. Collaborative concept mapping can be used to align the existing mental models to such an extent that a common vocabulary enables collaboration. In addition, it cannot be assumed that there is a common understanding concerning the borders of the work process to be coordinated. Concept mapping can also help to clarify this issue. In addition to the content dimension, concept maps provide a low-threshold entry into the world of conceptual modeling, since they do not predetermine the meaning of model elements, but rather allow the persons involved to define them during modeling. This facilitates the mapping of the individual mental models into the explicit representation and avoids the necessity of having to carry out a translation to a model with formally defined semantics in addition to the coordination with the other persons involved.

Within the scope of this component, participants are asked to describe all relevant aspects of the environment in which the work process to be reflected is embedded. This is done by individually writing each aspect on a separate card. When the collected individual aspects are brought together, the cards are arranged in turn on a common work surface. The aspects can be put into relation to each other. Cards with different terms for the same aspect are arranged in overlapping order. Hierarchical or causal relationships between aspects can be represented by drawing explicit connections, but also by the spatial arrangement of the cards. The example in Fig. 6.3, which is used throughout this section to explain the method, shows a concept map with relevant aspects for applying for a vacation in a company. The aspects were related to each other by spatial arrangement. The overlapping elements show aspects that are mentioned by several participants and are described using different terms.

Concrete implementation of components 2 and 3. Components 2 and 3 focus on the articulation and alignment of the perceived course of a work process and the associated interaction within this process. The modeling in component 2 is carried out individually by all persons involved, without interacting with others. This avoids overlapping effects and explicitly reveals different perspectives for the next component. The persons involved describe which of their work steps they see as contributing to the achievement of the work goal, with whom they interact, and in what form this interaction takes place. The negotiation of a common point of view in component 3 and the associated creation of a common model is again carried out by means of a structured procedure, which introduces more complex modeling tasks and guarantees a uniformly prepared model representation. In doing so, the previously created models are further used. The structuring scheme separates those

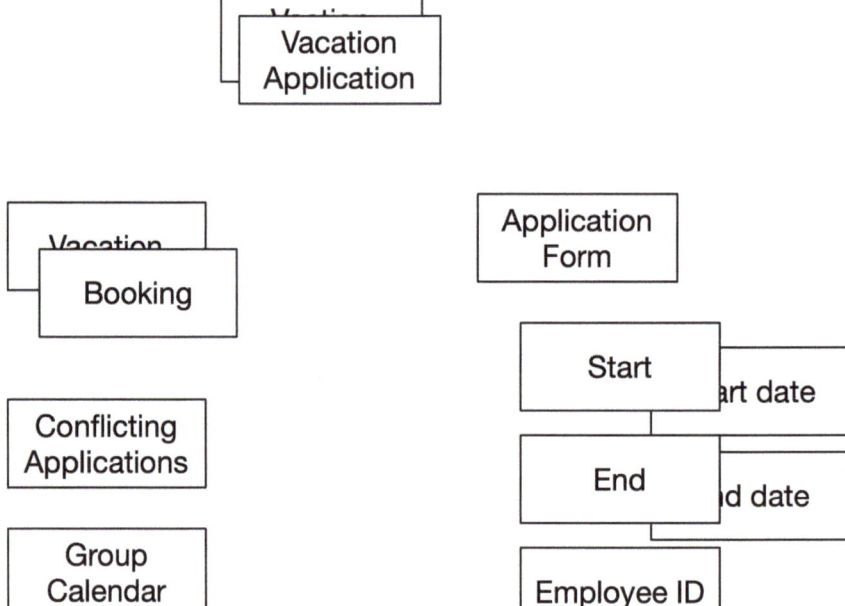

Fig. 6.3 Concept map on applying for a vacation

model aspects that remain in the individual worker's responsibility from those that are the subject of negotiation.

In this step, a structured form of representation with prespecified semantics is used to represent the work processes. It is based on current category schemes for the description of collaborative work processes. The categories WHO, WHAT, and EXCHANGE (M3) are used. WHO (blue in Fig. 6.4) refers to the actors in the work process. WHAT (red in Fig. 6.4) is used to describe active contributions in the scope of the work process. EXCHANGE (yellow in Fig. 6.4) is used in the context of

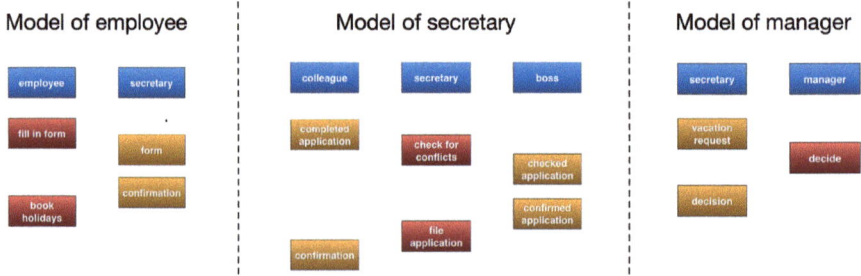

Fig. 6.4 Individual models in the presented notation

collaborative work processes to characterize the sharing or exchange of information or material between actors in the context of their own activities. For the sake of usability, these categories are not specified exactly and deliberately leave room for interpretation in concrete use, for example, a WHO element can represent a concrete person, a role, a department, or an entire organization. WHAT elements remain the responsibility of the individual participants. WHO and EXCHANGE elements are the subject of coordination in component 3 and must be developed toward a common understanding.

Individual articulation. In component 2, the persons involved individually describe with the help of the elements, what they contribute in the work process, who interacts with them, and in what form this exchange takes place. In order to support the articulation process, a structuring scheme was developed that prepares the models in a coherent form and allows them to be combined in the next step. As shown in Fig. 6.4, the structuring scheme defines the spatial arrangement of the model elements. Operative workers represent themselves through a WHO element, under which the perceived contributions to the work process are placed as sequentially arranged WHAT elements. For all other workers with whom an interaction is perceived, another WHO element is placed, under which the interaction is specified in more detail by EXCHANGE elements. Their vertical positioning determines whether an incoming resource is expected (placement above the dependent WHAT element) or provided (placement below the generating WHAT element).

Figure 6.4 shows three individual models for the example process described above, which were created according to this structuring scheme. In the example, it can be seen that at this point there may be divergent representations with regard to content, especially in the area of exchange elements (cf. "Application" vs. "Completed application" in the figure above). These divergences become explicitly visible in component 3 and are then subject of the negotiation of a common perspective.

Collaborative alignment. Collaborative alignment is based on the individual conceptional models created in component 2. Figure 6.5 shows an exemplary alignment process for two of the actors represented in the example. The common modeling again takes place on a common work surface (see Fig. 6.5 in the middle). The participant, who triggers the real work process, begins by describing his own contributions to the process and adding the corresponding model elements to the surface (steps 1–2 in the following figure).

The other participants intervene here only inquiringly to avoid misunderstandings or to disclose ambiguities. An active participation of the others takes place as soon as the first EXCHANGE element is used (steps 3–4). If a fundamentally common view of the work process exists, one of the participants should be able to introduce a correspondingly assigned EXCHANGE element at this point (steps 5–7).

If this is the case, the description process is continued by this person (from step 8). In the case of a basic fit, which differs, however, in the designation of the element, e.g., by different abstraction levels, this conflicting designation must

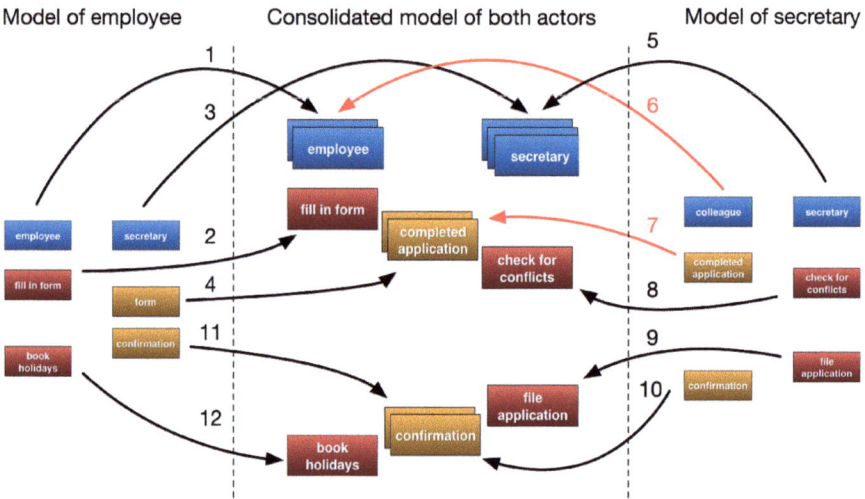

Fig. 6.5 Collaborative alignment

be resolved, or the semantic equivalence of the two elements must be represented by overlapping arrangement (e.g., step 7). If there is no element to be assigned, fundamental differences in the representation become visible. This may be due to a lack of awareness of the relevance of an exchange, which means that the addressed participant was aware of the interaction, but did not consider it relevant in the context of the work process. However, if a participant's perceived need for interaction is not reciprocated, this must lead to more in-depth alignment processes.

The initial alignment process ends as soon as all of the participants have explained their individual models and added them to the common model. This externalization phase is followed by a collaborative reflection phase, during which the work process is examined on the basis of the common model and discussed with regard to its adaptation to the individual views of the participants. Any necessary modifications are carried out at this point, after consensus has been reached among those affected.

The result of the application of the method now represents a consensual representation of the collaborative work process. Due to the limited expressiveness of the modeling language used, it is not possible at this point to map work variants or decisions that are otherwise common in process descriptions. The decision for a semantically limited modeling language was again made from a didactic point of view, since empirical evidence shows that inexperienced modelers can initially describe their views on a work process more simply in a narrative on the basis of a concrete case. Decisions regarding the concrete implementation of the work process have already been made in the case-based description. Thus, an explicit representation of the same is not necessary in the scope of the modeling. A complete description of the work process therefore requires a multiple execution of the method or its extension by further refinement steps, which, however, will not be considered here in detail.

In the sense of the formation of modeling competence, the focus in component 1 is on the introduction to the abstraction and conceptualization of perceptions of the real world necessary for modeling. In component 2, the representation and reflection of one's own perception of work, guided by structural aids, is captured in conceptual models and their description by means of given structural elements. Component 3 subsequently focuses on model understanding (of the other individual models), interpretation (with regard to their effects on one's own model), and negotiation (of the jointly justifiable view) of model content, which ultimately conveys the competence to influence work processes in a self-empowering way.

6.1.3 Raising Awareness of Process-Relevant Change Potential

In the following, the Value Network Analysis [3–5] is first discussed, as it was introduced in the field of knowledge management for the processing of performance relationships between networked actors [6–8], before its potential for process design (analysis and modeling) is detailed.

6.1.3.1 Value Network Analysis

If we consider, as previously mentioned, the added value of organizations and thus the level of performance-related exchange relationships between actors, tangible exchange relationships can be distinguished from intangible ones in the network of actors within the framework of work processes. Tangible exchange is determined by energy and material flows. Intangible exchange, such as knowledge, refers to cognitive processes and action-guiding information. If now participants and exchange relations are described, the structure of an organization or a network can be captured.

Exchange relationships represent the molecular level of economic activities. Thus, value creation does not only consist of tangible transactions but also of intangible transactions. These relate above all to cognitive exchange, since the sustainable success of an organization is based on the exchange of information, knowledge sharing, and open cognitive paths that enable appropriate decisions to be made (and thus the successful existence of an organization). However, knowledge and intangible elements behave differently than physical resources in business life, so they cannot be considered tangibles. Due to their proximity to living systems, they constitute a separate category of exchanges and differ from tangibles related to goods, services, and revenues.

Tangible exchange is defined as transactions involving goods, services, or revenues, e.g., physical goods, contracts, invoices, delivery and receipt confirmations, inquiries, requests, invitations to bid, and payments. It is essential here that knowledge-intensive products and services that generate income and for which payments are made as part of a service or product or on the basis of a contractual obligation are also regarded as tangible transactions.

Intangible exchange of knowledge and performance: Intangible exchange of knowledge and information supports core processes and thus the classic value chain but is not subject to any contractual obligation. Intangibles are "extras" or (small) courtesies that people exchange in order to build relationships and allow processes to proceed pleasantly or without disturbances. Intangible transactions include the exchange of strategic information, planning knowledge, business-operational knowledge, joint planning activities, collaborative design, and policy development. Intangible transactions are therefore not contractually agreed services for the benefit or support of organizations or their members. They can be extended from one person or group to another, for example, when an organizational unit requests an expert to work temporarily for them in a prestigious position. Recognition often helps in relationship work so that intangible benefits constitute genuine motivation factors for active participation and engagement in group activities.

Intangibles represent the core of all human action and thus also determine socio-economic action. Intangible transactions are deliberately seeded. They can be brought about and recognized. If one wants to understand how intangibles generate value, one must first understand how they become visible and work as negotiables in economic exchange relationships. They are often not immediately visible, but rather "packaged" in services or products. A typical example is to build an understanding for a customer situation (intangible) before offering a service (tangible). For a joint practice, the smooth running of processes is of immediate importance. Thus, those transactions are essential which (also) guarantee by means of intangibles that a common purpose of action is ensured. This must now be methodically taken into account.

In a Value Network, tangible and intangible values are generated by means of complex dynamic exchange processes between two or more individuals, groups, or organizations, which represent the object of reflective design.

6.1.3.2 Holomapping

The view of organizational value generation based on networking brings with it a new form of organizational modeling; every exchange requires a mechanism or medium as enabler for transactions. These can be tools such as e-mail or face-to-face interactions in communities of practice. As already mentioned above, typical intangibles pertain to knowledge to gain information from customers and feedback on (product) developments.

The representation of tangible and intangible exchange processes in a diagram with flow elements allows the mapping of the dynamics of living systems. First the participants or roles (also groups, teams, or organizational units, but not technical aids) are documented—they form the nodes of the network and are visualized through ovals. The participants send or supplement so-called deliverables to other participants. Arrows, which are labeled as the respective deliverable, indicate the direction deliverables take in the course of a particular transaction.

Transactions or activities are displayed as directed edges (arrows), which must originate with one participant and end with another. The arrow indicates movement and the direction in which something is happening between two participants. In contrast to participants, who are time-stable, transactions are time-limited and volatile. They have a starting point, a duration, and a conclusion.

Deliverables, on the other hand, are real "things" that move from one participant to another. A deliverable can be material (tangible), like a document or a table, or immaterial (not tied to matter), like a message or a request that is only verbally delivered. Deliverables can also be intangible, for example, when referring to knowledge about a certain fact (cognitive) or in the case of a favor (social/emotional). Arrows are only allowed in one direction—they cover a single transaction between participants. Bilaterally directed arrows are meaningless; in fact, they make it impossible to analyze the processes and exchange relationships.

An exchange occurs as soon as a transaction results in a deliverable that is returned. It does not necessarily have to be present in the practical world of action in organizations. However, if it occurs, a Value Network can establish itself, with transactions as molecular elements of value generation.

In the context of change processes, it is essential to empower those involved and thus to have the affected role holders create the communication map with tangibles and intangibles (holomap), as well as to process the data collected by them within the framework of the Value Network Analyses.

Within the scope of knowledge generation or knowledge collection at the beginning of the work on the network structure, each individual participant considers his/her role, which he/she then communicates to the other participants. In this way, relationships and interdependencies between the individual roles, which are often unknown, become more explicit and clearer. The roles are symbolized as nodes, and the exchange of material or immaterial values is represented in the form of lines connecting the roles. The modeling forms the basis for the subsequent analyses for the evaluation and processing of knowledge.

6.1.3.3 Exchange Analysis

The holomap shows how people use their work as a starting point for exchange analysis. Tangibles (material value flows) in the network refer to the material exchange between persons (typically goods, services, and sales revenue). They represent transactions based on contracts. Intangibles (immaterial, ideational value flows), in contrast to tangibles, are based on knowledge or a certain additional benefit. They are not contractually fixed or subject to a charge. Intangibles often collected are strategic information, process or planning knowledge, as well as existing emotional components such as mutual trust, common interest, need for knowledge, security, etc.—see also Fig. 6.6.

The exchange analysis examines a Value Network for its conclusiveness, robustness, and sustainability. It provides insight into the current structure and dynamics of the network. The following questions should support the exchange analysis: How do the values flow through the organization? Does a certain logic emerge? Is the relationship between the exchange of material and immaterial values balanced or does a certain type of exchange predominate? Does the pattern in the Value Network show reciprocal value flows or are there participants who receive more value flows

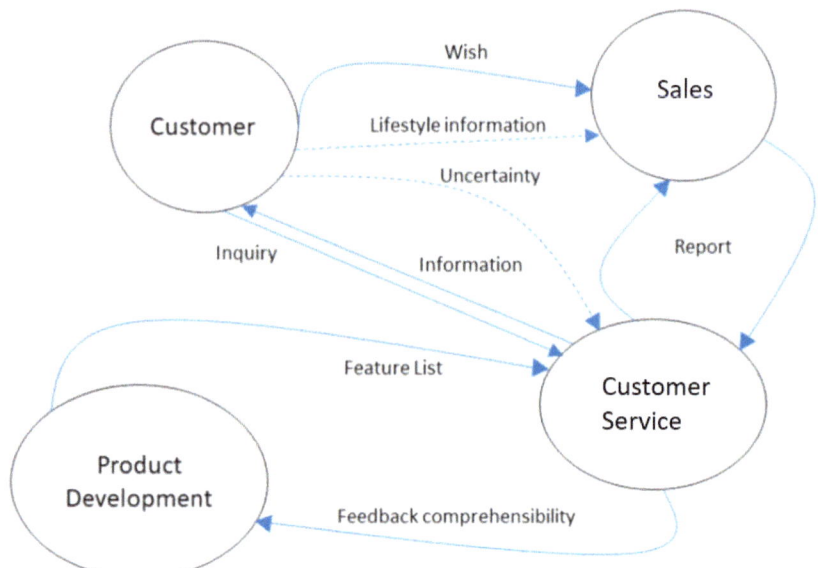

Fig. 6.6 Extract of a holomap for customer service

than they provide? Are there ineffective connections in the network that do not pass
on value flows?

These questions are intended to check whether the network fulfills its purpose,
whether missing end nodes or links can be detected, and how the structure of
the network can be optimized. They ensure a general overview of added value
and loss of value. The exchange analysis should serve as a stimulus for dialogue,
understanding complex systems, and promoting systemic thinking (cf. [9]). The
exchange analysis on customer service, under the assumption that the organization
is facebook, shows several findings: Customer service is tangible from the point
of view of product development as a sink—it only receives feature list. Sales
receives lifestyle information, but no trust-related information. The transmission of
uncertainty encumbers the relationship between customer service and sales as well
as between customer service and product development. This first evaluation may
be an indication of the information management shown in Fig. 6.6, where features
indeed allow for a certain form of feedback, but where these may be acknowledged
by users with requests reflecting uncertainty.

6.1.3.4 Impact Analysis

Impact analysis examines the impact of each individual value input on the participants and thus focuses on the recipients of value inputs. This analysis thus shows
which input triggers which reactions and activities and how this affects the material
and immaterial assets of the recipients concerned. The costs and benefits of value
inputs are then assessed as low, medium, or high.

In order to gain a better overview of these questions, the answers for each individual recipient of value inputs are entered into a table and the current situation analyzed. The table in Fig. 6.7 shows the impact analysis based on the insights gained from the exchange analysis of a customer service employee. The table shows who provides input for which activities and what effects are perceived in the form of material or immaterial value flows. The column entries for the general costs and risks as well as for the benefit of the input addressed are essential for the estimation of change potential.

The data from the initial evaluation (exchange analysis) thus form the basis for the two further analyses, whereby value-based detailed evaluations of transactions are carried out from the point of view of input received (impact analysis) and output transmitted (value creation analysis), and in this way provide insights for change processes.

For example, as can be seen in the table, it is explained when features enable a successful form of feedback, for example, to avoid requests that reflect uncertainty on the part of users. This is the case even if the current benefit of the presentation of features by customer service is estimated to be low due to a lack of comprehensibility.

The entries in the feature list table also show the reference point relevant to value creation, i.e., the quality of information provided to customers by customer service employees.

Based on the as-is analysis, strategic perspectives can then be derived and the table can be filled in again and serve as a comparison with respect to its planned, strategic activities (target analysis). In the present case, for example, a customer-oriented information service is of increased importance.

6.1.3.5 Value Creation Analysis

Value creation analysis analyzes how values can best be created, increased, and used. Like the impact analysis, the value creation analysis also considers the individual role in relation to the entire system. The difference from impact analysis is that, unlike with input, this time the sender or producer of output is considered in their role and with their related activities.

Each individual sender of value output is analyzed to determine how added value and value accumulation are realized in relation to the existing value output. A cost-benefit analysis will also be carried out for this purpose.

In the value creation analysis shown in the table in Fig. 6.7, the results of the work were used to analyze how values can be best created, increased, and used. The table shows the analysis based on data from a customer consultant's exchange analysis.

Performance indicators can be used to filter out the requirements placed on sales and product development from the analysis. The strategy developed from this can be outlined with the statement "availability or transparency of information." As a change measure, it could be decided to increase the identified value creation potential in the Value Network by expanding the tangibles of information flows between all functional units.

Customer service	From which role?	Which activities are triggered by the input?	Effect on the costs and tangible assets of the recipient	Effect on the costs and intangibles assets	What are the general costs / risks of the input?	What are the general benefits of the input?
What do we get (Deliverables)		Activity	Value-based effect	Intangible impact	Costs/ Risk	Benefit
Inquiry	Customer	Information	High effort, because translation required from inquiry → feature	Provision of associated feedback for the purpose of understandability to gain knowledge for product development	H in the case of unclear concerns / H for new requirements	M, because not always high, if no constructive feedback is possible
Uncertainty (Intangible)	Customer	Report to sales	Need to act	Negative relation to customer	H / L	H, because essential need for action evident
Report	Sales	Processing	Knowledge generation on customers (Customer Knowledge Management)	Achieving good customer relationships through knowledge of customers	M, depending on content / M	H, as an essential part of information flow
Feature list	Product development	Processing	Enabling customer-oriented information services	Knowledge gain about product	M, because required for product in any case / M, as comprehensibility possibly low when related to technology	H for comprehensible information, otherwise L

L=Low, M=Medium, H=High

Fig. 6.7 Extract from an impact analysis for customer service

Output of sender	Output for recipient	Added or increased value of the activity	Costs / Risks	Benefits
Feedback - Comprehensibility	Product development	Customer-oriented access Consideration of feasibility	H / H	H
Information	Customer	Dealing with customer needs Would also be interesting for potential customers	H / H	H
Report	Sales	Acquisition of customer data Would also be interesting for training department	H / H	H
For costs / risks and benefits: L=low M=medium H=high				

Fig. 6.8 Part of the case related (customer service) value creation analysis

After the presentation of the actual situation, the value creation analysis also makes it possible to derive strategic perspectives. Here the question should be asked "Which possibilities should still be used in the future to generate value optimization in value output?" With regard to the concrete question "What should be done to increase, expand, or optimize the value of output?", the table in Fig. 6.8 is filled out in a comparative manner to analyze the target situation.

The entries in the "costs/risks" and "benefits" columns are essential for decision support. Here, the assessment can be put into perspective, especially with regard to costs and risks in the target situation, if, for example, content should be included in training courses, since there is know-how for the creation of corresponding training materials and for the provision of effective mediation formats in the network (e.g., in the context "Report"—third table entry in the table). A target list usually takes into account knowledge about the feasibility or availability of resources and the associated costs for implementing measures, without anticipating a decision in this regard (see evaluation).

6.1.3.6 Evaluation

For the evaluation, tangibles and intangibles are evaluated in tabular form (impact analysis, exchange analysis, value creation analysis) according to their significance for the respective role(s). These evaluations reveal the effects on relationships and allow targeted measures to be taken.

So far, the exchange analysis has provided insight into the current structure and dynamics of the network. The implementation of the impact analysis allows all participants to deduce their own roles in the network in a context-sensitive way. The impact analysis also provides an overview of the effects each individual value transaction has on the participants. The value creation analysis allows decisions to be made on how values can best be created, increased, and used, and how they possibly affect other roles or should include them in the consideration. Based on the derived performance indicators, a strategy can now be developed to increase the identified value creation potential in the Value Network.

Typical results of an evaluation to increase added value include the consideration of missing exchange relationships, such as the ones related to the case in question:

1. Concrete inquiries to customers in order to better understand their concerns (especially those that lead to customer uncertainty) from the point of view of product development and sales—customer service plays a mediating role here, whereby the tangible report can also be upgraded and the feedback can contain concrete suggestions for the improvement or creation of features.
2. Feedback from customers concerning both the future handling and the previous handling of features, i.e., those issues which affect product development in particular. As soon as the comprehensibility of the presentation is explicitly addressed, an associated flow of information (back) to product development (and also to sales) can be ensured—another measure that facilitates customer-oriented access to the product.

Both measures show the necessity of networked representation of exchange relations. It is not necessarily the immediacy of exchange relationships, but rather the concatenation of exchange relationships that can bring about added value. If, for example, product development (e.g., software designers) were to start communicating directly with customers, a certain basis for discussion would first have to be established. Such measures could even be counterproductive to the strategic goal to be achieved and increase the existing uncertainty on the part of customers, thus adversely affecting the desired objective.

The additions to the network thus allow a context-sensitive system view of value creation through material and immaterial services that should flow between the actors involved. As shown in Fig. 6.9, the completed Value Network map forms the basis for further development planning. For the first time, it shows the inquiry to customers as well as the feedback for the purpose of comprehensibility as tangible deliverables, which are intended to increase the knowledge of those involved through the transparency and availability of information. In the long term, as an intangible exchange between customers and customer service, it is important to strive for a mutually secure relationship that can be expressed through customer loyalty to the organization. Only the open exchange of information enables sustainable customer knowledge management.

Value Networks view systems in their entirety and consider their complexity. They enable the holistic identification of both material and immaterial values. In any case, the latter indirectly determine the quality of material exchange relationships and must therefore be taken into account in the development of socio-technical systems. By means of Value Networks the focus on the individuals involved can be captured, which in turn gives them a sense of purpose and fosters their motivation to participate in reflection and actively take part in codesign. The surveys and analyses presented here allow the explication of individual roles and their directly or indirectly perceived contribution to the value creation of an organizational system by actors. This facilitates the clarification of roles and the understanding of correlations, since these are visualized graphically in holomaps by means of

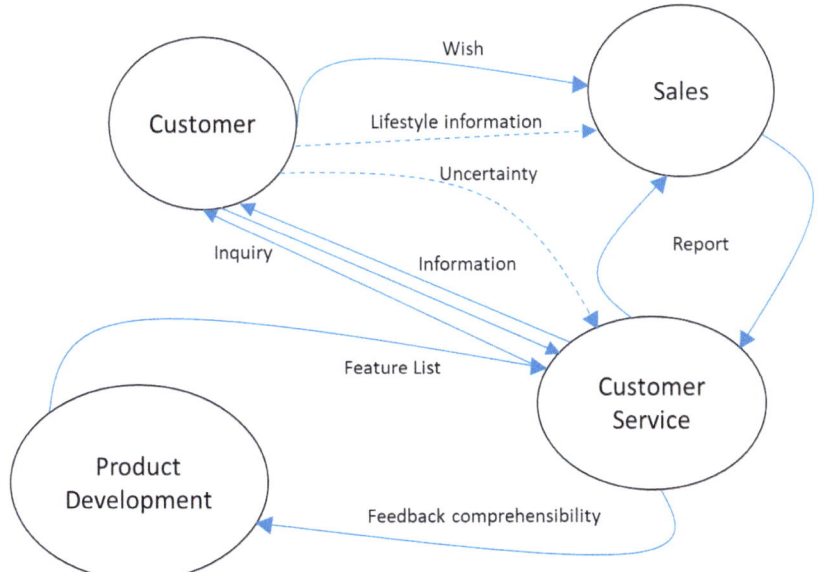

Fig. 6.9 Adapted network

value exchange relationships and are thus fed back role-specifically. As such, they represent a viable starting point for the participatory design of socio-technical systems.

6.1.3.7 Potentials for Process Analysis and Modeling

For the design of processes and their modeling, multiple potentials can be drawn from the Value Network Analysis:

1. The Value Network Analysis allows the representation of a situation as it is perceived by actors. The representation is based on roles, which are illustrated by nodes of a network of actors. Since each role holder can perform this analysis, individually perceived interaction patterns can be compared with the perception of other role holders. Thus, the Value Network Analysis allows the structured identification of differently perceived interaction patterns between actors from their individual point of view, whereby the different interaction patterns can also be presented cumulatively.
2. The recording and presentation of the actual situation represents a reference point from which change potentials can be tapped. This makes it possible for all participants to discuss changes in interactions on the basis of a common starting position in a way that is comprehensible.
3. The Value Network Analysis allows the determination of roles that are not necessarily functional in an organization, for example, in the organization chart. The definition of roles is based on the communication and interaction patterns

which are considered relevant within the framework of the fulfillment of tasks and the perceived organizational events. Thus, the focus is placed on the way of working and the interaction level.

4. Within the framework of the development of proposals for change, instead of demands from individual role holders, proposals are made to others in the sense of individual offers to the collective. Such an approach gives the addressee the choice of whether or not to exploit this potential. All offers are presented in the context of their origin and evaluated with regard to their organizational effectiveness by the respective proposing actors. They can then be coordinated collectively on this basis.

5. Interaction relationships are differentiated according to contractually binding services (tangibles) and not only from the respective role according to contractually regulated services (intangibles). This already makes it evident how tasks are handled, whether more so according to formal principles or interactions that promote successful process fulfillment, or according to informal principles. The same applies to proposed changes, which may also be in formal structures (as part of functional role descriptions), or at informal level (as voluntary contributions).

6. There are several ways to change an actual situation into a target state: (i) an informal (intangible) interaction becomes a formal part of a role (tangible); (ii) a formal (tangible) interaction is omitted or becomes an informal part of a role (intangible); (iii) a tangible or intangible relationship is newly introduced and complements existing interaction patterns.

7. Interaction relationships can be directly transferred into concrete process steps, as they represent the fulfillment of tasks by the role holders in chronological order. Thus, a process model, which focuses on the exchange of services between actors (in contrast to linearized functional steps), can be derived from a holomap.

Overall, Value Network Analysis is a diagrammatic/tabular technique for organizational development with the goal of process definitions or executable processes, which directly supports the mapping of interaction structures to communication-oriented approaches such as S-BPM [1, 10]. All information is generated from the point of view of the involved or responsible role holders.

Methodologically, one way of deriving process models from Value Network Analysis is tagging information using process-relevant metadata [11]. Tagging helps through classifying information represented in the VNA's holomap and analysis tables.

First of all, a VNA is performed along a specific role perspective. It refers to a fundamental process element, namely functional or organizational roles performing a set of tasks, that is part of the tagging scheme. Hence, role or task labels in a holomap can be annotated as such, e.g., providing a specific type of tag. The directed arcs between roles or tasks represent transactions; those depicted with dotted lines represent intangible transactions. They also represent fundamental process elements when being implemented in business operation. Both tangibles and intangibles can be part of process models, as they contribute to organizational value generation. When tagging transactions of the holomap, they can either refer to activities leading to the deliverable or action to be set by the receiver as denoted by the transaction, or data that is part of the transaction or the respective deliverable. They can be annotated with a specific type of tag, either activity or data.

Since process models also capture a temporal dimension, the start/end state and a set of activities or logically related tasks performed by a human role carrier, machine, or digital system need to be looked up in the VNA's holomap and analysis tables. The table entries supplement the declarative information from the holomap with procedural information, such as follow-up activities triggered by inputs from other network members. The same holds for manipulating input data and producing some output of value for customers or network partners.

Since business process models comprise roles, activities, input/output of activities, and the sequence of activities to produce an intended output, the tagging scheme addresses all these elements:

- Roles in terms of holomap nodes, e.g., tagging them with Subject or Actor
- Activities as indicated by holomap transactions, tagging them with Activity or Action
- Data as input or output of activities in terms of holomap deliverables (incoming and outgoing), e.g., tagging them with Data or Business Object
- Causal/Temporal relations referring to the sequence of activities, in terms of a holomap's directed links, e.g., by numbering transactions according to their sequence for process completion, while each transaction can be part of more than a single sequence

Besides tagging holomaps with fundamental process metadata like roles or data, the second type of tagging concerns the annotation of table entries when they refer to details of holomap elements. Both types of tagging are required for value-based process design (cf. [12], the way organizational change is managed (cf. [13]), sustainable development (cf. [14]) following a socio-technical systems perspective (cf. [15, 16]).

6.1.4   Structured Asset Records

In the following a procedure is described, which leads from a natural linguistic description to a formal behavior model. This approach is based on active sentences of natural languages. The process will be introduced on the basis of the Poly Energy Net (NET) project, an approach funded by the German Federal Ministry for Economic Affairs and Energy. The aim of this project was to develop a solution for a self-organizing distributed energy supply system. The following sections show how the associated software was developed, from a general description to a precise model, which was then converted in a first stage into a program based on process specifications.

6.1.4.1 General Information

The following steps, which lead from an informal description of a process to a formal model of the process flow, do not have to be performed in the order given. The steps rather serve the goal of a precise process description. If it turns out in one step that something had been forgotten in a previous step, or if it turns out that it is more advantageous to design subprocesses differently, this change is included in the step currently being worked on. The change is not reflected in the previous descriptions. To create a first draft of a process description, the procedures from Design Thinking described in the previous chapter can be used.

All documents of the previous descriptions are obsolete by default and no longer valid after completion of a more detailed description, except when a description explicitly states that a previous description is still valid (e.g., as an overview document). Experience has shown that it is not possible to keep several documents consistent. There should therefore only be one valid document, so that a formal behavioral model is available after the preparation has been completed. As a rule, changes should only be made to this model.

When creating a process model, one can also start with any step. For example, only active sentences can be used for a natural language description. Thus, the steps which transform a description in arbitrary form into an active description form are omitted. It can also begin with the identification of the actors and continue with the detailing of each actor, including communication with other actors. The concrete procedure depends on the circumstances and preferences of the parties involved.

6.1.4.2 Natural Linguistic Description of Processes

A process is described in a more or less structured way in natural language. There is no specification as to the structure of the document to be created or the vocabulary to be used. The creators of a process description can follow their preferences. Figure 6.10 shows an excerpt from the rough description of requirements for the energy management system.

The initial free use of natural language does not require any special methodological knowledge on the part of the participants. The need for such knowledge could be a major obstacle to the involvement of stakeholders from different departments.

Textual descriptions can be supplemented by suitable images. Figure 6.11 shows a functional structure of the system to be created. Such a functional structure is a first approximation to the specification of a process system.

Based on these more structural descriptions, a first process-oriented specification can be created. Figure 6.12 shows an excerpt of a process description.

This process description is supplemented by an illustration of the effects on a holonic energy network. Figure 6.12 refers to some elements (switches) in Fig. 6.13.

The tools used at the beginning for an initial requirement definition and process specification are not structured. Basically, texts and supplementary drawings of any kind can be used. In the following steps, this nontechnical description of a process is transformed step by step into a precise description of the process flow.

The holonic model

- The holonic model is a logical system that can be mapped to a physical system in the real world.
- The entire holonic supply system consists of holons.
- Within each holon, the same amount of energy is provided ("generated") as is consumed at any time.
- Holons consist of holonic (energetic) elements. These are:
    - holonic production and consumption elements
    - holonic connectors
    - holonic conversion elements
    - holonic storage elements
    - holonic guardians
- All holonic elements have a physical instantiation.
- Holonic elements have the ability to communicate with at least one holon manager. They are connected to at most one holon manager (to a holonic object).
- Holon managers can influence the behavior (e.g., generation, consumption) of holonic elements via control signals. All holonic elements that can communicate with the same holon manager form one holonic object.
- In each holon, there is an instance holon coordinator that can communicate with holon managers in its own holon and holon coordinators in other holons.
- Holonic objects can exist without being connected to a holon.
- Holonic elements can exist without being assigned to a holon manager ("free flying holonic elements").
- All holon managers and holon coordinators have a physical instantiation.
- Holons can dynamically merge into new holons or disintegrate into smaller holons according to certain holon rules. The rules are implemented by holon coordinators in interaction with holon managers.
- The rules for the holon formation are based on logical requirements and determining factors, which are defined by the physical instantiation of the holonic elements.
- Holons can dissolve. This is the case when there is no holon coordinator.
- There are also "non-holonic" elements, i.e. those that can neither be accessed nor are connected to the energetic system.

Fig. 6.10 Requirements for a holonic energy management system

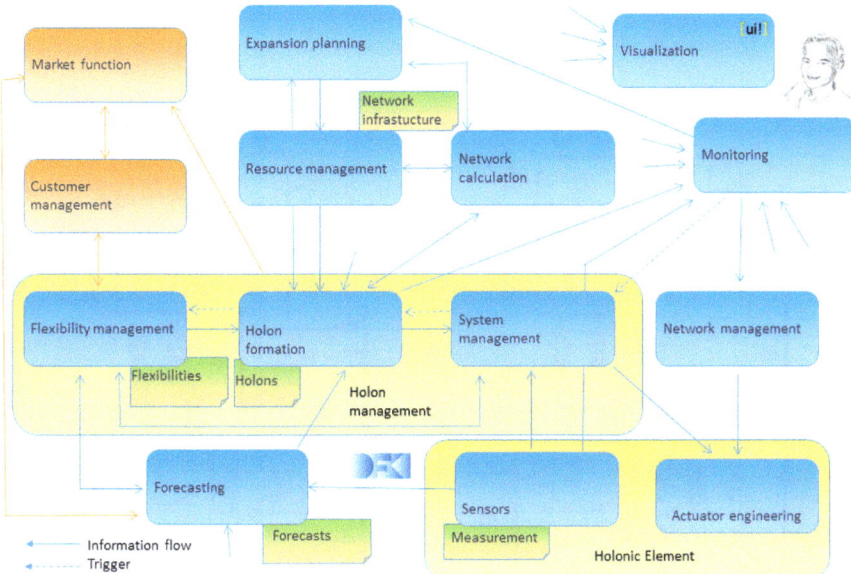

Fig. 6.11 Function blocks of a holonic energy management system

	In the holonic system
Trigger	Due to the failure of the local network transformer (in example A), a single network section in the low-voltage range can no longer be supplied by the higher-level medium-voltage network. This is detected by measuring and reporting a voltage drop to near zero in the affected network section (cf. PMU in Fig. 2.). It is assumed that the distribution bus bar in the local network stations is intact and that only the transformer as such has failed. The control center or network supervisor automatically reports the "voltage drop" result to the control station, which triggers the fastest possible supply (minimum possible supply of a consumer) with a process largely characterized by automated measurement and remote effects.
Procedure	By automatically querying measured values (at the PMUs in the network) and other fault information (e.g. from the involved local network stations involved), the control center identifies the location and, as far as possible, the cause of the fault. In the current case, it is determined that the transformer at A has failed. The control center informs one or more Holon Managers (HM) or Holon Coordinators in the affected network area. The Holon Coordinators and Holon Managers concerned communicate with each other and negotiate (also with neighboring Holon Coordinators) a new formation of holons which will enable the supply of as many consumers as possible even without the defective local transformer. The aim is to maintain such a supply (even without an emergency power supply system) until defective parts of the local network stations have been replaced. In the situation outlined in Fig. 2, it can be assumed that the holon management of the control center will propose the following new formation (cf. Fig. 3): • The holonic lines are to be switched as follows: ○ Switch 4 is to be closed and thus connects the distribution bus bar in the local network station A, which was previously supplied by the now defective transformer, to be supplied. ○ Opening or closing switches 5, 6 and 7 creates an island separated from the rest of the system. ○ Opening or closing switches 8 - 11 creates an island separated from the rest of the system. • The following holons are formed: ○ The island separated by switches 6 and 7 forms holon C and supplies itself. Apart from a domestic PV system, the only source of supply is the CHP, which is provided as an "emergency power generator" for a very critical consumer. The holon is to be operated in such a way that the latter is always fully supplied, further consumers can expect only a minimum supply. (Note: If this supply situation cannot be maintained, Holon C would probably soon disintegrate into smaller, sometimes very poorly supplied holons, or some of the consumers would be added to holon A). ○ The island separated by switches 8 and 11 forms holon B and supplies itself. Here, an extensive full supply is to be expected, since there are efficient branches in the holon (large BHKW, open-area-PV-plants, quarter storage). ○ All other holonic elements form holon A. Apart from a smaller BHKW and few domestic PV plants and associated domestic storage the local network station B secures the supply. If the control station accepts the holon formation, it initiates the corresponding switching processes and settings. The operating personnel is informed, drives to the local network station and disconnects the defective transformer from the distribution bus bar. The situation caused by the holon formation allows an optimal, as far as possible full supply of all consumers with sufficient energy source (sun, gas) until a replacement transformer can be installed or the existing one repaired. Note: If a supply as enabled by the new holon formation is not possible, this is recognized as an error situation and a new holon formation is triggered. As ultima ratio also here a net-replacement plant would also be used here.
Result	After the fault has been rectified, the operating personnel on site, including the network control center, restores the normal state (transformer supplies the distribution bus bar in local network station A). The measurement in the control center recognizes that a new, strong supplier is available, which triggers a new formation of holons. Note: This will likely lead to the situation involving holon A and B like before the occurrence of the use case.

Fig. 6.12 Dynamics of a holonic management system

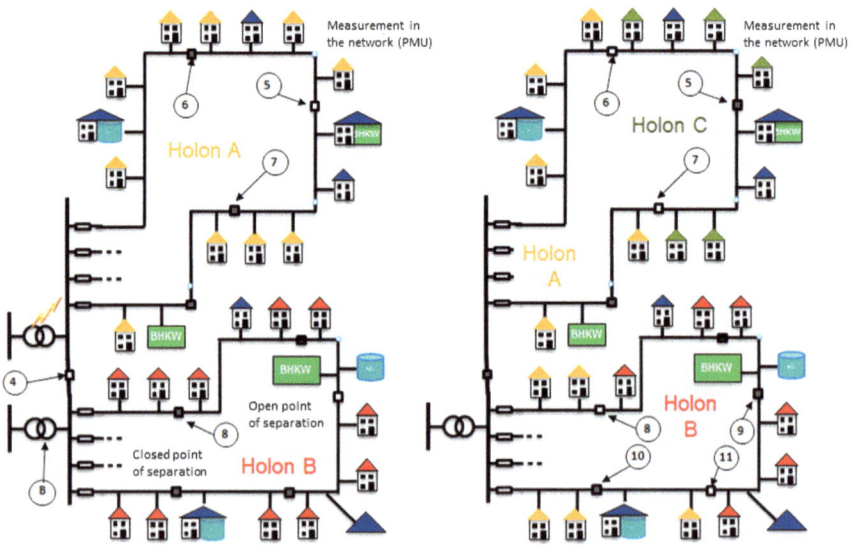

Source: B.A.U.M

Fig. 6.13 Example of a holonic energy management system

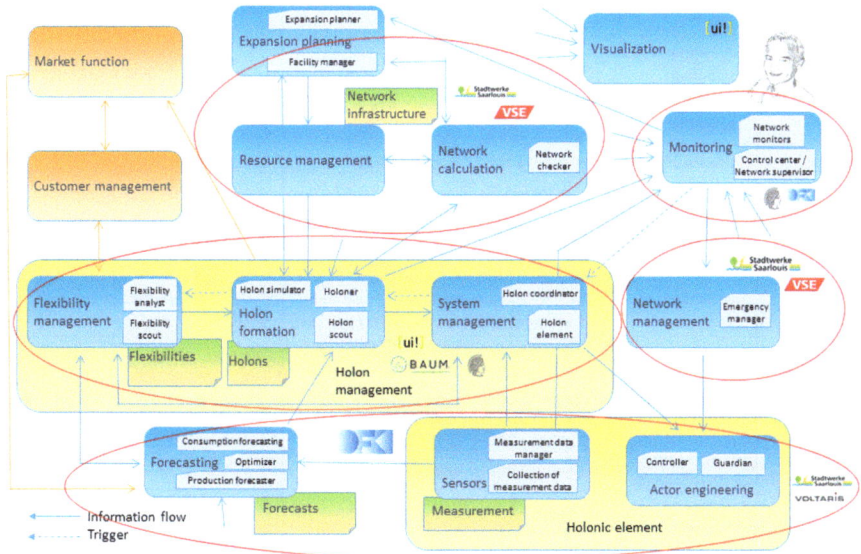

Fig. 6.14 Subject-oriented consideration of a holonic energy management system

6.1.4.3 Process Descriptions in Active Form

Informal process descriptions in natural language very often contain passive clauses (see also the above description). However, passive sentences do not contain a direct assertion about the performer of an action. Passive sentences are used when it is not important who the performer of an action is. However, this is not the case for processes. Process descriptions must include the performer of an action. All passive sentences must now be converted to active sentences. To do this, the active elements must first be identified. Active elements can be humans, software systems that run automatically and perform certain activities, physical systems, or any combination of these basic elements. Therefore, in our example, the control center can be a combination of software, people, and electrical systems. The software prompts an operator to read a specific measured value and enter it. Depending on the measured value entered, the software initiates the closing of a switch.

In order to avoid a process description being too dependent on the organizational and technical environment, abstract actors are introduced. Such abstract actors are entities that send messages, receive messages, or perform internal tasks. Figure 6.14 shows the function diagram with active elements assigned. These abstract active elements are called subjects, and the subjects are referred to in active sentences. Subjects play a role in processes.

The tasks of the identified subjects can be briefly described for better understanding, as shown in Fig. 6.15.

With the introduction of actors in the form of subjects, all passive sentences can now be replaced by corresponding active sentences. This makes the process description more complete. The table shown in Fig. 6.16 shows a process description

Identfier	Type (person, organization, component, (sub-) system, application)	Description	Specifics in this Use Case
Holon Manager (HM)	Software Service	The role of a HM describes a set of functionalities that are provided by one or more software components.	Examples of use-case-relevant functionalities are: - Identifying a Holon Coordinator - Acting in the role of Holon Coordinator
Holon Element (HE)	Component	Holar elements are production or consumption elements, conversion elements, storage elements or line elements. A HE always has a connection to the power system, a connection to the ICT system is optional, although the rule. A HE has at least one (usually IT-technical) control element, usually also the ability to provide information.	Examples of use-case-relevant functionalities are: - HE can send status information - HE can receive control commands
Holon Coordi-nator (HK)	Software Service	Holon coordinators perform the basic functions for operating a holon. They control holon elements in their own holon using the functions of a holon manager.	Examples of use-case-relevant functionalities are: - Determination of a permissible holon (if necessary, taking other goals intpo account) - Determine switching commands for establishing a holon - Initiate switching commands in a holon and monitor their implementation.
Control Box	System	A control box can receive and implement switching commands for holon elements.	
Control Center	Person/ Organization	Monitors networks and initiates measures to ensure optimal supply	Examples of use-case-relevant functionalities are: - Detection of network states - Communication of network states
Network Monitor	Software Service/ System	Monitors networks using specific services	Examples of use-case-relevant functionalities are: - Detection of network states - Communication of network states

Fig. 6.15 Tasks of identified subjects

with active sentences in tabular form. The numbering of entries already reflects the control flow. The number of follow-up actions is specified in the associated column. If the follow-up action depends on certain results of the action, this condition is described in the column follow-up action. Depending on the valid condition, there may be another follow-up action.

A table with the control flow of a process can be the starting point for a control flow-oriented process model. The individual actors are the swim lanes in BPMN or in a swim-lane-oriented EPK or in UML state diagrams. However, these modeling methods should only be used if no asynchronous events, such as the possibility

No.	Task	Indication	Follow-up action
1	Network monitor detects voltage drop in low-voltage network	Uses functions from the function group "Measure" for this purpose.	2
2.	Network monitor reports the situation to the control center		3
3.	Control center identifies and localizes the error	Uses functions from the function groups "Monitor" and "Measurement" (Remark: What happens if the control center cannot identify the error?)	4
4.	Control centre informs holon managers (HM) or holon coordinators in the affected network area	Attention: a single-point-of-failure or bottleneck may be present here; if necessary, it should be replaced by a decentralized mechanism.	5
5.	(where appropriate) Holon coordinators contact holon managers in the affected holons	Uses functions from the function group "Holon Management" for this purpose	6
6.	(if no Holon Coordinator acts) Holon Managers identify a HM to take over the coordination task		7
7.	Holon coordinator and affected holon manager identify a plausible new holon constellation	Uses function "Holon Formation" from function group "Holon Management"	8
8.	Holon coordinator reports the calculated proposal to the control center		9
9.	Holon coordinator goes into "alert" state and waits for feedback from control center		10

Fig. 6.16 Sequence in the holon system

of changing purchase orders, occur in a process and the parallelism of the agents is not to be modeled. In addition, the number of actors should not be too high. Swim lane representations are usually flat, i.e., there are no hierarchies of swim lanes. More than five swim lanes lead to confusing representations. Thus, a service process contains, as a minimum, the swim-lane customer, call center, first-level support, billing, and, where applicable, customer feedback. Experience shows that in real processes, there are usually about 10 actors or more involved. The swim lane diagrams even become confusing if the control flow has to cross several swim lanes to switch to another swim lane.

Control flows are not a manageable representation for cross-organizational or cross-company processes in a distributed environment. In a distributed environment, messages are the most vivid way to model the collaboration of individual actors.

6.1.4.4 Tabular Role-Oriented Description

In the last step before the actual process modeling, the process description is structured according to the actors. All sentences with the same actor as subject are summarized in a table. For this purpose, it may be necessary to supplement the process description with interactions between subjects. Phrases such as "informs subject xy" or "engages with" etc. are replaced by send and receive actions (see

No.	Subject (actor)	Verb	Object	Indirect Object	Outcome	Con-tinue with
	Network monitor					
1	Network monitor	measures voltage in the	low voltage network		voltage drop	2
					voltage rise	3
2	Network monitor	sends	(1) status black	to control center	sent	1
3	Network monitor	sends	(10) status green	to control center	sent	1
	Control Center					
1	Control Center	receives	(1) status message	from network monitor	received	2
2	Control Center	identifies and localizes	the error		error found	3
					error not found	?
3	Control Center	sends	(2) status	to holon coordinators	sent	4
4	Control Center	receives	(5) proposal	from holon coordinator		5
5	Control Center	checks	proposal		accepted	6
6	Control Center	sends	(6) V-accepted	to holon coordinators		7

Fig. 6.17 Sequence in the holon system (more precise)

Table in Fig. 6.17). Sentence no. 2 "Network monitor reports the situation to the control center" in Fig. 6.17 is converted into a send and a receive action. In the table shown in Fig. 6.17 this corresponds to sentence no. 2 "network monitor sends status black to control center" in the table section for the network monitor. The counterpart to this is sentence no. 1 in the table section for the control center.

After creating the behavior tables, a formal model can be derived in a suitable modeling language. A language should be used in which the aspects deemed important for the process under consideration can be clearly and precisely expressed. In our example, we have selected S-BPM. Figure 6.18 shows, in the left half, the network structure of the process considered. The rectangles with rounded corners represent the actors involved. The arrows between the actors are labeled with the messages exchanged. The numbers in the message names correspond to the sentence numbers in the table above. The diagram to the right of the process structure shows the behavior of the holon coordinator subject. The circles with the letters E and S are states of communication. Transitions from circles with an E are labeled with the messages expected in this state. The transitions to the S states are labeled with the messages sent in this state. All other transitions define local operations on local data.

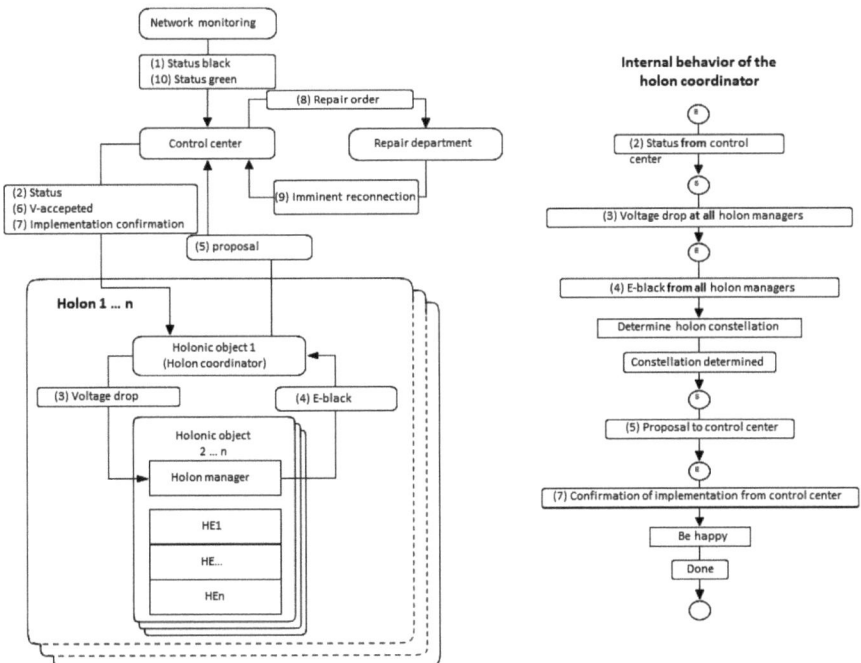

Fig. 6.18 Behavioral description of the holon coordinator subject

6.1.5 Process Modeling

6.1.5.1 Selection of the Modeling Language

The following lists some factors that should facilitate the selection of a suitable modeling notation or language. These include the determining factors of a BPM project, the language's manageability, and the support of downstream activities such as validation (see also [5–9]).

With regard to determining factors, the question "What are the properties of the subject matter to be modeled?" is of particular interest. The following properties should be decisive for the selection of a modeling language:

1. Asynchronous events: If such events exist, then a corresponding modeling language should offer the possibility to map the associated parallelization of processes or process steps in such a way that, if necessary, an execution reflects the parallelism. This means that the modeling language contains constructs for representing asynchronous events that explicitly contain this temporal quality. This allows a runtime environment to be configured accordingly at execution time.
2. Cross-organizational and cross-company: If an issue is relevant not only for a particular organization or one of its subsidiaries but also for networked partners outside the immediate areas of activity, such as other subsidiaries or the supplier

industry, then proven modeling mechanisms or language constructs should be available that enable the encapsulation of external issues. This makes it possible to embed external actors in an organization without having to know and represent their processes in detail.

3. Number of actors: At first glance, this parameter does not seem to be necessarily relevant for the selection of a modeling language. However, it becomes more important when it comes to the complexity of processes on the one hand, and the comprehensibility of the models on the other. After all, the instance-model relationship also plays into this factor. If there is a large number of actors involved, a notation should also have modeling mechanisms or language constructs that make them visible, as well as accessible aggregately or through other perspectives (e.g., functional view).

With regard to manageability, the question "How should the subject matter be described?" is of particular importance. The following properties or quality of a modeling language should be decisive for its selection:

1. Number of symbols: On the one hand, a limited number of symbols can make powerful models easily manageable, but on the other hand it can lead to an undesirable abridgement of facts.
2. Definition of symbols: The use of the symbols should be clear, i.e., objectively comprehensible for modelers. This facilitates effectiveness and efficiency in the creation of models.
3. Availability of tools for model description: The availability of digital tools for the simple and correct representation of subject matter determines the usability of a modeling language. A syntax editor for diagrammatic languages helps, for example, to create syntactically correct models and to structure complex situations in a usable way.
4. Possibilities of structuring models along a hierarchy: This feature allows networked issues to be viewed from a top-down perspective. This usually facilitates the legibility of models and thus increases the comprehensibility of illustrated facts for those not directly involved.

Regarding the support of further activities, the question "How is the support of the model for next steps?" is of particular interest. When selecting a modeling language, the following features of a modeling language should be considered in this context:

1. Validation tools: Can a model be validated? This means that a tool can be used to determine whether the notation and thus all of the language used has been utilized correctly in the sense of the syntax of the language and in the sense of the intention of the subject matter depicted.
2. Optimization tools: Can a process be optimized with the help of its model? Optimization follows initial modeling and validation and aims at the optimal distribution of tasks and the optimal use of resources. For this purpose, a tool

should be used to determine whether the notation and thus all of the language used allows, or actively supports, the optimization of modeled processes through corresponding constructs of the language, or through special mechanisms (e.g., through suggestions or reference models).

3. Tools for organizational embedding: Can the integration of a modeled process into an organization be realized with the help of a tool? This step is the first one to implement processes and requires that a tool can be used to determine which task or role holders or which organizational units should be able to carry out the illustrated activities in practice. On this basis, the corresponding assignments for the organizational implementation of process models can then be made (and changed again as required).

4. Tools for technical embedding: Can the integration of a modeled process into an IT infrastructure or information system architecture be realized with the help of a tool? This step is the second necessary step for the implementation of processes and requires the determination by means of a tool that the technical system can carry out the depicted activities in practice. On this basis, the corresponding assignments for the technical implementation of process models can be made (and adapted again as required).

5. Tools for commissioning and operation: Can the commissioning and operation of a modeled process in an organization be supported or ensured with the help of a tool? This step is necessary as soon as a process is switched to "productive," i.e., after it has been embedded in the organizational and technical infrastructure and has been transferred into the operational environment or has become operationally effective. In this context, a tool should help to support the introduction phase of a modeled process, i.e., to determine which process steps are transferred to operations and in which order. An appropriate tool should also support monitoring of implemented processes and thus help to ensure the operations of an organization and effectively support its further development. The latter can be done by means of annotations in process models, which mark obstacles to execution.

6.1.5.2 Modeling by Construction

When constructing a process model, modeling begins with a "blank sheet of paper." The information from the process analysis is used to describe the process step by step. The required activities include several different tasks, depending on the approach chosen:

1. Description of the processes and their relationships (process network).
2. Identification of the process to be described.
3. Identification of the actors or systems involved in the process.
4. Specification of the information exchanged between the actors or systems within the control, data, and message flow for processing business cases. This also includes the implementation of business rules, as they directly influence the behavior of actors and systems.

5. Description of the behavior of the individual actors or systems, in particular through functional steps and their temporal-causal relationship according to the modeled subject matter.
6. Definition of business objects or data and their use.

These activities are set in a certain order according to the selected language and lead to differently detailed representations of subject matter.

6.1.5.3 Modeling by Restriction

In addition to modeling by construction, there is also the possibility of modeling by restriction. This is based on general process models. A typical example is the communication-oriented approach as pursued with S-BPM. In the universal process model, each actor or system involved in a process can send a message to, or receive a message from, any other actor or system involved at any time. This message has the general name "message" and can transmit any media as a business object. The result is a universal process that is characterized by the number of its subjects. These are marked as boxes with subject 1... n. Their mutual interaction possibilities are marked by arrows between the subject boxes. This results in a similar initial behavior for each subject.

Within the framework of modeling by restriction, the following steps are taken to a detailed factual situation: (i) determine number of subjects and subject identifiers, (ii) reduce communication paths, (iii) specify message types, (iv) customize subjects' behavior, and (v) specify and refine business objects.

If other, for instance, function-oriented approaches are chosen, then basic structures can be generalized, for example, in the form of reference models. In doing so, behavioral patterns will also be used, such as previous events for functions or conditions that determine the further course of business processes after executing a function.

6.1.5.4 Combined Approaches

While in the construction of process models the modeling begins with a "blank sheet of paper" and is extended step by step with information from the process analysis, in the modeling by restriction, a generalized structure of process models and their components is assumed. A typical example of a combination of both approaches is the case corresponding to the middle-out approach. One instance of this case is to start with a construction and, as soon as a (recurring) pattern occurs, to use a reference model and reduce or concretize it.

Further application instances would be a pattern comparison and the start with recurring (routine) processes. The latter reverses the above-mentioned case and allows the embedding of special characteristics of process flows into generalized process architectures. The pattern comparison, on the other hand, represents a kind of control process in which the completeness or correctness of a model can be checked by means of a generalized pattern.

6.2   Quality Control: Validation and Optimization

Validation is closely related to modeling. In modeling the process flow is described according to the objective. This means that during the modeling activity the following question resonates: "Does the model correspond to the set qualitative and quantitative objectives?" The examination, whether a process model corresponds to the set goals, is called validation and/or optimization. This means that validation and optimization are constantly performed in the course of modeling. After the decision to complete the modeling process, a final check is made as to whether the overall model meets the set objectives.

Validation shows whether the process meets all requirements and achieves the intended results. It is also essential for a process whether the desired results are achieved with the least possible effort. Quality control in business processes, therefore, has two main tasks. It is intended to test the effectiveness and efficiency of processes. Effectiveness means that the process meets the requirements placed on it, i.e., delivers the desired result (output). The process is efficient if it can be carried out with as few financial and time resources as possible in order to deliver the desired result. This is to be achieved through optimization.

Both quality controls must be implemented as early as possible, before IT systems are developed at great expense, and later users are trained. Figure 6.19 summarizes the individual aspects of validation and optimization. The appropriate tools and reference models support the verification of a process model. For the validation, there are manual tools such as checklists or role-plays, while for the optimization, simulation software must be used. The results of the check are prepared and entered into "ToDo" lists for processing, i.e., modeling activities are started again. This cycle is repeated until verification leads to a result that is considered good enough.

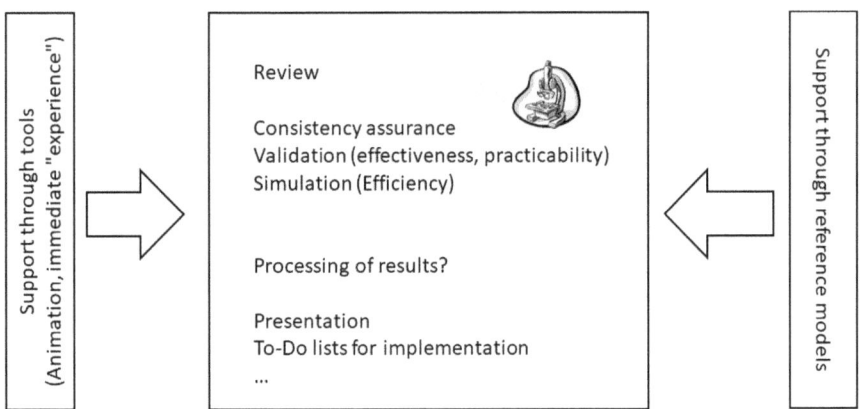

Fig. 6.19 Structure of the quality assurance of a process model

6.2.1 Validation

The prerequisite for validation is a model that reflects the subject matter to be represented. The model is checked whether it delivers the expected result according to the specified quality characteristics and whether the process contributes to the company objectives. This aspect is called semantic correctness. This results from the consensus of the managers and the technical and methodological experts who consider the model to be appropriate.

The semantic validity is to be distinguished from the syntactic correctness, which concerns the adherence to the fixed description rules, i.e., the description means are used according to the defaults of the modeling language.

6.2.1.1 Manual Process Validation

Figure 6.20 shows a general procedure for manual validation. Here the process documentation is checked with the help of checklists. The process documentation includes the description of the goals, inputs, results, triggering events, and of course, the model of the process. The process documentation should be checked by all parties involved in a process on the basis of the checklists.

The findings of the individual parties are consolidated and clarified in a joint workshop, and the necessary revisions are jointly determined. This cycle is repeated until it is jointly decided that no further revisions are necessary.

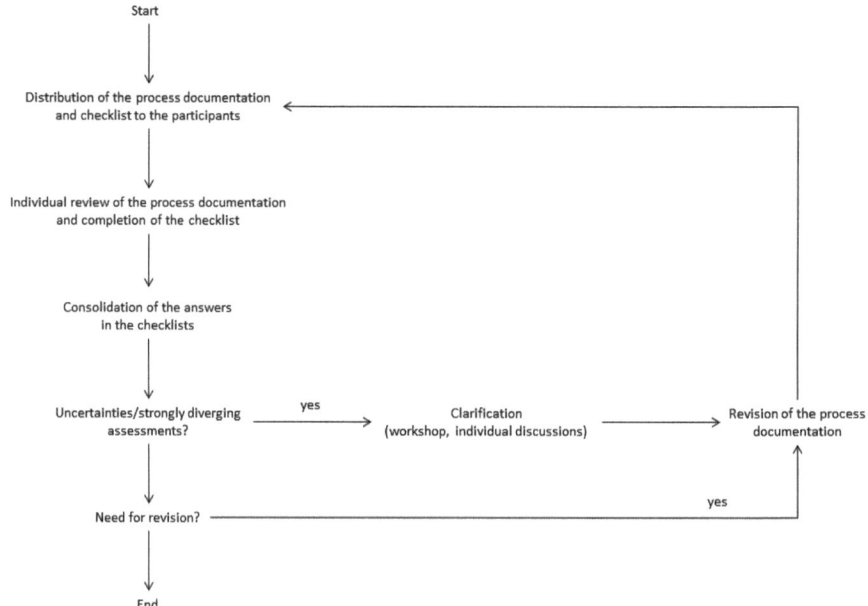

Fig. 6.20 Sequence of a manual process check

To prepare a review, the process description and a checklist, according to which the process description is to be verified, are distributed. This checklist contains questions to be answered by the evaluators regarding the process.

Examples of such questions are:

1. Does the process support the company's goals?
2. Are the objectives of the process defined?
3. Is the benefit of the process clearly described in the objective and is it clear what added value it delivers and for whom?
4. What risks does the process entail?
5. Is a process owner assigned?
6. Have the authorities of the process owner been defined and are these sufficient?
7. Are there any performance indicators with which the achievement of objectives can be evaluated?
8. Are the measurement procedures for the performance indicators clearly defined?
9. Are the target values for the performance indicators of the process systematically defined and do they provide an assertion about the value contribution of the process?
10. Does the process support the policy and strategy of the company or IT organization?
11. Is the process flow described?
12. Are the inputs and results of the process described?
13. Is it clear who (organizations, roles, people) provides which inputs and who receives which results?
14. Are the description conventions for processes adhered to?
15. Is it defined who is responsible for the individual steps of the process (organizations, roles, or persons)?
16. Is the procedure in the process aligned to the interest groups (e.g., customers)?
17. Is the procedure in the process clearly justified?
18. Are there sufficient tools for executing the process (checklists, work instructions, etc.), in addition to the process description?
19. Is the scope of the process clearly defined?
20. Are the relationships of the process to other processes described or defined?

The above list of questions is only exemplary and not complete. Companies often use lists with up to 100 questions.

Reading extensive process documentation and comparing it with long checklists is very tedious. Experience shows that the intensity of the check decreases with an increasing number of pages. The first pages are still read in detail. Then the accuracy decreases continually. In order to compensate for the weaknesses of a visual assessment, a more formalized version of the review, the so-called walk-through, was developed, whereby the walk-through refers predominantly to the process model.

6.2.1.2 Walk-Throughs

Similar to code inspection in programming, in a walk-through a process is discussed step by step with selected process participants. In order to make the step-by-step process more engaging, a formal process description can be run through with the help of a practical example. A process participant goes through the business process description step by step using a concrete example. For each process step, an expert asks specific questions in order to question the effectiveness of the process description.

For example, the understanding of technical terms, the technical necessity, as well as the completeness of the process description are questioned. In this way, the process description is evaluated. A walk-through is performed with about two to four process participants representing different user groups.

The "authors" of the process description (e.g., process managers) should remain in the background so that criticism can be formulated openly. All points of criticism and suggestions are collected, documented, and then evaluated with the process participants. This evaluation leads to a revision of the process.

The step-by-step analysis of a process can be supported by appropriate tools. The tool used shows the process model on the screen, and the current process step is highlighted in color.

6.2.1.3 Role-Plays

The next level for a tangible review of process models are role-plays. These are particularly useful when communication-oriented modeling languages are used. The actors are then already identified, and the roles are subsequently assigned to suitable persons. A game leader triggers the process and provides the necessary input. The individual role holders then execute these process instances according to the process descriptions. These "process flows" are observed by other affected parties, and the anomalies identified are noted. After a number of process instances have been executed, the findings are evaluated, and necessary adjustments are identified.

The execution of role-plays can be supported by suitable IT tools. The role owners of a role-play do not receive their role descriptions on paper. They are guided through the process by software that, in particular, implements the flow logic. This software is generated directly and automatically from the process model. The prerequisite for such an approach is that the semantics of the process modeling language used are clearly defined. This prerequisite is, for example, only partially met by BPMN and not at all in the case of EPCs. However, S-BPM entirely fulfills this requirement due to its clearly defined formal semantics.

Figure 6.21 shows what an IT-supported validation can look like. The advantage of an IT-supported role-play is that the preparation time is very limited and the process experience is very close to the subsequent productive process execution.

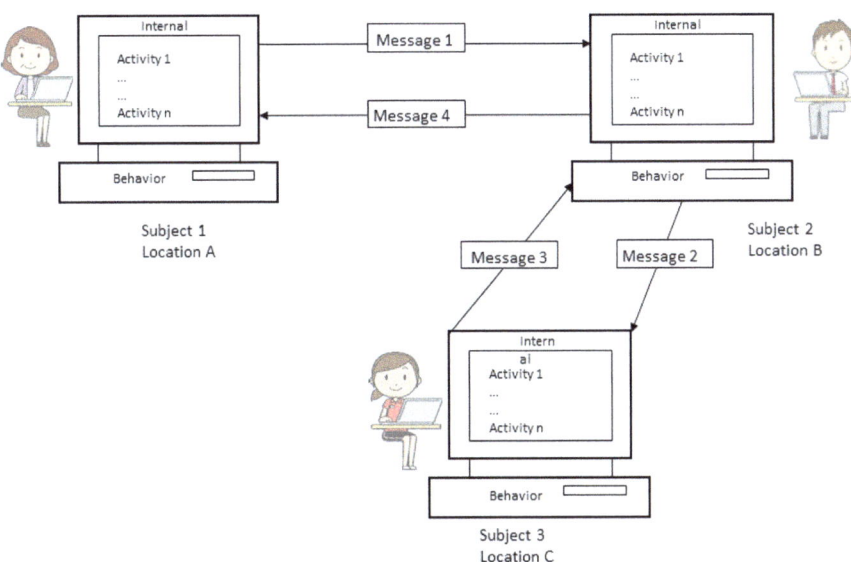

Fig. 6.21   Setting for an IT-supported role-play

6.2.2   Optimization

After checking the effectiveness (do the processes deliver the desired result at all?), it must be checked whether the result is achieved with the least possible use of resources. Optimization through manual testing, walk-throughs, or role-plays is only possible to a very limited extent. The knowledge gained in this way only provides an approximation for determining the resource requirements for an assumed number of process runs. A systematic determination of the resource and time requirements is only possible through simulation. However, the prerequisite for a simulation is that the process model can be executed.

When business processes are simulated, the business cases handled by a process are generated randomly according to an assumed probability distribution. As a rule, this is the exponential distribution with an expected value presumed or observed. Individual work steps are assigned the corresponding resources with the required work time. The required work time usually follows a normal distribution with expected values and standard deviations determined from observations.

Within the framework of simulation instances, information is provided on the execution capability of processes, on process weak points, and on resource bottlenecks. On the basis of the simulated Process Performance Indicators, various alternatives can be evaluated and a realistic benchmarking carried out in advance of cost-intensive process changes within a company.

Modern tools and simulation methods enable the analysis and optimization of processes with regard to costs, lead times, capacity utilization, or bottlenecks. In addition, the simulation of business processes forms a starting point for introducing activity-based accounting instead of the relatively inaccurate cost-plus pricing. The profits and losses of the individual departments thus become transparent at an early stage.

As already mentioned, conducting a simulation study requires a precise description of the process under consideration. This means that a formal method must be used to define the process flow. In addition, the most precise knowledge possible of the probability distributions, their parameters, and the examined performance indicators is required. In practice, simulations are not often used due to the high effort involved, although the findings can be compelling.

References

1. A. Fleischmann, W. Schmidt, C. Stary, S. Obermeier, E. Boerger, *Subject-Oriented Business Process Management* (Springer, Berlin, 2012)
2. N.M. Seel, *Weltwissen und mentale Modelle* (Hogrefe, Hogrefe, 1991)
3. V. Allee, Value-creating networks: organizational issues and challenges. Learn. Organ. **16**(6), 427–442 (2009)
4. M. Augl, C. Stary, Communication-and value-based organizational development at the university clinic for radiotherapy-radiation oncology, in *S-BPM in the Wild: Practical Value Creation* (2015), pp. 35–53
5. C. Kaar, C. Stary, Intelligent business transformation through market-specific value network analysis: structured interventions and process bootstrapping in geomarketing. Knowl. Process. Manag. **26**(2), 163–181 (2019)
6. C. Stary, M. Maroscher, *Wissensmanagement in der Praxis:-Methoden-Werkzeuge-Beispiele* (Carl Hanser Verlag GmbH Co KG, Munich, 2012)
7. C. Stary, Transactional value analytics in organizational development, in *Analytics and Knowledge Management* (Auerbach Publications, Boca Raton, 2018), pp. 221–250
8. I.A. Baum, C. Stary, Value network analysis for facilitator development in project-based learning. MethodsX **13**, 102846 (2024)
9. P.M. Senge, *The Fifth Discipline: The Art and Practice of the Learning Organization* (Doubleday/Currency, New York, 1990)
10. M. Augl, C. Stary, Stakeholders as mindful designers: adjusting capabilities rather than needs in computer-supported daily workforce planning, in *Designing healthcare that works* (Elsevier, Amsterdam, 2018), pp. 95–112
11. I.A. Baum, C. Stary, Creating business process intelligence through value network analysis: a tagging-based approach, in *AI and Data Analytics Applications in Organizational Management* (IGI Global Scientific Publishing, New York, 2024), pp. 109–138
12. F. Hotie, J. Gordijn, Value-based process model design. Bus. Inf. Syst. Eng. **61**(2), 163–180 (2019)
13. D. Binci, S. Belisari, A. Appolloni, BPM and change management: an ambidextrous perspective. Bus. Process. Manag. J. **26**(1), 1–23 (2020)
14. T. Helbin, A. Van Looy, Is business process management (BPM) ready for ambidexterity? conceptualization, implementation guidelines and research agenda. Sustainability **13**(4), 1906 (2021)
15. A. Fleischmann, W. Schmidt, C. Stary, *S-BPM in the Wild: Practical Value Creation* (Springer Nature, Berlin, 2015)
16. M. Neubauer, C. Stary, *S-BPM in the Production Industry: A Stakeholder Approach* (Springer Nature, Berlin, 2017)

Realization

7

With the specification of effective and efficient processes, the foundation for their implementation has been laid. Following these preparatory activities, we now deal with the implementation of process specifications in an execution environment and the handling of process instances in live operation. The implementation of a process specification as an executable process comprises the activity bundles' organizational implementation, IT implementation, and operation, including monitoring. Figure 7.1 shows the classification of these activities in the process management model.

Based on reflections on the documentation of elaborated process specifications, the following sections present selected methods for the activity bundles' organizational and IT implementation, as well as for operating and monitoring of processes.

The activities of the process management model provide the conceptual framework for the implementation of business processes in a working system. As already discussed in previous chapters, the activity bundles represent a certain standard classification criterion, but they can be performed in any order. Each of the phases contains a bundle of activities that are typical for accomplishing the respective tasks. Every business process is in a certain phase at any particular point in time—or in other words, in a certain state: either being modeled, put into effect, executed, or analyzed. The life cycle model thus defines a phase or state space for business processes.

7.1   Process Documentation

Since an organization's or company's business processes define how products and services are developed, manufactured, and delivered, it is useful to document these processes in a structured way. Documentation should be made centrally available to all employees. It must be available at the beginning of the implementation activities

© The Author(s) 2026   239
M. Elstermann et al., *Contextual Process Digitalization*,
https://doi.org/10.1007/978-3-032-06901-6_7

Realisation

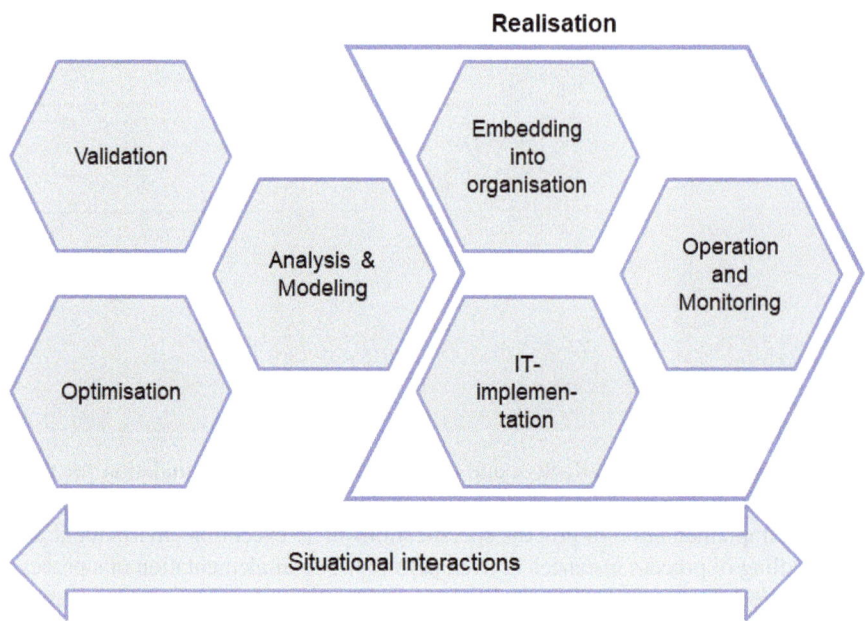

Fig. 7.1 Classification of implementation activities in the process management model

at the latest. Business process documentation is the result of activity bundles during preparation measures.

Nowadays, digital documents serve as the standard for documentation. Ideally, the provision of these documents takes place by means of a generally available intranet, with which a basic access control can also be designed. The documents themselves can be, for example, PDF files that cannot be easily changed (possibly also digitally signed), or HTML files that can be viewed via a browser.

For smaller organizations and companies, it is usually sufficient to use existing office software for creating and maintaining process documentation. For more extensive collections, the use of specific software, so-called *Business Process Management Systems* (BPMS), appears to be worth considering. In any case, the chosen form needs to support its users and the management systems based on it in the best possible way. The documents should also contain a unique identifier, a version number, and a date. In case a word processor is used, a style sheet is recommended in order to achieve a uniform appearance and uniformly defined structures. In addition, a list with all documents including their history is recommended to provide a general overview.

The process owner or process coordinator is responsible for ensuring that process documentation is up-to-date and complete. The process office specifies what the process documentation should contain and provides appropriate templates and explanations. In case a dedicated IT system (BPMS) is to be used, respective training of all employees—depending on their role—is strongly recommended. In the sense of change management, the employees should also be involved in the selection or development procedure in an adequate form.

Roughly speaking, the following content for a process documentation has proved to be useful, although not all items are relevant for every business process and additional items might be added where needed:

Aim of the process—a short descriptive text explaining the relationship of the process to overall business objectives (strategic contribution).

Trigger of the process—specifies which event starts a process instance and who can generate this event.

Input—a list with descriptions of the information, documents, and physical artifacts needed as input, including who provides it.

Output—a list with descriptions of the information, documents, and physical artifacts generated by the process; possibly also quality criteria per customer.

Area of validity and organizational determining factors—if necessary, delimitation to other business processes, or organizational restriction (e.g., only valid for the business area key accounts).

Definition of terms and abbreviations—abbreviations used in the document; Tip: if these are also consolidated in a company-wide directory, a glossary of the most important terms in a company, as well as uniform definitions in all process documentation, is obtained.

Overview description of the process model—a textual representation of the actors/roles and the process steps.

Process model—a (visual) representation created in an agreed modeling language; there should be uniform rules for the creation of process models to avoid uncontrolled growth (e.g., regarding colors and labeling of notation elements).

Technical determining factors—a list and description of technical tools required in the process; representation of IT support or dependencies; e.g., references to certain modules of an ERP system.

Feedback mechanisms—a description of how process participants can articulate problems during execution, e.g., incorrect or insufficiently modeled logic, or make suggestions for improvement. This should be a standard procedure implemented in Business Process Management.

Exceptions—possible exceptions from the process model, that is, activities that are not taken into account in the process model, since associated cases only occur rarely.

Interfaces to other processes—a representation of which other business processes require the output of a specific process, thus defining the customer of the process or their expectations.

Process Performance Indicators (PPIs)—a list, definition, and explanation of the planned Process Performance Indicators.

Performance measurements—a representation of how and when the performance indicators are to be measured and calculated, including references to other associated available documents.

Reporting—a representation of how and at what point in time Process Performance Indicators are reported and to whom, including references to other associated available documents.

Escalations—a definition of procedures to be started as soon as the tolerance range of performance indicators is violated.

Audits and compliance—a reference to appropriate guidelines. If individual activities are included in a business process for reasons of compliance, they should be documented in order to ensure that they are not eliminated as part of an efficiency optimization. It is advisable to highlight such activities in color in a visual representation. Furthermore, it has proven helpful in practice to document (in tabular form) in which business processes compliance with specific standards and legal regulations is necessary. Similar considerations apply to external requirements of compliance, e.g., quality standards, which have an impact on internal compliance issues, such as risk analyses and internal audits.

7.2   Linking Elements of the Enterprise Architecture

7.2.1   Overview

As mentioned in Chaps. 1 and 2, business processes are part of the enterprise architecture. Enterprise architectures address the internal aspects and structures of a company. They are essentially models of the internal structure of a company and cover not only organizational but also technical aspects, in particular the deployed IT infrastructure. When implementing the process models, it is now necessary to establish the relationship between the process model and the available resources. Figure 7.2 shows the individual steps from a process model to the executable process instance.

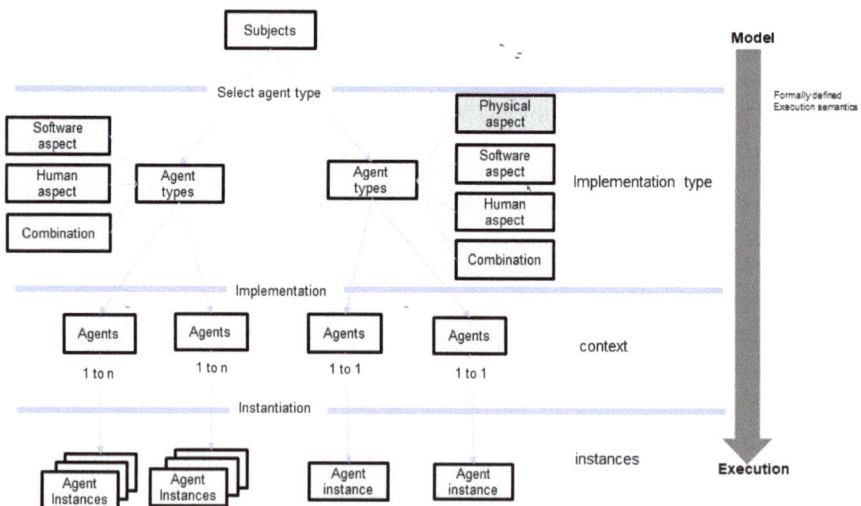

Fig. 7.2 From process model to process execution

In a process model, the actors, the actions, their sequences, and the objects manipulated by the actions are described. Actions (activities) can be performed by humans, software systems, physical systems, or a combination of these basic types of actors. We call them the task holders. For example, a software system can automatically perform the "tax rate calculation" action, while a person uses a software program to perform the "order entry" activity. The person enters the order data via a screen mask. The software checks the entered data for plausibility and saves it. However, activities can also be carried out purely manually, for example, when a warehouse worker receives a picking order on paper, executes it, marks it as executed on the order form, and returns it to the warehouse manager.

When creating a process model, it is often not yet known which types of actors execute which actions. Therefore, it can be useful to abstract from said model when starting to describe processes by introducing abstract actors. A modeling language should allow the use of such abstractions. This means that when defining the process logic, no assertion should have to be made about what type of actor is realized. In S-BPM, the subjects represent abstract actors. In BPMN, pools or swim lanes can be interpreted as abstract actors, while in EPCs roles can be used for this purpose.

In the description of the control logic of a process, the individual activities are also described independently of their implementation. For example, for the action "create a picking order" it is not specified whether a human actor fills in a paper form or a screen mask, or whether a software system generates this form automatically. Thus, with activities the means by which something happens is not described, but rather only what happens.

The means are of course related to the implementation type of the actor. As soon as it has been defined which types of actors are assigned to the individual actions, the manner of realization of an activity has also been defined. In addition, the logical or physical object on which an action is executed also needs to be determined. Logical objects are data structures whose data is manipulated by activities. Paper forms represent a mixture between logical and physical objects, while a workpiece on which the "deburring" action takes place is a purely physical object. Therefore, there is a close relationship between the type of task holder, the actions, and the associated objects actors manipulate or use when performing actions.

A process model can be used in different areas of an organization. The process logic is applied unchanged in the respective areas. However, it may be necessary to implement the individual actors and actions differently. Thus, in one environment certain actions could be performed by humans and in another the same actions could be performed by software systems. In the following, we refer to such different environments of use for a process model as context. Hence, for a process model, varying contexts can exist, in which there are different realization types for actors and actions.

In BPMN, the modeler can define for each task separately whether it is a so-called human task, service task, or user task. User tasks are performed by humans together with software systems, such as filling out a picking order on the screen. This means that the description of the implementation type in BPMN is part of the process logic. Since in BPMN pools and swim lanes can be interpreted as actors, care must be taken that no contradictions arise with the implementation type of tasks within, for example, a pool. For instance, in case the designer specifies that a pool is only executed by humans, this pool cannot contain any service or user tasks. Since the definition of the implementation type is part of the process logic in BPMN, it may be necessary to create a separate process model for each context.

In S-BPM, actors are not assigned to individual activities, but rather the actor type is assigned to an entire subject. In S-BPM, this assignment is not part of the process logic but is done instead for each process in a separate two-column table. The left column contains the subject name and the right column the implementation type. If there are several contexts for a process model, a separate assignment table is created for each of them.

The assignment of the implementation type forms the transition between the process logic and its implementation. Subsequently, it has to be defined which persons, software systems, and physical systems represent the actors and how the individual actions are concretely realized. These aspects are described in detail in the following subsections.

7.2.2 People and Organizations

For each context in which people are involved it is necessary to determine the respective action (activity) holders, and thus the concrete persons or organizational units that carry out the actions.

In companies and administrations there are people with different educations, qualifications, preferences, and interests. There are merchants, developers, craftsmen, etc. who will take care of the arising tasks. Organizations can therefore also be described as structured resource pools. Depending on the type and scope of the tasks, an organization forms units in which the respective specialists are combined. There are purchasing departments with procurement experts, or development departments that are made up of several development engineers and other specialists. The relationship between the persons and organizations in the organizational structure and the abstract actors in the processes can be established statically or dynamically.

Static Assignment
In the simplest case, the two-column table already mentioned provides information on which actor defined in the process (column 1) is assigned to which person (column 2). The second column can also contain an organization or organizational unit. Then, all its members are assigned to the abstract actor. Such a specification ensures that in case of illness or vacation any person from the organization can take over the arising tasks of the process. In addition, the workload can also be distributed dynamically if actions from several process flows (process instances) have to be handled.

With BPMN, pools, swim lanes, and individual actions can be assigned separately to an actor. It is important to ensure that there are no inconsistencies when using all assignment options. If a software system executes a swim lane as an actor and there is a human task in this swim lane, it is not clear what this means. Actors were therefore introduced in Bonitasoft's BPMN-based tool (see [1]). They are placeholders for task holders, to whom, similar to the subjects in subject-orientation, concrete actors are assigned.

In S-BPM, a complete subject is embedded into the organization, i.e., the assignment then applies to all actions of this subject.

Dynamic Assignment
In many processes, the assignment of the actors of a process to persons and organizational units cannot be determined statically. For a business trip application, the person handling the request can depend on whether the trip is domestic or international. While the process logic may be the same in both cases, the executor may differ, for example, because an employee has special expertise in international travel with visa issues.

In such cases, it makes sense to first determine and assign the persons or organizational units involved during execution of the process logic, for example, depending on data values in business objects (in this case, the travel request).

For a flexible dynamic assignment of physical actors, tables are usually no longer sufficient, but instead programming language constructs are necessary. Lawall et al. [2] shows how such a language can be used to embed subject-oriented process models into organizations. Since in BPMN the assignment of actors is possible via pools, lanes, and tasks, the description of the assignment is very complex here. Various BPMN-based tools such as Bonita [1] or Activiti [3, 4] integrate processes into the organization by programming this in Java or XML.

7.2.3   Physical Infrastructure

Particularly in manufacturing processes, physical systems are involved as actors. In this way, blanks can be delivered to a machine via a transport system, the machine processes the blanks, and the processed parts are then transported to the next processing step. If such a machine is regarded as a subject or pool, the delivered parts are modeled as messages to be received and the dispatched processed parts as messages to be sent. The modeler represents the processing step as a single task in a subject or pool.

7.2.4   IT Infrastructure

Digitalization in an economic system means implementing processes with the most comprehensive support possible through software systems. In corresponding scenarios, computer systems or machines carry out the activities for the most part;

human intervention is reduced as far as possible and sensible. Essential aspects thereby are:

- The control of the process flow:

The sequence of actions described in the process (control flow) is automatically controlled by computer programs.

- The execution of actions

Actions on data objects can often be performed fully automatically by appropriate computer programs.

Software systems are the means to merge the different types of actors. For example, during the control of the process flow, a process engine integrates human and machine operators at runtime in the processing of instances, according to the individual situation.

The following explanations deal with the control of the process flow and the manipulation of the associated business objects by Information Technology, although without going into detail about the integration of humans or physical systems as task holders. This will be covered in Sect. 7.2.5.

Control Flow
The process logic corresponds to the control flow logic of a computer program. The exclusive automated execution of the process logic by a computer program is only possible for highly structured processes. All conceivable process possibilities must be covered. No human intervention is planned. To avoid that the computer program's execution logic differs from the described process logic, it is useful if the computer program can be automatically derived from the description of the process logic. The following prerequisites must be met for such cases:

- The syntax and semantics of the language in which the process logic is described must be precisely defined.
- The description of the process flow must be available in electronic form.
- An implementation program must be available that reads the electronic form of the description of the process logic and generates a computer program in a suitable programming language, based on the precise semantics of the process description language.

The importance of distributed systems, which are already widely used today, continues to grow with the development of cloud and edge computing. This can mean that parts of a fully automated process are executed on different computer nodes of a distributed system. Since these can be based on different technologies, appropriate variants may have to be available for the automatic conversion of a process description into a computer program.

Thus, individual subjects of an S-BPM description of a process can run on different computer nodes of a distributed system. This can mean that the program code might need to be generated separately for each subject. This can, however, be avoided if the generated target code is available on preferably all the node types of the distributed system, and the target system has a framework through which the program parts running on different nodes can work together. The software components usually synchronize their collaboration by exchanging messages. Such an enabling programming language is, e.g., Java with the AKKA framework. It allows messages to be exchanged across computer boundaries. [5] has investigated this possibility on the basis of S-BPM models.

In BPMN, individual pools can be executed theoretically on different computer nodes. This requires that communication between the pools is possible across computer boundaries. A search for possibilities of a corresponding code generation tool for BPMN models in spring 2018 brought no results.

Activities and Data
In fully digitalized processes, computer systems also perform the activities contained in the process flow. This can be done using functions or services that are already available in existing application programs and can be inserted or called at the appropriate places in the program that implements the process control flow.

For the integration of newly developed software for activities, technologies such as Web services, REST interfaces, or simple APIs are often used. Database access for direct manipulation of data can be integrated analogously depending on the interfaces of the database systems used.

When using S-BPM, data belongs to a subject. Multiple subjects are not allowed to access shared data. If several subjects want to use the same data, e.g., stored in a database, it has to be "packed" into a subject. This subject receives the corresponding requests from other subjects, performs the desired action, and sends the result back to the requesting subject.

In software technology, activities together with their data are called classes. Several such classes can be combined to form services. In IT, this is then called a Service-oriented Architecture. The services are invoked according to the control flow of the process. Tasks in BPMN can be realized through services. Similarly, functions can be implemented within a subject in this way.

Microservices are a current concept for structuring software systems. Microservices describe an architecture in which individual small functional building blocks are independently programmed, tested, approved, and made available on different technical platforms on demand. Through their interaction by means of interfaces which are independent of the programming language, complex application software can be realized. In doing so, microservices usually communicate by exchanging asynchronous messages. This also corresponds to the concept of Reactive Programming, whose main characteristic is the coupling of program blocks by asynchronous messages.

In BPMN, pools can be implemented as microservices if all tasks in a pool are executed by the same actor.

In S-BPM, subjects are always assigned to a task holder and communicate via the asynchronous exchange of messages. Therefore, a process described in a subject-oriented format corresponds, in view of IT architecture, to a microservice-oriented structure that meets the requirements of Reactive Programming.

7.2.5 Combinations of Task Holders

Tasks are often not performed by a single type of task holder. With the increase of digitalization, the number of tasks performed exclusively by humans is decreasing continuously. Today, a warehouse worker often receives his picking orders via a tablet connected to an IT system. After he has assembled the goods, he also confirms task completion via the tablet. This action closes the commissioning task. The IT system updates the data and automatically triggers the subsequent task, such as preparing the shipping documents. The picking task is therefore carried out by humans and IT as types of task holders, a combination that is very common in business processes. The IT controls at least the process logic and manages the data while people enter data or operate machines.

Machines controlled by small computers with corresponding software are increasingly replacing machines as purely mechanical actors. These embedded systems control the mechanics and handle communication with other machines or higher-level business applications. Communication with other intelligent machines is referred to as horizontal communication, and with business applications as vertical communication. The latter links production systems with business processes and is an integral part of the Industry 4.0 initiative.

The following sections describe in more detail how the various task holders are integrated when implementing a process logic.

Combination of Humans with IT
The combination of people and IT in the execution of business processes is the core of their digitalization. The IT at least takes over the control of the process logic, i.e., it arranges the handling of the intended tasks by the respective task holders according to the process logic. In addition, tasks can be carried out directly by IT as task holders without the need to involve people. If a task can only be completed with human support, the software responsible for the control flow prompts the responsible human task holder via an appropriate user interface. This may concern not only the input of data but also the confirmation that the user has executed a manual action.

IT systems as control software and as actors for activities usually also store the data generated during process execution, both the content of business objects, as well as metadata, such as time stamps for the start and end of instances and execution steps.

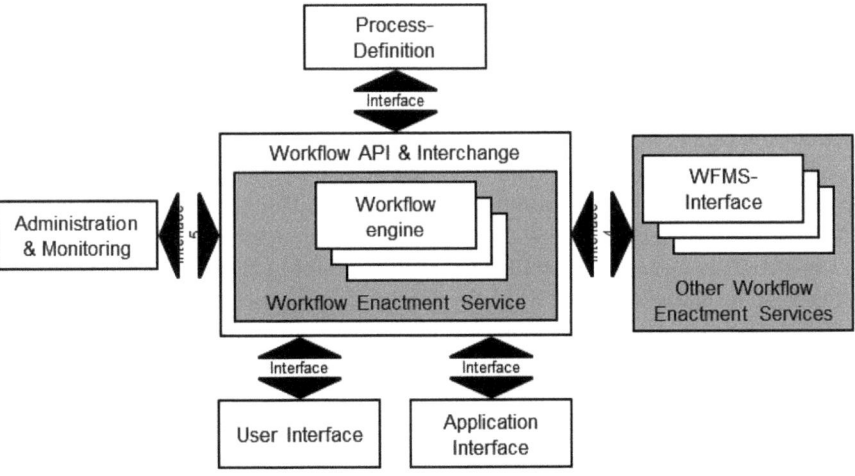

Fig. 7.3 Reference model for Workflow Management Systems (WFMS)

A comprehensive platform for implementing business processes executed by people and IT solutions is called a Workflow Management System (WFMS). The Workflow Management Coalition (WfMC) has developed a reference model for this purpose. Figure 7.3 shows the components and interfaces of the reference model [1].

The interfaces between the individual components are defined as follows:

• Process definition (Interface 1)

Interface between process definition, modeling tools, and the workflow engine (execution environment).

• User interface (Interface 2)

APIs for clients to request services from the workflow engine so that process progress and actions can be controlled.

• Application interface (Interface 3)

APIs that allow the workflow engine to call and use applications.

• Workflow Management System interface (Interface 4)

Standard interface for exchanging data with other workflow systems.

*   Administration and monitoring (Interface 5)

Interface for tools for process control and monitoring.

The essential components in the reference system of the WfMC are the workflow enactment service and the workflow engine. The actions and their sequence are defined in the process definition and controlled by the workflow engine.

In a company usually several instances of a business process run simultaneously. A process instance is created when the execution of a business process is triggered by an event defined for this purpose. Process instances follow uniform process descriptions but are executed independently of each other.

For example, two different customers can place an order. Each of these individual customer orders creates an independent instance of the business process "order processing."

The workflow enactment system uses workflow engines to manage the individual instances. A workflow engine provides the execution environment for a workflow instance.

Its main tasks are:

*   Integration of the instance into the organizational environment
*   Interpretation of the process definition
*   Control of the process instances
*   Navigation between sequential or parallel process activities
*   Interpretation of process data
*   Identification of user interfaces
*   Linking of the system to other programs/application systems
*   Linking of the system to other workflow systems
*   Superordinate control function

A workflow enactment service is a service that starts, manages, and executes one or more workflow engines. Workflow systems use application interfaces to access the functions of application systems that perform tasks defined in a process.

A worklist handler is a component that involves users in a process. It can be part of a Workflow Management System or defined and programmed by a workflow expert. Through the worklist handler the involved actors know which tasks they have to perform in which process instance.

Workflow functions can be embedded in other common applications, such as an e-mail program, so that users have a uniform user interface when handling process instances. For such an integration, there must be a communication mechanism between the workflow enactment service and the other applications.

The reference architecture also provides an interface for administration and monitoring. The software connected there serves to monitor the simultaneous execution of different instances of several business processes. On the one hand, this monitoring refers to the functional level of the processing of business cases, for example, with the recording and evaluation of response and processing times (see Sect. 7.3.3). On the other hand, the IT systems used must be monitored at the technical level, for example, with regard to load and malfunctioning behavior.

Most workflow systems currently available on the market only support orchestration, i.e., a single control flow of tasks. For BPMN, this means a workflow system can only execute the functions in a single pool. If several pools are used in a BPMN-based process description, a separate workflow engine is required for each pool. These workflow engines must then as a rule be connected by programming via Interface 4. Especially if a process should be executed on a distributed infrastructure, such structures can become complex and cost-intensive, as many software vendors charge license fees for each installed instance of the workflow engine. This increases not only technical complexity but also the costs.

Subject-oriented process descriptions are process choreographies, i.e., the subjects are independently executed in parallel, without central control for all subjects. To coordinate their individual activities, the subjects exchange messages asynchronously. An execution environment for subject-oriented defined processes is therefore, strictly speaking, a so-called multi-workflow system. Each subject corresponds to an orchestration performed by its own workflow system. The asynchronous exchange of messages between several workflow systems is realized in subject-oriented process management using the input pool concept. A number of multi-workflow systems have been developed for S-BPM.

Combination of Physical Devices and IT: Cyber-Physical Systems
In a process, actors can also be machines that perform tasks in a purely mechanically or electrically controlled way and fully automated without human intervention.

Machine control is carried out mechanically, electromechanically, or, in the case of the embedded systems already mentioned, increasingly by computer and software systems. Sensors monitor the physical condition of the machine and ambient conditions, and actuators such as servomotors, switches, controllers, etc. intervene with the operation of the machine. The control software largely determines what happens on and at intelligent machines and defines their vertical and horizontal communication with other systems.

Machines communicate with each other not only by exchanging data but also by forwarding and receiving physical artifacts. The message "workpiece to be deburred" can be realized by automatically transporting a workpiece from a metal-cutting production machine to a machine that deburrs edges. At the same time, the deburring machine can receive additional messages that contain a more detailed description of the workpiece and specify the type of deburring.

Combinations of physical and Information Technology components are referred to as cyber-physical systems (CPS). Since they bring together production and business processes, they are of particular importance for Industry 4.0 applications.

In BPMN, the modeler can model a task executed by a combination of humans and IT as a service task and describe an intelligent machine as a separate process in a pool. If there is a corresponding number of machines working together in a complex manufacturing situation, the use of numerous pools in BPMN can lead to representation problems. The reason lies in the horizontal arrangement of the pools: In case of a larger number, the message edges inevitably have to cross pools, which can be confusing. In S-BPM, on the other hand, a machine is always modeled as a subject, since the decision as to which type of task holder will execute the subject is first made in the implementation stage.

If a physical task holder is used in a process, there cannot be an arbitrary number of parallel instances of this process. A physical unit cannot be split logically, as is possible with IT or human actors.

Combination of Humans, Physical Devices, and IT
There are also scenarios in which people carry out certain tasks when intelligent machines are used. For example, a machine receives the workpiece via a transport system together with the associated information as a message, e.g., contained in an RFID device. Together the machine and an operator carry out the intended tasks in accordance with the information contained in the RFID device. The operator confirms the completion of his work via a user interface. The workpiece is then dispatched, and the updated accompanying information is transmitted to the other parties involved.

In such situations, the aim is to reduce the share of human labor and replace it with more sophisticated mechanics or improved embedded systems. This does not necessarily mean that changes to the process logic are required.

7.3   Execution and Monitoring

7.3.1   Putting the Process into Operation

After the definition of task holders and the implementation of the activities, the process has to be put into operation.

To this end, the task holders must be prepared by setting up the physical and IT infrastructure and by training the human task holders. IT-based task holders are loaded with the respective programs, and the mechanics of machines are configured accordingly.

During the go-live phase, it is important to establish the link with other processes. In a company, processes are integrated into a coherent network of processes. There should be no isolated processes. If, for example, a new process for shipping preparation is introduced, it needs to be linked to the order acceptance process. With communication-oriented process descriptions, this is done simply by exchanging messages. Another possibility is shared data, i.e., processes write data required by other processes into a shared database.

After the preparatory work, the process should be tested as an overall construct. An advantage would be a test environment that represents a realistic image of the operational environment. However, for cost reasons this is often not possible.

Irrespective of that, it is advisable to introduce the process step by step. It is an advantage if a process is described and implemented as a loosely coupled system of communicating task holders. The individual strands of action for the actors can be put into operation step by step. Since they are only loosely coupled to each other through asynchronous message exchange, other task holders can be initially simulated easily. With BPMN, pool by pool is thus put into operation. However, if the pools are very complex and include several swim lanes, the go-live phase is also complex. When using S-BPM, a system can be built by gradually adding the individual subjects and their behavior.

If modelers do not use several pools in BPMN, i.e., they define and implement a process exclusively in a control flow-oriented way, it can only be put into operation as a whole.

In the case of choreographies, i.e., when using subjects or several pools, the process can be executed, even though, for example, one pool contains software which is still faulty.

The messages sent to this pool can alternatively be received and worked on by people, and the result sent back by them as a message. The other pools recognize the described logic and flow (i.e., the observable behavior), although it is not yet implemented in its final form.

7.3.2   Process Instances

The actual execution of a process is referred to as a process instance. A process instance is created when the start event occurs. This can be a call from a customer who wants to order a product. In this case, a telephone salesperson explicitly creates an instance by starting the digital ordering process and entering the necessary data. When ordering in an online shop, the customer enters the order data himself and creates an instance as soon as he confirms the purchase. In both cases, an instance then runs through the processing steps and positions defined in the process logic.

Since a company normally has several purchase orders at any particular point in time, several independent process instances, which are in different processing stages, exist at the same time. Employees of a company are usually involved in several process instances and carry out the tasks assigned to them in these instances. They allocate, so to speak, a time slot of their working time to each process instance. This happens analogously with IT systems. The capacity of both the human resources and the IT systems can thus be divided into time slots in order to process several instances of the same process or different processes.

This cannot be readily done with physical or cyber-physical systems. Such a system can only be involved in one instance at a time. A machine cannot be instantiated several times; it is only available once. Only after a machine has completely finished a task or task sequence in a process instance, can it work for another process instance. A physical system is therefore assigned to exactly one process instance at a particular point in time. This fact is important when processes that can be easily instantiated because they do not contain physical task holders are linked to processes that contain physical components.

A manufacturing system almost entirely consists of physical or cyber-physical task holders. A process running in such a system is instantiated just once and exists as an instance until the whole production environment is switched off. A physical task holder cannot work in a time slot for a process instance 1, then do something for a process 2, and then continue working on process instance 1. The actions of a physical task holder for different process instances would not be independent of each other. If, for example, a valve for process instance 1 is to be half opened and then fully opened for process instance 2, the valve is of course also fully opened for process instance 1, which should not happen.

If a machine is assigned to a task in BPMN and the assigned pool can be instantiated several times, the machine must always be assigned to a single instance at runtime. The machine must always know which instance it is working for, in order to retrieve the correct data from the memory common to all instances, and then take the workpiece to be processed out of the workpiece container.

When using S-BPM, the machine is assigned to the corresponding subject. The latter receives the workpiece and the accompanying data as a message. The data also contains an identification of the associated higher-level process instance, usually the order number. With this, the machine knows for which process instance it is now working. The message by which a machine declares its work finished is transmitted to a subject instance of the triggering process instance.

7.3.3   Monitoring

In day-to-day business, process participants execute business processes according to the modeled design in the environment created during organizational and IT implementation, and consisting of personnel and technical resources.

Each business transaction runs in this execution environment as an instance. Transaction systems such as Enterprise Resource Planning (ERP) applications or workflow engines record the behavior of the instances in the form of entries in a log file (event log, audit log). A log data record contains, among other things, a unique instance identifier, a partial step identifier, and time stamps for the start and end. This results in raw data for the calculation of Process Performance Indicators (PPIs).

Reliable management information based on such key indicators is the prerequisite for continuous adaptation of process design with respect to increasing the degree of target achievement. The periodic ex post facto evaluation of a large number of instances over longer periods of time such as weeks, months, quarters, etc. primarily serves to identify structural improvement potential, for example, with regard to scheduled personnel deployment, process logic, or the degree of IT coverage. This traditional monitoring and reporting follows the concept of Business Intelligence with the principle "store and analyze" and the methods of data and process mining. The resulting changes are primarily of a medium- and long-term nature.

In order to meet the increasing real-time requirements, traditional process monitoring is supplemented by Business Activity Monitoring (BAM), which evaluates event-driven data almost in real time, reports results promptly, and thus enables short-term, instance-related measures [3]. An example is the prioritized processing of an ordering instance of an "A" customer once the system recognizes and reports that it lags behind the usual processing progress at a measuring point, and therefore the promised delivery date cannot be met (predictive analysis). BAM uses the concept of Complex Event Processing (CEP) with the principle "stream and analyze" and stream mining methods. This means that the system constantly searches for patterns of complex events in the stream of recorded individual events (e.g., set time stamps, passed measuring points), which only become relevant for certain purposes by linking the individual events.

A typical example is the recording of two transactions with the same credit card in Hamburg and New York. These simple single events (low-level events) are registered in the event stream as normal events. The CEP system only combines them into a complex event if both transactions take place within a short period of time, in this example about 3 hours. In this case, an event pattern of geographical distance and time frame would lead to classification as a complex event of "assumed credit card fraud."

Business activity monitoring is intended to monitor a large number of data sources permanently and simultaneously. Event data generators include applications that execute process instances (e.g., ERP, CRM, workflow engines), and which provide other information from inside or outside the enterprise, such as surrounding conditions, weather, and traffic data. Increasingly, this also includes (sensor) data produced by smart phones and devices that are part of the Internet of Things. BAM analyzes and aggregates the flood of data using defined rules and transmits the results to entitled and interested recipients.

Figure 7.4 juxtaposes traditional and Business Activity Monitoring. The activities listed in the left column serve as attributes for comparison.[1]

The timing and type of exploitation of the recorded/registered data depend on the design of the monitoring and reporting according to the user requirements. Utilizing the pull principle, the user can retrieve the desired evaluation at any time. According to the push principle the system generates evaluations on a time-controlled basis, e.g., daily, weekly, monthly, and quarterly at specified times, and informs the predefined recipient group accordingly. If limits or tolerance thresholds of Process Performance Indicators of individual instances are exceeded at runtime, alarm messages can also be transmitted by push to those responsible, or other processes can be started, e.g., an extensive escalation procedure with corrective measures for the case in question.

Management cockpits containing dashboards dominate for the presentation of evaluation results. These usually include representations in the form of tachometers, traffic lights, and bar or pie charts. For space-saving displays with high information density, word graphics such as spark lines or bullet graphs are also used.

---

[1] Ibid., p. 231.

Criteria for Comparison	Process Monitoring		
	Traditional Monitoring *←complements*		**Business Activity Monitoring**
Measurement	Instance and other data from heterogenous sources		
Analysis Trigger & point in time	Request (pull) Time (push) Ex post facto		Event (push) Real-time/near real-time (low latency)
Concepts & Methods	Business Intelligence → Operational ← Intelligence Store and analyze Classic Database Requests OLAP/Data Mining/Process Mining		Complex Event Processing Stream and analyze Continous Database Requests Stream Mining
Reporting & Presentation	Ad hoc Periodically Addressee: upper & top management		Permanently (very short refreshing intervals) & by exception Addressee: operational management process participants
Cause Analysis, Decision, Action	Usually mid-term/long-term		Immediately/short-term

Fig. 7.4 Properties of traditional and business activity monitoring

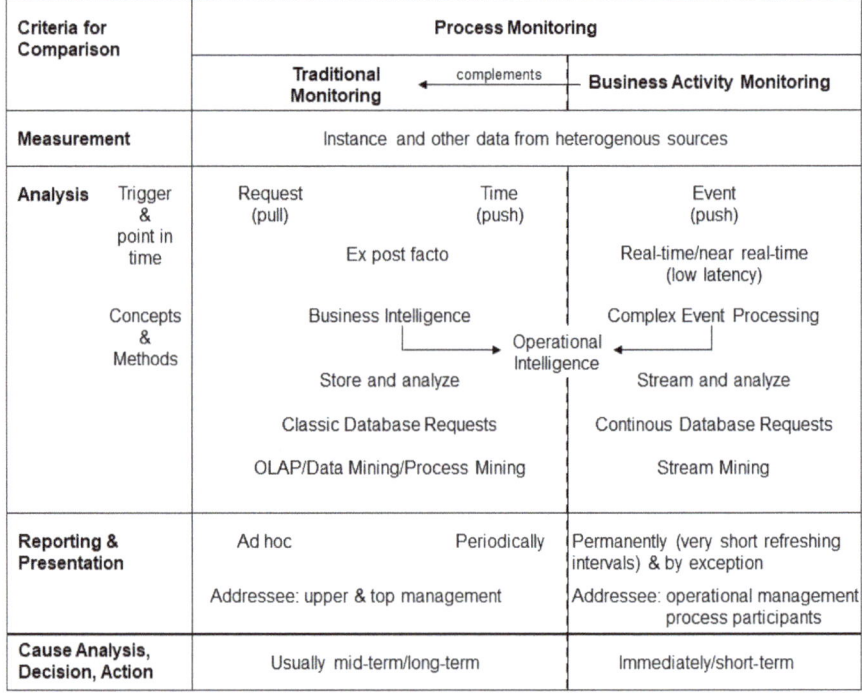

Fig. 7.5 Instance report (overview)

Examples of evaluations and their presentation are:

- Lead time of running and completed instances. The status is expressed in traffic light colors, depending on the deviation from defined target values or tolerance ranges (see Fig. 7.5).

Fig. 7.6 Instance report (single instance)

- Lead time of a running instance (absolute value and comparison with average), chronological sequence and duration of individual steps for each process participant (cf. Fig. 7.6).

- Sequence of process steps of a running instance with time stamps for the completion of a step, i.e., for the transition from one state to the next (see Fig. 7.7).

- Number of instances of a process per time unit, minimum, average, and maximum processing time per process participant and step (see Fig. 7.8).

7.3.4   Process Mining

Process mining is a special form of evaluating process data. Log files are thereby used to extract process-related information from the transaction data of central IT systems (e.g., ERP, CRM, and SCM) and thus visually reconstruct and analyze the actual process flow. This allows insights to be gained into the actual behavior of executed process instances [4]. Hence, process mining concepts and tools deliver valuable information for analysis and continuous improvement of processes (see Section 7.3.5). The most common and frequently analyzed business processes are purchasing, sales, accounts payable, and accounts receivable, as well as ticketing systems (e.g., in IT service management).

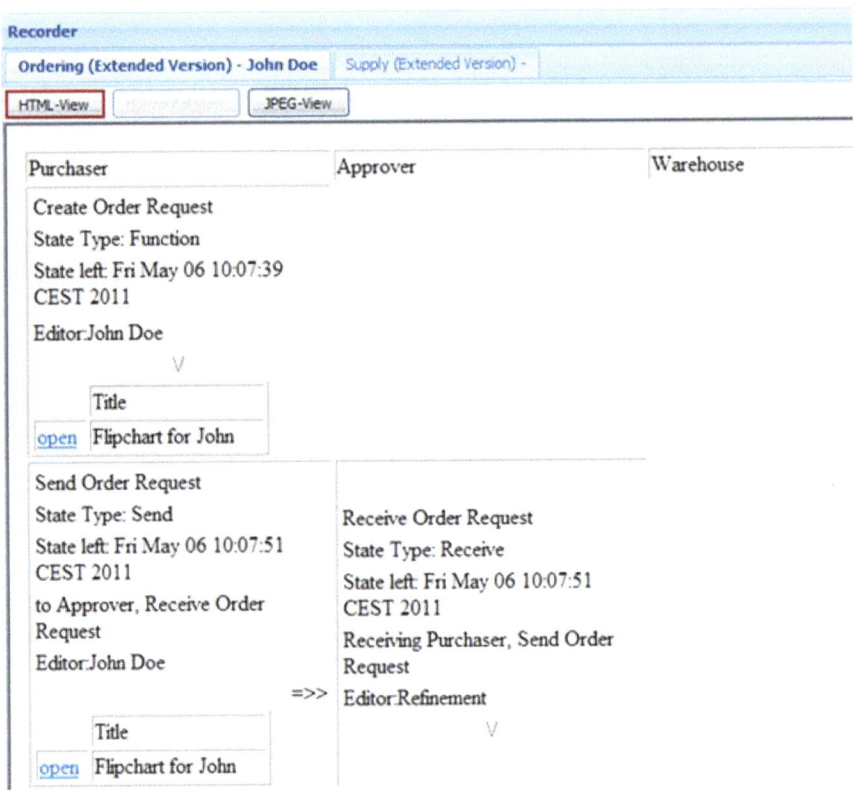

Fig. 7.7 Instance report (current processing status)

An event log contains sequentially recorded events (trace) with attributes such as case ID, activity, timestamp, resource, and business objects (data elements). Depending on the process, additional information can be added, such as the name of a customer or vendor, order quantity and value, delivery quantity, etc. Fig. 7.9 shows an extract of an example of an event log.

Combining such protocol data for process execution with process models allows identifying three essential types of process mining approaches ([4], p. 33 ff.):

- Discovery: Algorithms reconstruct the actual process flow and its manifold variants from the log data (without additional information). This allows the formal description of processes that are already in day-to-day operation ("lived") but not yet documented.
- Conformance: Algorithms compare an existing, valid process model with the actual process as it is derived from the log data. Any discrepancies that are detected can provide clues for optimization and uncover abuse or violations of compliance rules.

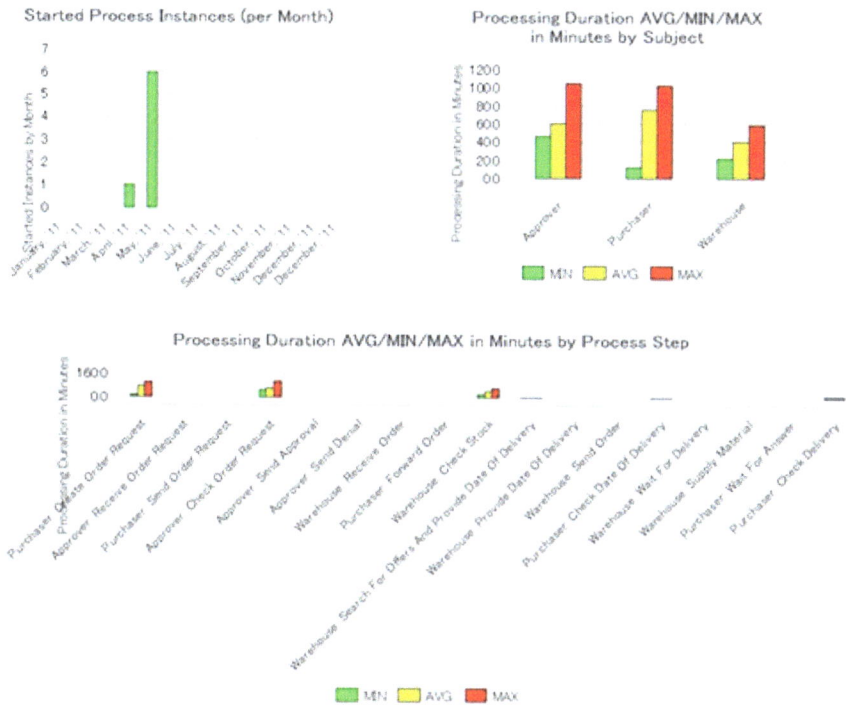

Fig. 7.8 Process report

- Enhancement: In this case, existing models are adapted to the observed reality of process execution (repair) or further aspects, such as duration, are added to the model (extension).

In particular, the conformance check should be carried out as part of Business Activity Monitoring during the runtime of instances, in order to promptly detect violations and mitigate their consequences, e.g., stopping a bank transfer in the event of irregularities in the release of payments.

The following example is taken from the process mining tool provided by Celonis SE (www.celonis.com). It shows selected mining results for an ordering process (purchase to pay) that is handled by an ERP system. The analysis of the associated event log for a given period has produced the following information (see Fig. 7.10):

- 279,020 instances of the process with a net order value of €539,180,072.
- 107,688 instances followed the normal process flow (happy path), starting with the creation of a purchase requisition and ending with the posting of the invoice (see CaseID 10002 in Fig. 7.9). The average lead time is 27 days. Process variant 1 covers 39% of all instances; in addition there are 527 other variants.

CaseID	Activity	Timestamp
10001	Create purchase order	01-01-2009, 8:35 am
10001	Print and send purchase order	03-01-2009, 12:13 am
10001	Goods receipt	07-01-2009, 07:01 am
10001	Scan invoice	09-01-2009, 2:00 pm
10001	Book invoice	10-01-2009, 10:30 am
10002	Create purchase requisition	02-02-2009, 1:17 pm
10002	Create purchase order	04-02-2009, 9:15 am
10002	Print and send purchase order	07-02-2009, 4:41 pm
10002	Goods receipt	27-02-2009, 6:53 am
10002	Scan invoice	28-02-2009, 1:00 pm
10002	Book invoice	13-03-2009, 11:59 am
10003	Scan invoice	13-04-2009, 10:00 am
10003	Create purchase order	17-04-2009, 3:47 pm
10003	Print and send purchase order	17-04-2009, 5:30 pm
10003	Goods receipt	27-04-2009, 4:23 pm
10003	Book invoice	30-04-2009, 8:50 am

Fig. 7.9 Extract from event log (Image taken with permission of Celonis SE (www.celonis.com))

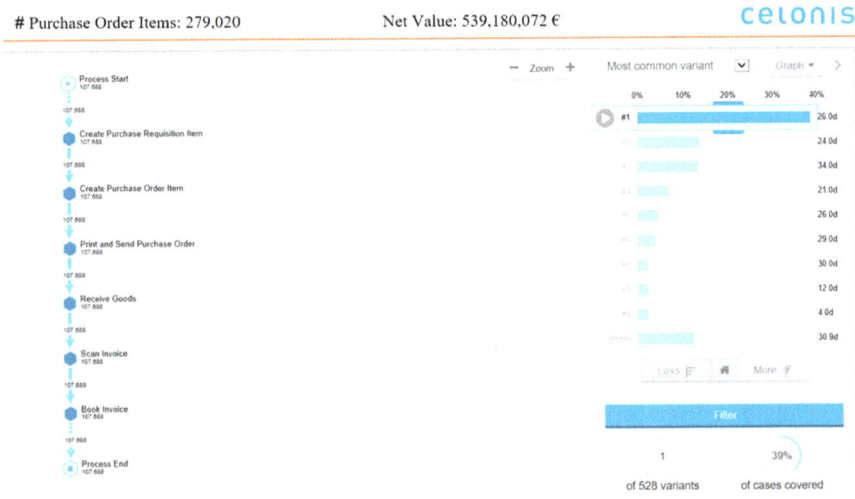

Fig. 7.10 Overview of process variants (right) and happy path (left) (Screenshot of Celonis Viewer/Variant Explorer with permission of Celonis SE)

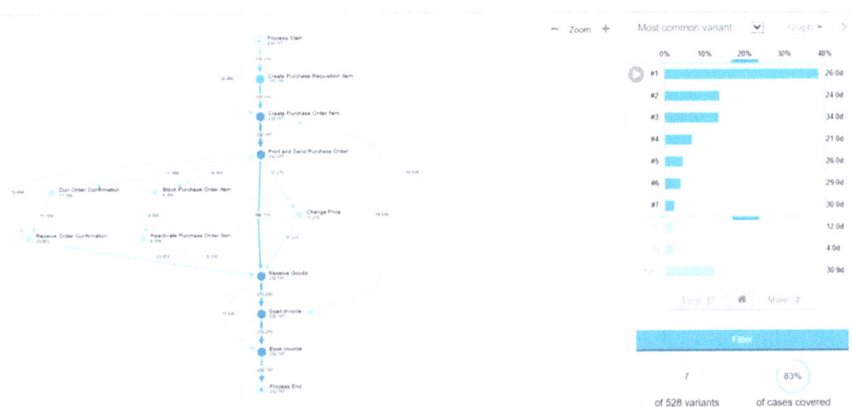

Fig. 7.11 Display of the seven most frequent process variants (Screenshot of Celonis Viewer/Variant Explorer with permission of Celonis SE)

Fig. 7.12 Display of additional information (Screenshot of Celonis Viewer/Analysis with permission of Celonis SE)

If the scope is expanded to include the seven most frequently occurring process variants, 83% of all instances are covered. The process graph now also shows the seven paths with the corresponding frequencies (see Fig. 7.11). Alternatively, the average duration of paths and state transitions can be displayed. With regard to the process flow, it can be seen that a considerable number of instances (18,938) begin with the scan of the invoice and only then is an order created in the system (see CaseID 10003 in Fig. 7.9). This is an indication of so-called maverick buying, i.e., departments procure something without prior involvement of the purchasing department. In a next step, this usually undesirable process behavior can be specifically investigated in order to eliminate its root causes.

With the display of complementary information, processes can be examined in greater depth. Figure 7.12, for example, provides information on the number of order instances distributed over months with the respective values as well as their distribution among suppliers.

The presented analyses cover only a small part of the extensive capabilities of the Celonis environment. In addition to the default evaluations provided by the system, users can define their own evaluation scheme on the basis of their individual data models by using a large number of existing analysis components, such as various diagram types, Process Performance Indicators, and OLAP tables. Furthermore, the software allows executing individualized process evaluations with the help of the Process Query Language (PQL).

Additional functions allow, for example, the comparison of the actual process flow with the one intended in the model (conformance check), or the parallel visualization and thus the comparison of different behaviors of the same process, e.g., in two branch offices (benchmarking).

The future of process mining lies in the combination of process analysis with intelligent algorithms. For example, the Celonis Proactive Insights Engine (Pi) integrates machine learning and Artificial Intelligence techniques, enabling automated identification of process weaknesses and their causes for users. Building on this information, the user can retrieve intelligent recommendations for process improvements.

Given the described features, process mining plays an important role in the context of Robotic Process Automation (RPA), in particular when it comes to assessing RPA potential of processes and developing respective applications.

7.3.5 Continuous Improvement

The aim of monitoring, evaluating, and reporting process instances is to generate and provide management information on process behavior. The addressees can analyze it, investigate the causes of deviations from target values, and derive short-, medium-, and long-term needs for action and restructuring measures.

In the following, we discuss typical changes in process design, the goal of which is to have positive effects on process behavior with respect to optimization. For illustration, we refer to the loan application example in Chap. 5.

Parallelism and overlapping execution. Logically and technically independent activities can be executed completely or partially simultaneously and by different task holders. Although the number of different activities can increase as a result of the splitting, executing these in parallel often accelerates the process. For example, a review step in loan application processing could be broken down into the creditworthiness check for the customer and the value check for the object to be financed, and these could be run in parallel.

Aggregating activities. Aggregating as the opposite of splitting means that activities that were originally carried out separately and by different task holders are now carried out by a single task holder. This reintegration of tasks reduces the division of labor and thus, for example, reduces interfaces. The number of activities in a business process and its model decreases as a result of the grouping and the sequence of steps in the relationships between the activities change. In the credit application process, the (re-) combination of the two checking steps could again be reasonable, in case the automation of the customer creditworthiness check previously described outweighs the time gained through parallelism.

Changing the sequence. The sequence of events in relationships between activities, or between groups or bundles of activities, can possibly be reversed, which may have advantages in terms of time, cost, or capacity. In the loan application example, the creditworthiness check should be accomplished before the value check of the object to be financed, because the latter is not necessary, or the entire process ends, if a potential customer is not creditworthy. The sequencing of checks contrasts to running them in parallel. Therefore, in order to choose one of these variants, it would be helpful to know how often an application is rejected due to a lack of creditworthiness, and thus how many resources are wasted through a parallel object value check in these cases.

Elimination of activities. Verbal discussions, process mining, path analyses, and simulation experiments can reveal activities that are not needed (dead paths), activities that are very rarely carried out, and activities in which hardly any value is added or that are inefficient. The number of activities of a process decreases due to elimination, and the structure of the relationships changes. An example of eliminating low-value-adding activities could be the omission of an additional credit application approval by the department management for amounts over €200,000 as mentioned in Sect. 5.2.

Elimination or reduction of cycles. When business transactions are iterated along cycles of activities, the lead times of processes are generally increased, which often leads to waiting times during execution. With path analysis, such cycles can be identified and localized, and possibly eliminated by changing the process design. During loan application processing, for example, the loan officers may repeatedly have to ask the prospective customer for information because there is a lack of sufficient details to assess the financing project. If the electronic application form requires input (mandatory form fields, annexes, etc.) for such information, the workflow system can prevent the submission as long as information is missing. Although this does not ensure that the applicant will provide the correct information in a complete and valid manner, the probability that he will do so increases, and the number of enquiry loops necessary due to missing details will most likely decrease.

Insourcing and outsourcing. Under certain circumstances, it may make sense to have entire business processes, or parts of them, carried out by specialized external service providers rather than by the own organization. External partners might accomplish tasks in a more cost-effective way and/or much faster, e.g., due to economies of scale. In this way, fixed costs can often be replaced with variable costs through the use of partner services. For example, instead of employing its own experts for property valuation, the bank could, on a case-by-case basis, engage an architectural firm. If the right conditions are in place, the reverse route can also bring advantages, for example, in case previously outsourced activities can be organized more economically internally, e.g., because interfaces and transaction costs are no longer necessary.

Automating. Technical progress opens up possibilities to have manual work steps supported by IT applications and machines, e.g., robots, or to have them executed completely automatically. This is particularly relevant for time-consuming, less motivating, and error-prone activities. In order to implement automation options, the development and market for corresponding technologies need to be continuously monitored. In doing so, suitable solution modules can be identified and included in process adaptations. As an example, the credit bureau's Web service can be used for obtaining customer information. Its integration not only fosters automation but is also an example of partial outsourcing.

Reduction of interfaces. Naturally, process execution based on the division of labor has interfaces on the organizational and technical levels. It involves various organizational units and external partners, who often use heterogeneous IT systems and tools to generate and exchange intermediate results which are sometimes linked to different media. The consequences are media disruption and associated duplication of work effort, transmission errors, loss of time, costs, etc. Reducing the number of interfaces counteracts these deficiencies. It can be achieved through organizational changes such as reintegration or elimination of activities and changes in the allocation of tasks to task holders. On the technical level, integrated IT systems such as Enterprise Resource Planning software and workflow applications are helpful. In the loan application example, the partial transfer of signature authority to the processing level has changed the tasks assigned to the clerks and the department management. As a consequence, one branch of the process flow could be eliminated, and the corresponding set of interfaces reduced.

Since many of the mentioned optimization approaches are mutually interdependent, the effects of a measure on other design factors must always be taken into account. For example, outsourcing of process parts can increase the number of interfaces and increase efforts for service management. These effects counteract the advantages of outsourcing and always require an assessment of associated advantages and disadvantages.

References

1. M. Lankhorst et al., *Enterprise Architecture at Work* (Springer, Berlin, 2017)
2. A. Lawall, T. Schaller, D. Reichelt, Integration of dynamic role resolution within the s-bpm approach; s-bpm one-running processes, in *Proceedings of the 5th International Conference on Subject-oriented Business Process Management. S-BPM ONE*, Springer (2013)
3. W. Schmidt, Business activity monitoring (BAM), in *Business Intelligence and Performance Management: Theory, systems and industrial applications* (Springer, Berlin, 2013), pp. 229–242
4. W. Van Der Aalst, *Process Mining: Data Science in Action*, vol. 2 (Springer, Berlin, 2016)
5. F. Krenn, C. Stary, Exploring the potential of dynamic perspective taking on business processes. Complex Syst. Inform. Model. Q. **8**, 15–27 (2016)

Tools

8

To be truly practical, individual activities in the activity bundles should be supported by digital tools . These tool suites offer applications for various activities in business process management covered by activity bundles. They provide tools for analyzing, modeling, reviewing, optimizing, implementing, monitoring, etc. Figure 8.1 shows the respective types of tools that could be used for individual bundles of activities. The functions of the individual tools are highly dependent on the respective modeling methods (see Chap. 3).

In the following sections, the characteristics of tools for supporting the respective activity bundles are described and illustrated with a few examples. This is intended to give an impression of the basic functions of the various tools. It is not a systematic investigation and evaluation of individual tools, nor is it intended to provide anything close to a comprehensive overview of the tool landscape. For individual modeling methods, there are usually several tools, the number and availability of which are constantly changing, so any detailed comparison would quickly become outdated. The tools presented are arbitrarily selected, and no judgment is associated. However, they are generally well-suited to perform the intended tasks.

The selection of tools for a business process management project is heavily dependent on the organizational environment. This includes, for example, the qualifications and preferences of the individuals or organizations involved in the project, which often impose requirements on the software to be used.

The following descriptions, therefore, merely guide selection in cases where such given factors are absent.

8.1 Process Capture and Modeling Tools

The central process management activity is to define a process strategy and related process logic (see Fig. 1.2). This defines the requirements for the later process

© The Author(s) 2026
M. Elstermann et al., *Contextual Process Digitalization*,
https://doi.org/10.1007/978-3-032-06901-6_8

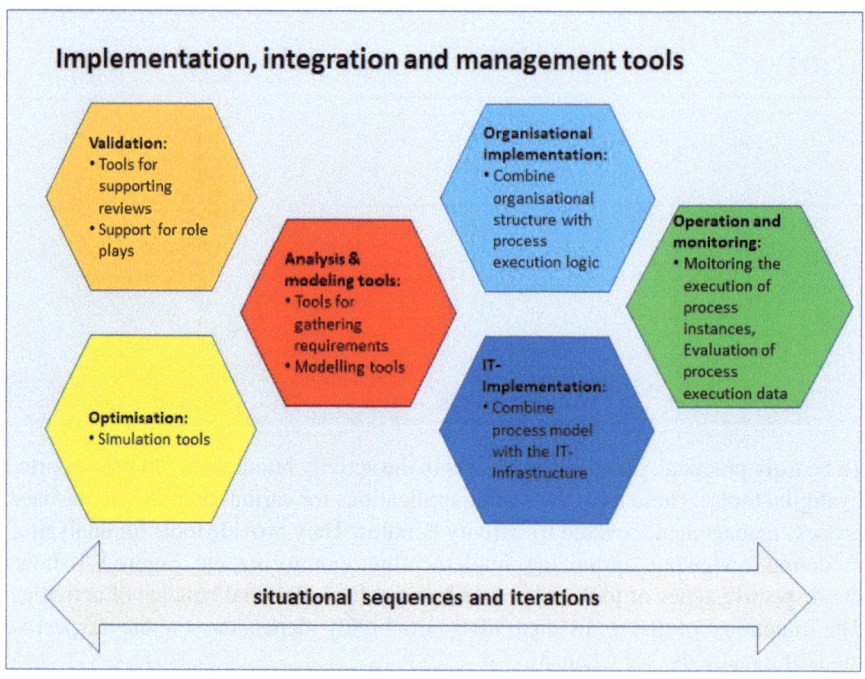

Fig. 8.1 Tools for capturing and implementing business processes

implementation.[1] What input does a process or process participant receive, how does it interact with its environment (other processes, etc.), in what order are the individual activities performed, or what result does it produce to satisfy customer needs?

When analyzing the individual modeling tools, particular attention is given to the following aspects:

- **Description of complex process systems:**
  Processes are generally very complex, especially when organizational or even company boundaries are crossed. No process exists in isolation. It is embedded in a landscape of other processes. For example, a delivery process is preceded by a corresponding ordering process. To describe this complexity clearly, hierarchization concepts and formal abstraction mechanisms are necessary (see Sect. 4.1 in the chapter). The applied modeling tool used should contain or support such structuring concepts.

---

[1] If the definition is part of a development project, these tools are essential and automatically crucial for the conception or design in process implementation.

- **Natural language annotations in models:**
  Every process model, no matter which method is used to create it, often requires additional information, usually added in natural language to provide a better understanding, primarily for people who are not directly involved in modeling activities. A modeling tool should thus offer the possibility to add such annotations at any point in the model.
- **Printing on common paper formats:**
  Models are created digitally on a screen, which, due to scrolling functionality, operates on an arbitrarily large canvas. For discussions or control tasks, it is still practical, and sometimes even necessary (e.g., for compliance reasons), to have models and the natural language annotations available on paper or in a format inspired by traditional paper sizes (e.g., an A4 PDF). This means that it should be possible, through appropriate printing functions, to split a model onto multiple pages in a meaningful yet simple manner. In addition to process discussions, such a function is also necessary when the process model, along with annotations, is part of the tender documentation for the actual digital implementation. Therefore, there should be an easy way to insert models into documents using common office tools.
- **Exchange of models between different modeling tools:**
  Different tools are used for the individual activity bundles; ideally, each should be able to access the results of other tools. For instance, in addition to the process model, the description of the organizational structure must be accessible for organizational implementation. To achieve this, the respective tools' storage structures need to be compatible.
- **Representation of various model aspects:**
  Process models cover various aspects, e.g., tools should be able to represent the structure of processes and process actors, the dynamics of process flow, and the structures of the data used in a process.
- **Type of implementation:**
  Essentially, modeling tools can be realized as stand-alone applications or as Web applications. In a stand-alone application, the tool is installed locally on the user's PC and is limited to that device. The models can thus be stored in a protected environment, but must also be exported and transported if they need to be used elsewhere. In Web-based implementations, the application's front-end runs as a local app in the browser, while the actual program and data storage run on a dedicated computer on the network (server), which a service provider may own. This allows multiple geographically distributed participants to access and edit a model description simultaneously.

According to the author's practical experience, the features mentioned in tools for business process management are essential for describing complex process systems in an industrial environment.

The handling of the respective graphical editors and other operational functions is not addressed, as they depend on the individual user's preferences and are subject to frequent changes.

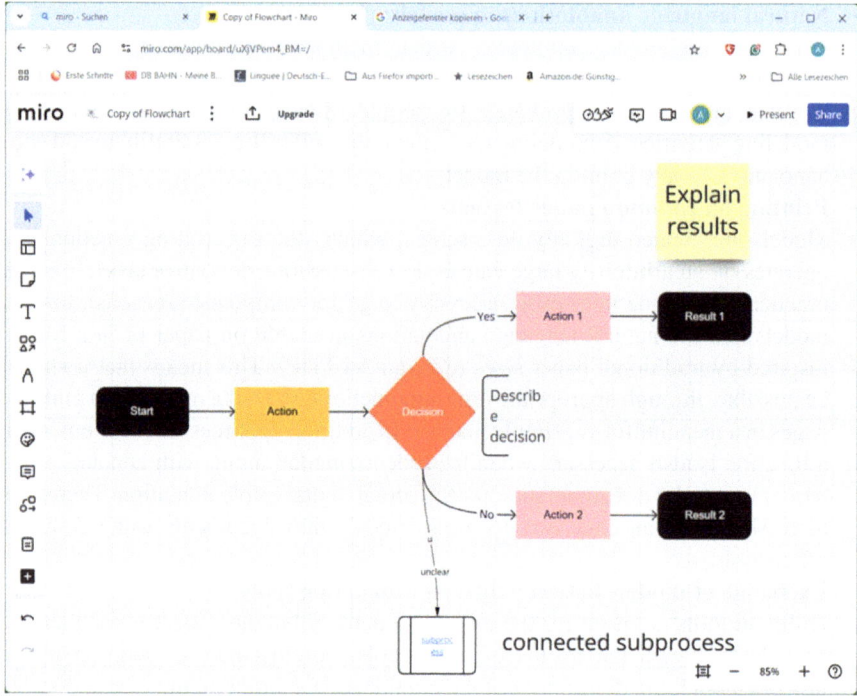

Fig. 8.2 Tool for drawing flowcharts

In the following, arbitrarily selected tools for the modeling methods from Chap. 3 are briefly explained based on the mentioned aspects, and their functionality for individual activity bundles is illustrated with examples.

8.1.1   Modeling Tools for Flowcharts

Since flowcharts belong to the first generation of process description methods, numerous tools are available for them. Figure 8.2 shows, for example, Miro,[2] a free Web-based tool available in a reduced version, with a simple flowchart.

On the left side, the symbols allowed for the flowcharts are visible. The possibility of process hierarchies is supported by enabling a link to the corresponding process description to be inserted into a subprocess symbol. Figure 8.2 shows the use of the subprocess symbol in the "unclear" branch of the decision ("linked subprocess").

---

[2] https://miro.com/de/diagramm/

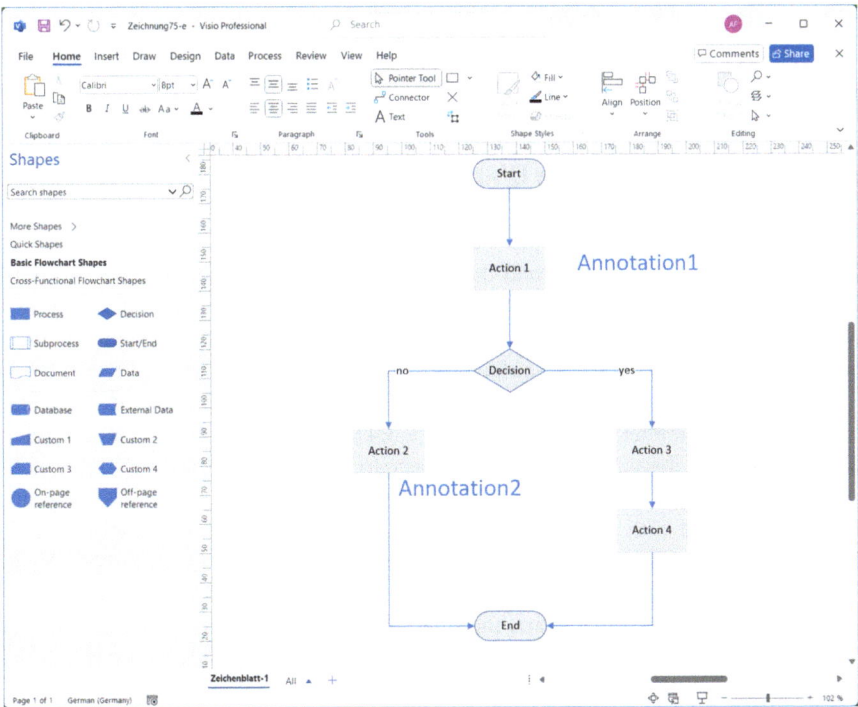

Fig. 8.3 Creating flowcharts with the universal drawing program MS Visio

Natural language annotations are inserted directly into the image, meaning that longer comments are only possible to a limited extent. As shown in Fig. 8.2, there are several ways to insert text into the graphic.

For exporting the description, only JPG and PDF formats, which are pure graphics, are available. A process model cannot be directly embedded into an Office document but must be inserted via copy and paste. The tool assumes an arbitrarily large canvas . To prepare the size of an export model, the user must manually split it into appropriate DIN A4 pages. The tool allows for the description of process logic in the form of flowcharts, but there are no functions to describe the data structure used. A publicly accessible definition of the storage format used could not be found, so the created model descriptions cannot be easily reused in other tools.

Another modeling tool examined is based on the Visio diagram-drawing tool by Microsoft . This tool can be purchased as a stand-alone application or as an extension to Microsoft Office. Figure 8.3 shows a simple flowchart created using the corresponding symbol palette in MS Visio.

When using MS Visio with the available standard shapes (standard symbol palette) for flowcharts, similar limitations apply to the Miro tool described above, mainly due to the flowcharts' restrictions. Since MS Visio can contain any symbol palette, it is possible to model the respective data structures through suitable diagram variants. The graphics with the descriptions of the data structures can then be linked to the process elements where the respective data are used. However, this must be done manually, as this approach has no automatic support.

8.1.2   Modeling Tools for UML Diagrams

UML includes 14 different types of diagrams. In particular, there are diagrams for modeling (data) structures and diagrams for dynamic aspects such as Activity Diagrams . An example of a Web-based drawing tool for creating Activity Diagrams is Lucidchart. A screenshot of the user interface could not be included, as a permission request from the manufacturer was not answered.

Activity diagrams are similar to flowcharts, but also provide elements to model distributed and parallel processes (see Sect. 3.4). This allows abstraction concepts like those in flowcharts, such as subprocesses, to be used.

Natural language explanations can be added as text annotations in a diagram. Diagrams created with Lucidchart can be converted into formats like PDF, JPEG, etc. In the premium version, it is also possible to export the code to the MS Visio format and thus continue editing the diagram. The author could not test the quality of this conversion. In Lucidchart, the diagrams can have a maximum size of one drawing sheet (DIN A4), which facilitates printing and forces structure through the use of subprocesses. Lucidchart also allows for the modeling of data structures, including the typical UML Class Diagram notation . The corresponding symbol palettes can already be used when modeling Activity Diagrams (the symbol palette bar is located on the left side of the user interface). Data structure diagrams can be linked to Activity Diagrams through connections (links).

Figure 8.4 shows the creation of a UML Activity Diagram with MS Visio. The properties described for MS Visio when used for flowcharts also apply here.

8.1.3   Modeling Tools for Event-Driven Process Chain Diagrams (EPC)

Event-driven Process Chain diagrams are essentially flowcharts supplemented with additional information (see Sect. 3.3). Adding this extra information, such as the data used or the organizational units executing, is supported by all tools (see the lower half of the symbol bar in the ARIS Basic tool[3] in Fig. 8.5).

Complex processes can be structured through the Process Interfaces available in EPCs, supported by ARIS Basic. ARIS Basic also allows the integration of various documents, including videos.

ARIS Basic is a Web-based tool, meaning multiple people can work on a model simultaneously. The models are stored in the associated ARIS Cloud. Process

---

[3] https://www.softwareag.com/de_de/platform/aris/process-design.html

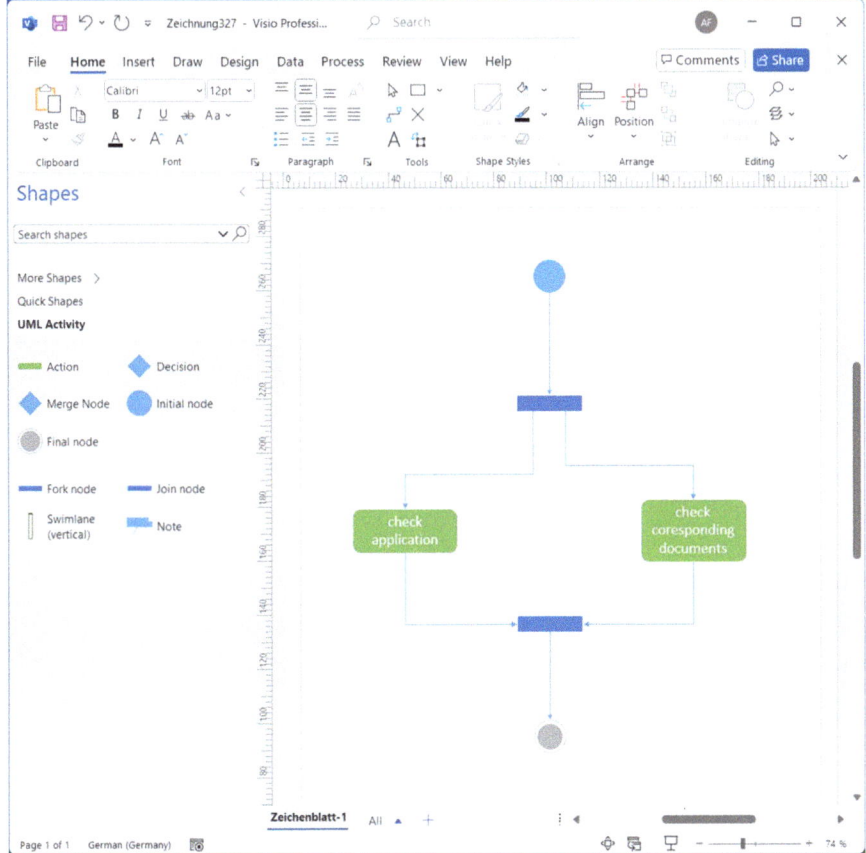

Fig. 8.4 Creating UML Activity Diagrams with the universal drawing program MS Visio

models can only be exported graphically in PNG format, saved locally, and then printed. The author could not find any other export formats in ARIS Basic. The author could also not determine how a process model with the added information can be compiled into a complete document.

EPKs can also be created using corresponding palettes with MS Visio. This software is widely used, and many users are familiar with it, so the training effort to use it is likely to be low. Figure 8.5 shows the user interface for creating EPC diagrams with MS Visio (Fig. 8.6).

8.1.4 Modeling Tools for BPMN Diagrams

A Google search shows that there are many modeling tools based on Business Process Model and Notation (BPMN). As described in Sect. 3.5, BPMN only

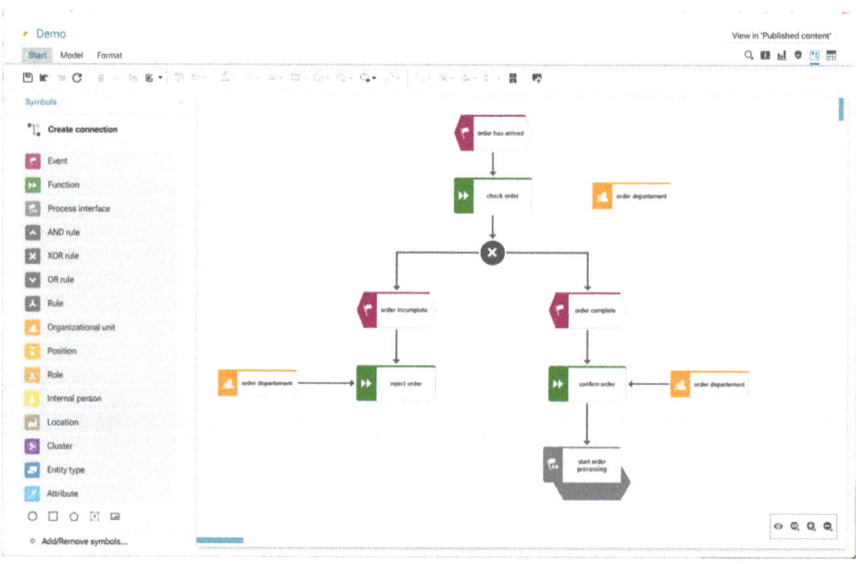

Fig. 8.5 Creating EPC diagrams with the ARIS Basic tool

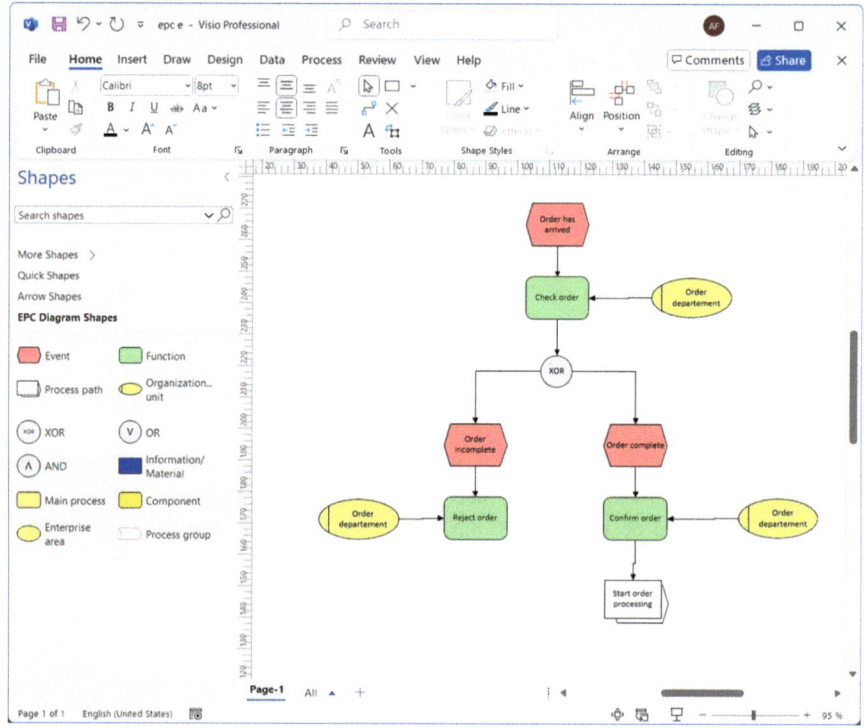

Fig. 8.6 Creating EPC diagrams with the universal drawing program MS Visio

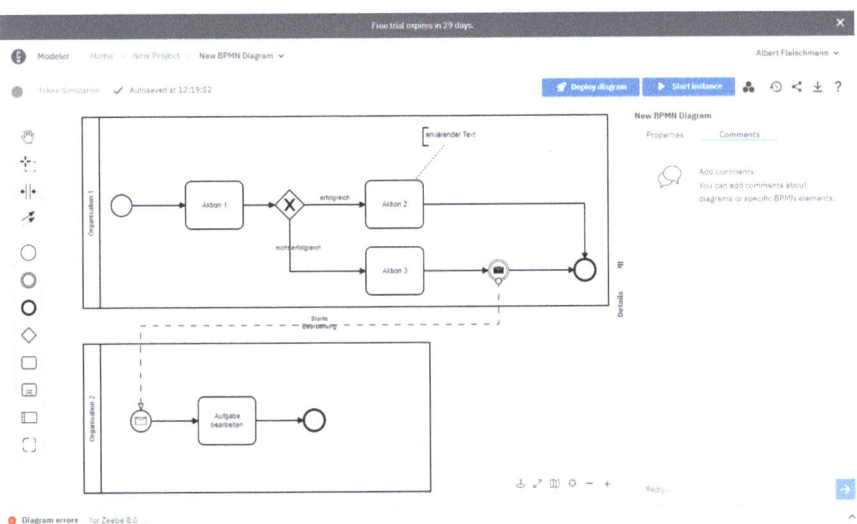

Fig. 8.7 Creating BPMN diagrams with a BPMN-specific modeling tool (Camunda Modeler)

supports hierarchies to describe workflows within a pool , and even then, only within a lane. There is no way to describe complex communication structures between pools; therefore, such functions are not included in the respective tools. Figure 8.7 shows a simple BPMN diagram with two pools. The example was created using the Camunda Modeler.[4] In this tool, text annotations can only be added directly within the diagram (see "explanatory text" in Fig. 8.7). Larger documents, such as PDF files, cannot be added.

The model must be exported to print, e.g., in PNG format. When creating a model, care must be taken to ensure that it can be read when printed on a standard page. A drawing canvas in the modeling tool corresponds to a DIN A4 page when printed.

The Camunda Modeler focuses on modeling the flow aspects of a business process. Although it is possible to model that specific data is required for actions (BPMN standard), the structure and properties of this data must be defined using other tools.

The Web-based tool allows for the download of created process models in the BPMN-XML standard format so that models can theoretically be processed further with other tools. However, this is often challenging in practice. MS Visio also includes shapes to create process models in BPMN (see Fig. 8.8). The same characteristics apply to using MS Visio for flowcharts or activity diagrams. However, MS Visio uses its format to save models, so models saved in BPMN-XML cannot

---

[4] https://camunda.com/de

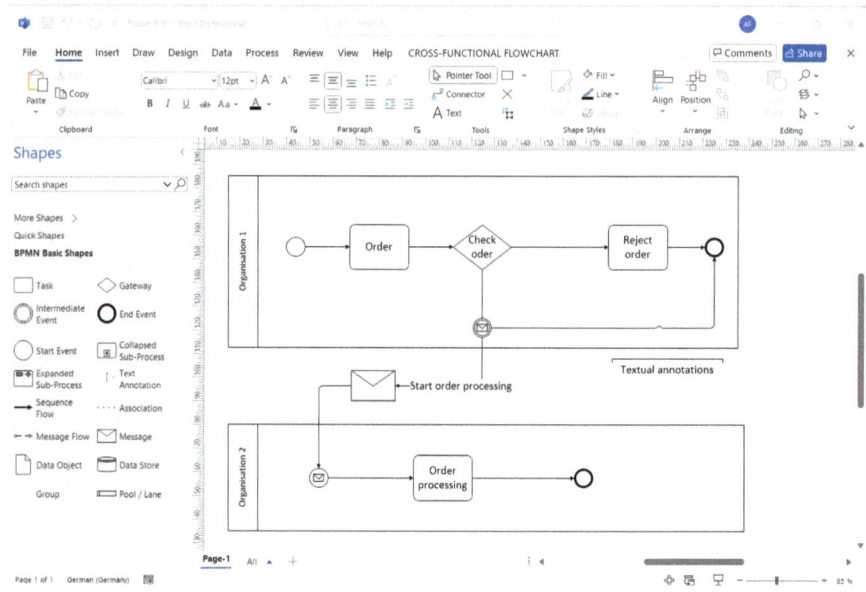

Fig. 8.8 Creating BPMN diagrams with the universal drawing program MS Visio

be imported natively. Likewise, MS Visio does not allow models to be saved in this format.

8.1.5   Modeling of PASS Diagrams

Section 4.1 explains the capabilities of the subject-oriented modeling language PASS (Parallel Activity Specification Schema) for the hierarchical description of complex process systems. These capabilities are supported to varying degrees by different tools.

With the Eclipse-based development environment , the Metasonic Suite, which is part of Metasonic One by Allgeier Inovar, process systems can be described hierarchically.[5] Figure 8.9 shows a process system created with the Metasonic Build modeling component included in the suite, consisting of three processes. These are interconnected through message exchange. Each subprocess consists of the respective subjects that exchange messages. If messages are sent to subjects in another subprocess, these subjects are modeled as so-called external subjects. In Fig. 8.10, this is the subject "Lieferant" (in English: Supplier).

For each subject, a behavior is defined (see Sect. 3.6), in which the execution order of sending, receiving, and internal operations is specified. Figure 8.11 shows

---

[5] https://www.allgeier-inovar.de/de/produkte/ecm-loesungen/metasonic.html

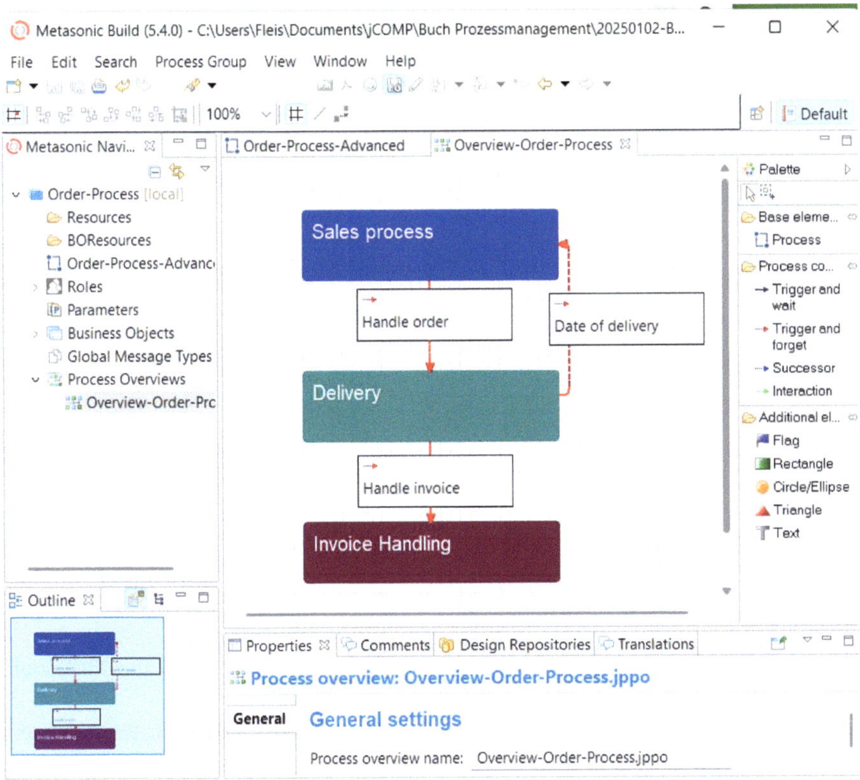

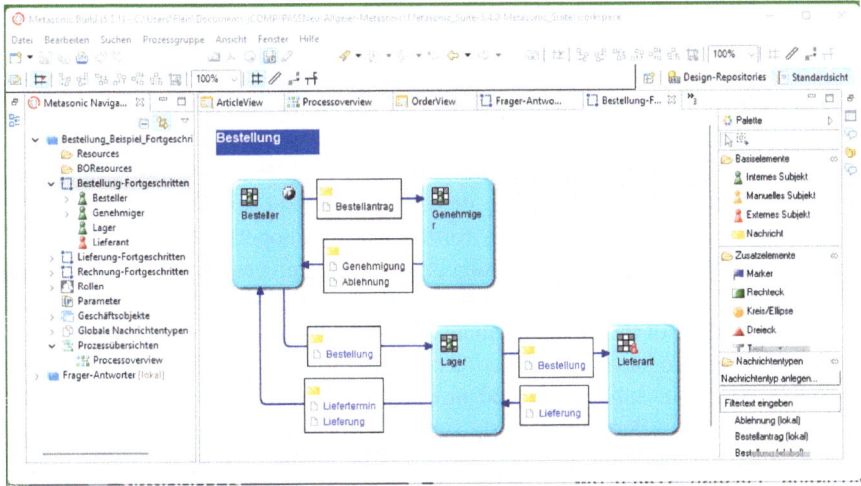

Fig. 8.9 Structural description of complex process systems in the Metasonic Suite

Fig. 8.10 Subject Interaction Diagrams (PASS SID) created with the Metasonic Suite

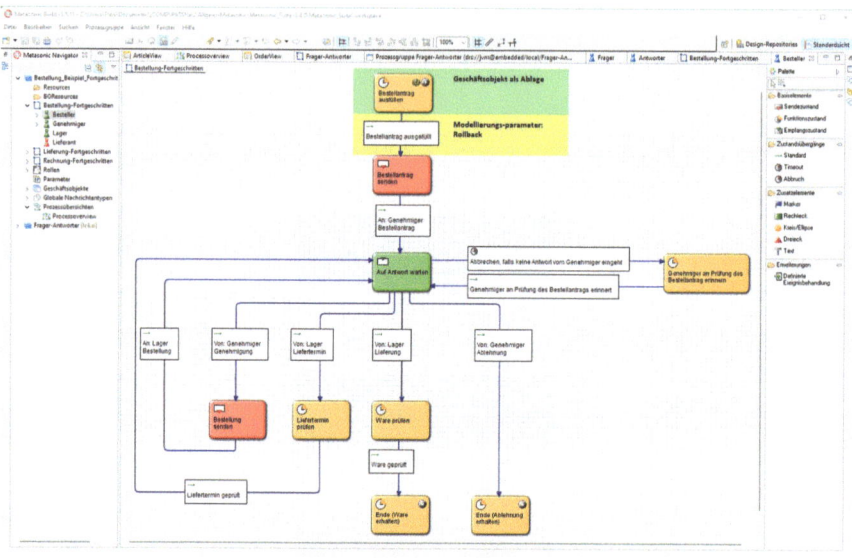

Fig. 8.11 Subject Behavior Diagrams (PASS SBD) created with the Metasonic Suite

a behavior diagram created with Metasonic Built which is part of the Metasonic Suite.

Allgeier Inovar offers a tool for behavior description called Metasonic Process Touch, which has a unique feature.[6] The modeling surface is a table on which the building blocks representing the individual symbols in the behavior description are used to specify subject behavior (see Fig. 8.12). Modeling together at a table supports collaboration among those involved in a process, i.e., the representatives of the involved subjects. Models created on the table can be further edited on the computer, and vice versa.

The Metasonic Suite allows the input of text for each modeling element. Thus, subprocesses, subjects, messages, and states can be annotated. Process models can be exported as PDF files. In these PDF documents, all comments are also included in the appropriate places. Complex graphics are automatically split and spread across multiple pages, naturally making the graphics only partially legible. The XML format in which the tool stores the models can be read directly. However, since this is the manufacturer's proprietary format, it is not supported by other tools. The definition of data objects (business objects) used in a process is also possible with the Metasonic Suite. Figure 8.13 shows the tabular notation used. The first column contains the name of the object attribute, the second column contains the type, and the third column contains the restrictions.

Another tool for subject-oriented modeling of business processes is based on MS Visio. This tool does not natively support PASS, but with appropriate external

---

[6] A video about it can be found at https://www.youtube.com/watch?v=Yz2oRLQyHmw.

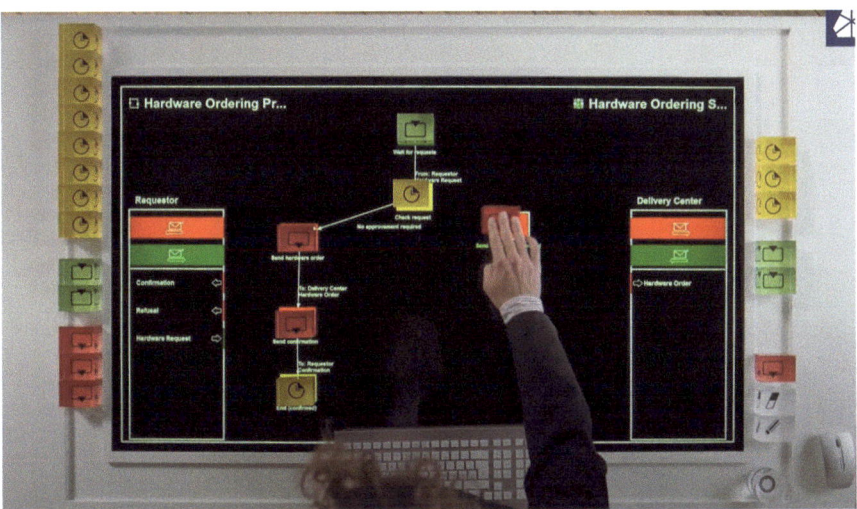

Fig. 8.12 Creating Subject Behavior Diagrams (PASS SBD) with the Metasonic Touch tool

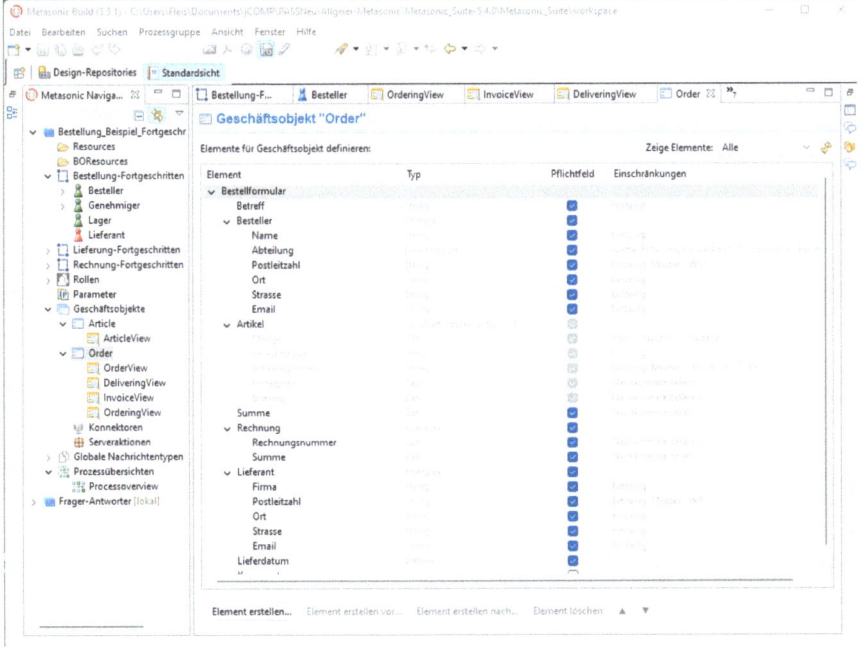

Fig. 8.13 Business objects created with the Metasonic Suite tool

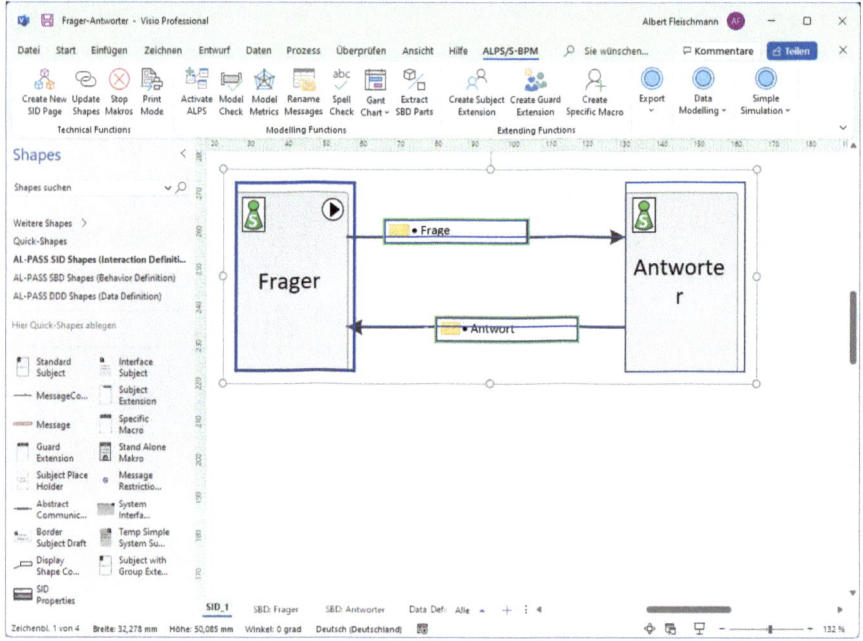

Fig. 8.14 Subject Interaction Diagrams (PASS SID) created with the MS Visio tool

symbol palettes that can be freely downloaded,[7] the functionality can be easily
added. MS Visio is not only extended with passive symbols but also actively
supports modeling with embedded program code. This includes many automations,
such as message name management, as well as verification tools for checking
syntactical correctness. Figure 8.14 shows the subject interaction diagram (SID) of
a simple question-answer process. On the left side of the image, the usable symbols
are visible. The upper toolbar shows the possible operations that can be executed on
a model, such as simple simulation runs (see Sect. 8.3). The corresponding behavior
diagram (SBD) of the subject "Frager" (in English: Questioner) in the same tool is
shown in Fig. 8.14.

8.2   Validation Tools

When describing processes, the objective is usually to create an effective process
model, that is, an attempt is made to achieve the desired result with the process
model while minimizing the effort involved. Based on the start event and the
associated inputs, the process model describes the logical and temporal sequence of

---

[7] https://subjective-me.jimdofree.com/visio-modelling/   or   https://github.com/I2PM/PASS-
Modeling-Stencils-for-Microsoft-Office-Visio

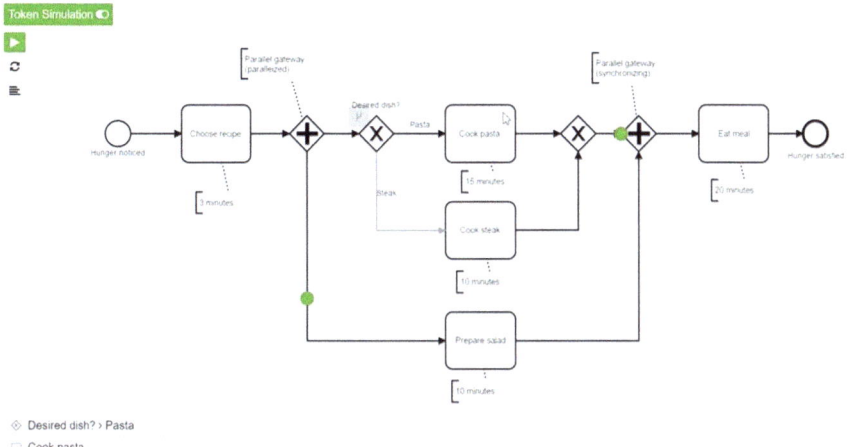

Fig. 8.15 Token simulation in Camundas BPMN tool

operations that are carried out by actors, e.g., on business objects, in order to achieve the desired result. The process model is still largely considered independently of its realization. The validation activity bundle checks whether the process model contains all actions in a meaningful sequence and the necessary business objects. Validation therefore considers the aspects *actors*, *actions*, and *objects* in the process. The aim is to examine whether all possible sequences of actions have been considered and described with the actors, and whether the model contains all the necessary business objects with their structure. Depending on the description method for process models, these aspects are considered with different weights. In BPMN, for example, the focus is on the sequence of actions. The actors are partially considered by the Pool and Lane constructs. Business objects are only superficially integrated into a model. BPMN itself does not support a precise description of business objects.

So far, no computer system can truly capture reality independently. For this reason, checking whether a model correctly depicts all aspects that are important for the respective use case is, in principle, a manual task in which process participants can receive the model's content and label it as correct or incorrect.

Based on the properties of the modeling languages used, the corresponding tools support these activities with the aspects of actions, actors, and business objects to varying degrees. There is often a kind of "play-through" of the process.

For example, a plug-in for the Camunda Modeler supports checking the sequence of actions within a process, that is, within a pool. Collaboration of several groups through message exchange is not supported. Figure 8.15 shows a process model with the respective tokens for the process flow. The parallel gateway splits the process into two parallel execution sequences. This is illustrated by the two tokens (green dots). One token has already reached the merging parallel gateway, while the second token is about to execute the "Prepare Salad" action. Data objects and actors are not considered in this token simulation.

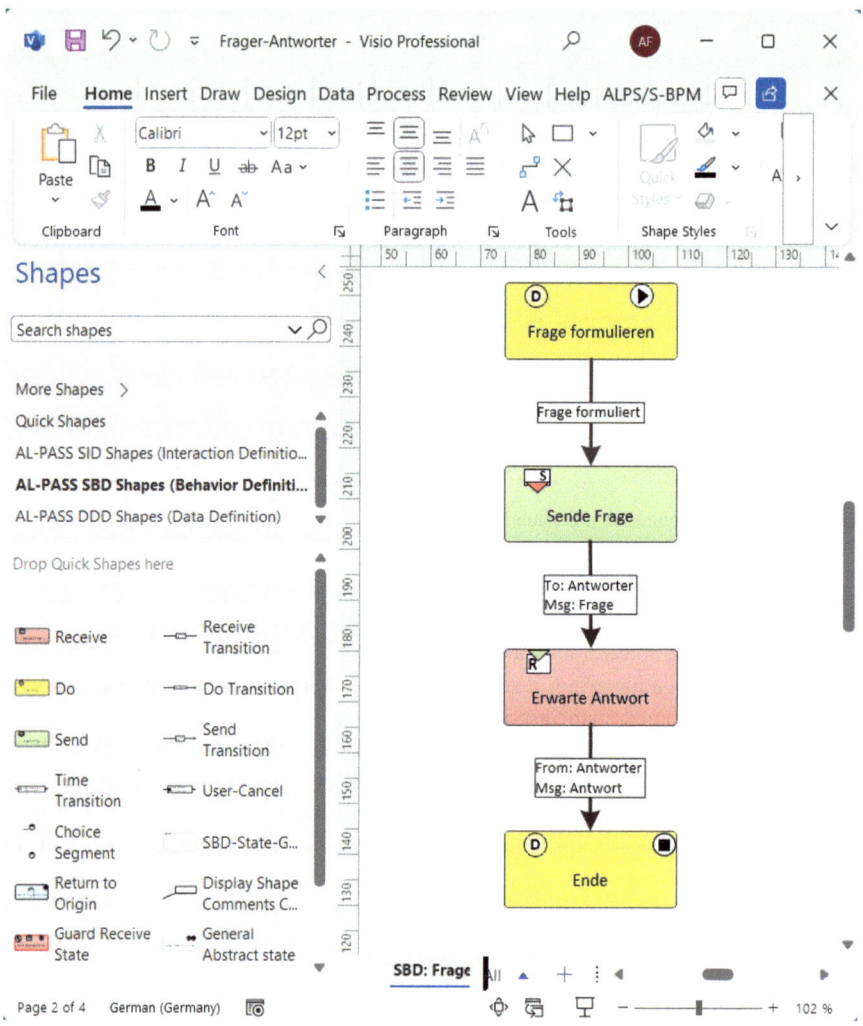

Fig. 8.16 Subject Behavior Diagrams (PASS SBD) created with the MS Visio tool

In the Metasonic Suite, process validation is supported by the Metasonic Proof component. Since Metasonic uses subject-oriented modeling with PASS as a paradigm, different users can adopt and execute the behavior of individual subjects. A process can be tried out in an IT-guided role-playing game. The proof component generates an executable version from the PASS model. Figure 8.17 shows what a validation looks like. The "Fragen-Antworter" process (in English: questionnaire-responder) of Sect. 8.1.5 (see Figs. 8.15 and 8.16) is used as an example. For this purpose, the model already available in MS Visio was modeled with the Metasonic Suite. This was necessary because the different storage formats do not allow a direct transfer from MS Visio to Metasonic.

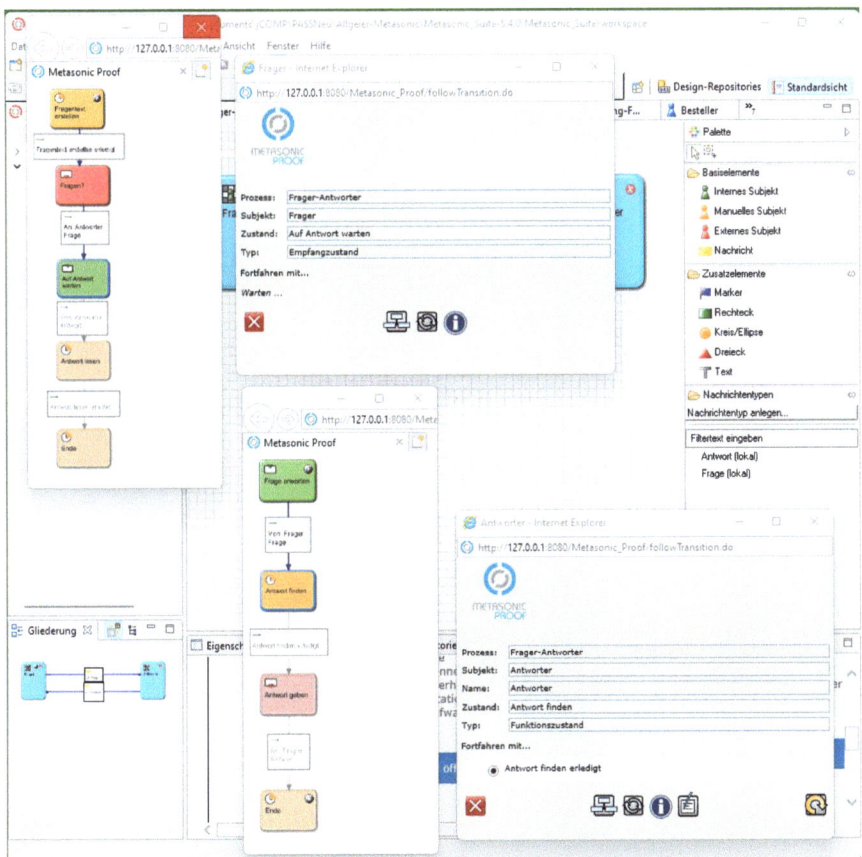

Fig. 8.17 Validation with role play supported by the tool Metasonic Proof

The upper half of Fig. 8.17 shows the inputs for the subject "Frager" (in English: Questioner) and the lower half for the subject "Antworter" (in English: Responder). The paths of the subject behavior that have already been run through (with the respective status colors) and those that have not yet been run through (grayed out) are displayed next to the masks for the user interaction. The user interactions show which subject is being operated, which state it is in, what the next state should be, and also whether data input is required (the button on the far right leads to the input of parameter values). This is the case with the "Antworter."

After clicking on the button to enter the parameter values, the input screen for the "Answerer" displays the question text and the field to enter the answer (see Fig. 8.18). The validator checks the behavior and the respective data requirements. Of course, the values entered can also be calculated by software functions in the implementation or recorded by sensors. The validator thus "simulates" software functions, sensors, and human input. Validation in the Metasonic Suite, therefore, makes it possible to check whether the sequences and data of the model correspond to the intentions for the process model.

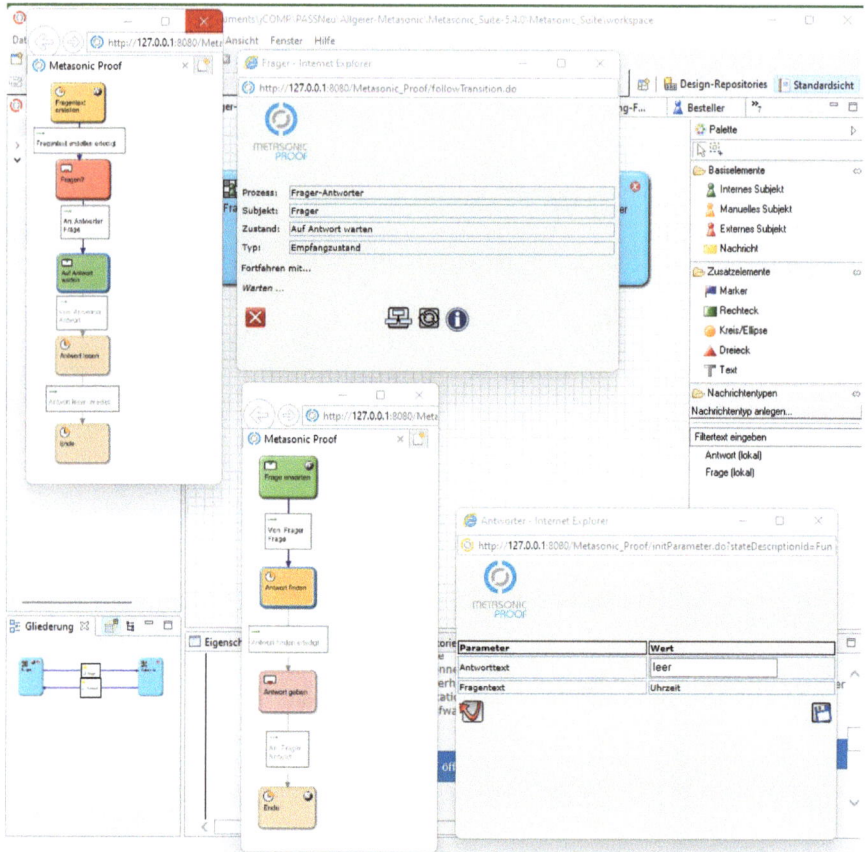

Fig. 8.18 Input of parameter values for validation using the Metasonic Suite

8.3   Optimization Tools

Optimization examines the resources required for the execution of the process or the execution system of the modeled process. This involves determining which resources are available and how long it takes to execute the process. The costs for the execution of one or more process instances over a certain period of time are then calculated from the costs per time unit and resource.

The Camunda tools do not support simulations, which is why SAP's Signavio product is used here as an example of simulation with BPMN models.[8] The upper part of the Signavio Simulator user interface shows the process model to be analyzed. The necessary parameters can be specified in the lower part. The

───────────────

[8] www.signavio.com

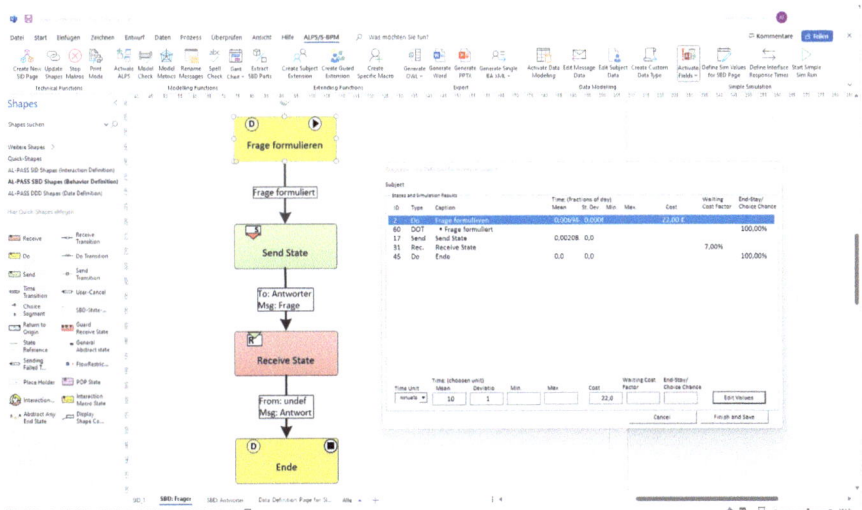

Fig. 8.19 Batch input of simulation data using the tool SiSi

processing times of the actions in the process model are also visible there (a screenshot could not be inserted as a release request remained unanswered).

The Simulation with the Signavio tool supports inputs for the costs and duration of individual activities, the general labor costs of a resource per hour, as well as the probability of choosing a path for X-OR decisions. As well as fixed values and different probability distribution functions can be entered, especially for the duration of activities. The results of a simulation run are displayed through the process model. There, the process is executed 100 times in 5 days. The "Defer application" action is executed 57 times, and the application is approved 43 times. The summary on the right-hand side of the user interface shows that the process does not contain any resource bottlenecks.

For subject-oriented modeling, the Simple Simulation (SiSi) (see [1]) tool is available as part of the MS Visio stencils mentioned in Sect. 8.1.5. It allows PASS models to be supplemented with the following information, for example: Duration of activities or their distribution (do and send states), duration of the transmission of messages, fixed costs of an execution (do and send states), labor costs that a subject causes per time, proportion of waiting times in a receiving state that should be taken into account for the costs,[9] probabilities for passing through paths after branches in do states. Data can be entered individually or as a batch for multiple states. Figure 8.19 shows the batch input of the data required for the simulation in the Sisi tool.

---

[9] If a real person has to wait for something in a process instance, but the time is productively available in another process, then this proportion is 0%. However, if they are blocked by waiting, then this waiting time, which is calculated by simulation, must be added to costs accordingly at 100%.

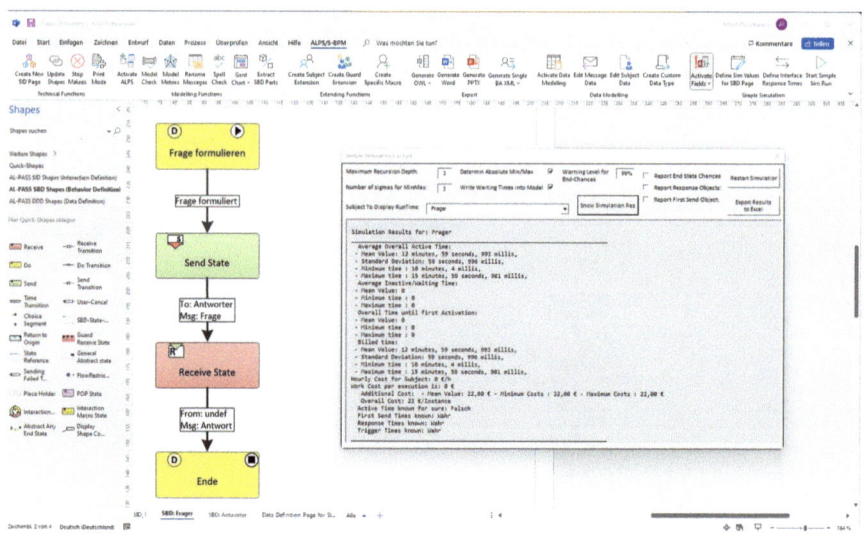

Fig. 8.20 Simulation results produced by the tool SiSi

The starting of the simulation and the first output or display of errors are done via a simple window, as shown in Fig. 8.20.

Both Signavio Simulator and SiSi's simulation results can be exported in MS Excel format for further processing and analysis.

One of the main differences between the two tools lies in the subject-oriented nature of PASS, which makes it unnecessary to list activities by resource in the analysis, since the entire model has already been designed according to the actors. A more in-depth comparison between the two tools and their possible uses can be found in [2].

8.4   IT Implementation

Business processes are socio-technical systems, that is, people, machines, and software systems are involved in their execution. The focus is usually on the process logic realized with IT, into which human activities, physical devices or machines, and existing or newly created software modules are integrated. This combination of such elements of a business process can be interpreted as IT implementation and supported by suitable tools. The starting point is the implementation of the process logic, the business objects used in it, and the software functions that perform the desired actions on them (see also Sect. 7.2). Physical components such as sensors, actuators, or even complex machines, as well as people as users, are then integrated into the resulting software system.

In the following, we look at the aspects of process logic, business objects, software functions, and physical objects. Due to its importance for business processes, a separate chapter is dedicated to the integration of people (see Sect. 7.2.2).

8.4.1   Process Logic

Depending on the modeling language used, the process logic described can be implemented directly into a largely executable program using the capabilities of suitable tools (see also direct vs. indirect execution in Sect. 4.2.1). Today, platforms with this capability are also referred to as low-code platforms, where this implementation requires very little (low) programming effort.

The author is unaware of any low-code platforms for EPK models. This also applies to UML activity diagrams.

For BPMN, there is a standardized XML format to store models, including a description of flow semantics. The latter is defined in natural language. BPMN-based tools can therefore execute the process logic immediately, which already enables validation and simulation (see Sect. 8.2). Tools that make this possible are offered by companies such as Camunda, Bizagi, and Bonitasoft. In most cases, only one function needs to be called in the modeling environment.

However, these processes must not contain any message exchange for automatic execution. With Camunda, for example, this must be programmed explicitly. This is supported by templates.[10]

8.4.2   Forms and Business Objects

In the process logic that is executed on a corresponding IT platform, people must be involved in individual actions. For example, they are asked to enter the required data via suitable forms (parts of the graphical user interface of the execution platform). The follow-up action is activated only once this has been completed. With BPMN-based tools, these forms can be described directly in the modeling environment and assigned to the individual activities in which the input request is to take place.

When defining the forms, the tools also create the corresponding business objects in which the input is initially stored.[11]

For PASS-based tools, a slightly different approach is used, as the data objects used in the flow logic are part of the model. The models defined with the PASS diagrams also contain the description of the required data objects (see Fig. 8.32 for the Metasonic Suite and Fig. 8.21 for MS Visio). The data objects used in the process are therefore part of the model and are saved together with the process description in

---

[10] See the corresponding videos on the Camunda Web site https://camunda.com/de/.

[11] For users, the separation of form (= GUI for individual users) and business objects (= data object for storage and transport) may be irrelevant, as the former can only be accessed via the latter.

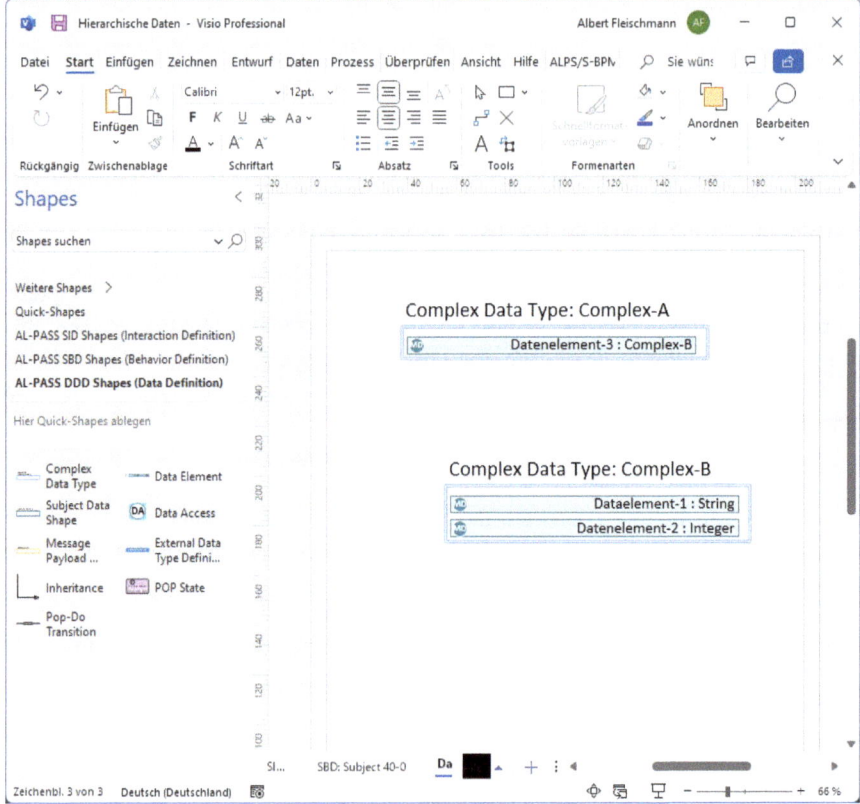

Fig. 8.21 Creating business objects and data types with the ALPS Shapes in Microsoft Visio

an OWL format (see Sect. 4.2.2.5). In BPMN, the data structures used in a process are not part of the XML storage standard.

The Metasonic Suite also generates a form proposal from the business objects required in a function (see Fig. 8.22).

8.4.3 Embedding of Software Functions

During the execution of the process logic, the values are assigned to the defined business objects by user input , access to previously saved data or calculations. Values of business objects can also be saved in order to use them in subsequent process sequences or to perform calculations on them. These operations on the business objects are related to the activities in the process flow. They are executed when the execution platform is in this activity during the process flow. Each action in a process flow within a digital execution platform is a software function. The functions mentioned are usually standard functions that are added to the

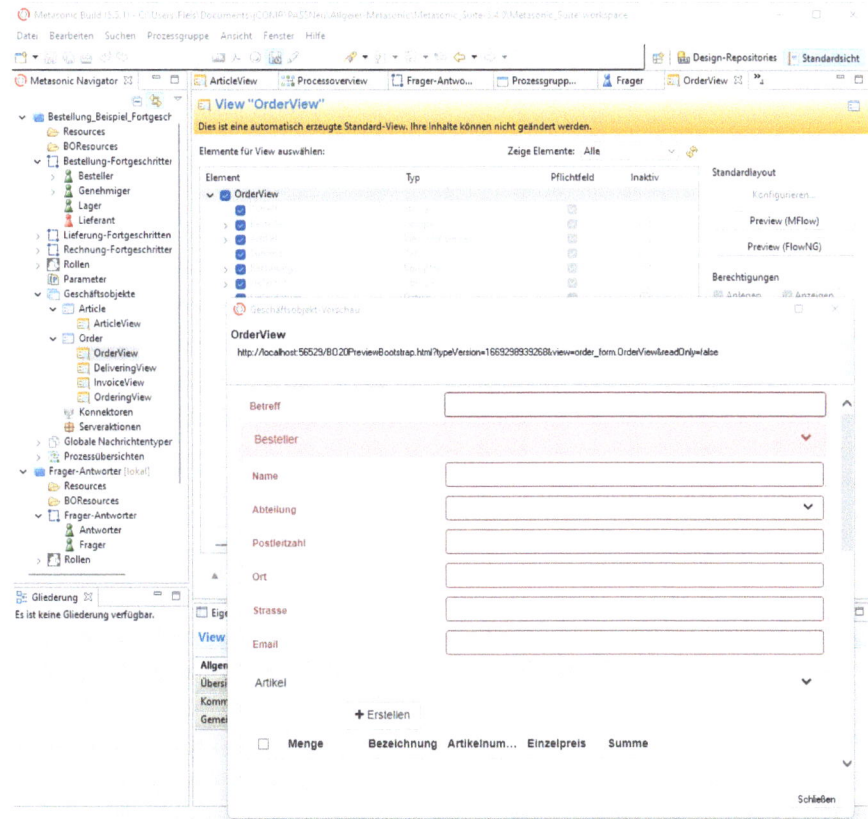

Fig. 8.22 Creating forms with the Metasonic Suite

process model automatically or simply by drag-and-drop (Low Code). In addition, however, there are usually a large number of functions or accesses to special systems depending on the use case and, above all, on the IT systems used by the executing organization. These are not provided as standard and must be individually supplemented, configured, or, in some cases, developed.[12]

BPMN-based tools generally support the integration of corresponding software modules. They allow the input of paths to software libraries in almost all common programming languages (Java, Python, C++, C#, etc.). Frameworks such as Spring

---

[12] This is also usually the point at which advertising promises from platform providers prove to be unrealistic, because the development is correspondingly complex and usually cannot be carried out by non-experts. As mentioned above, these supplementary descriptions of a process model are usually explicitly limited to a platform or a single instance for a specific company and its IT ecosystem. Simple use in a different context is almost impossible.

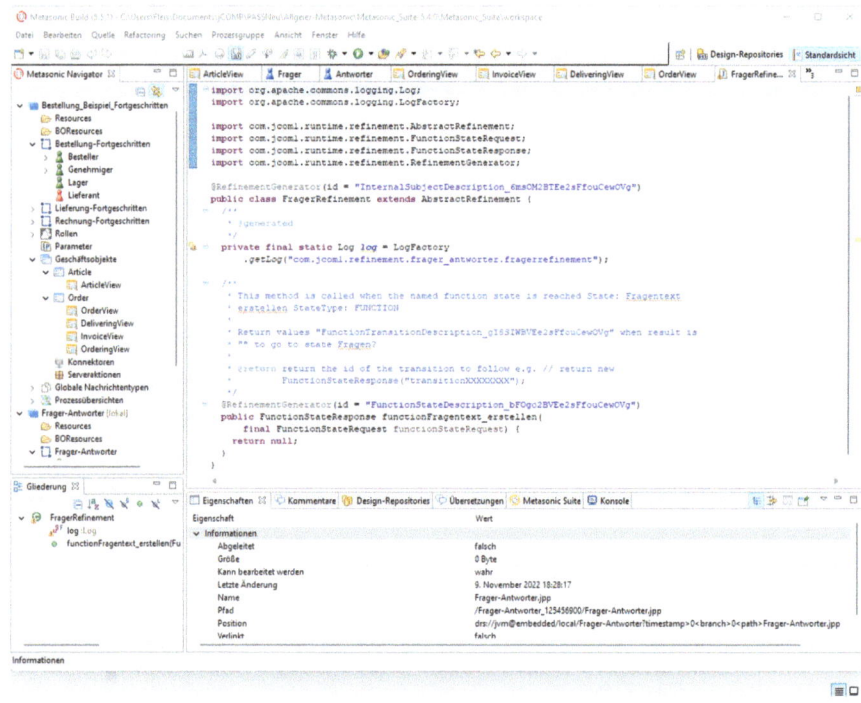

Fig. 8.23   Including software modules (Refinements) into the Metasonic Suite

or programming interfaces such as REST can also be used to integrate software functions into a process logic.

In the Metasonic Suite, external software modules or connectors are integrated via so-called refinements. A refinement can be added to each state. The refinement of a subject, that is, the specific software module, can give access to all the subject's business objects, forms, and software functions within a process instance. Figure 8.23 shows how, for example, the corresponding implemented function can be inserted into the Do-State "Fragetext erstellen" (in English: Create text for question). Of course, other available programs or system calls can also be integrated here. The Metasonic Suite also offers a wide range of options for integrating external software modules or connectors.

8.4.4   Physical Objects

Physical components such as sensors, actuators, or even complex machines can also play a role in business processes and must be integrated accordingly. This is the case, for example, when activities are carried out by physical components or machines.

This integration should already be taken into account in the models of the process to be implemented. However, it must also be supported in implementing tools, especially when it comes to automation, and the corresponding machines also need to be specifically controlled (see, for example, the challenges discussed in sect. 4.3.1).

If there are corresponding software drivers, often called connectors, that exist for these components, they can be integrated in the same way as software modules. This can be done in the same way for physical components.

If there are no suitable connectors, integration can take place indirectly. In this case, the workflow system prompts a person to perform a certain action and communicate the result to the workflow system via a corresponding form. Therefore, the integration of a physical device takes place via an organizational integration (socio-technical).

8.5   Tools for Organizational Implementation

Once a model for an effective and efficient process has been created, it must be embedded in the respective environment, that is, the socio-technical system, in which the process is to be executed. The individual activities of a process are carried out by task carriers, which can be either people, machines, computer programs, or combinations of these (see Sect. 7.2). We refer to the assignment of tasks to the execution carriers of tasks as organizational implementation. It must be described formally. The assignment of task owners depends on whether the process logic is executed according to specifications (work instruction), computer-controlled (workflow engine), or a combination of both. In the case of execution according to the specifications, the corresponding work instructions must be created. Tools that support their creation are not considered here. Ideally, the process models themselves can function as the corresponding instructions.[13]

Our focus is on digitalization, scenarios in which the process logic is computer-controlled. The assignment of task owners, in this case users of the corresponding software platforms, to the individual tasks must be formalized here. However, this is only supported by very few tools and then mainly as a person's direct assignment to individual tasks.[14]

The Metasonic Suite is the only one of the modeling tools presented in Sect. 8.1 that supports the assignment of persons to task areas, in this case to subjects. A role can be assigned to a subject in the modeling tool. This can be seen as a task area in an organization. Several subjects can be assigned a role. The assignments define the area of responsibility of a role. Figure 8.24 shows how the

---

[13] This is one of the strengths of subject-oriented description, especially with PASS, in which the behavior diagrams already represent concrete descriptions for individual task areas and can also be passed on individually.

[14] This is mostly due to the use of modeling languages that only follow task-oriented logic.

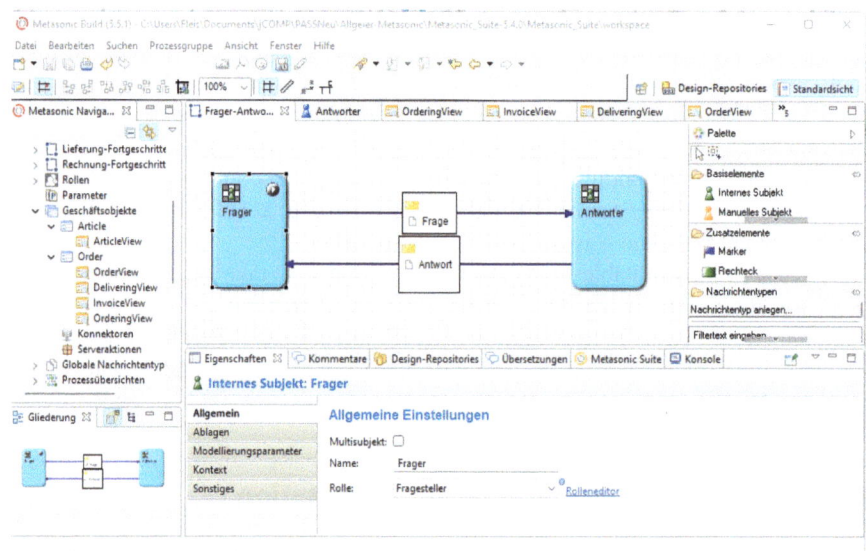

Fig. 8.24 Assignment of roles to subjects

role "Fragesteller" (in English: questioner-role) is assigned to the subject "Frager" (in English: Questioner). The Questioner role was previously created with the role editor.

The role is the link to the organizational structure. The Metasonic Suite is based on LDAP Directories (Lightweight Directory Access Protocol). It includes an editor to manage the organizational structure consisting of users, groups, and roles. This organizational description must reflect the roles assigned to the subjects in the modeling tool. Figure 8.25 shows how the roles that have already been used in the modeling tool and assigned to the subjects that are created in the directory.

By assigning roles to groups and specific users to groups, the employees who will perform the subject behavior are assigned to each subject. This assignment, which is managed in the Metasonic Suite Editor, makes it easy to change the way a process is embedded in the organization, for example, when new employees are hired, released from work, transferred, or entire organizational units are regrouped.

A similar assignment takes place in the Camunda suite, but not based on subjects, but on an activity basis or on the basis of the permission to start a process with the first activity. In addition, Camunda distinguishes between two cases with regard to technical authorization when assigning task owners, which are relevant for data security.

- Situations/activities in which authorization is required:
    - An REST API can only be used to a limited extent, even after authentication.
    - A Web application can only be used by users to a limited extent, even after authentication.

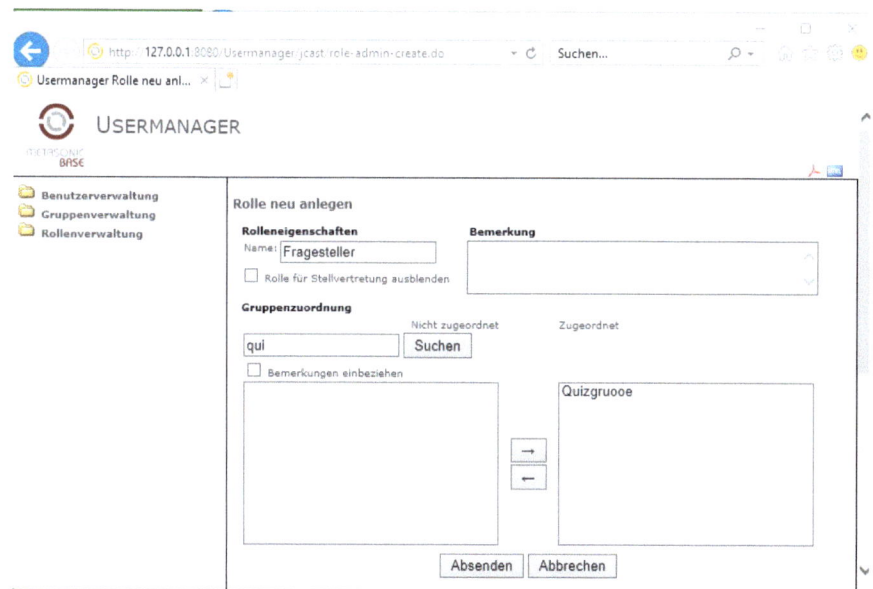

Fig. 8.25   Creation of a role in the Metasonic Suite

Process Definition Authorizations				Create new authorization +
Type	User / Group	Permissions	Resource ID	Action
ALLOW	⠿ accounting	ALL	invoice	Edit Delete

Fig. 8.26   Assigning roles to groups in the Camunda Suite

- – Untrusted users can execute queries and commands on the Workflow Engine.
- Situations in which authorization is not necessary:
  - – An external application can call the Workflow Engine via an API method in a fully controlled manner within the process.
  - – Users have full access to the Workflow Engine via the Web application after authentication.

The assignment of task owners in Camunda is heavily dependent on the applications in which the individual processes are embedded. Figure 8.26 shows how the "Invoice" process is assigned to the "Accounting" group.

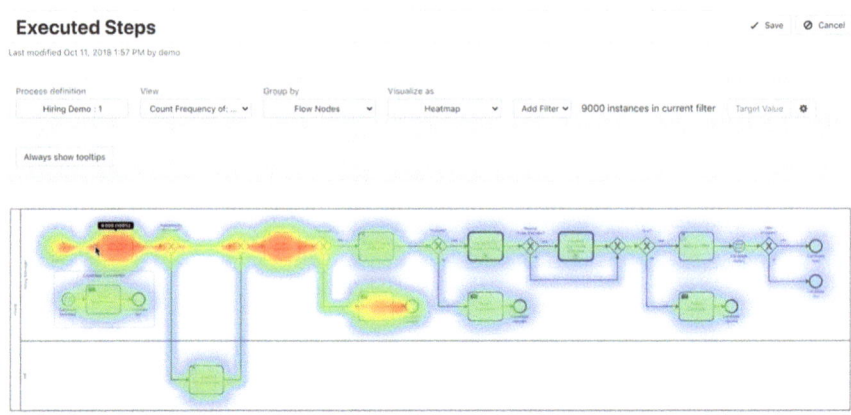

Fig. 8.27 Heatmap overlay on a process model in Camunda to analyze how often certain actions are executed

8.6   Tools for Operation and Monitoring

Almost all business process management platforms generate data during the execution of processes that can be used to assess the effectiveness and efficiency of processes. In addition to classic individual Process Performance Indicators (PPIs) that relate to a single instance, such as the duration of a run, there are also many data that are independent of the specific task of a process. Examples include the number of instances for a process within a particular period or the average execution time across several process instances or actions. This data can then be evaluated using appropriate analysis tools, in the simplest case with MS Excel.

With Camunda tools, the execution information of processes is stored in a database by the workflow engine. The data is then exported from there in a format that is understood by the Elasticsearch[15] tool. Elasticsearch is then used to perform the desired analyses. Figure 8.27 shows an analysis of the frequency with which the actions of a process are executed. A so-called heat map is used, which is placed above the process model. The color green means a low number, and red means a high number of executions of the individual actions. Several of such reports, as shown in Fig. 8.27, can be combined by Camunda to form a dashboard (see Fig. 8.28).

The Metasonic Suite also provides process data from process instances for analysis in a database. If, as with Camunda, there are no predefined analysis tools, the log data must be analyzed with external software.

---

[15] www.elasticsearch.com

Fig. 8.28 Combining several reports into one dashboard in Camunda Optimize

8.7   Interaction of the Tools

The individual activities from the described activity bundles are carried out with the support of the respective tools. Depending on the procedure, the system switches between the activities. This means that the results of the individual activities are saved and picked up by other tools and enriched with further information. For example, the process models created with modeling tools are picked up by simulation tools, enriched with data on processing effort, resources, etc., and used in simulation runs. For organizational implementation, the information from the process models is merged with the information on the organizational structure. Connectors are used to integrate software functions or physical devices.

Figure 8.29 shows how the individual tools for the respective activity bundles interact to implement processes. A central aspect here is the storage format for the process models and the importance of the stored model for the process flow (flow semantics). In addition to the process flow, the storage format should also contain the required business object structure. The tools needed are placed around the storage format with the associated process semantics.

There is no standard for the storage and execution semantics of process models. There is an XML-based storage format for BPMN, but only partial formal semantics [3]. However, this does not cover the exchange of messages between pools.

As a result, tool manufacturers cover these gaps with proprietary formats to enable an integrated tool suite. This, in turn, has the disadvantage that tools from different manufacturers are only partially interoperable and can only be used together in business process projects.

With S-BPM, an attempt is made to define both a storage structure and execution semantics (see Sect. 4.2.2.5). This creates the prerequisite for selecting a vendor-independent tool for a business process management project.

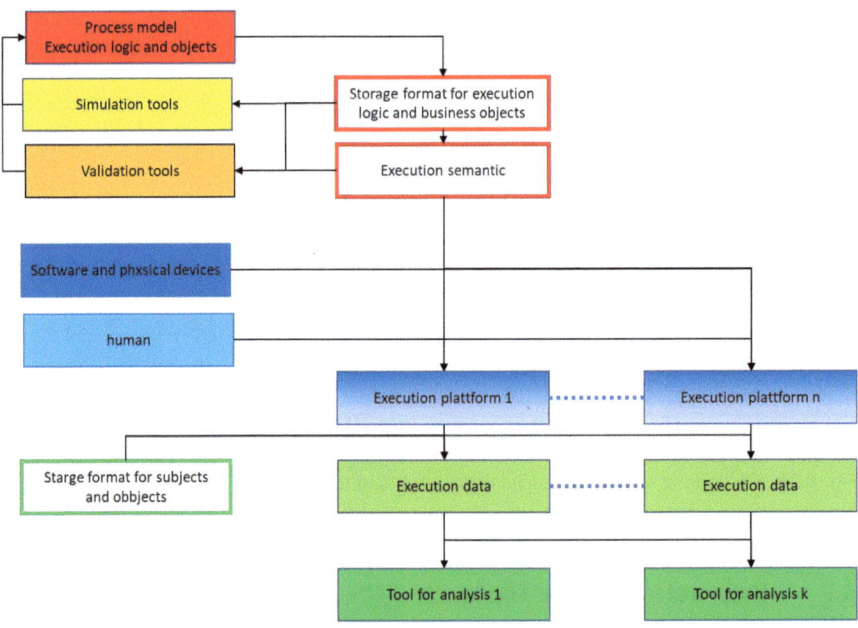

Fig. 8.29 Interaction of Tools for Modeling and Implementation

8.8   Tools for the Management of the Digitalization Process

Therefore, the respective activities within the activity bundles are carried out in a suitable sequence, and the tools used or described in the previous sections should support this. Of course, the individual tools must first fulfill their respective purpose well.

However, the changes between the activity bundles are much more important. The description of a sequence in which individual activity bundles should be executed can be referred to as a process model or process management life cycle. There are different approaches for such process models.

In the so-called *waterfall model*, the activity bundles are executed in the order *analysis modeling*, *validation*, *optimization*, *implementation*, and *operation monitoring*.

In reality, this rigid sequence can rarely be adhered to. It is almost always the case, for example, that you want to adapt the process model and therefore switch back to analysis. For example, if it is determined during implementation that a change to the process model is necessary because a single process action is to be executed by two different organizational units and must therefore be split into two actions. Switching between the tools for the individual activity bundles requires that the memory models within the activity bundles match each other (see Sect. 8.7). If this is not the case, it may be impossible to make subsequent changes because all the work in between must be started again. This is because the modified process model is technically not considered a change to the original model, but a completely new one for which all supplementary descriptions regarding access from and to other IT systems, graphical user interfaces (GUIs), or user mappings would have to be recreated.

Complex processes are further complicated because several groups are involved in their development, each working on a specific part of the overall process. If these groups are to act reasonably flexibly and independently of each other to achieve results more quickly and not always have to wait for other groups, then it should be permitted and possible to work on the respective part of the process in different activity bundles at a certain point in time.

The ease of switching between activity bundles also depends on the modeling method. With flowchart-oriented methods, the process actions to be executed are strongly linked to each other by the control flow, so changes to the model or its implementation must be closely coordinated, and switching between activity bundles becomes difficult.

The Camunda tools are designed for orchestration, meaning that process development must be centrally controlled. Although several parties can work centrally on a BPMN model, a process must be deployed centrally.

In communication-oriented models, at least some models are loosely coupled via their communication relationships. For example, BPMN pools and S-BPM subjects can be processed very independently of each other. Only the communication protocol between the pools or subjects needs to be coordinated.

The respective tool suites support these more technical aspects for switching between activity bundles. The Camunda suite allows multiple versions of a process to be executed, i.e., there are parallel process instances based on different process model versions. It is possible to transfer process instances of one version into process instances of the other model or process version. To implement this, a corresponding mapping function is defined (see Fig. 8.30).

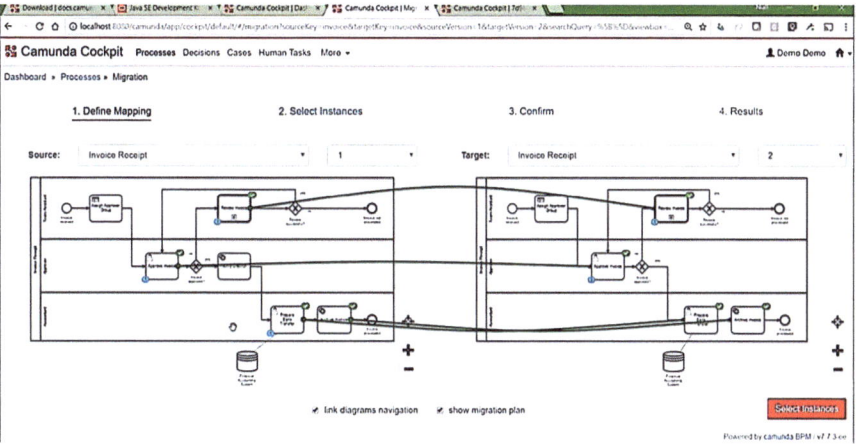

Fig. 8.30 Migration of process instances in Camunda from one (process model) version to another

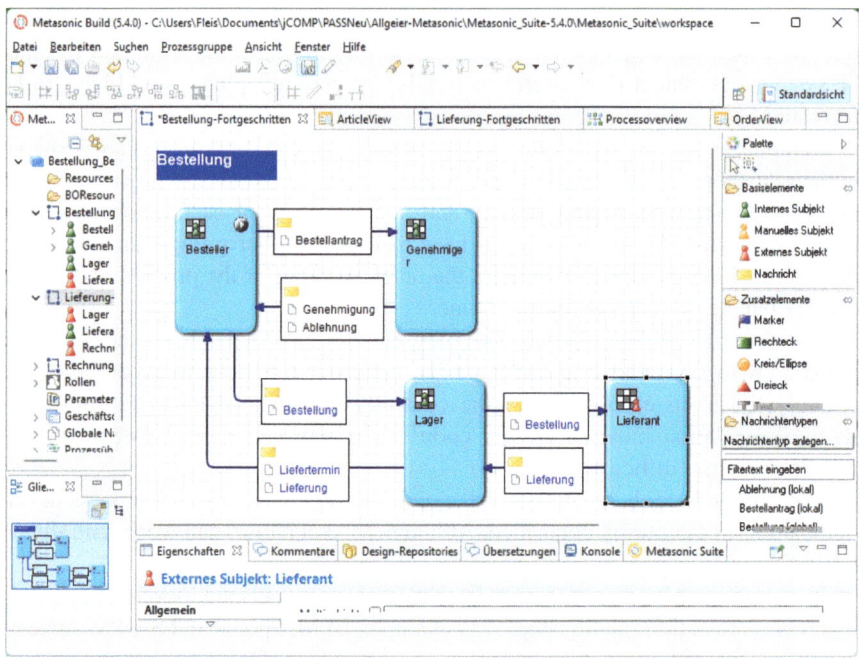

Fig. 8.31 Independent development of subprocesses: Ordering process

This migration option allows a process to be continuously changed and existing process instances to be transferred to newer versions. Based on information on the Internet, this is the only functionality that directly supports iterative process development.

The process networks supported in the Metasonic Suite allow subprocesses to be developed almost independently of each other. Only the communication protocol between the respective external subjects must be coordinated (see Sect. 4.1). Figure 8.31 shows the process "Bestellung" (in English: Order) with the external subject "Lieferant" (in English: Supplier). This subject is part of the "Lieferung" process (in English: Delivery) (see Fig. 8.32) and is used here to link the process "Bestellung" with the "Lieferung" process under consideration. Complementary to the subject "Lager" (in English: Warehouse) of the "Order" process is an external subject in the "Delivery" process. Although all process models are linked, they can be adapted and changed individually. Analogous modeling options are also included in the MS Visio-based modeling tool.

The situation is different for review and approval workflows and requests for acknowledgments, automatic revision, and archiving of results within the respective activity bundles.

None of the tool suites examined directly supports these activities, making it difficult to establish various process development processes. This makes it more difficult to set up and expand a management system for process optimization.

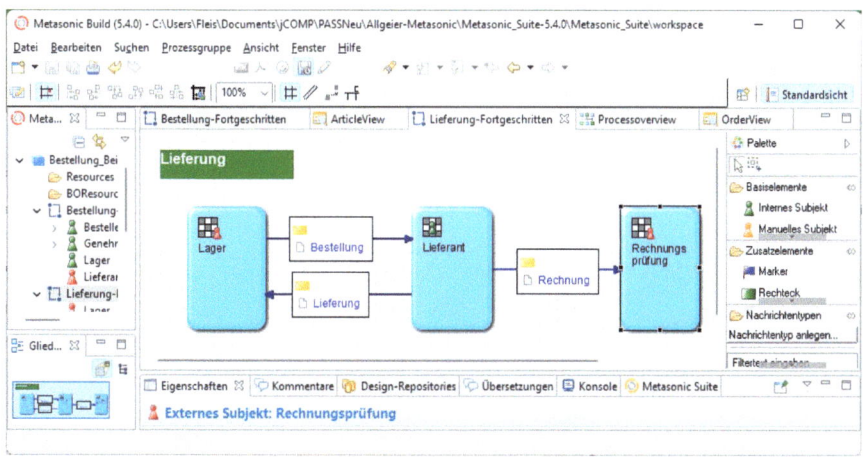

Fig. 8.32 Independent development of subprocesses: Process Delivery

References

1. M. Elstermann, J. Ovtcharova, Sisi in the alps: A simple simulation and verification approach for pass, in *Proceedings of the 10th International Conference on Subject-Oriented Business Process Management*, ed. by C. Stary, S-BPM One '18, New York, NY (Association for Computing Machinery, 2018)
2. M. Elstermann, O. Piller, A comparative study of simulation tools for business processes, in *Subject-Oriented Business Process Management: Dynamic Digital Design of Everything – Designing or being designed?*, ed. by M. Elstermann, S. Betz, M. Lederer. Communications in Computer and Information Sience (Springer, Berlin, 2022)
3. F. Kossak et al., *A Rigorous Semantics for BPMN 2.0 Process Diagrams* (Springer, Berlin, 2014)

Industrial Use Cases

9

The previous chapters present basic concepts, ideas, and methods that are necessary for the successful digitalization of processes. They are based not only on elaborated theory but also on many years of industry experience and good practices.

In this chapter, three case studies are presented in which the concepts, methods, and languages of the previous chapters were applied in operational practice in order to design and improve key business processes.

For each example, the extent to which the propagated advantages of the methods in this book were shown to be valid, such as simple, distributed, and incremental modeling, and IT integration, is also examined.[1]

An important point that should become clear from these case studies and is therefore made at the beginning is that the individual aspects of the previous chapters are not strictly separated from each other and are not implemented separately. In practice, they flow into one another and need to do so.

The first two case studies show projects that were implemented at ENGEL Austria GmbH. The first project is a classic improvement project to reduce lead times in production. The second project deals with the introduction of a driverless transport system in the area of intralogistics.

ENGEL is a traditional manufacturer of injection molding machines from Austria and was founded in 1945 by Ludwig Engel. After introducing the first injection molding machine in 1952, ENGEL has developed into a company with a total turnover of 1.5 billion euros by 2022. The fully owner-managed company employs around 7,000 people worldwide in 9 production plants and over 85 subsidiaries. ENGEL is highly customer-oriented with a focus on flexibility and innovation [6].

The third case study shows the design and introduction of a Manufacturing Execution System (MES) at the company Peneder. The Peneder Group is a family-run company with locations in Atzbach and Fraham (Upper Austria) and sales offices in several European countries. Founded in 1922 as a farrier's workshop, Peneder

---

[1] The reports and analyses are based on previous work by the authors such as [1–4], and [5].

© The Author(s) 2026
M. Elstermann et al., *Contextual Process Digitalization*,
https://doi.org/10.1007/978-3-032-06901-6_9

has developed into a company with 400 employees. Today, the internationally active group of companies is made up of three divisions: Fire doors and gates, construction and architecture for industrial and commercial buildings, and facility management and facility services (FIX). In the 2021/22 financial year, the Peneder Group generated an operating performance of 111 million euros [7].

9.1   Case Study 1: Optimization of Logistics Processes to Reduce Throughput Times

9.1.1   Initial Situation

ENGEL's focus on customer needs and the ongoing development toward shorter delivery times led to the definition of a company-wide goal: to reduce the total process lead time by 30% for all variants of one of the standard components. A project team was created to survey and analyze the existing production processes and implement the necessary improvements. At the time the project was launched, there was hardly any explicit information on the overall process, the individual process steps, or the process actors involved available.

At first, it was only known that the process involved two production sites in different countries (hereinafter referred to as Factory A and Factory B) and consisted of three relevant product groups:

- Product 1: Product 1 was the finished frame, the initial component of each injection molding machine. The frames were assembled in factory A and consisted, among other things, of Product 2. The total lead time for Product 1 included order processing, production, and delivery of components (Product 2) and sub-components (Product 3).
- Product 2: The so-called raw frame with oil tank. This main component was still mechanically unprocessed and was assembled in Factory B out of Product 3. There were several dozen variants of Product 2, depending on the customer's requirements.
- Product 3: A type of building kit made from saw cut parts, which were sawn from bar material in factory A for the respective variant.

Figure 9.1 shows a high-level diagram of the supply chain. The starting point was the customer order for an injection molding machine. The finished product 1

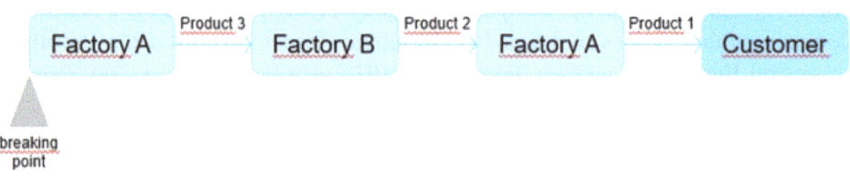

Fig. 9.1 High-level diagram of the supply chain between factories A and B

was delivered to the assembly line in factory A, which was considered a *customer* within the company.

This process was controlled by *order*, which was exchanged between the factories. When an order arrived at a factory, it was recorded and a *production order* was created with a corresponding delivery date. The order was effective as an *order* only once it was recorded. If this entry process took longer than two working days, the production order would not arrive on time in the production of the respective factory, as the order lead time was set to two working days.

In the initial situation, approximately 95% of all orders between factories were entered too late, i.e., more than two working days passed between the arrival of the order in the system and the actual entry. These orders had to be manually processed with enormous additional effort, resulting in an internal delivery reliability of only 39% for product 2. This resulted in problems with production planning in factory A and delays in the production of product 1.

9.1.2 Approach

A time frame of just 10 weeks was set for the process improvement project in order to achieve the specified target of reducing throughput times by 30%. The two factories were located in two different countries with different languages and corresponding cultural and geographical distances.

The tight time frame led to further restrictions for the project: new software solutions or technologies could not be introduced, as such an introduction would have required far-reaching changes and corresponding strategic decisions as well as a lot of personnel, money, risk management, and time. This meant that changes to existing processes had to be implemented within the existing organizational structures and IT environment. Only after the original project goal had been achieved would it have been possible to implement further measures necessary for additional improvements.

Apart from a coarse-grained description of the material flow between the factories, no explicit process information was available. Therefore, the first step of this optimization project was to map the as-is process in order to obtain more detailed knowledge about material and information flows and all factors that could have influenced the production processes.

First, an attempt was made to document and analyze the already established production process using the value stream analysis (VSA) methodology according to [8] or [9]—a standard tool for documenting and analyzing production processes. For an initial mapping of the process, it was necessary to select a suitable, representative product that includes the basic production steps and covers most of the material flow. Ultimately, it was decided to use a variant of product 2 for an initial as-is analysis. This selection was based on an ABC analysis of all product variants and the corresponding work plans. The selected variant for product 2 accounted for 30% of the total production and had the most complex work plans and the highest total lead time of the three defined product groups.

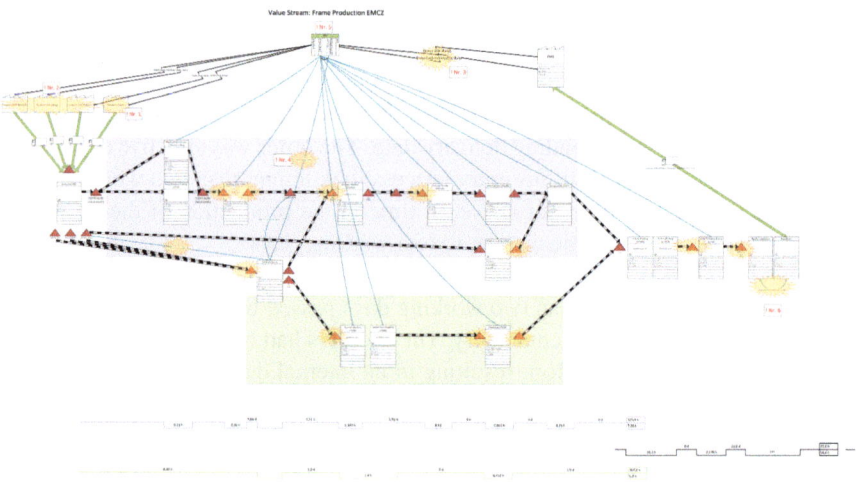

Fig. 9.2 Value stream analysis of the production process of product 2

By tracking the material flow at plant level through both factories, collecting relevant KPIs (inventory, production throughput times, customer cycle, etc.) and personally interviewing the responsible employees, we were able to create a value stream map (VSM) for product 2. Figure 9.2 shows the VSM of the production process and its hierarchical structure.

The results of the value stream mapping were as follows:

- The production process of product 2 consisted of two main steps: Manufacturing the base frame and manufacturing the oil tank. Once the oil tank was completed, it was mounted on the frame to produce product 2.
- The oil tank and the frame were manufactured separately. This means that there was no coordination between the two production lines once the order was processed.
- Due to a lack of production planning, unfinished stock piled up with long waiting times. Only about 10% of the total lead time was production time.
- Through optimizations in production planning and work schedules, the lead time could be reduced. However, the identified improvements were not sufficient to achieve the specified target.
- Great potential in the order processing of the information flow was identified.

In addition, more specific information about the ordering process between the factories was obtained and the process description was expanded accordingly:

- The demand for product 1 comes from Factory A, from where an order for the required variant of product 2 is sent to Factory B.

- The order for product 2 is processed, and the procurement of the required components, including product 3, begins.
- Factory B now orders product 3 from Factory A.
- The order for product 3 is recorded in factory A, the parts are cut to size and sent to factory B.
- As soon as product 3 arrives at Factory B, production of product 2 begins, and the finished product 2 is then delivered to Factory A.
- As soon as product 2 arrives at Factory A, production of product 1 begins.
- This process is the same for every machine, regardless of the variant of product 1.

The relatively simple value stream analysis has already identified two potentials: the lack of production synchronization and the non-optimized order processing. However, production synchronization was directly linked to the respective production planning process. After a brief analysis of the planning process, we came to the conclusion that long-term improvements were only possible if the procedures in the "planning" process were completely reorganized and restructured, and the mindset itself was changed. Although this would have been a necessary change, it could not be implemented within the time frame of the project. Instead, the focus was placed on the ordering process and its optimization potential, as this was seen as a likely "quick win."

According to our experience from previous applications, the VSA focused on production processes and was primarily suitable for describing a relatively linear material flow between individual physical manufacturing steps. The value stream map we created showed that many problems existed in the interactions and exchange of information, but it did not provide a satisfactory basis (for our application) for capturing and describing them. The Value Stream Map created in the course of the value stream analysis lacked relevant process information in order to map the overall process and the corresponding information flow in detail and to understand it correctly. This included, for example, the following circumstances:

- No information about the interactions between the parties involved
- No information about which steps in the process were automated and which steps were performed manually
- No specific information on the transactions used in the SAP ERP[2] system
- No information about the timelines of the information flow
- No verification of the information provided

This was the starting point for choosing a new approach for a comprehensive process survey: an additional method to describe the information flow at a level

---

[2] Enterprise Resource Planning (ERP) system—the central IT system for business planning in every company by default.

of detail that allows a precise analysis to be carried out and, above all, the above-mentioned points to be clearly mapped, understood, and discussed.

The method of subject-oriented business process management (S-BPM) was used as an additional modeling tool (see [10])(see Sect. 3.6). This choice was based on previous experience and above all on problems that had occurred in similar contexts with other modeling languages (including Flowcharts/Swim lane diagrams, eEPC, BPMN, etc.) when these were occasionally used alongside VSA in the company. These process models had two shortcomings: Some of them provided an overview of the process but were not detailed enough for a thorough process analysis, while others were so detailed that it became very difficult to maintain an overview or to read and understand the model.

One of the experiences mentioned in past projects was that the people involved in the processes, their individual approaches, their knowledge, and their experience are a decisive driving force and essential for successful processes—a realization that other experts have made too, e.g., [11] or [12]. Another experience is that the way in which the information flow is organized between process actors has a significant influence on business process performance (see also, for example, [13]).

These are important circumstances for which the methods of subject orientation and the approaches presented in the previous chapters of this book are viewed as very well suited.

The next step was to conduct more detailed personal interviews with the relevant process participants and, on this basis, to create a subject interaction diagram (SID) of the actual situation of the logistics and production processes, which—as expected—was very complex. Approximately 40 subjects were involved in the production, production planning, and logistics of all three products in both factories. A sketch of the final version of the resulting actual SID can be seen in Fig. 9.3. The SID shows the general communication structure of the process, i.e., which subjects (rectangles) exchange which messages (on the arrows) with each other. The specific names of the subjects or the content of the exchanged messages are not relevant for understanding the approach taken.

To differentiate between the two factories, the corresponding subjects were color-coded in green for Factory A and orange for Factory B. In addition, subjects representing functionalities of SAP systems were marked by hatching (gray) to highlight those parts of the existing process that were already digitalized.

Although the same ERP system was used in both plants, it was divided up according to the three application areas for a more structured visualization: SAP System A, SAP System B, and SAP System A Material planning.

Due to the large number of subjects involved and the complexity of the entire process, it would not have been practicable to collect and model all subject behavior diagrams (SBDs) without a defined framework for our next steps, nor was it necessary for the question to be clarified.[3] To define such a framework, the SID was

---

[3] Engineered, detailed SBDs can help to verify the content of the SID or make it more consistent. However, the effort involved should be well thought out and appropriate resources (time) should be available.

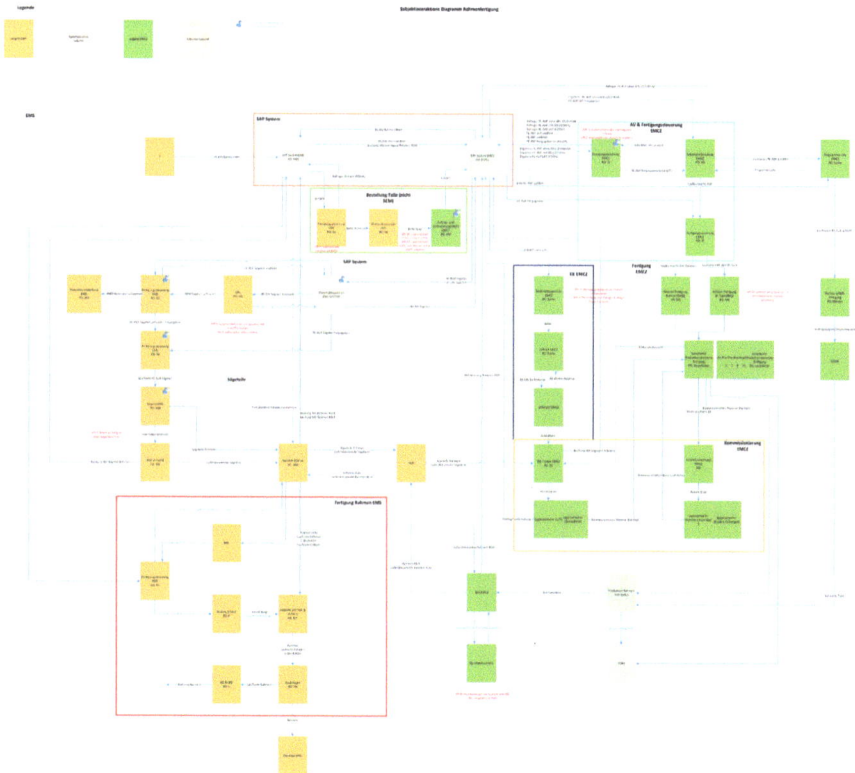

Fig. 9.3 Sketch of the communication structure (subject interaction diagram) of the production and ordering process

used for identifying and analyzing the main nodes and bottlenecks in the process for the corresponding product (Fig. 9.4). Individual subject behaviors were modeled in detail only as necessary within the defined framework.

The most striking part of the process was the order processing itself. The processing of the order of product 1 by factory A, the order processing and procurement of product 2 by factory B, and the production of product 3 in factory A involved up to 12 subjects (3 SAP systems and 9 persons/roles) and took up to 15 working days. In addition, only 65% of product 2 production was completed on time because order processing took too long and orders were received too late in the production center (approx. 95% of all orders). This had a direct impact on the production of product 1 and on process stability. The delivery times could only be met with a great deal of effort in production. It was decided to focus on this material procurement process (a subset of the modeled subjects), as this process was very cumbersome and time-consuming relative to the complexity of the components provided (product 3).

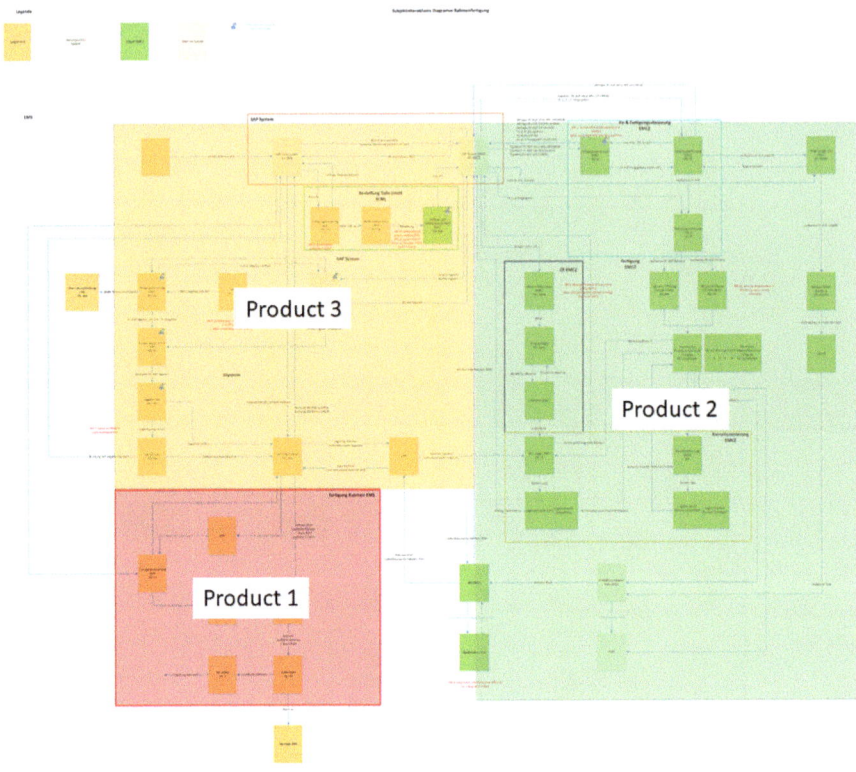

Fig. 9.4 Connection between the communication structure and the different products

The framework for this process survey is defined as follows: The focus was on the logistics departments of Factory A and Factory B. This included the production of product 3 in Factory A, as it was organizationally integrated into logistics and was therefore part of the process and production of product 2 in Factory B. The material procurement in Factory A and the actual assembly of product 1 in Factory A were no longer part of the survey (see Fig. 9.4 for a visualization of the process and the corresponding products).

The relevant process steps were examined by directly interviewing the employees involved in individual interviews or by accompanying the employees during their own process and at the same time modeling the subject behavior diagrams for the interviewees to see. This allowed the process flow for product 3 (see arrows in Fig. 9.5) to be described in detail relatively quickly and efficiently, extensive information about the SAP ERP system and the transactions used to be documented, and the interviewees to be able to directly accompany the process modeling and verify the model.

Once the SAP transactions were clearly described in the SID and the employees' SBDs, and a dummy order was followed through the system, the various steps of the

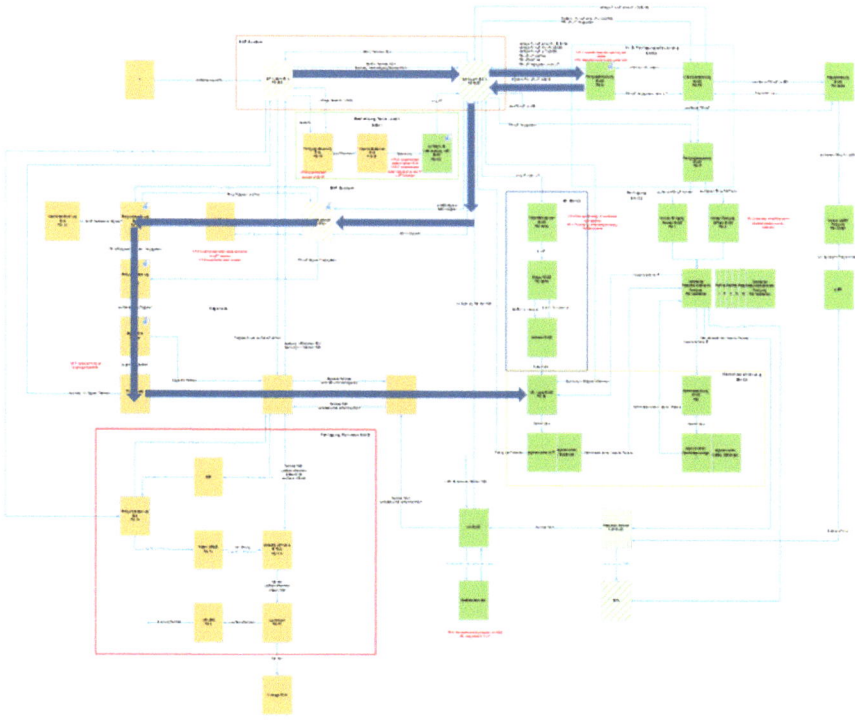

Fig. 9.5 Communication structure (SID) of the process for the production of product 3

SAP system were also modeled. This allowed us to differentiate between automated (digital) and manual steps, to verify the process model, and to document the actual process lead times (process lead time).

Figure 9.6 visualizes the process behavior of an employee who handles the processing of production orders in Factory B. This employee checks whether production plans are available for planned production orders. All planned production orders are then combined with available production plans according to a defined set of rules and released for production. The employees do this manually for each production order, with several thousand orders per day. Product 3 alone causes a total workload of around seven hours per day.

The total effort for the survey, all interviews, and the time required to complete and review the process models amounted to around 200 working hours. Given the complexity of the process models and the level of detail examined, this is a relatively small amount of work compared to other process optimization projects.

With the detailed knowledge now available about the subjects involved and the data documented in the SAP system (order times, delivery times, etc.), a schedule was created for the process. This schedule contained all organizational

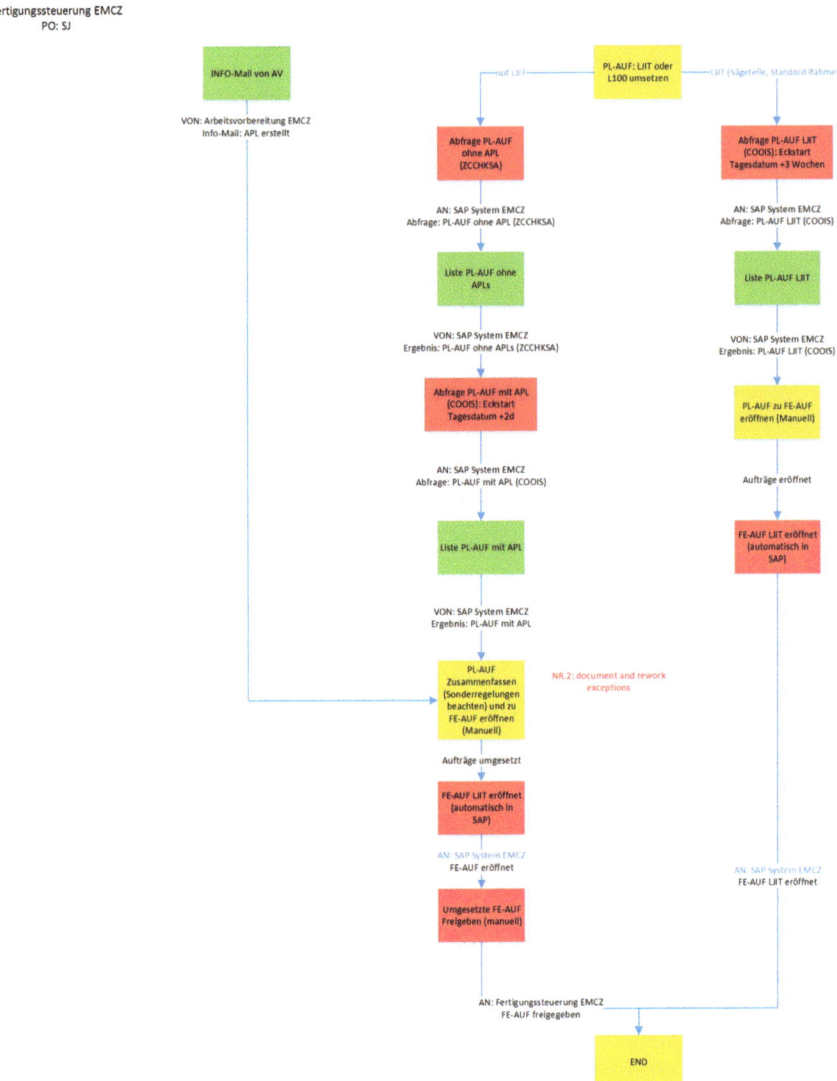

Fig. 9.6 Example of a behavioral description (SBD) of an employee

and production steps and their respective lead times. For example, the lead time for one of the product 1 variants, from order acceptance in Factory B to delivery of the finished product 1 to the assembly line in Factory A, was approximately 30 working days (Fig. 9.7).

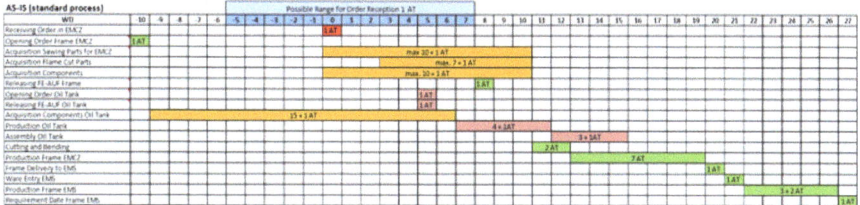

Fig. 9.7 Process schedule in the initial process

9.1.3 Results Achieved

As a result of the analysis, the existing work plans were revised, updated, and improved in collaboration with the employees. This resulted in shorter lead times for the same work steps and a reduced number of work steps due to merging. In this case, a reduced number of work steps means both fewer subjects and fewer behavioral states in the subject behaviors. During the analysis, several similar process steps were also identified that are performed differently in Factory A and Factory B. For example, in one factory, certain necessary process steps were executed manually, but in the other factory, they could be executed automatically by the SAP system. In addition, existing automated SAP batch jobs were interrupted if the required manual entries were missing. These batch jobs were scheduled at two defined times during the working day. If the manual input was missing at this time, the entire order had to wait up to an entire working day. This could happen several times for each order for different jobs, which could ultimately lead to a delay of several working days.

The subject descriptions provided precisely defined processes (SBDs) that specify all relevant process steps in the SAP system, in particular all required SAP transactions, the worker executing these transactions, and the interaction between the system and employees. Based on this detailed process documentation, necessary changes to the system for an optimized target process were identified and described. The adjustments to the ERP system required for realizing the target process were implemented directly by the IT department to create new standardized, digitized, and automated processes, to revise process steps, and to streamline the processing schedule of existing batch jobs for both factories. This included steps such as order acceptance, order entry, order opening, order release in both factories, and delivery of production paperwork to production. Automated order processing allowed for order-based and timely processing of product 3 at Factory A, which in turn allowed for the introduction of KANBAN inventory with defined critical parts, reduction of noncritical parts inventory, and shipping of externally purchased parts directly to manufacturing.

Another achieved result was a new stock strategy and a reevaluation of the stock, which made it possible to revise the entire stock and implement a KANBAN system for critical parts of product 3. The newly created KANBAN stock and

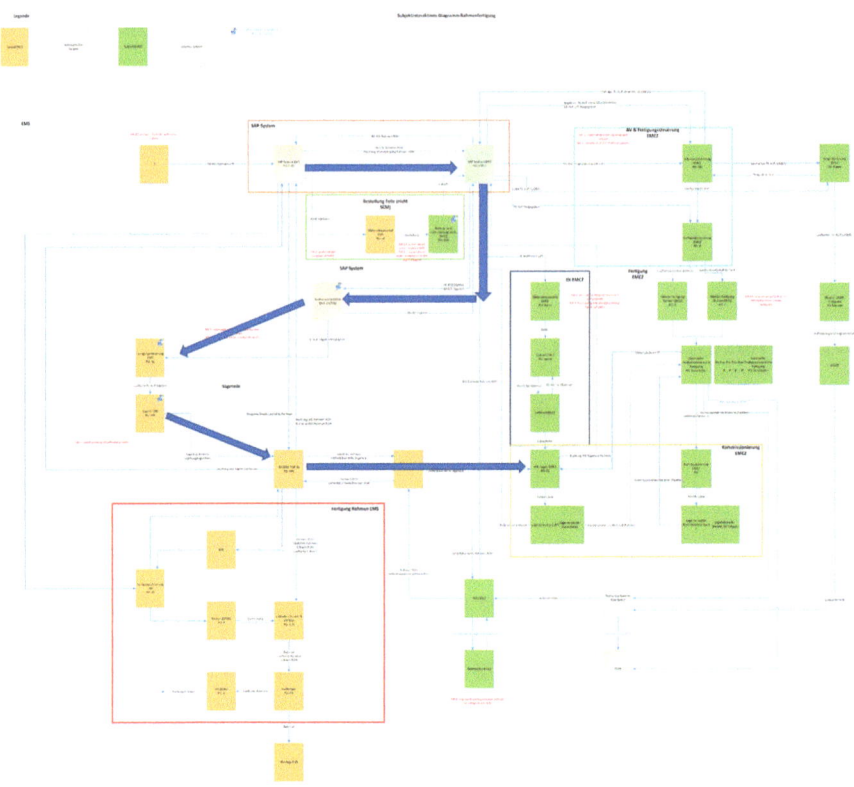

Fig. 9.8 Communication structure (SID) of the optimized process for the production of product 3

the higher value of the parts resulted in an overall increase in stock value of approximately 209%, which at first glance is a huge figure but only corresponded to an absolute increase of approximately   10,000 of the existing stock value. This new strategy increased availability and reduced delivery times for all purchased parts. The interruptions in the production of product 2 due to missing parts could originally last up to 15 working days. After the implemented changes, all required components were available within one working day either directly on site or via the safety stock at the supplier's site. This meant a huge improvement in process stability and reduction in work in progress against a comparatively small increase in inventory.

The restructuring and digitization of previously manual processes led to a standardized process and a reduction in the number of subjects involved from 12 down to 8 (see Fig. 9.8). Fewer subjects led to fewer interfaces in the process, which in turn reduced process complexity and increased process stability and transparency. In addition, employees were freed from time-consuming and repetitive tasks.

The increased degree of digitization and the newly planned process led to a new process lead time of 2 days for order processing from the original 5–10 days. Thanks to the detailed and clearly defined process, the IT department was able to implement the process changes in the existing system environment within just 3 working days. The production and shipping process for product 3 was reduced to 3 days from the original 5–6 days. This means that we were able to reduce the total lead time of product 3 from 11–15 working days by 87% to 2 working days. These changes led to increased on-time delivery for product 3: delivery reliability increased to 89% just 4 weeks after implementation and to 97% after one year.

The relatively long time required for order processing for product 3 in the initial phase meant that most orders arrived at Factory A too late or at very short notice. The newly created automated SAP processes led to a faster processing of orders from Factory A within the departments of Factory B. This resulted in a shorter order time for product 3 and an earlier start of production of other components required for product 2. The result was a reduction from an initial 95% of orders being registered late to just 12%, which in turn greatly increased process stability and process quality and reduced the need for troubleshooting in both factories. The total lead time of the production and ordering process of product 2 was reduced by 7 working days (approx. 38%), from 19–23 days to 12–14 days.

The conversion of manual work into automated, digitized processes in the SAP system led to a reduction in the workload of the employees involved from 5–6 hours to up to 1 hour per day. The employees now only had to process orders manually for very specific components or special cases that could not be covered by the SAP system. The effects of these changes add up to a calculated process cost reduction of around 65,000 per year. The implemented improvements and corresponding changes at the process level reduced the lead times for products 2 and 3 and led to a shortened total lead time for Product 1: from 26–33 working days to 18–20 working days. This is an overall reduction of approximately 60% for the entire ordering and production process (see Figs. 9.9 and 9.10).

Not only was the target of a 30% reduction in lead time achieved. By digitalizing and automating the process steps and the corresponding information flow, this reduction could even be more than doubled. This also led to a reduction in work in progress with a total value of several hundred thousand euros over the entire process.

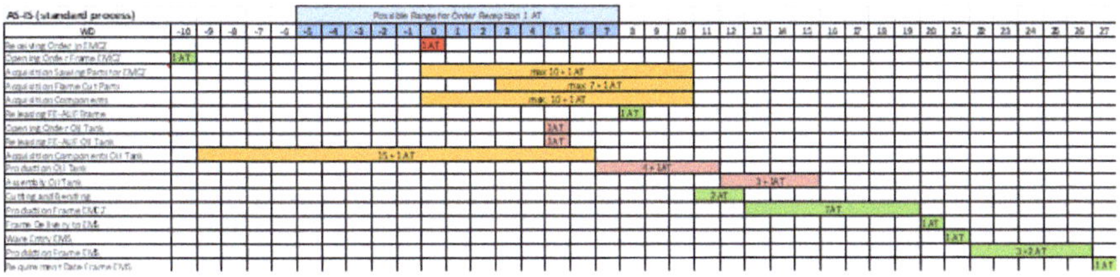

Fig. 9.9 Time table of the initial process

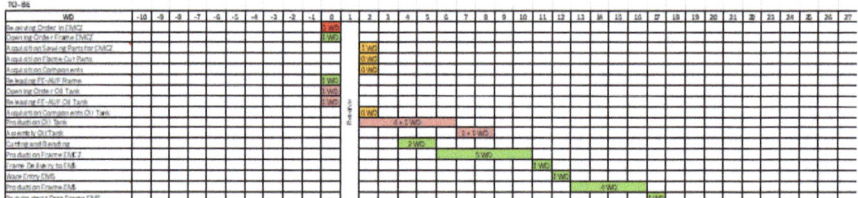

Fig. 9.10 Time table of the reworked process

These results show that it was possible to significantly reduce lead time and manual workload by optimizing and digitizing the information flow. The increased degree of digitalization and the associated process transparency could help to achieve further improvements and to better understand the processes in future analyses (see [14]).

9.1.4   Conclusion of the Method Application

Simplicity of Modeling The small number of symbols of the PASS Notation enabled process participants to understand the notation after only a 10-minute introduction. That introduction mainly focused on understanding and creating SBDs so that process participants could articulate the process from their own point of view (i.e., only their own subject). The goal was to enable them to structure their SBDs around the three key issues: *"What do I need from others?"* (Receive), *"What do others need from me?"* (Send), and *"What do I need to do?"* (Do). SBDs of other subjects were disclosed only upon request, in order to keep the mental overhead for stakeholders at a minimum.

The combined approach of interview and modeling enabled the process participants to create a direct reference between their mental model of the process and the S-BPM model. This also reduced the post-interview documentation effort because the process models were the direct result of the interviews. No intermediary textual description was required. During the interviews the process participants began to (verbally) verify and correct the model by themselves. This can be seen as a confirmation that the short introduction to S-BPM was sufficient to understand and contribute to the process models.

Distributed Modeling Every interview involved modeling the behavior of only those subjects that the respective interviewee was responsible for. This was a major advantage for the project, as individual interviews are easier to schedule than collaborative workshops involving all process participants from different countries at the same time. The one-on-one interviews also led to a more efficient modeling process because they eliminated the idle time of process participants not involved in the current process part. These factors also increased the overall motivation and acceptance of the participants regarding the process survey and modeling.

On the other hand, this approach also presented a disadvantage. The chronological sequence of the overall process across all subjects and messages became very difficult to follow without in-depth and detailed process knowledge. While this effect could be somewhat mitigated by arranging or naming the subjects in chronological order, this was only feasible for SIDs with a small number of subjects and few process loops. To make the chronological sequence more comprehensible, the S-BPM model was additionally represented in a (highly simplified) swim lane diagram.

A large number of subjects and messages also reduces the readability of the process model—a problem that, naturally, every modeling method faces once a certain level of process complexity is reached. The arrows representing the messages become increasingly difficult to follow in terms of their direction (i.e., sender/receiver subject) and their content. To alleviate this issue, a standardized naming convention for subjects and messages was introduced in earlier S-BPM application projects: Subjects were assigned a name and a unique number. Messages were labeled with a name and given a prefix indicating the sender and receiver (e.g., "02_03 MessageName" for a message from "02_Subject" to "03_Subject").

Continuous Changes Throughout the course of the project, the process models were continuously extended, revised, and corrected. Older versions of the model were not discarded but merely adapted and saved as new versions, following the approach of incremental change. Adjustments to represent the target process were visualized by adding or removing individual subjects, subject behaviors, or messages. As a result, the effort required to implement these changes was relatively low. The model thus served not merely as documentation of an (interim) result but as an integral working tool.

IT Implementation The process model described concrete processes, including the individual process steps within the ERP system (SAP)—specifically, all necessary SAP transactions and the interactions between the system and the employees. The detailed graphical representation enabled the IT department to directly implement the required new processes, adapt existing ones, and optimize the process flows. The implemented changes within the existing system environment were carried out by a single IT specialist within one working week (approximately 38 working hours). In response to the management's skeptical question as to when these changes would actually be implemented, the project team was able to reply: "They've been running for two weeks." The changes included process steps such as order confirmation, order release in all plants, and the distribution of production orders in the ERP system. As previously mentioned, the implemented automation made it possible to manufacture the products on time.

9.2 Case Study 2: Implementation of an Automated Guided Vehicle System (AGVS)

The second project at ENGEL Austria concerned the digitalization of processes in intralogistics, which were necessary for the implementation of an automated guided vehicle system (AGVS). An incremental strategy was followed throughout the entire project, supported by S-BPM methods for process and interface analysis, planning of the individual development stages of the new process, and communication between stakeholders.

9.2.1 Initial Situation

ENGEL pursued a strategy aiming at a high degree of vertical integration and was capable of manufacturing all product components in-house. Production was coordinated in the manufacturing control system via a Manufacturing Execution System (MES). Internal transport systems supplied the workstations with the necessary raw materials and semi-finished products in a four-shift operation. In autumn 2018, the company launched a pilot project to implement an automated guided vehicle system (AGVS) with the aim of supporting internal transport and easing the workload for forklift operators. Implementing such an AGVS in a production facility posed a significant risk for ENGEL, as it required high investment costs and affected a central, production-critical process. To reduce the risk of the pilot project, it was decided that the AGVS should be implemented in several small steps, which were easier to validate. Defining the future target processes and the necessary implementation steps required capturing and describing the existing (as-is) processes. However, at the start of the project, no explicit process documentation existed for the affected transport processes and their control.

9.2.2 Approach

The goal was to document the processes at every stage of the project in a way that was comprehensible for the whole project team. That team consisted of internal logistics planners, machine operators, forklift drivers, IT staff, and the external suppliers of ENGEL's MES and AGVs. However, due to differences in the team members' work environments, jargons, training, and experience, constructing a shared understanding about the processes was expected to be a challenge.

Based on positive experiences from previous projects, S-BPM/PASS was chosen as the modeling approach. For data collection, the same approach of individual interviews and modeling methodology as in Case Study 1 was applied. If it became apparent during an interview that additional subjects were necessary in the process, they were added to the SID and an interview with the respective process participant was arranged to model the corresponding SBD.

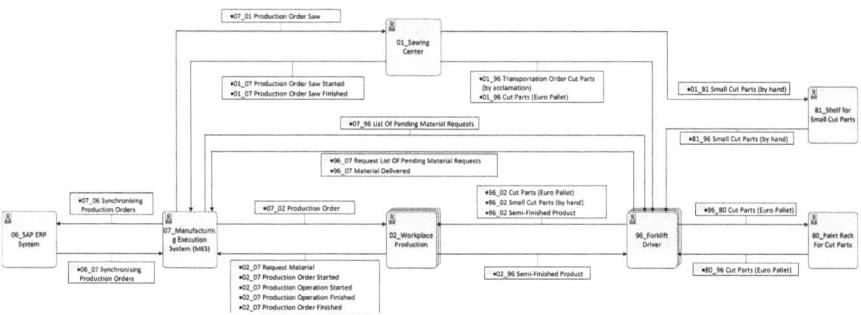

Fig. 9.11 Subject Interaction Diagram of the as-is process (Step 0)

The following findings were made based on this approach:

1. The logistics processes at ENGEL were highly information-intensive and were fundamentally controlled through interactions between machine operators, fork-lift drivers, and the MES. Using Subject Interaction Diagrams (SIDs), all process participants (subjects) and their interactions were described, regardless of whether they were humans, machines, or software applications.
2. The separation of subject behavior (SBD) and SID reduced the risk of process participants being overwhelmed by a flood of (irrelevant) details and prevents control flow problems. A SID provided an effective basis for communication within the very diverse project team.
3. The SIDs allowed for the representation of a modular process structure in which subjects and messages could be easily changed, deleted, or extended without the entire process needing to be completely remodeled for each iteration.[4] This supported the approach of incremental introduction of the AGVS, as the as-is process model gradually evolved into a target process model.

The following provides a detailed description of the steps taken.

Step 0: Modeling of the As-Is Process
The first implementation stage of the project (referred to as "Step 0" within the project) consisted of capturing and documenting the as-is process of internal material supply. The resulting process description was intended to serve as a foundation for a shared understanding of the process. The as-is process described in Step 0 is outlined in Fig. 9.11 (the specific labels of the subjects are not relevant for understanding the project): As shown in the model, production orders were exchanged to coordinate between the SAP ERP system and the MES. When a

---

[4] This is an indicator supporting the hypothesis that the subject is the natural modularization concept for process descriptions—as opposed to arbitrarily chosen task boundaries or attempts to introduce more flexibility in process descriptions through the concept of subprocesses.

production order was triggered, the employee in the sawing center received the task of cutting the required material. Small parts were stored on a shelf near the sawing workstation and later collected by a forklift driver. Large parts were temporarily stored on Euro pallets on a shelf and also transported by the forklift drivers. The forklift drivers were informed by the respective employee at the saw when transport was required. After delivering the material, the forklift driver manually confirmed in the MES that the material was available at the designated workstation.

Machine operators received their production orders via the MES and were able to organize the production sequence within their work queue themselves (e.g., to optimize setup times). They reported the status of every production order back into the MES and triggered orders for raw materials (or cut-to-size parts) for new production orders. Transport requests were initiated either by the machine operator or by the forklift driver who received a list of required materials on a mobile tablet from the MES. The forklift driver manually decided which transport request to process first, based on a predefined set of rules (e.g., planned delivery date).

Based on the SID, several areas of the process were identified where automation and digitalization could lead to improvements. One such area concerned the available transport capacity (forklift fleet and forklift drivers). The forklift drivers were primarily occupied with "simple" transport tasks—such as moving standardized Euro pallets and small parts. However, forklift drivers were most effectively deployed when handling more complex transport tasks, such as oversized components (several meters in length) and heavy materials (weighing up to several tons). Every time a small part (individual items weighing up to 15 kg) was transported by forklift, valuable transport capacity was wasted.

Another opportunity for improvement was identified in the handling of transport orders. Manual prioritization led to errors in the process, which resulted in additional coordination efforts and even production delays. The large number of transport orders, for example, made it very difficult for forklift drivers to consistently follow the prescribed prioritization rules. One reason for this was that the list of transport orders used by the forklift drivers was not a true transport list. It was a modified list of production orders in which a field labeled "material required" was manually filled in by the machine operator when the material was requested. As a result, forklift drivers received no explicit information when changes to production orders affected the sequence of transport orders or required re-prioritization. While the planned start time (date and time) was technically visible, with several hundred orders per day, it was simply not feasible to manually check for changes. Additionally, communication between forklift drivers and machine operators took place informally—by phone or face-to-face. This meant that machine operators would often attempt to direct the delivery of materials themselves, fearing that it might not arrive on time. However, this could result in excessive material being delivered to the workstations, which not only restricted workspace but also tied up valuable transport capacity needed for other orders.

Based on the analysis of the as-is process, the decision was made—and formally approved—to introduce an AGV system in order to automate standardized transport tasks as far as possible. In the long term, at least 80% of all internal transports

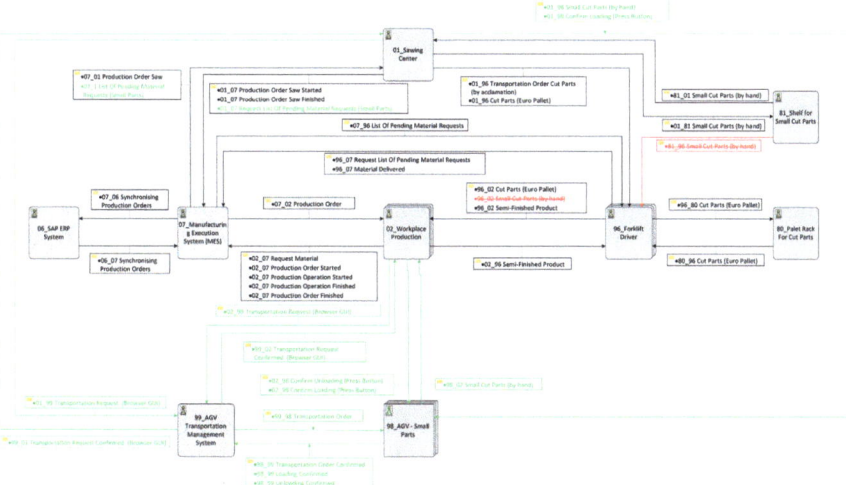

Fig. 9.12 Subject Interaction Diagram of the to-be process (Step 1) (added elements in green; removed elements in red)

were to be handled by the AGV system. A pilot project was launched to implement the system and to monitor the resulting process changes incrementally. After each project phase, the effects, required effort, and benefits were to be reviewed in order to decide whether to proceed with the next step. For this approach, three broad stages were defined and later executed accordingly.

As part of the development of the implementation stages, the project team also created a corresponding requirements specification for the AGV system to be implemented. This specification served as a basis for communication with various AGV providers and ultimately for selecting one of them.

Step 1: Automated Guided Vehicle System for Small Parts

In Step 1 of the project, an AGV system for transporting small parts within the production facility was introduced. Figure 9.12 shows the updated process model, highlighting the changes in the process flow compared to the as-is process from Step 0 (see Fig. 9.11). The changes are marked in different colors (green for "added," red for "removed"). In the new process, small parts were transported by the AGV system, which was suitable for loads of up to 100 kg. Transport orders were created and managed via a standardized graphical user interface. This browser-based user interface was a pre-configured, tested solution provided by the AGV supplier and could be used without additional software installation. As a result, every workstation equipped with a computer could be directly connected to the system. As soon as a machine operator required materials, they created a transport order via the user interface, which was then automatically processed by the AGV control system.

From a technical perspective, it would have been possible to implement automated loading and unloading of the transported materials during Step 1. However, it was decided that the AGV should be loaded and unloaded manually by the machine operators, as the necessary automation would have required additional, highly costly investments. After the loading process, the respective employee confirmed the loading by pressing a button directly on the AGV, which then proceeded executing the next transport order.

During the implementation phase and the first weeks of operation, extensive practical experience was gained in deploying the AGV system within an active production environment—particularly regarding the acceptance of this new technology, order management, route planning, and more. The outcome of the efforts in Step 1 was that all transport orders for small parts were processed by the AGV system. Consequently, it was decided to proceed with Step 2.

Step 2: Automated Guided Vehicle System for Large Parts
In Step 2, the transport of raw materials for large parts between selected workstations was to be implemented. As in the previous steps, the changes were developed and presented through a process model, which again formed the basis for communication between the project team and the involved departments. The most important part was the verification of the planned process by the employees affected in logistics and production. The key question to be answered was both simple and complex: "Do you and your work benefit from this new process?" This was of particular priority in Step 2, as the necessary process changes deeply affected the transport process within intralogistics and had far-reaching consequences. Here, the graphical process model proved indispensable as a "common language" for effective communication.

In the new process, all parts weighing up to 1.500 kg were transported on Euro pallets. The raw material was cut in the sawing center and manually loaded onto the pallets at designated loading stations. The saw operator then created a transport order by scanning the unique production order number, which was linked to the loading station number. This triggered a transport order, and the large-parts AGV system transported the pallet to a pallet rack, which was directly managed by the AGV system. Each machine operator could now digitally request the required production order from the rack via the user interface at their workstation. The transport was carried out by the AGV system and automatically reported as completed once the pallet was delivered to the respective workstation. The corresponding process model is shown in Fig. 9.13. The incremental changes, this time compared to the process model from Step 1, are again highlighted in color (added elements in green; removed elements in red).

Step 3: Automated Control of Transport Orders
In Step 3, the AGV system was directly integrated with the existing MES to automatically generate and manage transport orders. This means that the MES now automatically created a transport order whenever a production step was reported as complete and the material or semi-finished product was required at another workstation. Ideally, this could eliminate any manual transport between

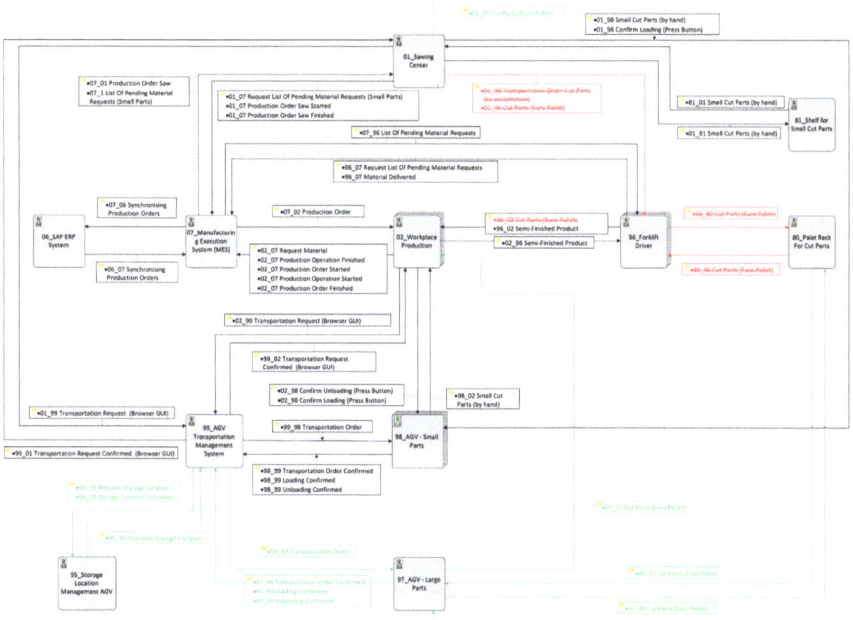

Fig. 9.13 Subject Interaction Diagram of the to-be process (Step 2) (added elements in green; removed elements in red)

workstations. If a workstation was not connected to the AGV infrastructure, a forklift driver was automatically notified via the MES. The corresponding process model for Step 3 is shown in Fig. 9.14. All changes, this time compared to Step 2, are again highlighted in color (added elements in green; removed elements in red).

9.2.3   Results Achieved

In the described pilot project, an incremental strategy was used to reduce the risk associated with introducing the AGV system and the significant process changes involved. The fact that all three planned steps were successfully implemented shows that each preceding step was completed successfully.

One of the main tools for implementing this strategy was the subject-oriented modeling method, which is based on the flow of information between process participants. Additionally, the approach supported modular process structures. Changes in the logistics processes between project steps could be represented by selective modifications in the existing process model. It was not necessary to completely remodel the altered process models. The loose coupling between the subjects made it possible to reuse the same SID with only a few changes by adding or removing individual elements. Behavior diagrams unaffected by changes could be

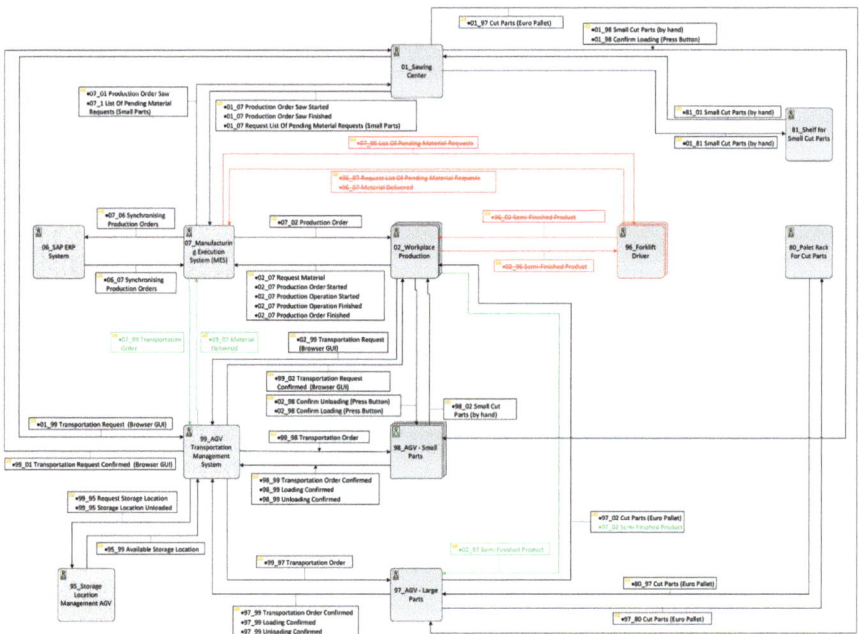

Fig. 9.14 Subject Interaction Diagram of the to-be process (Step 3) (added elements in green; removed elements in red)

left completely unchanged. This saved time in the planning and validation of each process change. The process analysis, modeling, and elaboration of all individual project steps required approximately 160 working hours.

Project steps 1 and 2 were implemented in 2020 and were operational.[5]

Further detailed data and process analysis , based on experiences from stages 1 and 2, showed that far-reaching and complex changes to existing data structures within the ERP system would have been necessary to reach the initially requested level of automation (stage 3). The very high implementation cost resulted in a non-acceptable amortization time. The implementation of stage 3 was therefore suspended. This shows that the incremental strategy used to reduce the involved risks of the transformation has proven to be successful.

9.2.4   Conclusion of the Method Application

Simplicity of Modeling All participants were able to learn and understand the notation very quickly and actively took part in creating the process model—

---

[5] A demonstration can be found at the following link: https://www.youtube.com/watch?v=Mpds0goQpzo. The AGV supplier published the project as a reference ("Success Story").

regardless of their prior experience or training (ranging from IT specialists to forklift operators). One of the main tools used for implementing the incremental strategy was the S-BPM approach. This enabled the creation of a common project language to describe the information flows between process actors within a modular process structure.

Distributed Modeling Changes between the individual project steps did not require a complete redesign of the process models. The loose coupling of the subjects via the messages made it possible to adapt the already created SIDs individually with only a few modifications, without jeopardizing the overall consistency of the model.

Subject behaviors are defined as self-contained within their respective subjects, and it is not necessary to know the subject behaviors to model a complete SID. This enabled the project team to describe the processes without knowing every detail. For example, it was neither necessary nor possible to describe the subject behavior of the FTS ("AGV Transportation Management System" in Fig. 9.12). However, it was possible to specify the system's interactions and the required information exchanged, which in turn formed the basis for defining the system interface.

Continuous Changes The relatively quick and straightforward visualization of the possible project steps and the required changes provided additional support in communicating the necessary modifications and requirements—both internally and externally. This saved a great deal of time and effort in planning and validating each project step. Additionally, the implementation costs for each step could be estimated more accurately.

IT Implementation The S-BPM/PASS models served as an important communication tool within the project team. This was primarily due to the easily readable SIDs, which were used for every step of the project. This facilitated the collection and communication of requirements for the development of human-machine and machine-machine interfaces. Additionally, the process models were used to verify the concept prior to implementation.

9.3   Case Study 3: Implementation of a Manufacturing Execution System

9.3.1   Initial Situation

In spring 2020, Peneder Bau-Elemente GmbH launched an extensive improvement program for the production of fire protection elements. Based on the company's strategy to modernize production comprehensively, increase resource efficiency, and achieve the planned growth targets, all planning, logistics, and production processes were to be examined for potential improvements. Over several months, extensive process analyses were conducted, resulting in the identification of numerous opportunities for improvement with varying levels of implementation effort.

As the improvement opportunity with the greatest potential but also the highest implementation effort the project team identified the digitalization of the entire production system through the introduction of a Manufacturing Execution System (MES). A dedicated "Digitalization" project team was established with the goal of digitalizing production and all supporting processes (such as production data acquisition, machine data collection, production and capacity planning, materials management, logistics, etc.) in order to create more structured, efficient, and transparent production processes.

The introduction of an MES is a resource-intensive change with far-reaching consequences for all areas in a company. Switching between different MES solutions involves an even greater effort, and the implemented system must meet the company's requirements and remain operational for decades. This means that as many current and future requirements as possible need to be known in advance when choosing a suitable software solution—which also applied to Peneder. Additionally, the implementation of the MES had to work in two distinct ways: firstly, it had to be possible to integrate the MES into the existing process and software structures; secondly, existing processes needed to be adapted to better and more efficiently fit in the new digital MES environment.

To define the correct requirements for a new system a detailed understanding of the processes is essential. All relevant process information as well as interfaces between systems, machines, and people are crucial for designing a production-supporting MES. At the start of the project, however, no explicit, up-to-date process documentation was available. Similar to Case Study 2, the project team consisted of various employees from all departments: production staff, IT consultants, production planners, quality management, and more. Here too, it was indispensable to create a common basis for communication to avoid misunderstandings. This was the reason for employing subject-oriented process modeling. Additional challenges arose because, within the same time frame, a complete redesign of a production area, the construction of a new powder coating oven, and modernization of the control system for the conveyor technology were planned. Resulting changes had to be considered in the MES requirements as well, since a new workstation structure with a different layout impacts the master data in the ERP system, which the MES is intended to access. Likewise, for continuous machine data acquisition, the conveyor system was to be connected to the MES. Accordingly, the resulting MES-conveyor technology interface had to be defined, while also taking into account a planned but not yet implemented modernization of the conveyor technology.

9.3.2 Approach

Similar to the previous projects, individual interviews were conducted with the project participants. The process model and its development were displayed live on a large screen for everyone involved. This approach had already proven successful in the past, as the interviewees could directly see how their respective knowledge was being represented in the process model.

Before the interviews commenced, every participant received a brief, prepared introduction to the S-BPM/PASS notation. This explanation was the same for everyone, regardless of role or prior experience with process modeling:

"The processes are modeled using subject-oriented business process modeling (S-BPM). This means the focus of the process representation lies on the perspective of the participants and their position within the overall process. The graphical representation is therefore shown on two levels. The SID depicts the process participants (abstractly: humans, machines, systems, etc.) and their interactions. The SBD describes the concrete actions of the process participant (subject) from their own perspective. The subject behavior is modeled using three states. To aid differentiation, the states are color-coded (freely selectable): Receive (I need something to be able to work), Send (someone needs something from me to be able to work), Do (what must I do)."

This brief description evolved over numerous S-BPM projects in which it was applied. Time and again, it has been shown that a more extensive explanation was not necessary to understand the process models—and in fact, most participants did not wish for one.

The process models developed during the interviews were used to establish a common understanding of the processes and to describe the interfaces between employees, production machines, software applications (both custom solutions and COTS), the ERP system, sensors, and track and trace systems. During the modeling process, necessary or desired adjustments to the processes were incorporated directly into the process model. This means that the as-is processes were not separately documented and analyzed before implementing changes. Instead, the to-be processes were modeled directly from the outset.

This direct transition to to-be process modeling had not been planned initially. However, during the process survey, it came very naturally to the interviewees to not only describe their daily work but also to articulate very detailed changes that would improve or facilitate their tasks. Many of these proposed changes had a direct impact on the use of the new MES, which led the project team to decide to model the possible to-be processes simultaneously with the as-is processes.

In the beginning of the data collection and modeling phases, a process model was created for each individual production area (i.e., one SID each for logistics, metalworking, powder coating, etc.), as this was a natural way in which the team leaders described their processes and areas. Every team leader explained their work as a continuous process from start to finish, without dividing it into individual subprocesses. The resulting (area-specific) process models comprised over 80 individual subjects in total, with a corresponding number of subject behaviors, and several hundreds of messages exchanged between the subjects (see examples in Figs. 9.15, 9.16 and 9.17).

For modeling using the PASS notation, basically any tool capable of displaying shapes and arrows could be used. During the data collection phase, a simple,

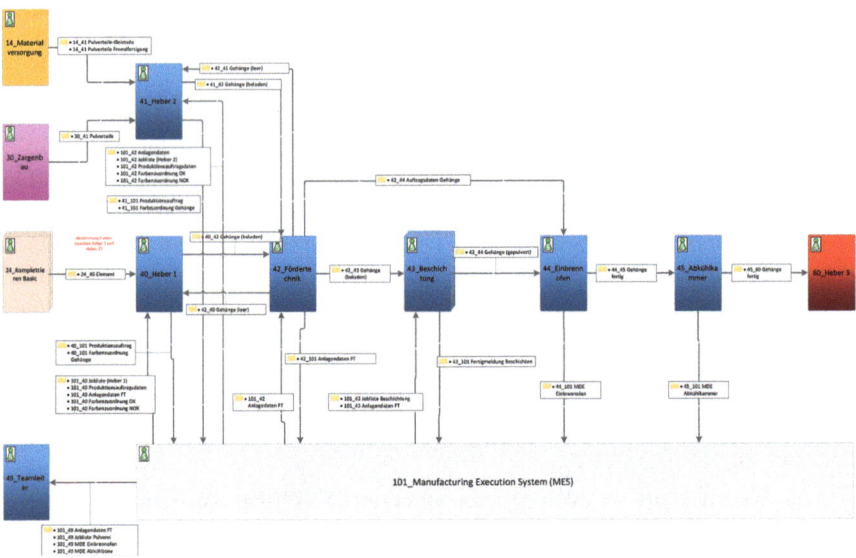

Fig. 9.15 Process powder coating (SID)

specialized MS Visio plug-in for subject-oriented PASS modeling was employed[6] (cf. Sect. 8.1.5). Besides offering more convenient operation and support to maintain model consistency, an additional advantage of the plug-in is that the graphical process model can be directly exported into a Microsoft Word document that contains all subjects, subject behaviors, messages, and states. However, the resulting documentation spanned over 140 pages and was too extensive and complex to be easily understood by third parties not involved in the data collection (e.g., software providers).

Nevertheless, the textual descriptions complemented the graphical model and helped identify relevant interfaces between the process actors. This was particularly useful for the planned machine data acquisition, as it enabled the description of individual machine controls and integrations. The resulting process model served as the foundation for creating a requirements specification document, which communicated the demands for the various interfaces both internally, between production and IT, and externally with the different software providers. The graphical process models directly depicted the desired target processes. The current as-is processes were also explained in textual form within the specification document. Additionally, to enhance understanding, specifically requested MES functions (e.g., workflows, reports, dashboards, etc.) were described using a use case notation. Based on these use cases, function-specific "sub"-process models were derived from the overarching process model (see Fig. 9.18).

---

[6] https://subjective-me.jimdofree.com/visio-modelling/

Fig. 9.16 Workstation "Lift
1" (SBD)

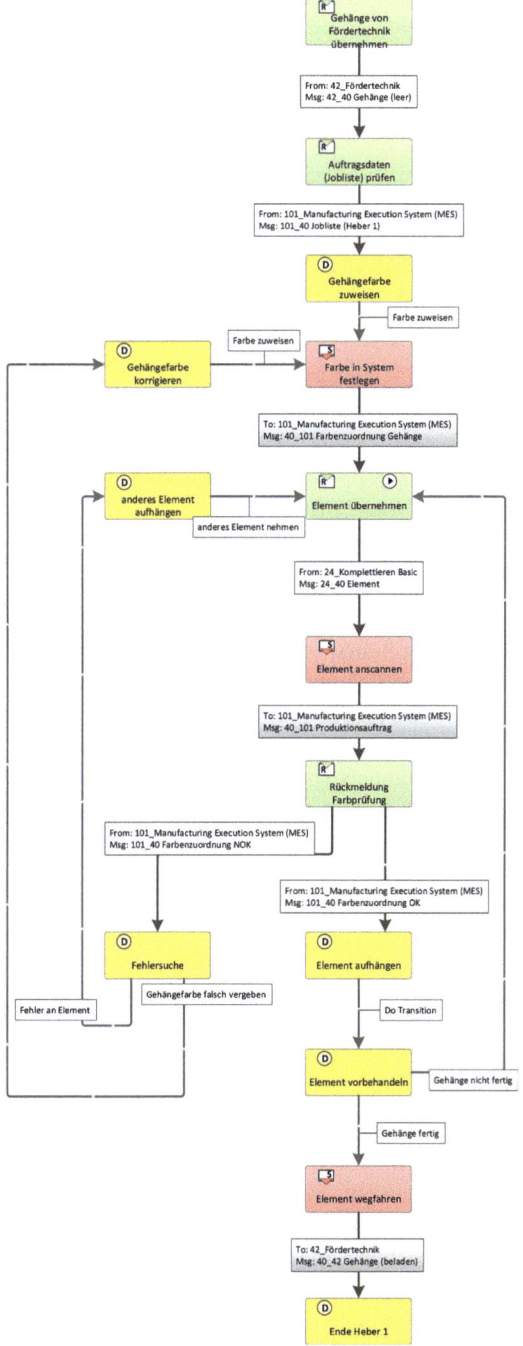

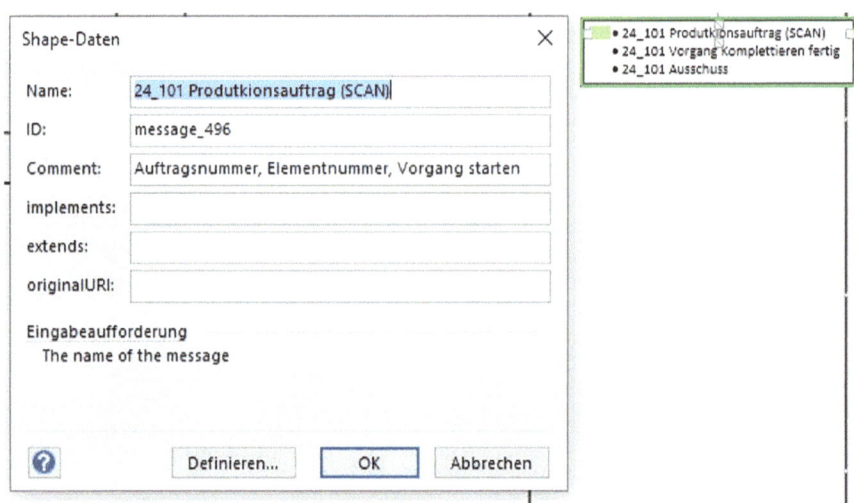

Fig. 9.17 Example: data input for the message "Production Order"

The total effort for process elicitation and modeling amounted to approximately 90 working hours, with an additional 160 hours spent finalizing the requirements specification document. This was a relatively low workload considering the large number of process participants, the high level of detail in the models and the specification, as well as the fact that the elicitation had to start from scratch. The requirements specification and process models were sent to all relevant MES suppliers. Based on the specification, the suppliers were asked to provide feedback on which requirements could be met, whether these were included in the standard functionality or needed to be addressed through custom features, and to submit a corresponding offer. The goal was to enable a comparison of the individual scopes of service, implementation costs, and ongoing expenses.

9.3.3   Results Achieved

Thanks to the requirements defined in the specification document, it was possible to compare the received software proposals in terms of functionality and pricing, ultimately leading to a well-founded decision regarding implementation and procurement. With the selected supplier, the requested implementation was reviewed and validated in detail during so-called solution workshops. During these workshops, the supplier's project team noted that the level of detail in the process models and interface descriptions was exceptionally high and significantly supported the solution design. Open questions could be clarified within a matter of hours, or even minutes, whereas similar issues in other implementations often required entire working days.

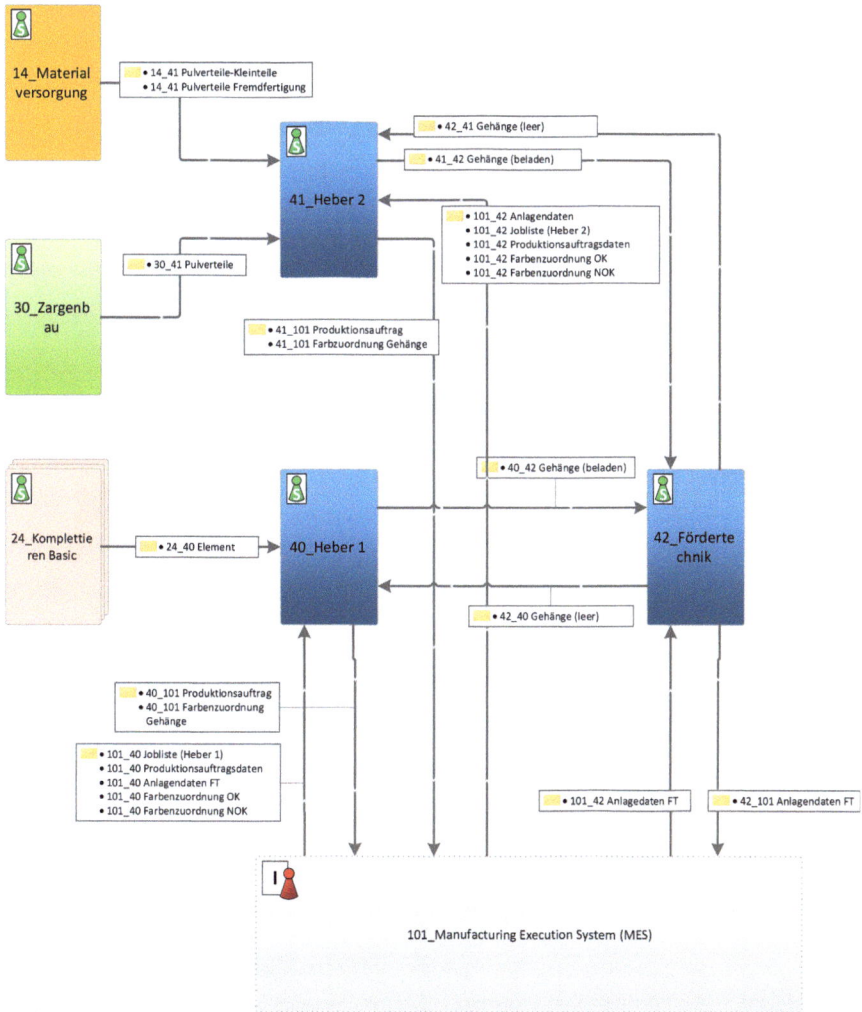

Fig. 9.18 Powder coating "sub"-process (SID)

By autumn 2022, approximately 90% of the production digitalization had been completed. At this point it was evident that the projected annual savings of around 100,000 would be achievable. This is largely the result of employees being provided with relevant, clearly prepared information regarding the current production orders directly from the MES. Previously, a significant amount of production time had been spent on organizing and manually evaluating order data. The realized improvements were derived directly from the process model and implemented accordingly.

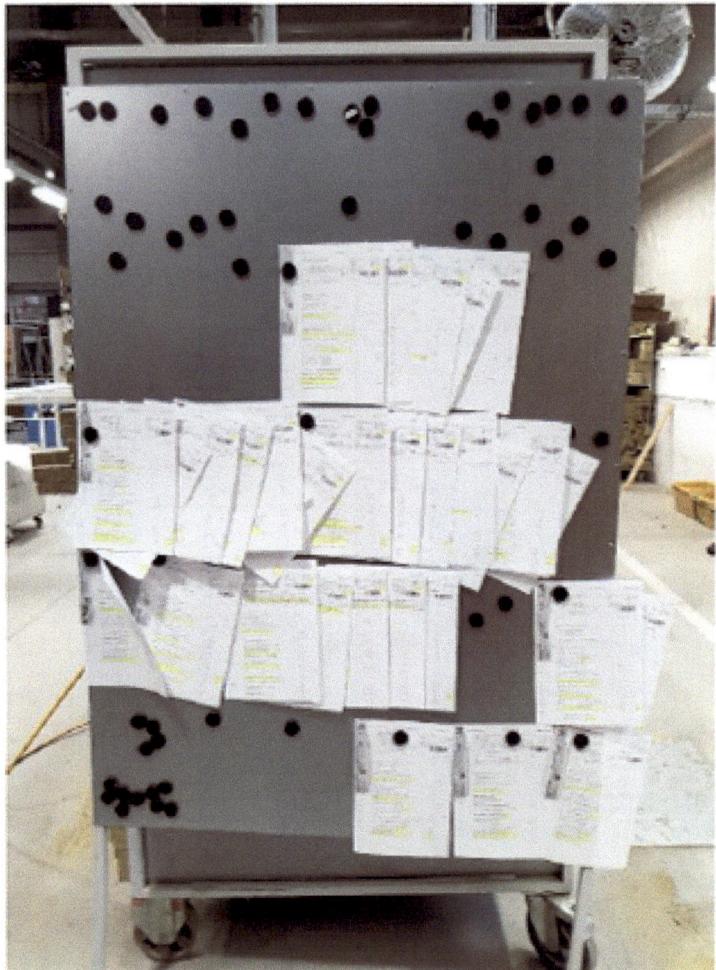

Fig. 9.19 Provision of order data in paper form

Here are some examples of implemented improvements to better understand the digital transformation:

- **Requesting order data:**
  Before: At a workstation, several employees received various components for final assembly. After receiving the component, one of the employees searched for the corresponding printed order documents on a magnetic wall (see Fig. 9.19).
  After: By scanning a bar code attached to the product, all order data is automatically displayed on a screen (see Figs. 9.20, 9.21 and 9.22).

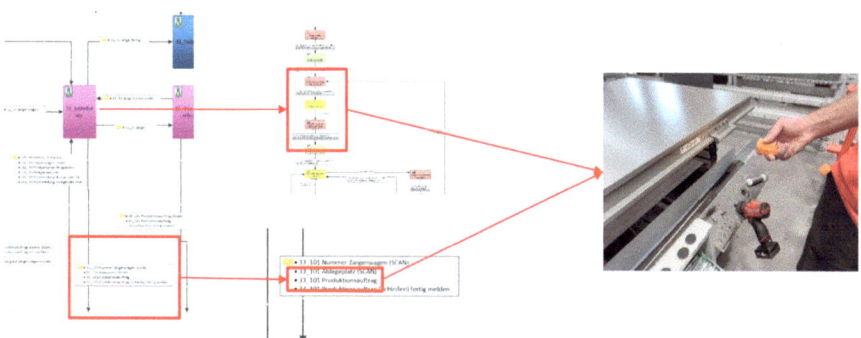

Fig. 9.20 Requesting order data via SCAN and MES

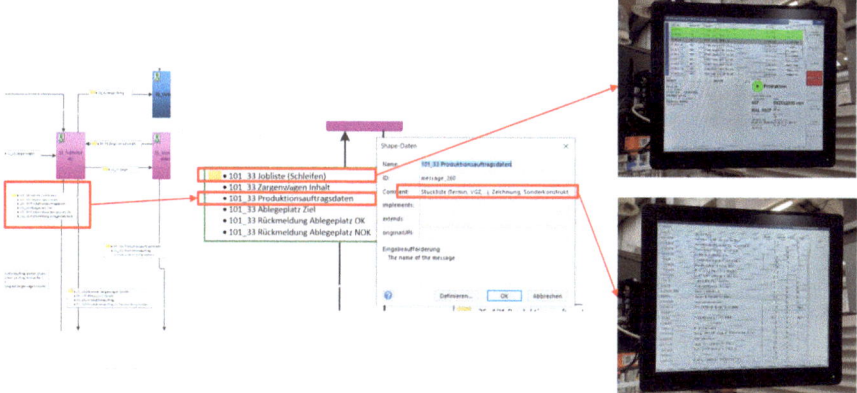

Fig. 9.21 Providing order data via MES on a Screen

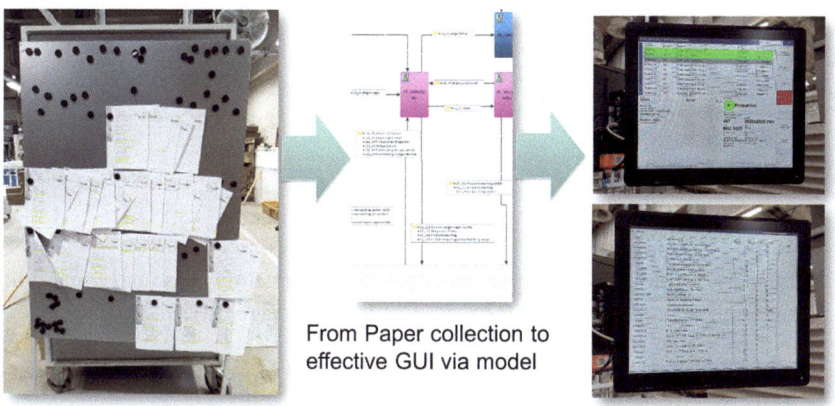

From Paper collection to effective GUI via model

Fig. 9.22 Digital transformation of the process

Fig. 9.23 Manual counting of special parts (sample list)

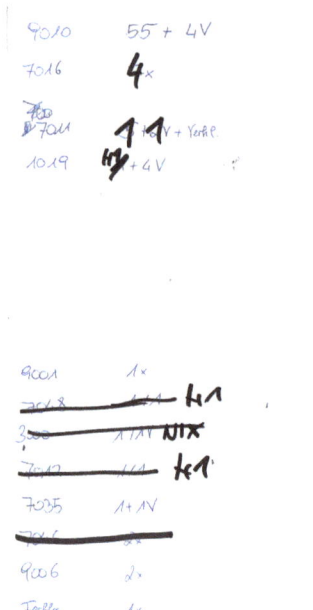

Fig. 9.24 Automatic report for special parts

ORDERNUMBER	MATERIALTEXT	MATERIALNUMBER	Elementnr	STK	FARBTON	Produktionsbeginn
550924237	Gfl.FN00 ST-1R	521017334POS_001.FX-GFL	164	2	RAL 7016	30.09.2022
550924239	Gfl.FN00 ST-1L	521017334POS_004.FX-GFL	165	2	RAL 7016	30.09.2022
550924217	Gfl.FN30 ST-1L	521015540B1/-101.FX-GFL	036	3	RAL 7047	30.09.2022
550924374	Gfl.FN30 ST-1R	521015540B1/-106.FX-GFL	037	3	RAL 7047	30.09.2022
550924373	Gfl.FN30 ST-1L	521015540B1/-102.FX-GFL	038	3	RAL 7047	30.09.2022
550924375	Gfl.FN30 ST-1R	521015540B1/-107.FX-GFL	039	3	RAL 7047	30.09.2022
550924224	Gfl.FM30 ST-1L	5210174240G1-18*.FX-GFL	046	3	RAL 9004	30.09.2022
550924225	Gfl.FM30 ST-1R	5210174240G1-19*.FX-GFL	047	3	RAL 9004	30.09.2022
550924226	Gfl.FM30 ST-1R	5210174240G1-20*.FX-GFL	048	3	RAL 9004	30.09.2022
550924227	Gfl.FN30 ST-1R	5210174240G1-LAG.FX-GFL	049	2	RAL 9004	30.09.2022
550924240	Gfl.FN30 ST-1L	521017334POS_5.1.FX-GFL	079	2	RAL 9010	30.09.2022
550924241	Gfl.FN30 ST-1R	521017334POS_5.2.FX-GFL	080	2	RAL 9010	30.09.2022
550924238	Gfl.FN00 ST-1R	521017334POS_002.FX-GFL	081	2	RAL 9010	30.09.2022

- **Counting Special Parts:**
  Before: An employee spent approximately one hour per day manually searching through all order documents (around 150 pages) to identify and count special parts (see Fig. 9.23).
  After: An automatic report in the MES evaluates all parts and summarizes them on just a few pages (see Fig. 9.24).

Vor Beschichtung								×
Auftrag	Materialbeschreibung	Status seit	Plandtart	Startzeitpunkt ▾	Element-Nr	Traverse	Norm	☰
550952482	Zar.FN30 UF-1L	15.11.22, 14:11	15.11.2022	15.11.22, 14:11 387		12	RAL 9010	
550952483	Zar.FN30 UF-1L	15.11.22, 14:11	15.11.2022	15.11.22, 14:11 387		12	RAL 9010	
550952511	Zar.FN30 UF-1L	15.11.22, 14:11	15.11.2022	15.11.22, 14:11 377		12	RAL 9010	
550952512	Zar.FN30 UF-1L	15.11.22, 14:11	15.11.2022	15.11.22, 14:11 377		12	RAL 9010	
550952513	Zar.FN30 UF-1L	15.11.22, 14:11	15.11.2022	15.11.22, 14:11 377		12	RAL 9010	
550952059	DFT90 -2 GF/BAE Links	15.11.22, 14:09	15.11.2022	15.11.22, 14:09 085		2	RAL 9010	
550952057	DFT90 -2 GF/SLE Links	15.11.22, 14:08	15.11.2022	15.11.22, 14:08 083		2	RAL 9010	
550952244	Gfl.FN30 UF-1L	15.11.22, 14:00	15.11.2022	15.11.22, 14:00 082		26	RAL 9010	
550952206	Gfl.FN30 UF-1R	15.11.22, 14:00	15.11.2022	15.11.22, 14:00 076		26	RAL 9010	
550952356	Zar.FN00 UF-1R	15.11.22, 13:55	15.11.2022	15.11.22, 13:55 405		12	RAL 9010	
550952357	Zar.FN00 UF-1R	15.11.22, 13:55	15.11.2022	15.11.22, 13:55 405		12	RAL 9010	
550952358	Zar.FN00 UF-1R	15.11.22, 13:55	15.11.2022	15.11.22, 13:55 405		12	RAL 9010	
550952276	Gfl.FN30 UF-1L	15.11.22, 13:52	15.11.2022	15.11.22, 13:52 080		29	RAL 9010	
550952246	Gfl.FN30 UF-1R	15.11.22, 13:52	15.11.2022	15.11.22, 13:52 079		29	RAL 9010	
550952274	Gfl.FN00 UF-1R	15.11.22, 13:51	15.11.2022	15.11.22, 13:51 081		29	RAL 9010	

Fig. 9.25 Dashboard powder coating

- **Sequence of Colors in Powder Coating:**
  Before: To prepare the required colors in powder coating, an employee had to walk along the conveyor system several times per hour to read the color labels attached to the transport trolleys, ensuring the correct color was prepared.
  After: A dashboard displayed on a screen directly at the powder booths shows the status of the conveyor system and the required colors in the correct sequence (see Fig. 9.25).

The structured and timely provision of necessary production data, tailored to each specific workstation, reduced organizational effort throughout the entire production process and significantly increased transparency in manufacturing. In the future, all production orders would also be started and completed at their respective workstations, enabling precise recording of processing times. Additionally, these digitalization steps could save up to 800,000 sheets of paper annually—a factor that also supported the company's sustainability goals and CO^2-neutral production.

9.3.4   Conclusion of the Method Application

The derivation of the requirements specification and necessary technical specifications based on the process model could be carried out relatively easily. The 45-page document comprised general objectives, fundamental requirements for the overall process, as well as several use cases and user stories to illustrate the planned application. Although these descriptions were labeled differently, they were direct excerpts from the modeled subject behaviors. The complete process models were also included in an appendix to the requirements specification.

Simplicity of Modeling
None of the participants involved in the data collection (i.e., the leaders of the various production teams) had prior knowledge or experience in process modeling or process management. Similar to case studies 1 and 2, the interviewees received a

brief introduction to the notation. The team leaders verbally described the workflows occurring at the individual workstations. A modeling expert simultaneously created graphical models. Despite the very simple explanation, all participants were able to read, interpret, and even verify the emerging process model ("[...] that's why we still need a green box here, because I'm waiting for [...]"). At the same time, during the modeling phase, the team leaders began to describe their optimized target process by modifying the process model.

With increasing complexity of the process model, the same issues arose as in the previous projects: the messages and their chronological sequence could only be followed with a high level of detailed knowledge, at least within the SID. However, due to the very linear production process, this was less pronounced in Project 3.

Distributed Modeling
Thanks to the subject-oriented approach, each team leader could be interviewed individually, resulting in self-contained, syntactically correct process descriptions. With other common approaches, such as the classical modeling workshop, the simultaneous presence of all team leaders (six team leaders in the production area) would have been necessary. Since the team leaders report their productive (operational work in production) and nonproductive hours (e.g., time spent on projects), this would have had a direct impact on the weekly plant report and the associated key performance indicators. To make the process model clearer and easier to read, the SID was divided into several sub-SIDs, i.e., one sub-SID per manufacturing area. The connections between the individual sub-processes were established via so-called interface subjects. An interface subject is a subject without subject behavior and is used as a placeholder. Figure 9.15 shows one production area (depicted in blue), which is connected via interface subjects to four other areas (depicted in orange, green, pink, and red).

Continuous Changes
As in Projects 1 and 2, the process models were revised and gradually refined over multiple iterations during the data collection phase, following the concept of incremental change. Changes to the target process were represented by adding, removing, or modifying individual subjects, subject behaviors, and/or messages. To improve the traceability of the models for the software suppliers, only specific use cases were presented in the requirements specification, in the form of the aforementioned sub-processes. These process segments were essentially "cut out" from the overall SID by deleting subjects, messages, and subject states that were not relevant for the description. It was not necessary to remodel the individual process segments (cf. Fig. 9.18)

IT Implementation
The 140-page process description, automatically generated from the models, was not directly usable for achieving the project goals. Although the software vendors regarded the process models as precise, structured, and fundamentally understandable, they requested a more compact and traditional requirements specification for

preparing offers and defining deliverables. During the implementation phase, the project team received very positive feedback from the software supplier regarding the level of detail and clarity of the process descriptions. Data specifications (such as workstation structures, data hierarchies, etc.) were discussed and defined in several brief online workshops (each lasting up to one hour)—activities that the software provider normally indicated would require several person days spread over multiple weeks. This enabled the setup of an initial baseline system in the test environment just four weeks after the first technical workshop—a step that directly reduced project lead time and project costs (the software supplier billed by project hours).

9.4   Summary

In the described projects, the use of process models varied significantly. The individual processes were analyzed, improved, and the application specifications were derived directly from the process descriptions. Unlike in usual practice, the primary purpose of the created process models was not documentation. Creating documentation is generally regarded as a burden, something that is due at the end of a project or process implementation and does not contribute directly to productivity. This, however, was not observed in these three projects. Instead, process modeling was actively used as an operational tool throughout the change process, rather than as a final documentation step. The PASS models created were living documents that continuously evolved, and their creation process was an essential part of understanding and structuring complex matters. They served as central reference points for all stakeholders—not just at the end of a project or project phase but throughout the entire project duration. The process models were focal points for ongoing discussions about process adjustments during the implementation phase and beyond, supporting continuous improvement.

References

1. C. Moser, U. Kannengiesser, M. Elstermann, Examining the PASS approach to process modelling for digitalised manufacturing results from three industry case studies. Enterp. Model. Inf. Syst. Archit. Int. J. Concept. Model. **17**, 1–24 (2022)
2. C. Fleischmann, K. Riha, G. Stangl, Logistics processes modelled in s-bpm and implemented in sap to reduce production lead times, in *Proceedings of the 8th International Conference on Subject-Oriented Business Process Management*, S-BPM '16, New York, NY, Association for Computing Machinery (2016)
3. C. Moser, K. Ríha, Digitalization of information-intensive logistics processes to reduce production lead times at ENGEL austria GmbH: Extending value stream mapping with subject-oriented business process management, in *Digitalization Cases, How Organizations Rethink Their Business for the Digital Age*, ed. by N. Urbach, M. Röglinger (Springer, Berlin, 2019), pp. 293–312
4. C. Moser, U. Kannengiesser, Incremental implementation of automated guided vehicle-based logistics using S-BPM: experience report of a digitalization project at ENGEL Austria, in *S-BPM ONE*, ed. by S. Betz (ACM, New York, 2019), pp. 3:1–3:6

5. U. Kannengiesser, H. Müller, Industry 4.0 standardisation: Where does S-BPM fit?, in *Proceedings of the 10th International Conference on Subject-Oriented Business Process Management, S-BPM ONE 2018, Linz, April 05–06, 2018* , ed. by C. Stary (ACM, New York, 2018), pp. 11:1–11:8
6. ENGEL Austria, Engel – hersteller im bereich kunststoff-spritzguss, (2022)
7. Peneder Bau-Elemente GmbH, Peneder - ein familienunternehmen mit dynamik, (2022)
8. M. Rother, J. Shook, Sehen lernen–mit wertstromdesign die wertschöpfung erhöhen und verschwendung beseitigen. dt. ausg., 1.0. (2004)
9. K. Erlach, Wertstromdesign, 2., bearb. u. erweit. aufl (2010)
10. A. Fleischmann, W. Schmidt, C. Stary, S. Obermeier, E. Börger, *Subject-Oriented Business Process Management* (Springer, Berlin, Heidelberg, 2012)
11. I. Liappas, Vom business zu den prozessen, in *AGILITÄT durch ARIS Geschäftsprozessmanagement* (Springer, Berlin, 2006), pp. 43–55
12. G. Riempp, *Integrierte Wissensmanagement-Systeme: Architektur und praktische Anwendung* (Springer, Berlin, 2012)
13. N. Kock, J. Verville, A. Danesh-Pajou, D. DeLuca, Communication flow orientation in business process modeling and its effect on redesign success: results from a field study. Decision Supp. Syst. **46**(2), 562–575 (2009)
14. P. Parviainen, M. Tihinen, J. Kääriäinen, S. Teppola, Tackling the digitalization challenge: how to benefit from digitalization in practice. Int. J. Inf. Syst. Project Manag. **5**(1), 63–77 (2017)

Conclusion

10

Finally, we summarize our key findings and the framework for holistic digitalization of processes and their further development. We embed these in initial situations from corporate practice and clarify the relationship between process management activities and socio-technical system design. Those responsible for organizations ultimately learn about the success-critical factors of a holistic approach.

"It's always been this way and it's always worked well!" becomes "What was organized in which way and how did it work?" and is finally transformed into "This is how we want to implement our organizational structure and develop it further in a self-directed manner." This is a value that underpins individual actions and ultimately organizational added value. The chapters of this book target individual and collective value creation. They convey successful concepts and procedures for stakeholder-oriented organizational design and development based on digital technologies in business and academia.

In addition to the decomposition of complex issues into manageable, i.e., configurable entities, the findings reveal the variety of development approaches of socio-technical systems, especially when they are modeled based on the communication between interacting actors and components. Thus, the design of such systems primarily focuses not on data structures and their modeling, but rather on coherent behavioral patterns and task bundles in the sense of functional collaboration and social cooperation.

Agility, resilience, value-based design, and composable business operations can be represented within the framework of process-based modeling of behavioral patterns and task bundles through the interaction of autonomous units. The resulting network-like enterprise architectures allow the assignment of technologies as a means and link between human actors or systems for the execution of tasks. Process models create the necessary transparency of processes as well as the usability of information and data exchanged within organizations and with external partners. Structure and behavior complement each other and can be implemented in an integrated manner.

© The Author(s) 2026
M. Elstermann et al., *Contextual Process Digitalization*,
https://doi.org/10.1007/978-3-032-06901-6_10

This complementarity allows for the design and implementation of the necessary adaptability of organizations in digital transformation projects in order to secure their socio-economic value. The reflection and design-oriented penetration of product developments and behavioral patterns of networked role carriers are crucial for the achievement of both content-related and economically sound goals through digital transformation processes. The latter are determined by stakeholders such as customers, suppliers, or employees, who articulate requirements that organizations need to address holistically and with continuous collaboration among the stakeholders involved. This development is likely to be accompanied by disruptive changes, as triggered by the Internet of Things, cyber-physical systems, and digital twins. To deal with them, focused while holistic development techniques and technologies, as presented in the previous sections, need to consider the behavior of system actors and components from different perspectives and in their mutual context.

However, stakeholder-oriented, holistic system design must, as demonstrated conceptually and practically, follow the principle of simplicity on several levels:

- Simplicity in acquiring and presenting knowledge about structures and processes, in terms of aspects relevant to stakeholders and their concerns
- Simplicity in presenting and developing a system architecture with participating system components and stakeholders, both the entire system as well as the consideration of individual system components and their details, including interactions with others
- Simplicity of transformation projects through behavioral models as a reference point for initial digitalization and the subsequent, ongoing adaptation of organizational processes or economically relevant task bundles

A crucial tool for implementing this principle, in order to also consider heterogeneous system structures, is the choice of levels of abstraction. They must provide a sufficient overview of concurrent processes, as well as in-depth behavioral analysis within the framework of application- and stakeholder-oriented modeling, albeit economic considerations. Only then do they represent a transparent basis for implementation and further digitalization steps.

Design and implementation can be intertwined once modeling approaches allow for automated execution of represented behavior. Thereby, models created by participants represent reference points that, initially designed according to individual ideas, can be experienced in their implementation by all involved stakeholders. Building on this, extensions towards machine and artificial intelligence can be made in a structured form. Such extensions can affect both technologies that are attributable to the context of cyber-physical system development and the economically relevant development of organizations. Hence, organizational or social behavior of participants can be addressed by using models that extend the scope of action of participants in certain situations.

In both cases, the automated execution of behavior models is crucial, as it allows for simulations, which are essential for estimating organizational and thus economically relevant effects before processes are put into operation.

As empirical evidence from the practical use of modeling languages and development techniques in research and corporate projects shows, not all measures and tools in the context of organizational transformation with digital technologies are equally helpful, even with a high degree of standardization of notations and an integrative consideration of different perspectives. This means that holistic organizational design should take a differentiated approach, starting with planning, which should consider core competencies and interpersonal communication as well as economic conditions and technological capacities. The design and especially the implementation process should be characterized by diversity and variability—guided by "be open as long as possible which role carrier or system perform which job." The demonstrated case created the respective evidence and should motivate organizational leaders to contribute to the innovation capacity and economic sustainability of their organization through the active design of structures and processes. The associated task profile is particularly characterized by the following features:

- Learning to increasingly delegate responsibility to those involved without neglecting the joint economically/technically and socially relevant goal-setting.
- Role-centered modeling and corresponding digital implementations—they increase the reliability of results in multidimensional transformation processes.
- Resilient structuring of tasks through adaptable behavior models—these are established as the subject of continuous, creative discussion.
- Promoting conflict and communication skills, namely, as a constructive discussion of behavior and interaction models—these enable the transparency of processes that promotes resilience and innovation.

As soon as the courage to change behavior becomes apparent, further use of technology is worthwhile in order to ultimately focus on multidimensional key performance indicator systems such as the Balanced Scorecard. With the help of the transparency provided by the models, organizational and learning processes can be reflected and (re-)designed from a financial perspective in connection with relevant behavior patterns.

When represented in executable business process models, dynamic changes can become organization practice in the course of sustainable development.

Index

© The Author(s) 2026   341
M. Elstermann et al., *Contextual Process Digitalization*,
https://doi.org/10.1007/978-3-032-06901-6